Commercial Banking
Practice and Policy

Oliver G. Wood, Jr.
University of South Carolina

D. Van Nostrand Company
New York Cincinnati Toronto London Melbourne

To my Mother
and
the Memory of my Father

D. Van Nostrand Company Regional Offices:
New York Cincinnati

D. Van Nostrand Company International Offices:
London Toronto Melbourne

Library of Congress Catalog Card Number: 78-420
ISBN: 0-442-29535-9

Manufactured in the United States of America.

Published by D. Van Nostrand Company
135 West 50th Street, New York, N.Y. 10020

10 9 8 7 6 5 4 3 2 1

Preface

The period 1973–1975 marked the worst crisis for America's bankers since the Great Depression. The prime rate rose to 12 percent; liquidity was squeezed to dangerous proportions; and loan losses, especially in the area of real estate, attained alarming levels. The crisis reached a climax with the failure of the Franklin National Bank on October 8th, 1974. Nevertheless, the problems that beset the banking industry in this period had some positive benefits. Banks that had been known as "go-go banks" now want to be known as conservative banks. Bankers, with some heavy prodding by the regulatory authorities, are paying more attention to liquidity management and capital adequacy. In banking, there truly has been a swing "back to basics."

This book emphasizes the fundamental concepts and definitions in banking. It is intended as an introductory text for undergraduate courses in commercial banking. In addition, bank educational directors should find it useful in providing trainees with an overview of commercial banking. In this regard, it could be the text for a formal class or simply given to trainees for outside reading and study.

To facilitate learning, each chapter begins with a short statement of purpose and a list of the major areas to be covered; headings and subheadings are employed extensively; trends and historical perspective in every major area are provided through data presented in tabular form; and, for those who wish to explore the various topics in greater depth, there is an extensive list of references at the end of each chapter.

Bankers today realize that the services offered by other financial institutions are becoming similar to their own and, therefore, more competitive. Chapter 1 underscores this point in the "modern theory of financial intermediation," which explains that the similarities among financial intermediaries are more significant than the dissimilarities. The balance of the book is divided into seven parts.

Part I details the responsibilities and the reports of bank management. Chapter 2 contains an outline and description of the organizational framework for the acquisition and utilization of bank funds and a summary of the duties and responsibilities of the primary managerial positions. Chapter 3 outlines the nature of the principal reports that must be submitted to the banking regulatory authorities and those that must be provided to the shareholders, in addition to developing a profit planning and reporting system similar to that used by many banks. Chapter 4 reviews each of the major income, expense, and profit items in the income statement.

Part II describes the sources of bank funds. Chapter 5 discusses the types of deposits and the significant shift in recent years in the relative proportion of time and savings deposits. Chapter 6 discusses the types of bank capital and the concept of capital adequacy in addition to explaining various types of bank nondeposit liabilities and the concept of liability management. A simple model integrating asset and liability management is presented.

A bank's liquidity management is discussed in Part III. Chapter 7 deals with the management of the bank's money position or cash assets. In Chapter 8, short-term or seasonal liquidity needs are considered separately from long-term or cyclical liquidity needs.

The six chapters comprising Part IV deal with various aspects of loan management. Chapter 9 is an introduction to the general considerations that bear upon loan management. Chapter 10 discusses the essential principles in credit analysis needed for making sound business loans. Chapters 11–14 describe the four primary types of bank loans—short-term business loans, term loans, consumer loans, and real estate loans.

The two chapters in Part V are concerned with investment management. Chapter 15 summarizes the primary types of securities eligible for bank investment along with the general considerations that shape portfolio policy. The concepts of the "interest rate cycle" and "yield curve analysis" are introduced in Chapter 16 as important topics relating to the execution of investment policy.

Part VI discusses the various regulations of the banking structure. Chapter 17 is concerned with regulation of banking entry; Chapter 18 deals with bank mergers. Chapter 19 deals with the multibank and one-bank holding company movements.

Finally, banks in the future will face great opportunities and challenges. Congress is now considering bills that would increase the financial powers of nonbank financial institutions and, consequently, increase the competitive pressures on banks. Part VII represents an effort to provoke thought about the opportunities and challenges in the banking world of the future. Chapter 20 presents some estimates of the absolute and relative sizes of the various financial intermediaries in 1980 and 1985 and Chapter 21 explores several banking service areas that may prove fruitful in the coming years.

Many people contributed in numerous ways toward the creation of this book. The author benefited considerably from the comments and suggestions of Norman J. Collins, Senior Vice-President of Florida National Banks of Florida and former President of Robert Morris Associates; Robert T. Perdue and William C. Barksdale, Vice-President and Vice-President and Administrator of Commercial Loans, respectively, of the South Carolina National Bank; H. J. Almers, Senior Vice-President of Southern Bank and Trust Company, Greenville, South Carolina; and Dr. Olin S. Pugh, Professor of Banking and Finance, University of South Carolina. Valuable assistance in compiling the tabular material and in proofreading the manuscript was provided by David Bernthal, Charles Davis, Charles Rhue, Alvin Wall, James Wheeler, and Patricia Ross. Virginia Van Seters, Associate Editor, Bureau of Business and Economic Research, assisted in editing an earlier draft of the manuscript. Excellent typing assistance was provided by Linda Mellin, Sharon Flanagan, Gloria Nicholson, Briggs Hubbard, and Vonnie White. The author thanks Dr. James F. Kane and William F. Putnam, Dean and Associate Dean, respectively, of the College of Business Administration at the University of South Carolina for providing an environment conducive to writing and research. A special debt of gratitude is owed to my colleagues Dr. James L. Athearn and Dr. Robert J. Porter, for their encouragement and counsel throughout the project. Finally, the author wishes to thank Phil Desper and Bruce Williams, publisher and developmental editor, respectively, of D. Van Nostrand Company for their very excellent assistance.

Oliver G. Wood, Jr.
Columbia, South Carolina

Contents

CHAPTER

1

Financial Intermediation In Our Economy

Commercial banks, as financial intermediaries, have contributed substantially to the economic growth and development of the United States.[1] Over the years, banks have provided funds for financing the construction of factories, schools, and highways. They have assisted embryonic business enterprises and corporate giants alike with various forms of credit as these firms sought to increase the supply of goods and services available to our citizens. At the same time, banks have helped to undergird the demand for goods and services by enabling consumers to purchase and enjoy such items as automobiles, appliances, boats, and homes in advance of the time that they could earn income and pay for them in full. Banks have financed college educations and aided families faced with staggering medical bills. By providing funds to in-

[1]A financial intermediary may be defined as an institution that acquires funds by creating claims on itself in the form of deposits and shares and that, in turn, creates credit (the obligation to repay funds in the future) as it provides loanable funds to borrowers.

vestors and consumers, banks have served to stimulate and facilitate growth in both the aggregate supply of, and aggregate demand for, goods and services.

Banks also have contributed to our nation's economic development by serving as depositories and by providing an efficient and low-cost means of exchange. Only at a few times in our history have people had to worry about the safety of their funds. Moreover, the large-scale acceptance of the use of demand deposits to effect payments at an early stage of our economic development permitted and encouraged specialization and thereby accelerated economic growth. In sum, commercial banks deserve much credit for the fact that the United States has become the most affluent and industrially advanced nation in the world.

In this chapter we shall (1) examine the role of financial intermediaries in the circular flow of economic activity, (2) note the general functions of financial intermediaries, (3) discuss the specific functions of nonbank financial intermediaries, and (4) consider briefly the specific functions of commercial banks.

The Circular Flow of Economic Activity

Let us see, in simplified terms, how financial intermediaries, including commercial banks, fit into the economic system. This can be accomplished with the aid of a familiar economic model—the circular flow diagram. The principal advantage of using the circular flow diagram is that it depicts and relates in one diagram all the major functions performed in an economy—production, distribution, and consumption. A circular flow diagram gives the "big picture" of an economy as it attempts to provide its citizens with goods and services. Usually, the circular flow diagram is introduced on the second or third day of class in a course concerned with the principles of ecomomics. It is customary to develop the model for a "simple economy" without financial intermediaries before proceeding to a discussion of an "advanced economy" with financial intermediaries.

Simple Economy

The term *simple economy* means an economy that performs no saving and undertakes no capital investment. In other words, people spend everything that they earn for consumer goods and services, and no provision is made for replacing or increasing the stock of capital. It is assumed also that there is no governmental sector and that only family units are consumers of goods and services. In reality, of course, businesses are also consumers. Finally, it is assumed that no pool of savings exists from prior periods.

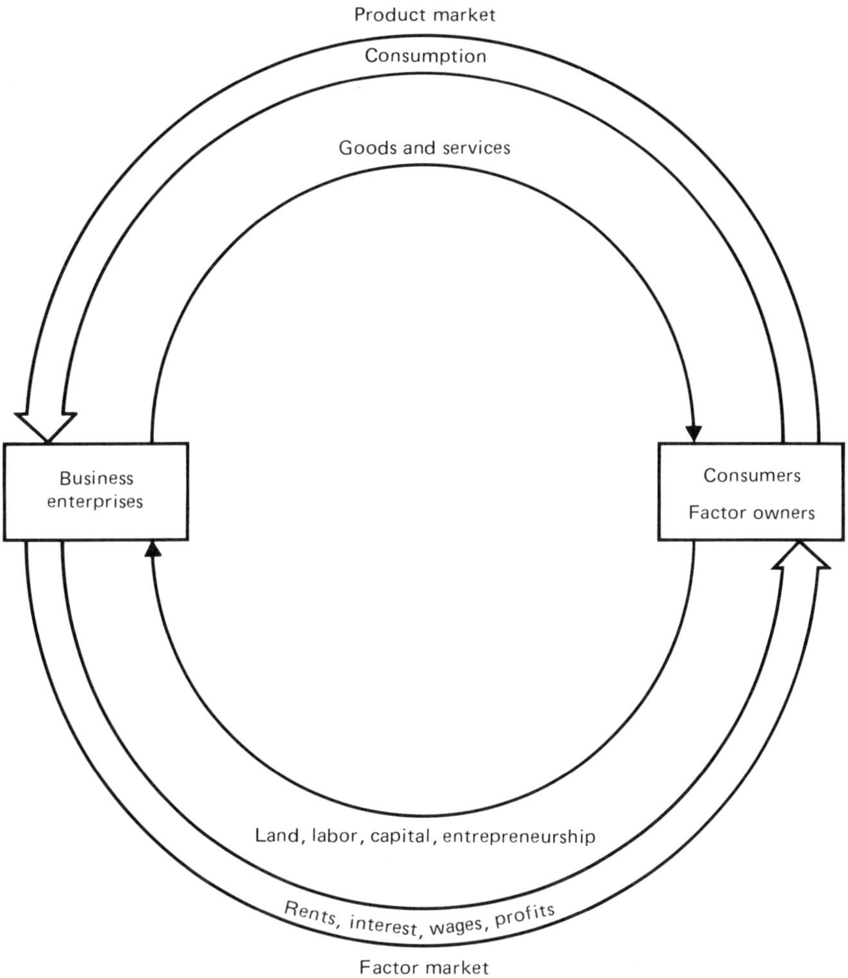

Figure 1-1 Circular Flow Diagram for a "Simple" Economy

As shown in Figure 1-1, the production of goods and services is performed by business enterprises that acquire resources to produce goods and services from the factor owners. These resource owners provide land, labor, capital, and entrepreneurship to businesses in return for payments in the form of rents, wages, interest, and profits, respectively. Wearing their second hat as consumers, factor owners, in turn, use their income to acquire goods and services from the businesses.

If all resources in the economy are fully employed, enough income is generated to enable consumers (factor owners) to acquire all the goods and services their resources have helped to produce. The outer flow of income to the factor owners matches the flow of expenditures from consumers to pay for goods and services. Moreover, if several other assumptions were made, it could be stated that the *product market* would be in equilibrium with the *factor market*; that is, the top half of the diagram would be in equilibrium with the bottom half.

Advanced Economy

The circular flow diagram for the simple economy does not take into account several important aspects of the economy. First, some consumers may not want to spend all their income on goods and services; that is, they may want to *save*. Second, other consumers may wish to acquire more goods and services than their current incomes allow them to purchase. Third, some businesses may want to replace or to acquire additional capital.[2]

If some consumers decide not to spend all their income, other things being equal, they short-circuit the smooth functioning of the economy. Businesses will take this as a signal to reduce production because they do not want inventories to pile up in their warehouses. Cutting back on production reduces the flow of payments to the factor owners, who, unfortunately, as consumers, find that their efforts to save become difficult as income declines.

Although a surfeit of funds may exist in the hands of some consumers, there may exist simultaneously for other consumers and businesses a demand for these funds to finance the purchase of consumer durables and capital goods. If these demanders are able to acquire savings and to channel them back into the spending stream, the level of economic activity will be sustained, and there will be no cyclical fluctuations or unemployment of human or nonhuman resources.[3]

Figure 1-2 depicts the *advanced economy* and the paths that savings take as they find their way into the hands of businesses and consumers that demand funds. Consumers who desire to save essentially have two options: (1) they may place funds directly in the organized security markets in exchange for stocks, bonds, and other securities issued primarily by business enterprises, or (2) they may acquire deposits, shares, or other claims issued by financial intermediaries.[4]

Organized security markets and financial intermediaries serve as links between suppliers and demanders of funds. In addition, there are

[2]Business enterprises in the United States finance the bulk of their capital requirements themselves from retained earnings (savings).

[3]At this point, in order to facilitate the discussion, it is assumed that financial intermediaries serve only as conduits of funds between savers and spending units such as consumers and businesses. As will be explained later, all financial intermediaries have the ability to create loanable funds and thereby to augment the supply of savings available to finance investment and consumption expenditures.

[4]Of course, consumers and businesses could also save by hoarding currency or coin or by the direct purchase of resalable assets.

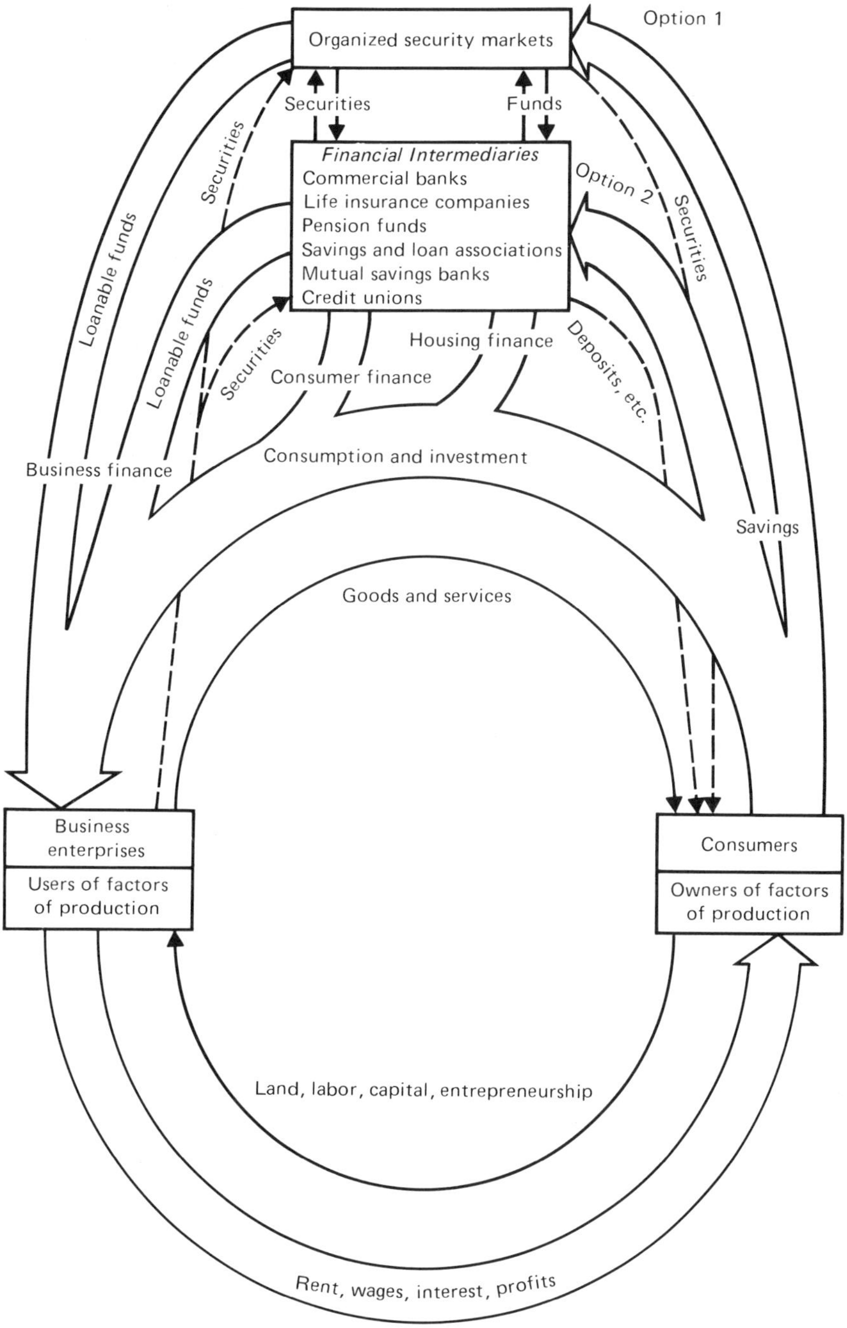

Figure 1-2 Circular Flow Diagram for an "Advanced" Economy

links between the organized security markets and the financial intermediaries themselves. The latter may issue or buy securities in the organized security markets, thereby further improving the efficiency of the process of providing funds to creditworthy investors and consumers.

Although this representation of the financial linkages in an advanced economy abstracts from the complex interrelationships that exist in a financially sophisticated economy such as the United States, it does indicate the vital role that organized security markets and financial intermediaries play in facilitating growth in aggregate supply and aggregate demand. Sometimes, in emphasizing the need for the stabilizing influences of monetary or fiscal policy, it is easy to forget that the private sector, through security markets and financial intermediaries, already has done much to assist the economy toward full employment by providing funds to investors and consumers who wish to purchase goods and services. In spite of the built-in economic stabilizing influence of security markets and financial intermediaries however, adjustments through public policy are needed occasionally to smooth the flow of economic activity.

General Functions of Financial Intermediaries

Financial intermediaries perform three general functions in our economy: (1) they create loanable funds for creditworthy borrowers, (2) they reduce risk exposure for financial claimholders, and (3) they provide liquidity for financial claimholders.

Loanable Funds

In our simplified discussion of the circular flow diagram, financial intermediaries appeared to perform only one major function, that of conduits of funds from savers to consumers and investors. However, the *modern theory of financial intermediation* rejects the idea that these intermediaries channel funds from savers to borrowers.[5] Rather, all intermediaries, bank and nonbank alike, are considered to be capable of credit *expansion*, that is, of augmenting the total supply of loanable funds.

The *supply of loanable funds* available during a period such as a year may be defined as consisting of several elements:[6] (1) *current saving* (S), that is, the part of current income that is not spent for goods and

[5]For a more complete discussion of the modern theory of financial intermediation, see Murray E. Polakoff, ed., *Financial Institutions and Markets* (Boston: Houghton Mifflin, 1970), chaps. 3, 6, 26.

[6]This discussion is derived largely from Polakoff, pp. 37–38.

services and is not hoarded (H),[7] and (2) the net increase in the amount of credit provided by the banking system. Since banks ordinarily create credit (acquire loans and securities) by expanding their liabilities in the form of demand deposits, it is possible to measure this source of loanable funds by changes in the money supply (ΔM).[8] Therefore, the supply of loanable funds (SLF) is equal to $TS - H + \Delta M$. As may be seen, within this framework there is no recognition that nonbank intermediaries also can create, that is, expand the supply of loanable funds. However, this fact may be explained quite easily by use of this supply-of-loanable-funds equation.

Suppose a nonbank intermediary such as a savings and loan association increases its dividend rate on savings deposits and therefore induces the public to reduce some of their idle money balances and add to their savings and loan deposits. This shift in funds represents dishoarding. Savings and loan associations now have the ability to make mortgage loans or purchase securities, thereby increasing the supply of loanable funds. Whereas commercial banks increase the supply of loanable funds by increasing demand deposits and only to the extent that the newly created funds are not hoarded, nonbank financial intermediaries augment the supply of loanable funds by inducing dishoarding; that is, they reduce the demand for money.[9] According to the modern theory, the important point is not that commercial banks increase the supply of loanable funds by means of creating claims (money) on themselves, but that all intermediaries, bank and nonbank, are capable of creating loanable funds.

The ability of financial intermediaries to create credit and expand the supply of loanable funds contributes greatly toward the smooth functioning of our economy. Stated differently, they help to bridge the gap between production and consumption. The excess demand by creditworthy investors and consumers for goods and services is translated into an effective demand for goods and services by intermediaries who expand the supply of loanable funds to augment current income available for purchases.

The modern theory of financial intermediation has two important implications for bank policy. First, banks must be aware of the close substitutability between the claims on nonbank intermediaries and those on banks in the form of demand, time, and savings deposits. Second, banks must recognize that funds obtained from nonbank intermediaries are no different to the borrower than those received from a bank; that is,

[7]Hoarding may be defined as the difference between the amount of money desired to be held and the amount available to be held. Therefore, current saving (S) equals total savings (TS) minus hoarding (H), or $S = TS - H$.

[8]The banking system can augment the supply of loanable funds through money creation (ΔM) only to the extent that the additional funds are not hoarded.

[9]The ability of all financial intermediaries to create credit is enhanced to the extent that saving from current income is used to acquire more claims on these intermediaries.

they all command goods and services in the marketplace. In sum, there is little basis in theory for distinguishing among classes of financial intermediaries.

Risk Exposure

One of the reasons that financial intermediaries have been successful in attracting funds is that they reduce the exposure to risk that savers ordinarily would face. Without intermediaries, savers would have to evaluate the *credit risk* (the chance of nonpayment at maturity) for each borrower to whom they entrusted their funds. This, of course, would take time and specialized knowledge on the part of savers. By employing experts in credit analysis and by applying uniform credit evaluation standards to borrowers, intermediaries are able to place funds in the hands of those businesses and consumers who are most likely to repay the funds on schedule, thus limiting (or averaging down) the chance of loss to individual savers. Also, through diversification of their asset holdings, intermediaries further reduce the risk faced by individual savers. The federal government has gone one step further and reduced the chance of loss for many savers by establishing insurance for funds placed in commercial banks, mutual savings banks, savings and loan associations, and credit unions.

Liquidity

When savers place funds in intermediaries, they benefit from the law of large numbers. When intermediaries issue money claims to a large number of savers, it is possible to predict within fairly narrow limits the expected number of claims that will be cashed in over a period of time as well as the expected future inflow of new funds. Acting independently, individual savers may participate in the everyday economic processes of production, distribution, and consumption with some degree of certainty that they can liquidate their claims on financial intermediaries without a delay. As an example of this importance, it is known that the level of investment and consumption spending in the economy is a function of the degree of liquidity of money claims on financial institutions. If individuals and businesses had some doubt about their ability to liquidate these claims on short notice, spending for capital and consumer goods would diminish until confidence was restored. Part of the decline in investment and consumption during the Great Depression may be traced to the inability of many intermediaries to meet the demand for funds from their claimholders.

Thus the importance of financial intermediaries to the smooth functioning of the American economy should not be underestimated. Economic historians probably would state that the rapid and large-scale development of financial intermediaries in this country was an essential and necessary condition for our nation's meteoric economic rise during this century. Saving, investing, and spending have been encouraged and facilitated by our system of financial intermediaries. On the other hand, the economic development of Russia and the South American, African, and Asian countries has been retarded by the relatively undeveloped financial intermediaries in these areas. Because it is recognized that financial intermediaries perform functions that are important to the economic and social well-being of all its citizens, the federal and state governments in the United States have chosen to encourage and protect these institutions through numerous statutes and regulations.

Specific Functions of Nonbank Financial Intermediaries

Thus far, no specific distinctions have been made among the various financial intermediaries in the economy. Let us look now at the specific functions of five major nonbank financial intermediaries: (1) life insurance companies, (2) savings and loan associations, (3) private noninsured pension funds, (4) mutual savings banks, and (5) credit unions.

Life Insurance Companies

Like all financial intermediaries, life insurance companies receive funds in return for a promise to pay. The terms of this promise to pay, however, differ from that generally offered by other intermediaries. Life insurance companies promise to pay their policyholders under such conditions as death of the insured, surrender of the policy, or at the end of a specified period of time.

In the course of issuing these specialized promises to pay, life insurance companies in the United States at the end of 1976 had accumulated $320.6 billion in assets (Table 1-1). Of this total, $96.6 billion were invested in mortgages, $123.1 billion in bonds of business enterprises, $25.8 billion in loans to policyholders, and $34.5 billion in equities.

Savings and Loan Associations

The concept for savings and loan associations originated in 1831 when a group of citizens in Frankford, Pennsylvania, met to form a cooperative home-financing society. Their purpose was to accumulate savings from association members in order to allow other members to buy homes. Today, savings and loan associations or building and loan associations, cooperative banks, or homestead associations, as they are sometimes called, employ full-time professional staffs to attract savings.

Table 1-1

Total Assets of Major Financial Intermediaries, Selected Years, 1960–1976 (billions of dollars)

Year End	Insured Commercial Banks	Life Insurance Companies	Savings and Loan Associations	Mutual Savings Banks	Noninsured Pension Funds	Credit Unions	Total
1960	255.7	119.6	71.5	40.6	33.1	5.7	562.2
1965	374.1	158.9	129.6	58.2	59.2	10.6	790.6
1970	572.7	207.3	176.2	79.0	97.0	18.0	1,150.1
1971	635.6	222.1	206.0	89.4	106.4	21.1	1,280.8
1972	732.8	239.7	243.1	100.6	117.5	24.8	1,458.2
1973	827.1	252.4	271.9	106.7	126.5	28.4	1,620.6
1974	906.3	263.3	295.5	109.6	133.7	31.9	1,746.5
1975	944.7	289.3	338.2	121.0	145.2	38.0	1,876.4
1976	1,011.1	320.6	392.0	134.7	160.4	44.9	2,063.7

Source: *Federal Reserve Bulletin*; Securities and Exchange Commission, *Statistical Bulletin*; U.S. Savings and Loan League, *Savings and Loan Fact Book*.

Most of the funds placed in savings and loan associations are in passbook deposit accounts. In practice, associations honor a depositor's request to redeem his account on demand. If a liquidity problem arises, however, existing contracts require passbook account holders to wait until sufficient funds are available. Recently, savings and loan associations have attracted a large amount of funds through the sale of large-denomination savings certificates that have maturities usually ranging from 30 days to 6 years. At the end of 1976, savings and loan associations had savings capital of $336.0 billion and assets of $392.0 billion, of which $323.1 billion consisted of mortgages. Savings and loan associations provide, by far, the largest amount of funds to finance home purchases.

Private Noninsured Pension Funds

Private noninsured pension funds are financial entities established mainly by corporations to provide retirement of deferred profit-sharing benefits to employees. The word "private" is used to distinguish these pension funds from those established by a governmental unit; the word "noninsured" denotes the fact that the funds are not accumulated with insurance companies. Pension funds are financial intermediaries because they collect funds from corporations and frequently their employees in return for a promise to pay an income to these employees when they retire. These contributions provide the basis for an expansion of loanable funds and the acquisition of earning assets. At the end of 1976, assets of private noninsured pension plans totaled $160.4 billion, of which $93.4 billion were common stock, $39.1 billion were corporate and other bonds, and $2.4 billion were mortgages.

Mutual Savings Banks

The first mutual savings bank was founded in Scotland in 1810 by the Reverend Mr. Henry Duncan. The idea quickly spread to this country with the founding in 1816 of the Provident Institution for Savings in the Town of Boston and The Philadelphia Savings Fund Society, both of which today are among the nation's largest mutual savings banks.

As financial intermediaries, mutual savings banks issue claims on themselves in the form of deposits and promise to redeem these claims within a specified length of time.[10] In practice, withdrawals are paid in full on demand. The assets acquired by mutual savings banks usually are of a long-term nature. At the end of 1976, 473 mutual savings banks in the United States had deposits of $122.8 billion and assets of $134.7 billion, of which $81.6 billion were mortgages. The savings bank industry is concentrated in the northeastern section of the United States.

Credit Unions

A credit union is a cooperative self-help thrift and loan society composed of individuals bound together by some tie such as a common employer; membership in a labor union, a church, or a fraternal order; or residence in a well-defined geographic area. Members purchase savings shares in the credit union and receive dividends, which recently have been as high as 6 percent at many of these institutions. Only members enjoy the privilege of borrowing from a credit union. Loans usually are for the payment of current expenses or the purchase of consumer durables, but some credit unions finance homes or real estate.

The first credit union in the United States was formed in 1909. Credit unions, however, did not become significant in terms of assets until the 1960s. Between 1960 and 1976, assets to credit unions rose from $5.0 billion to $44.9 billion. At the end of 1976, there were 22,608 credit unions in operation.

Credit unions perform valuable services for their members. They provide a convenient place for members to save and borrow. Interest rates may not exceed 1 percent per month on the unpaid balance, which, on an annual basis, is less than that charged at most retail credit outlets and by bank installment loan departments. As intermediaries, credit unions provide not only an above-average return on savings but also a below-average cost to consumers.

[10]Some savings banks now offer conventional checking accounts, the so-called NOW (negotiable orders of withdrawal) accounts. Savings banks also offer a variety of other services, including savings bank life insurance, safe deposit boxes, funds collection for customers, traveler's checks, credit cards, and 24-hour-a-day withdrawals through cash-dispensing machines.

Specific Functions of Commercial Banks

Commercial banks perform five principal functions in our economy: they (1) hold deposits, (2) provide a payments mechanism, (3) create money and credit, (4) provide trust services, and (5) provide other services.

Deposits

Deposits or claims on commercial banks are held for at least four reasons: (1) to carry out everyday transactions, (2) as a reserve against future contingencies, (3) to finance future purchases, or (4) because the deposit holder does not want to hold savings in the form of equities, debt instruments, or claims on nonbank intermediaries in view of his expectations concerning business trends, interest-rate movements, and price trends. Transactions balances usually are held in the form of demand deposits, which, as their name implies, are claims on banks that must be met without delay. These working balances are held by their owner to carry out the everyday business routine, such as buying goods and services and paying workers. Some demand deposits are held as compensating balances, that is, deposits that represent a portion of a loan granted to the deposit holder.[11] The amount of working balances held in banks is primarily a function of the volume of transactions that must be effected within a short-run time horizon, the ease with which these balance holders can acquire loans, and the opportunity cost of holding noninterest-bearing funds.

Bank balances also are held as a reserve against future contingencies. These precautionary balances may be held in the form of demand, time, or savings deposits.[12] Precautionary balances may be held by individuals, for example, to meet possible future medical expenses or simply to provide for retirement. Businesses hold precautionary balances to meet fixed expenses if strikes by employees reduce output or if a recession occurs and sales turn downward or just as part of the firm's overall liquidity position.

Bank deposits may be held to finance future expenditures. Sometimes balances are accumulated by individuals to purchase a high-priced item or service, such as a piano or a trip to Europe. Businesses

[11]Depending on credit conditions, compensating balance requirements may vary from 0 to 25 percent of a loan. For example, if a borrower received a $100,000 bank loan at 8 percent with a compensating balance requirement of 20 percent, the borrower would have use of only $80,000; hence the effective interest rate on the loan would be 10 percent.

[12]Savings deposits are interest-bearing balances held by individuals, corporations, governments, or nonprofit organizations evidenced by a passbook. Time deposits is a general heading for all other bank interest-bearing deposits. By agreement between the bank and a borrower, some savings or time deposits serving as compensating balances might be designated as noninterest-bearing.

might accumulate balances to finance a small plant addition or to purchase another business. Balances held for this finance motive may be in demand, time, or savings accounts.

Finally, bank balances are held as an alternative to holding equities, debt instruments, or claims on other financial intermediaries. Income recipients must make two decisions: (1) what percentage of income to consume or save and (2) in what form to hold the amount that is saved. As shown in the circular flow diagram, funds not consumed (saved) may be placed in the securities markets in exchange for equities or debt instruments or they may be placed in financial intermediaries in exchange for deposits or other claims. The form in which to hold savings depends on the saver's expectations with respect to the business cycle, interest-rate movements, price trends, or other factors. For example, if interest rates are expected to rise, that is, if the prices of debt instruments are expected to fall, savers might prefer bank deposits to debt instruments. On the other hand, if the economy is about to recover from a recession, savers might shift from bank balances to equities in anticipation of a rebound in these issues. In theory, a saver should allocate funds among savings forms until the expected marginal return from each form is equal.

Regardless of why funds are held at banks, the accumulation of these deposits results in an increase in reserves, which gives an individual bank the ability to create money and credit equivalent to its excess reserves.

Payments Mechanism

In addition to serving as custodians of demand deposits, banks also perform the valuable function of transferring these balances among accounts when they are directed to do so by means of checks issued by deposit holders. Banks provide a payments and collection system largely to attract deposits.

The amounts spent for tellers, bookkeepers, computers, postage, checks, forms, and advertising in connection with the payments system is a large percentage (perhaps a third) of total bank costs.[13] It is estimated that banks recoup only a fraction of this expense through service charges. To an extent, bank borrowers subsidize bank deposit holders and check writers.

Money and Credit

A unique characteristic of a commerical bank is its ability to create money (demand deposits). When a commercial bank makes a loan or an

[13]The Federal Reserve Act of 1913 directed that the central bank provide a national clearing system for checks. Most of the Federal Reserve's expenses are incurred in discharging this responsibility.

investment, it creates liabilities on itself in the form of demand deposits as it creates the obligation to repay the money on a specific future date (credit).[14] When a nonbank financial intermediary makes a loan or an investment, it creates credit in exactly the same way that a bank does, but, in the process of credit creation, the nonbank financial intermediary transfers to the borrower demand deposits that it has in its commercial bank account or currency that it has in its vault.

After a borrower receives the demand deposits created by the bank, he will use them to accomplish the purpose for which he was granted a loan. If the borrower is a business, it might have received a loan to purchase newly produced capital equipment (investment), or to pay its employees (distribution), or to purchase office supplies (consumption). If the borrower is a consumer, he might use the proceeds to purchase an automobile or a boat (consumption). If the borrower is a state or local government, the proceeds might be used to finance the construction of a hospital (government spending). Use of these funds to purchase goods and services usually stimulates businesses to increase the utilization of resources in order to produce more goods and services. The act of production, of course, creates income in the hands of factor owners, who are also consumers. Because they have more income, consumers then are in a position to buy more goods and services.

Trust Services

A *trust*, essentially, is a fiduciary relationship involving property. The sharp growth in income and wealth in this country has created a great need for the long-run safekeeping and management of vast amounts of property. Commercial banks, in order to attract and to retain large individual and corporate deposits, moved into the business of providing trust services and, therefore, are fulfilling an important need in the economy. As of December 31, 1975, banks were administering $770.9 billion in trust assets. Trust assets at several banks are greater than the bank's own assets.

The trust business may be divided into two segments: personal and corporate. Most banks with trust departments provide only personal trust services. Although the corporate trust business is growing, it still is concentrated primarily with banks located in large metropolitan areas. Personal trust services may include estate and trust planning, serving as executor and/or trustee under a will, serving as guardian of a minor or a person ruled incapable of managing his own financial af-

[14]There are three primary ways that a bank lends money: (1) by crediting the borrowers demand deposit account, (2) by issuing a cashier's check, or (3) by paying out currency. Because of its convenience to both the bank and the borrower, the first method is used customarily. Regardless of which form the loan takes, eventually demand deposits will increase at a bank or banks somewhere, as the borrower purchases goods and services with the loan proceeds.

fairs, providing investment counseling and management, providing tax counseling and tax return preparation, and serving as custodian of securities, which also may involve the collection of dividend and interest income.

In the area of corporate trust services, a bank may serve as trustee of pension and profit-sharing plans. Under such an agreement, the bank receives the funds from the corporation, invests them, collects the income, and pays out the benefits. Banks also may serve as the trustee for a bond issue. This involves, first, ensuring that the corporation as a bond issuer fulfills all its obligations to the bondholders. In effect, the bank represents the interests of the bondholders. Second, as trustee for the bond issue, the bank receives the necessary funds from the corporation to pay any interest and principal payments that are due.

Other corporate trust services involve stock transfer and registration. As stock-transfer agents, the bank will maintain stockholder records and handle stock transfers. As registrar, the bank seeks to ensure that the stock is not overissued. Most corporate stock cerificates are, therefore, signed by both the stock-transfer agent and the registrar.

Finally, corporate trust departments have had active roles in many of the corporate mergers and takeover bids that occurred in recent years. A corporation interested in absorbing another company or, perhaps, only in taking a position in the stock, could place funds with a bank trust department that would take custody of any tendered stock and make payment to the tendering stockholders.

Other Services

The list of other services provided by banks is extensive. Many services are given primarily to attract deposits. Some of these are provided free to customers; others are performed for a fee. Because of rising costs, many banks, with the aid of better functional cost data, recently have begun to evaluate the profit contribution (negative or positive) of all bank services.

A partial list of miscellaneous services provided by banks includes Christmas Clubs, traveler's checks, bill collection for customers, wire transfers of money, business and financial advice, credit cards, safe deposit boxes, lockboxes, and foreign exchange. Numerous banks have affiliates that perform travel agency functions, mortgage banking, factoring, and data processing, and that provide all types of insurance, courier services, and equipment leasing.

Suggestions for Additional Reading

Dobson, Steven W. "Development of Capital Markets in the United States." Federal Reserve Bank of Dallas, *Business Review* (April 1976), pp. 1–11.

Flannery, Mark J. *An Economic Evaluation of Credit Unions in the United States*. Research Report No. 54. Boston: Federal Reserve Bank of Boston, February 1974.

Goldsmith, Raymond W. *Financial Institutions*. New York: Random House, 1968.

Harless, Doris E. *Nonbank Financial Institutions*. 4th ed. Richmond, Va.: Federal Reserve Bank of Richmond, October 1975.

Institute of Life Insurance. *Life Insurance Fact Book*. New York: Institute of Life Insurance (Annual).

Jacobs, Donald P.; Farwell, Loring C.; and Neave, Edwin. *Financial Institutions*. 5th ed. Homewood, Ill.: Richard D. Irwin, 1972.

Krooss, Herman E., and Blyn, Martin R. *A History of Financial Intermediaries*. New York: Random House, 1971.

Nadler, Paul S. *Commercial Banking in the Economy*. 2nd ed. New York: Random House, 1973.

National Association of Mutual Savings Banks. *National Fact Book: Mutual Savings Banking*. New York: National Association of Mutual Savings Banks (Annual).

Polakoff, Murray E., ed. *Financial Institutions and Markets*. Boston: Houghton Mifflin, 1970.

Robinson, Roland I., and Wrightsman, Dwayne. *Financial Markets: The Accumulation and Allocation of Wealth*. New York: McGraw-Hill, 1974.

U.S. Savings and Loan League. *Savings and Loan Fact Book*. Chicago: U.S. Savings and Loan League (Annual).

PART

I

Responsibilities and Reports of Bank Management

CHAPTER

2

The Functional Framework and Responsibilities of Bank Management

In Chapter 1, the five principal functions performed by commercial banks in our economy were discussed.[1] To perform these functions efficiently, the individual commercial bank should organize its personnel within a "functional framework" that has clear lines of authority and responsibility and that contains explicit job descriptions for everyone. No business, be it the corner service station or the Bank of America, can function effectively unless everyone involved knows where he fits into the organization, what his job is, and to whom he reports.

In this chapter we shall (1) discuss the functional framework for the organization of a commercial bank, (2) explore some of the considerations that influence the bank's organization structure, and (3) note the responsibilities and functions of bank directors, bank director committees, and the principal executive officers of the bank.

[1]Not all banks perform the trust function or provide the same services, of course.

Probably no two banks in the nation are organized in the same manner. All banks, however, have two common objectives: (1) the acquisition of funds and (2) the utilization of funds. The specific banking functions of holding deposits and providing for a payments mechanism and other services are related to the acquisition of funds. The creation of money and credit, of course, is the principal way in which funds are utilized.

Bank Functions Designed to Acquire Funds

In the market for funds, the individual bank faces intense competition from other banks, nonbank financial intermediaries, and the savings instruments available in the organized security markets. Gone are the days when a bank could hang out its shingle and acquire sufficient funds to meet the needs of all its creditworthy customers. Today, the acquisition of funds involves considerable planning and expense. Many banks have reacted to the growing competition for funds by creating a separate staff marketing function with the specific responsibility of planning and developing programs for funds acquisition. The responsibility for implementation of these programs rests with line personnel, such as new-business development officers, branch managers, and tellers. Let us examine the functions of the marketing department in a modern bank and see briefly how line personnel carry out programs developed by the marketing group.

Functions of the Marketing Department

Bank marketing departments perform at least five functions: (1) research, (2) program development, (3) advertising, (4) public relations, and (5) facility design.

Research. The basic idea of the "marketing concept" is to determine what the public needs and wants and to supply it. After defining the geographic limits within which it plans to operate, a bank must determine the financial needs and requirements of the individuals, businesses, and governmental units comprising its market area. This involves marketing research. A bank's marketing research staff is an intelligence-gathering group that is continually "taking the pulse" of the marketplace in order to verify the degree of success of existing programs, or to plan new ways to acquire and utilize funds. An example of a current bank marketing research effort by many banks stems from the competition for passbook savings deposits. In this regard, a bank's marketing research staff could survey the market to determine the public's awareness of interest-rate differentials among financial intermediaries and the public's attitude toward various savings plans that the bank could offer.[2] Given this information and other economic and financial characteristics of the community, the marketing research staff then could recommend the types of savings instruments to emphasize and estimate the expected savings inflow if a particular program were adopted. Other tasks often performed by the marketing research group include the conduct of branch-location studies and the preparation of applications to the supervisory authorities for new banking offices (in those states permitting branch banking).

Program Development. Once the market for a new service has been verified and evaluated, the next step is program development. Many banks have taken a cue from the defense industry and assigned the task of instituting a new service to a project manager who will report directly to the head of the marketing department. Because the implementation of a new program usually requires changing several forms, systems, the flow of work, and perhaps the addition of equipment and people, the project manager must be familiar with virtually every aspect of the bank's operation. The project manager must ensure that an information and training program is developed and coordinated. In addition, he must ensure that the advertising campaign associated with the new service is developed and executed on time. The project manager's responsibilities end when he turns the program over to the functionally responsible department. Most of the bank charge-card programs adopted during the late 1960s were instituted via the project-manager system.

Advertising. Most banks today employ an advertising agency or a staff specialist to develop and coordinate the bank's advertising program. Even if an advertising agency is retained, an advertising specialist is still needed to serve as liaison between the bank and the agency. The bank's director of advertising, as he or she is usually called, must ensure that the agency fully understands the nature of the banking market served, set schedules for specific campaigns, and convey effectively to the agency what management's philosophy and objectives are.

An important part of the advertising specialist's duties is to develop an advertising budget and to allocate funds among the various promotional media. A fundamental principle is that funds should be spent on advertising up to the point where the marginal benefits equal the marginal costs. Similarly, within the total advertising budget, funds also should be allocated among the different media based on the marginal principle. The advertising director's task is complicated by changing economic and financial conditions and by competitive moves of other financial institutions.

[2]Recently, several banks have employed behavioral scientists to assist in the conduct and evaluation of surveys dealing with the public.

Public Relations. Closely related to the advertising function is the public relations function. The public relations or information officer is concerned with providing information to the public, customers, shareholders, and staff, and with representing the bank and its point of view to the various broadcasting and publications media. Usually this officer is called on to write speeches or comments presented by the bank's president and other officers. In addition, the public relations officer may plan, coordinate, and distribute the bank's external publications such as the quarterly and annual reports.

Facility Design. Finally, the importance of modern and attractive facilities to the acquisition of funds must not be overlooked. In years past, banks built massive, fortlike buildings with interiors dominated by steel bars, wire cages, multilock safes, and heavy, ponderous vault doors to impress the public that their deposits were physically safe. In lieu of building "Greek temples," banks now emphasize deposit insurance to their customers as a means of protection. As for decor, banks today employ a variety of architectural styles, materials, and colors in the design of their facilities. The marketing department is the logical choice to coordinate and control the bank's physical image.

Clearly, the head of the marketing department occupies a very important place in a modern bank. Ideally, he should report to the president or chief executive officer, and should be a permanent member of every senior management committee. He would not be able to develop a marketing plan for the bank without full knowledge of the bank's objectives as determined by the board of directors and senior management.

Functions of Line Personnel

Although the marketing department is responsible for the development of specific plans and programs to acquire funds, it usually does not implement them or participate directly in the programs. Instead, the plans are carried out by the bank's public-contact personnel, depending on the particular program involved. Among those who actually go to the public in connection with funds acquisition programs are new-business development officers; trust business development officers; branch managers and teller staff; international banking officers; national account officers; and installment, commercial, and mortgage loan officers. As a general rule, bank officers, regardless of their functional duties, direct their business development efforts toward corporate customers. The tellers and other nonofficer staff customarily are concerned in their business development efforts with individuals. This is not to underestimate the value of individual account relationships, for a substantial number of such deposit accounts provide stability to the bank's supply of funds. The impact of a single individual depositor's withdrawal, however, is far less than that of the typical corporate account. Still, the individual deposit customers are a potential market for installment loans, safe deposit boxes, the Christmas Club, trust business, and other fee services offered by the bank.

In the search for business funds, many organizational alternatives exist. At the heart of each approach should be a well-planned and organized officer-calling program. Such a program involves the periodic visitation with a prospective source of new deposit funds by an appropriate bank representative. In many banks, the task of calling is a portion of every public-contact officer's responsibilities. The work of these officers is directed not only toward the acquisition of new customers for the bank, but also toward retaining present customers and expanding their use of the bank's services. Over time, bank officers normally become knowledgeable about their customers' businesses and industry relationships. As a result, the bank can offer a high quality of corporate financial assistance and counsel.

Bank Functions Designed to Utilize Funds

We shall now examine briefly the functional framework through which funds are utilized. Parts III, IV, and V contain more detailed discussions of the ways in which banks employ their funds.

The management of bank funds or assets involves the allocation of the bank's resources among competing uses, such as cash, fixed assets, loans, and investments. Traditionally, banks have allocated the bulk of their funds among four principal types of earning assets: (1) commercial loans, (2) consumer loans, (3) mortgage loans, and (4) investments.

Commercial Loans

As we saw in Chapter 1, commercial banks have played a vital role in facilitating the economic development of the United States by supplying credit to business and industry. Historically, commercial loans have had first priority in the use of bank funds.

Within the bank's organizational structure, the board of directors sets broad loan policies for commercial lending. Banks with assets of $25 million or more usually have a commercial loan group headed by a senior officer who is responsible for setting operational policies for the commercial lending function. These include the establishment of guidelines with respect to the mix of loans by industry and geographic region within the portfolio, interest rates, compensating balance requirements, and maturities. Within the commercial loan group are several junior loan officers and usually a credit department, which must evaluate and make recommendations regarding credit requests.

Consumer Loans

Since World War II, few bank functions have grown as rapidly as the consumer loan operation. The concept of "buy now, pay later" has become deeply ingrained in the American public's life style. Consumer loans are made to individuals for a variety of purposes: the purchase of automobiles, appliances, furniture, mobile homes, boats, and campers; to pay taxes, educational and medical expenses; and for home repair and modernization.

Just as with commercial loans, broad consumer loan policies are established by the board of directors. Most banks today have a consumer or installment loan group headed by a senior officer who has functional reponsibilities for carrying out the board's policies. Under this department head are consumer loan officers who have the day-to-day task of making and administering consumer loans.

Mortgage Loans

To perform mortgage lending on a large scale, a bank must have knowledgeable personnel in the areas of real estate appraisal, law, and taxation. Today, most medium-sized banks have mortgage loan departments staffed with specialists in these areas. Again, the board of directors must determine to what extent the bank wishes to participate in mortgage lending. Usually participation depends on the availability of time and savings deposits and of mortgage lending specialists. If a mortgage loan department is established, it will be headed by an experienced officer in real estate credit, and there will be several other public-contact officers to handle the myriad details involved in granting mortgage credit.

Investments

Most banks have an investment committee composed of several members of the board of directors and the senior investment officer. This committee will ensure that the bank's investment portfolio is in keeping with the board's written investment guidelines. In large banks there is an investment group staffed by specialists in investing and trading in Treasury, municipal, and corporate securities. Besides handling the bank's own portfolio, the investment department will buy and sell securities for other financial intermediaries, businesses, and individuals. Within the investment section, large banks usually have a separate underwriting department that is concerned with the underwriting of certain eligible debt issues.

Supporting Services

In our discussion of those groups engaged in the acquisition and use of funds, little mention has been made of certain other bank functions, whose purpose it is to provide administrative support. Yet, without the existence of the operations and control, audit, and personnel staff, the people and tools required to accomplish the tasks of acquiring funds and using them profitably would be overburdened with tasks not directly related to their principal functions.

Operations and Control

The basic purpose of the operations and control function in a commercial bank is to provide service and support in the form of efficient systems, accounting procedures, records, forms, and equipment to ensure the operation of the bank within the requirements of law and appropriate regulatory authorities. To discharge these responsibilities, the cashier, who is usually the senior operations officer in a nationally chartered bank, normally designates several subfunctions. Typical of these are data processing, accounting or control, systems, line operations, and purchasing.

Data Processing. In terms of numbers of people and expense involved, the data-processing organization is the largest staff group under the cashier. The principal task of this group is to process by computer the large volume of checks coming into the bank daily. Some of the other banking tasks handled by computer are loan accounting, investment records, shareholder files, budgets, income and expense statements, equipment inventories, personnel and payroll information, security transfers, trust accounting, and the bank's general ledger. The substitution of electronic equipment for clerical workers in banking has led to a heavy investment in computers. Because of the expense incurred in equipment, techniques continually must be devised by the data-processing head to increase the computers' utilization and to force down processing costs. A programming and systems staff becomes a necessary result of this effort.

Accounting. The accounting or control staff is that group concerned directly with the day-to-day management of the bank's central accounting activity. This group maintains the appropriate records for income, expenses, and budget. Insurance programs relating to the bank's property and the safeguarding of depositors' funds or securities against embezzlement or unexplained loss often are responsibilities assigned to this group. This function also is concerned with the bank's tax planning and returns. Because of the flow of information on all aspects of the bank that passes through this area, it is the logical group to prepare the variety of reports required by senior management. In addition, the cashier refers to the accounting and control staff for the periodic information required by the Comptroller of the Currency, the Federal Reserve, the FDIC, or the state banking department.

Systems. The work of a bank, like that of any other organization, is actually completed by many small groups of people requiring varying amounts of space, equipment, and forms. A process adopted by larger banks to study and develop more efficient ways of performing various tasks is that of *systems analysis.* A system's staff is used in the continuing effort to provide improved service and support to all bank functions by the development and implementation of improved internal processing techniques and procedures. Because cost controls work-measurement programs, new equipment evaluation and standardization and forms design and control are routine assignments for a systems group. "People" costs continue to be a heavy portion of total bank expense. It is the responsibility of the systems staff, in conjunction with department heads and first-line supervisors, to develop better work processes and to utilize current technology to help management control such expense.

Line Operations. "Line operations" is a banking term covering those subfunctions concerned with the day-to-day processing and accounting for checks, deposits, loan payments, the routing of checks payable by other banks to their proper destination, the teller function, the settlement of accounts between banks, the collection of drafts and notes, and the operation of the safe-deposit-box program. In brief, these functions provide the detailed support necessary to service efficiently the processes of funds acquisition and use. A major concern of the line operations staff is physical security and the application of proper measures to safeguard customer funds and the bank's assets.

Purchasing. The responsibility for purchasing the bank's supplies and equipment rests with the purchasing department, which is usually adjunct to the operations and control group. The purchasing department, typically, is responsible for inventory records of bank furniture and equipment.

Audit

The principal purpose of the internal auditing function is to assist all members of bank management in the effective discharge of their responsibilities by furnishing them with objective analyses, appraisals, recommendations, and pertinent comments concerning the procedures and activities that are reviewed.[3] Unlike other major bank functions, whose heads report to the president or chief executive officer, the bank's general auditor reports to the audit committee of the board of directors. This places him in the position of being able to bypass active

[3]Internally sponsored audits essentially involve checking bank procedures, whereas *examinations* by the banking regulatory authorities entail the valuation of bank assets and compliance with banking laws and regulation.

management and go directly to the board on matters relating to actions or policies of management that have an impact on the directors' liability or responsibility under banking law.

The general auditor provides support to other bank departments through the scheduling of audits and written reports to management. Such reports enable those responsible either to note the adequacy of their procedures or to institute corrective action. Always, the state of maintenance of internal controls is examined to limit the opportunity for fraud.

Personnel

The basic purpose of a bank's personnel department is to contribute to the profit-making and customer service objectives of the bank by ensuring the effective acquisition, development, deployment, and retention of the bank's human resources. In order to provide for intelligent manpower planning, executive recruitment, and salary administration throughout the organization, the head of the personnel department ideally should report to the president. It is primarily through the effective use of the bank's human resources that the bank's objectives are met.

Among the activities of the bank's personnel staff are recruitment, job description writing, job evaluation, salary surveys, employment studies, the negotiation and administration of employee benefits, payroll accounting, maintenance of personnel records, training programs at various levels, and the coordination of enrollment of staff members in various banking schools. To provide service and support to all levels of management, it is necessary that the personnel function cross organizational lines and be accessible to any and all persons within the bank. A very close working relationship with all other functional heads is needed to supply the people and managerial techniques necessary for these departments to accomplish their objectives.

Some Considerations Influencing the Bank's Organizational Structure

Even though banks may use the same terms to describe functions or services performed, their organizational structure may be entirely different. Three important factors influence every bank's organizational structure: (1) the nature of the market served, (2) its size, and (3) the applicable laws regarding branching. The plan of organization for the Seattle-First National Bank, with assets of $5.3 billion, is shown in Figure 2-1. This plan is representative of an organizational structure for a large bank with many branches and a wide range of services.

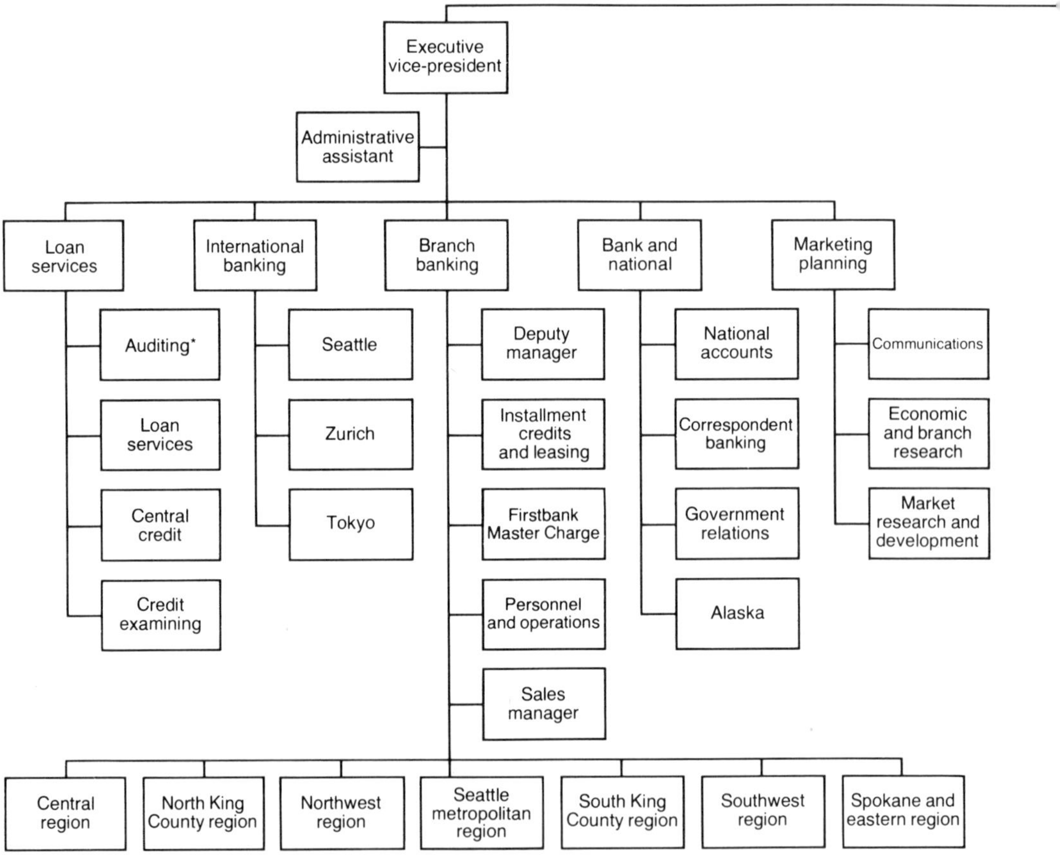

*Audit reporting responsibility direct to Board of Directors.

Figure 2-1 Plan of Organization, Seattle–First National Bank

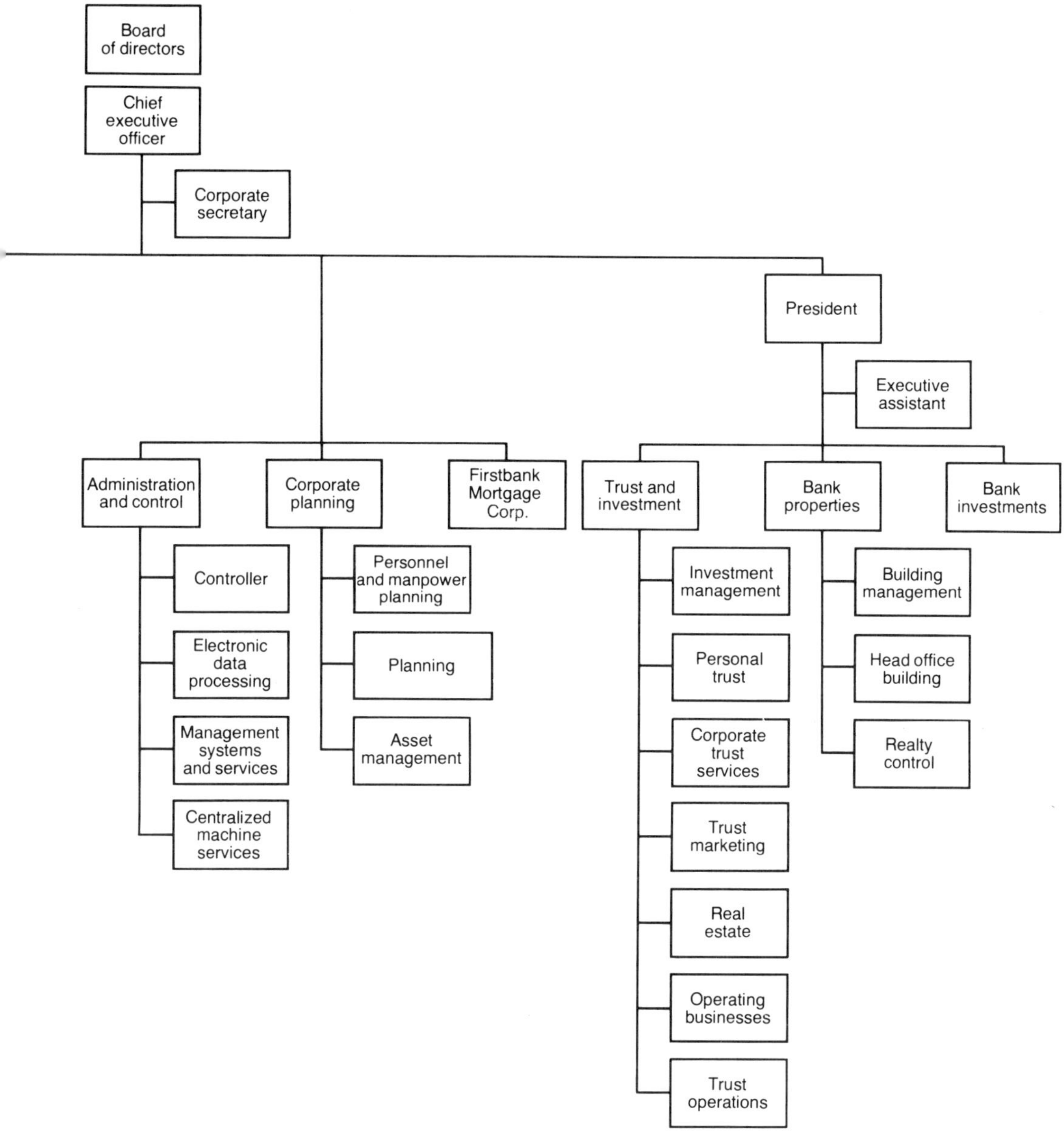
Board of directors
Chief executive officer
Corporate secretary
President
Executive assistant
Administration and control
Corporate planning
Firstbank Mortgage Corp.
Trust and investment
Bank properties
Bank investments
Controller
Electronic data processing
Management systems and services
Centralized machine services
Personnel and manpower planning
Planning
Asset management
Investment management
Personal trust
Corporate trust services
Trust marketing
Real estate
Operating businesses
Trust operations
Building management
Head office building
Realty control

The Nature of the Market Served

The financial needs of the market within which a commercial bank operates dictates, to a large extent, the alignment of functions in the bank's organizational structure. On December 31, 1975, 12,456 or 86.6 percent, of the 14,384 commercial banks in the United States had deposits of $50 million or less. Therefore, because of their size, the vast majority of the banks deal primarily with small business and individual depositors and borrowers. These banks feature such services as small business loans, accounts receivable financing, and small denomination certificates of deposits for their business customers; and installment loans, savings deposits, and safe deposit boxes for their individual customers.

If a bank were located in an agricultural community, emphasis organizationally would be placed on serving the agribusiness sector and its special needs. With a considerable portion of loan volume and income dependent on agriculture, the functional head of this loan area would be a senior officer with several junior loan officers under him.

Specific industries also call for the full-time attention of certain bank specialists. For example, Republic National Bank in Dallas and First City National Bank of Houston have divisions that are concerned solely with the petroleum industry and its special financial problems. Similarly, First National Bank of Memphis and Union Planters National Bank of Memphis have commodity divisions that specialize in handling the unique requirements of buying, selling, and hedging for cotton producers. First National Bank of Chicago and Continental Illinois National Bank and Trust Company of Chicago have had their commercial loan divisions organized along industry lines for many years. Other banks have special divisions listed on their organization charts concerned with international banking, state and municipal finance, insurance, and transportation. Seattle-First National Bank has a department devoted to serving the banking needs of Alaska. Specialized departments such as these exist primarily, of course, in the larger metropolitan banks. Obviously, each smaller bank is equally concerned with its community and its specialized needs, but it does not specify them in its organizational structure.

Citibank was a pioneer in organizing its services into groups on a worldwide scale based on the size and location of its customers. The major groups and their functions are (1) International Banking Group—manages overseas banking activities; (2) World Corporation Group—serves multinational corporations, whether based in the United States or abroad; (3) National Banking Group—provides financial services for U.S.-based corporations, except multinational accounts; (4) Merchant Banking Group—offers governments, corporations, and financial institutions throughout the world financial consulting and advisory services, and in the United States, this group participates in the underwriting, distribution, and trading of federal, state, and municipal securities; (5) Consumer Services Group—provides a wide range of services to individuals; and (6) Investment Management Group—provides various fiduciary services to individuals and businesses. These banking groups are almost self-contained organizations designed to provide complete financial services and counseling.

The national division of a large metropolitan bank offers an illustration of a department organized to serve specific geographic areas. For example, the National Division at the Manufacturers Hanover Trust Company of New York is subdivided into the following service districts: Greater New York, Southwestern, Mid-Western, Western, New England, Mid-Atlantic, Central, South Atlantic, and Southern. By concentrating on serving the firms and banks in a particular area, a banker in a particular division becomes more familiar with the nature of business and banking in his region, thereby permitting the bank to provide better services.

Size

As a bank succeeds in attracting funds and in employing them profitably, growth ensues. With an expansion of assets, loans, and deposits, problems of internal bank management and control increase. The bank finds that it can no longer function effectively and efficiently with many officers performing as "jacks-of-all-trades." It must hire specialists in certain functional areas, such as commercial and installment lending, investments, personnel, and marketing.

Size does not just cause a need for specialization; it may be a result of specialization. In today's competitive banking market, financially sophisticated individual and corporate customers demand a number of specialized services, such as cash flow analysis, investment counseling, lockbox arrangements, international banking services, and trust services. Banks that can provide a variety of needed services obviously stand to grow faster than those that do not.

When a bank hires specialists, the bank's organizational structure is altered significantly. Lines of authority and responsibility are changed. The number of officers reporting to the president probably will be reduced if several senior or executive vice-president positions are created as a result of growth. As may be seen in Figure 2-1, size apparently has caused Seattle-First National Bank to create an executive vice-president position that is on the same level as the president. Both positions report to the chief executive offecer.

Branching Laws

The laws governing whether a bank may have more than one physical place of business vary considerably among the states.[4] Most states limit

[4]Branch banking will be discussed further in Chapter 17.

branch banking. Illinois and Texas, for example, permit no branch banking. Ohio permits a bank to branch but limits branching to the county in which the head office is located. Nebraska limits additional outlets for a bank to "facilities" that may be located up to 2,600 feet from the main office. These "facilities" are limited in function to accepting deposits and loan payments. On the other hand, California, Arizona, and the two Carolinas, for example, permit statewide branch banking.

The geographic dispersion of a bank's branches has obvious implications for its organizational structure. Where branching is permitted, a system for controlling and coordinating the various offices must be created. One approach to branch management is to group the branch officers by geographical location; that is, all offices in a specified area are placed under the administrative control of a group or regional vice-president (see Figure 2-1). Branches also may be grouped on the basis of size of office, with total deposits and loans outstanding as determining criteria. Another approach is to control the branches through the principal banking functions whose managers are located in the headquarters office. Under this concept, the functional heads, such as those for commercial and installment lending, have officer counterparts in the branch offices. These branch officers are responsible to the major functional head rather than to the city executive for the manner in which they discharge their duties. In small branch banks, the best approach may be to have each branch office head report to the bank president directly. In these circumstances, the branch officer, operating within the bank's overall policies, is responsible for all activities in his office.

Responsibilities, Duties, and Liabilities of Bank Directors

The final responsibility for the success or failure of a commercial bank rests with the board of directors. These men and women usually are selected to serve because of their prestige in the community and because they control, indirectly or directly, a considerable volume of deposits that may be placed in the bank. As a rule, the directors are involved deeply in their own business or professional activities and participate to a great extent in many civic and community projects. Selection as a bank director places another demand on the time of a busy individual.

The person who takes his selection as a director lightly is in for a surprise. In return for the honor, fees, and psychic rewards that bank directors receive goes the responsibility for all phases of the bank's operation and exposure to criminal and civil liabilities if they are negligent in the discharge of their duties.

Responsibilities of Bank Directors

Bank directors are responsible to the bank's depositors and shareholders and to the appropriate supervisory authorities.

To Depositors. With respect to depositors, a bank's directors must ensure that adequate funds are available to meet withdrawals and that there is adequate capital to absorb possible loan defaults or a decline in security values. Depositors also have a right to expect directors to employ only capable and honest officers and personnel to run the bank. Although the FDIC insures deposits up to $40,000 per depositor, the safety of funds beyond this amount depends largely on the care and diligence of the active managers, who process deposit transactions and make the bank's loans and investments.

To Shareholders. Like all shareholders, people who own bank stocks expect a reasonable return on their investments. They have a right to expect that the directors will exert positive leadership in supervising the bank's affairs. In the competitive banking environment that exists in most communities today, bank profits are not generated accidentally; they are the result of hard work and imaginative planning. New programs and better services to attract depositors and innovative financing arrangements to attract sophisticated borrowers do not just happen; they must be conceived, developed, and implemented. Because bank directors are usually successful in their own lines of endeavor, they can be the source of many ideas that can be translated by the bank's staff into profit-making programs. Often it is said that "behind every successful man is an inspiring and devoted wife." A good case could be made that "behind every highly successful and profitable bank is a hard-working and devoted board of directors."

To Supervisory Agencies. A national bank is examined three times in a two-year period. In the interim, a bank's directors essentially are surrogates for the supervisory authorities. They must oversee and audit the bank's affairs to ensure compliance with the many statutes and regulations that apply to the banks. When the bank examiners do arrive, their task is simplified greatly if the bank's directors have discharged their responsibilities fully. If discrepancies and questionable practices are discovered, however, it is the directors who are responsible for ensuring their elimination. Examination reports are forwarded to directors, who must note in the board's minutes what corrective action they have taken with respect to each shortcoming and problem area. It should be clear to bank directors, therefore, that "an ounce of prevention is worth a pound of cure."

Duties of Bank Directors

To discharge their responsibilities, bank directors must assume certain duties. These duties either are set forth in the banking statutes or are derived from common law by virtue of the director's fiduciary relationship to the bank's depositors and shareholders. In this regard there are six duties that bank directors must perform: (1) assure that realistic goals are set for the bank, (2) formulate broad policies to achieve these goals, (3) select management, (4) create committees, (5) develop business, and (6) supervise the bank's operations.

Goals. Robert Townsend, in his best-selling book *Up the Organization*, states that the first task of management is to set the goals and objectives of the organization. Preferably, the goals should be formulated in a short and succinct statement that can be remembered easily by everyone in the company. At every opportunity all officers and employees should be reminded of this statement of objectives. Townsend credits much of the success of his company, Avis, to the fact that it has a very short and simple goal: ". . . . to become the fastest-growing company with the highest profit margins in the business of renting and leasing vehicles without drivers."[5]

There is considerable merit in this goal-oriented approach to the management of a bank. A bank's directors cannot establish policies if they do not have a clear concept of their goals. In this regard, directors and active management should formulate a short statement that sets forth the bank's short-run, or intermediate, objective. For example, one bank adopted as its goal during its eighth year of operation "$100 million in deposits by our tenth anniversary." Every director, shareholder, officer, and employee of the bank knows this goal. It permits everyone concerned to relate to a common purpose and to know that each of his fellow employees is striving toward the same objectives.

It is recommended also that directors and active management establish annual and three- or five-year profit objectives for the bank. These profit objectives should be in written form and discussed frequently at staff meetings. A progress report on profits should be a regular part of each directors' meeting. In order to achieve the bank's profit goals, a detailed plan should be established outlining the amount of deposits and loans, by type and source, that the bank must acquire to attain its profit objectives. Comparison of the present volume and types of deposits and loans with the volume types necessary to achieve the profit goal should be an integral part of management's monthly report to directors.

[5]Robert Townsend, *Up the Organization* (New York: Alfred A. Knopf, 1970), p. 129.

Policies. To achieve the publicized short-run, or intermediate, goal and the profit objectives of the bank, the directors must formulate written policies or guidelines for themselves and the bank's staff to follow. For example, a policy must be outlined with respect to the lending function. Such a policy should include the types of loans the bank wishes to make, the territory, from which the loans are to come, and the action to be taken with respect to slow loan charge-offs. Without such a policy, there could not be a unified effort to achieve the profit goals. Loan officers would not know what types of loans to encourage or to solicit, and neither would the personnel officer know what special qualifications he should look for in recruiting prospective loan officers. Without written guidelines, an overzealous loan officer might expose the bank to unnecessary risks in order to achieve the desired profit level.

The same basic rationale applies to the investment function. If the directors believe that the bank's tax position and liquidity requirements permit an aggressive investment policy with respect to intermediate or long-term municipal securities, the policy should be so stated in written form and incorporated in the board minutes and, preferably, also in a bank policy manual.

Other bank policies adopted by the directors might deal with the risk and insurance program, employee-customer lunches, the nature of the bank's profit-sharing and pension plan, sick leave, vacations, and salary review. A clear statement of policy from the board of directors does much to remove many of the uncertainties that reduce operating efficiency and might short-circuit the bank's profit objectives.

Management. Directors should not be involved intimately in the day-to-day operations of the bank. Rather, it is their duty to select capable officers who can implement the policies that the board has established. In addition to selecting the bank's principal officers, the directors must set their salaries and fringe benefits. Directors should try to stay abreast of the bank salary picture and to reward management commensurately with their effort and contribution toward the bank's goals.

Committees. Primarily because of their overall responsibilities for the bank's operation and because of the limited time that they have to devote to the bank's affairs, bank directors must create committees in order to reduce their work load to more manageable proportions. The requirements for creating committees to oversee the lending, investment, audit, and trust areas usually are specified in the bank's bylaws and the applicable statutes under which the bank operates. Committees also are a device for most efficiently utilizing the special talents of a board member in a particular functional area. For example, if one board member is a professional accountant, he would be a logical choice for a seat on the audit committee.

Business. By virtue of their prominent role in the community, directors have an opportunity and a duty to seek and to develop business for the bank. Especially in small banks, the directors usually are responsible, in one way or another, for substantial deposits and loans. Because their names appear on every statement of condition that is published, the public tends to associate various directors with their banks. In their normal, everyday business contact with the public, directors are more or less expected "to put in a good word" for their banks.

Along this line, it is beneficial for the directors to set personal annual goals with regard to business development. This is especially desirable in the case of a new bank, which must get off to a good start. For example, the directors of an established bank might decide that their personal goal is to increase their bank's share of deposits by two percentage points this year. In a community with $200 million in deposits, this would amount to $4 million, which, when divided among ten directors, amounts to a rather reasonable and attainable goal of $400,000 each.

Bank Operations. In addition to the above specific duties, directors are accountable for all the bank's operations. They carry out this duty by attending periodic meetings at which they receive detailed reports about the bank's operations. After hearing these reports, they should question the bank's executive officers about specific items and should satisfy themselves that problem areas are receiving proper attention from management. In addition to handling committee duties and attending board meetings, directors should visit the bank frequently and discuss the bank's operations informally with various senior and junior officers. This display of interest on the part of the directors will contribute toward a general alertness in the bank.

Liabilities of a Bank Director

Bank directors are exposed to both criminal and common-law liabilities as they carry out their responsibilities and duties. With respect to these liabilities, "directors of a national bank may become personally liable for losses sustained by the bank due to a statutory breach in which the directors participated or to which they assented, a failure to exercise the requisite degree of care and prudence under the common law or a breach of duty to conduct the affairs of the bank with the utmost loyalty".[6]

Criminal Liabilities. Statutory liability of bank directors is predicated on provisions contained in the National Bank Act, the Federal Reserve

[6]The Comptroller of the Currency, *Duties and Liabilities of Directors of National Banks* (Washington, D.C.: The Comptroller of the Currency, 1972), p. 2.

Act, and applicable state statutes. Violation of the federal statutes usually carries a maximum fine of $5,000 or imprisonment of not more than five years, or both. *Duties and Liabilities of Directors of National Banks*, published by the Comptroller of the Currency, contains a partial list of the criminal laws applicable to national bank directors. Violations for which directors, officers, agents, or employees may be prosecuted include the following:[7]

1. False entries, false reports, etc.
2. False certification of checks.
3. Theft, embezzlement, or misapplication by bank officer or employees.
4. False representation as to FDIC coverage.
5. Violation of prohibition of loans to bank examiners.
6. Violation of prohibition of loans of trust funds to directors.
7. Violation of prohibition of director receiving fee for procuring loans, etc.
8. Violation of prohibition of political contributions and expenditures.
9. Violation of prohibition of participation by financial institutions in lotteries.

Common-Law Liability for Negligence. Directors may be held personally liable under the common law for negligence. As it pertains to bank directors, common-law negligence may be defined as the failure to exercise ordinary care and prudence in the administration of the affairs of a bank. In carrying out their duties, directors are not liable, for example, for bad judgment that results in a loan default. Directors are liable, however, if they fail to use ordinary care in the initial investigation of the creditworthiness of the borrower, or if they do not use reasonable diligence to collect the loan, once there are serious doubts about its repayment. Moreover, a director who fails to attend directors' meetings may not plead ignorance as a defense against liability arising from transactions that are made without the use of ordinary care and prudence.

Handling the Liability Risk. There are three possible methods of handling the statutory and common-law liablity risk that directors face: (1) avoidance, (2) prevention and control, and (3) transfer.

The first alternative would be to avoid the risk of liability by not becoming a bank director. If a potential director cannot devote the time and energy to discharge his responsibilities satisfactorily, then the first alternative is clearly best for both him and the bank.

The second way that a director might deal with the liability risk would be to take positive action to prevent and to control the possibility of loss. In this regard, all the director would have to do is exercise

[7] *Ibid.*, pp. 8–10.

the ordinary care and prudence demanded by common law, and study and familiarize himself with the statutory provisions dealing with his job and the affairs of the bank.

A third approach to dealing with the liability risk would involve transferring a portion of it to an insurance company. Several companies offer a director and officers liability policy for banks whose directors and officers are subject to liability under statutory or common law. Typical limits on this coverage run from $400,000 to $10 million, with a minimum deductible of $20,000 and a 5 percent participation by the insured bank in losses in excess of the deductible. Clearly, this third method of handling the director's liability risk would not be a substitute for, but rather a desirable complement to, the second alternative.

Responsibilities and Duties of Bank Director Committees

In order to divide the workload of overseeing the bank's operations and to discharge certain statutory responsibilities, a number of standing committees must be formed. These may include (1) the executive committee, (2) the loan committee, (3) the investment committee, (4) the audit committee, (5) the trust committee, and (6) the salary and employee relations committee.

Executive Committee

The executive committee of a bank is usually empowered by the bylaws to decide on all questions of policy between regularly scheduled board meetings. These powers do not include the declaration of dividends or the adoption, amendment, or repeal of the bylaws. The executive committee must file copies of its minutes with the board of directors, who, in turn, must ratify any actions taken by the committee.

Loan Committee

The primary function of the loan committee is to screen loan applications above a certain limit as specified in the board's written loan policy. At small banks this limit may be as low as $25,000, while at larger banks it may be $1 million or more. The loan committee itself may have a loan limit, in which case loan applications above that amount would be sent to the full board of directors. In addition to individual loan applications, the loan committee periodically reviews the composition of loans, interest rates charged, and security requirements. In smaller banks the executive committee and the loan committee may be combined.

Investment Committee

The functions of the investment committee involve matters of portfolio policy, including the types and maturities of securities in which the bank should invest. As with the loan committee, the investment committee should operate within a written investment policy for the bank. The types of investment decisions that a bank's investment committee might make would include the degree of participation the bank would have in a local municipal bond issue or the extent to which the bank should purchase long-term governments if the economic circumstances and yield-curve analysis warrant.

Audit Committee

The audit or examination committee is a very important means by which the directors assure that the bank is operating within the applicable banking statutes and regulations. It is recommended highly that this committee appoint an outside CPA firm to audit the bank's books at such times as it may believe necessary and at least annually. The audit committee then would review the CPA firm's report and make any necessary examinations itself in order to be satisfied with regard to the bank's financial condition and procedures. The president is not a member of the committee.

Trust Committee

The primary function of the trust committee is to oversee the administration of the bank's trust accounts and the investment of the funds in these accounts. At some banks with large trust departments, there may be a trust administration committee and a trust investment committee. Trust committees with investment responsibility make essentially the same type of decisions that the bank's regular investment committee does, except that they have different goals and a different set of statutory constraints.

Salary and Employee Relations Committee

Some banks have a salary and employee relations committee, which is charged with the responsibility of reviewing and determining annually senior management's salaries and employee benefits. The competition among banks, financial institutions, and industry for experienced officers and personnel is keen. A successful bank officer continually will receive offers to join other firms. It is imperative, therefore, that the salary and employee relations committee apprise itself of conditions in the job market and make every effort to match salary and benefits with performance.

Responsibilities and Duties of the Executive Group

The executive group of a typical bank consists of the chairman of the board of directors, the president, and one or more executive vice-presidents. As a group, these men are concerned with the development of the bank's objectives and image, the staffing of key officer positions, the bank's position on important social issues, and the bank's relationship with political parties and the various levels of government.

Chairman of the Board of Directors

The chairman of the board is responsible for making the board a viable and contributing entity in the bank. The position of chairman carries a great deal of prestige. Through his leadership ability, a strong and energetic chairman can inspire the board and enhance the image of the bank significantly within the community. Much of the chairman's time is spent on civic activities, such as heading the local United Fund or serving on community development boards. Typically, the chairman serves on the boards of other corporations and, in this capacity, usually can obtain significant deposits for the bank.

President

The president's responsibilities and duties within the bank depend on his background, his ability, and the size of the bank. If the president has experience in banking, he may assume much of the responsibility for the administration and overall supervision of the bank's operations. On the other hand, if he does not have a banking background, he may serve the bank best by being an "outside" man and concentrating on business development and community activities. In small banks, the president ordinarily must oversee the bank's internal operations, make loans, and carry the major burden of the bank's public relations effort. National banking law and most state banking statutes require that the president be on the board of directors.

Executive Vice-President

If a bank has an executive vice-president, he usually is involved intimately in the day-to-day affairs of the bank. The executive vice-president will assume many of the president's duties and will make many daily operational decisions. On important matters he will consult the president. In most small- to medium-sized banks, the president and executive vice-president operate as a team and divide the duties of running the bank.

Suggestions for Additional Reading

The American Bankers Association. *A Bank Director's Job.* Washington, D.C.: The American Bankers Association, 1970.

———. *Bank Public Relations and Marketing.* Washington, D.C.: American Bankers Association, 1967.

Baughn, William H., and Walker, Charls E., eds. *The Banker's Handbook.* Homewood, Ill.: Dow Jones-Irwin, 1966, chaps. 1–11, 52–66.

Berry, Leonard L., and Capaldini, L. A. *Marketing for the Bank Executive.* New York: Petrocelli Books, 1974.

The Comptroller of the Currency. *Duties and Liabilities of Directors of National Banks.* Washington, D.C.: The Comptroller of the Currency, 1972.

CHAPTER

3

Bank Reports and Profit Planning

As fiduciary institutions regulated by one or more levels of government, commercial banks are required to submit many reports and data to their appropriate supervisory agencies. These *external reports* provide the necessary information for the supervisory authorities to ensure that banks are operating in such a manner as not to jeopardize the safety of the public's funds and the smooth working of our financial system. In addition, banks are required by law to report certain information to their shareholders.

As profit-seeking institutions, banks also generate a considerable number of *internal reports* on the many aspects of their operations. These reports assist management in its analysis of the profitability of various services, functions, and offices and the performance of personnel in the key functional areas.

In this chapter we shall (1) note the primary reports that must be submitted to the banking supervisory agencies and to shareholders and

(2) discuss a system of bank profit planning and internal reporting that may be used by management.

Reports to Supervisory Authorities

Statement of Condition

As required by the FDIC Act, each insured state nonmember bank shall make to the FDIC, each insured national bank and each insured district bank shall make to the Comptroller of the Currency, and each insured state member bank shall make to the Federal Reserve Bank of which it is a member four reports of condition (*call reports*) annually on dates selected by the Chairman of the Board of Directors of the FDIC, the Comptroller of the Currency, and the Chairman of the Board of Governors of the Federal Reserve System, or a majority thereof. These call reports shall be submitted on two dates selected within the semiannual period of January to June inclusive and two dates selected within the semiannual period of July to December inclusive. The first two call reports shall be the basis of a certified statement filed in July showing the average semiannual assessment base for federal deposit insurance. The second two call reports shall be the basis of a certified statement filed in January that shows the average assessment base for the second semiannual period.

The correctness of each call report shall be attested by the signatures of at least three of the directors of the bank other than the officer making the declaration, with the declaration that the report has been examined by them and that to the best of their knowledge and belief it is true and correct. Call reports must be published in a newspaper where the bank is established. The information in the call report is usually rearranged for presentation to shareholders. The format in Table 3-1 is suggested by the FDIC as a guide for the preparation of statements of condition sent to shareholders of state insured nonmember banks. When required by their respective regulatory agencies, a bank must also submit with its report of condition a report of condition of each affiliate, such as computer service corporations or real estate subsidiaries that own bank properties.

Report of Income and Dividends

A bank must submit annually to its appropriate regulatory authority a report of its income and dividends for the twelve-month period ending December 31. Banks usually rearrange the data in the income statement for presentation to shareholders. The format in Table 3-2 is suggested by the FDIC as a guide for the preparation of income statements sent to shareholders of state insured nonmember banks. Each of the items in the income statement will be examined in detail in Chapter 4.

Table 3-1

Statement of Condition for
All Insured Commercial Banks in the United States
(millions of dollars)

	December 31	
	1975	1976
Assets		
1. Cash and due from banks	129,024	130,230
2. Investment securities		
(a) U.S. Treasury securities	81,011	96,866
(b) Securities of other U.S. Government agencies and corporations	33,299	34,306
(c) Obligations of states and political subdivisions	100,802	103,486
(d) Other securities	7,404	7,360
3. Trading account securities	5,332	7,882
4. Federal funds sold and securities purchased under agreements to resell	37,345	45,843
5. Loans, net	493,635	518,569
(a) Loans, total	502,290	524,750
(b) Less allowance for possible loan losses	8,633	6,181
6. Bank premises and equipment	15,598	16,686
7. Other real estate owned	1,909	2,888
8. Investments in subsidiaries not consolidated	1,993	2,303
9. Customers' acceptance liability	8,688	9,154
10. Other assets	27,757	35,480
11. Total assets	943,796	1,011,053
Liabilities		
12. Deposits:		
(a) Demand deposits	321,423	333,816
(b) Time deposits	459,326	496,908
13. Federal funds purchased and securities sold under agreements to repurchase	52,190	70,320
14. Other liabilities for borrowed money	4,651	5,128
15. Bank's acceptances outstanding	9,276	9,762
16. Mortgages payable	774	794
17. Other liabilities	27,080	16,958
18. Total liabilities	874,720	933,687

Table 3-1 (Continued)

	Capital Accounts		
19.	Capital notes and debentures	4,408	5,123
20.	Equity capital:	64,664	72,243
	(a) Capital stock:		
	Preferred stock	48	47
	Common stock	15,565	16,214
	(b) Surplus	26,713	28,883
	(c) Undivided profits	21,182	25,268
	(d) Capital reserves	1,156	1,830
21.	Total liabilities, reserves, and capital	943,796	1,011,053

Source: FDIC, *Annual Report* and unpublished data.
NOTE: Details may not add to totals due to rounding.

Other Reports

Besides the statement of condition and the income statement, banks are required to submit numerous other reports. Some of the principal ones are described below.

Report of Deposits, Currency and Coin, Loans, and Securities. After the close of business each Wednesday, member banks must submit a "Report of Deposits, Currency and Coin, Loans, and Securities" to the Federal Reserve Bank or branch holding their reserve account (see Figure 7-1). This report provides the Reserve bank with the data for computing required reserves.

Trust Department Reports. Each bank that exercises fiduciary powers must submit annually to its cognizant regulatory agency a report of condition of its trust department. In addition, each bank that operates a collective investment fund in connection with its fiduciary activities must file a financial report of the fund. This report must contain a list of investments in the fund showing the cost and current market value of each investment; a statement showing purchases, with cost; sales, with profit and loss, and any other investment changes; income and disbursements; and an appropriate notation as to any investments in default.

Reports of International Operations. National banks possessing a capital and surplus of $1 million or more may establish foreign branches, purchase stock in corporations engaged in foreign banking, and acquire ownership of foreign banks. National banks operating foreign branches must furnish information concerning the condition of such branches to the Comptroller of the Currency on demand, and

Table 3-2
Statement of Income for
All Insured Commercial Banks in the United States
(millions of dollars)

	1975	1976
1. Operating income:		
(a) Interest and fees on loans	43,380	51,626
(b) Income on federal funds sold and securities purchased under agreements to resell	2,295	1,984
(c) Interest and dividends on investments:		
1. U.S. Treasury securities	4,441	5,975
2. Securities of other U.S. Government agencies and corporations	2,349	2,414
3. Obligations of states and political subdivisions	4,918	5,133
4. Other securities	533	854
(d) Trust department income	1,602	1,794
(e) Service charges on deposit	1,555	1,635
(f) Other service charges, collection and exchange charges, commissions, and fees	1,654	2,182
(g) Other operating income	3,832	7,037
Total operating income	66,558	80,634
2. Operating expenses:		
(a) Salaries and wages; pensions and other employee benefits	12,687	14,743
(b) Interest on deposits	26,246	34,994
(c) Expense of federal funds purchased and securities sold under agreements to repurchase	3,323	3,312
(d) Interest on other borrowed money	377	666
(e) Interest on capital notes and debentures	294	344
(f) Occupancy expense of bank premises, net:	2,325	2,763
Gross occupancy expense	2,755	3,260
Less rental income	430	497
(g) Furniture and equipment expense (including depreciation)	1,533	1,720
(h) Provision for loan losses	3,612	3,688
(i) Other operating expenses	7,185	8,487
Total operating expenses	57,581	70,717
3. Income before income taxes and securities gains (losses)	8,977	9,918
4. Applicable income taxes	1,793	2,291
5. Income before securities gains (losses)	7,184	7,627
6. Net security gains (losses), less related tax effect	37	194
7. Income (before extraordinary items, if any)	7,221	7,822
8. Extraordinary items, less related tax effect	34	26
9. Less minority interest in consolidated subsidiaries	[a]	[a]
10. Net income	7,255	7,847

Source: FDIC, *Annual Report* and unpublished data.
[a] Less than $500,000.
NOTE: Details may not add to totals due to rounding.

every member bank investing in the capital stock of banks or corporations described above must furnish information concerning the condition of such branches to the Board of Governors of the Federal Reserve System on demand.

Reports on Security Devices. Because of numerous bank robberies in recent years, Congress passed the Bank Protection Act of 1968. Pursuant to this act, banks are required to file with their appropriate regulatory agency as of the last business day in June of each calendar year a statement certifying to compliance with certain minimum security standards.

Summary of Deposits. The FDIC requires that each insured bank report its deposits, by type, and by county, on June 30. Summaries of this deposit data are a valuable source document for bank marketing research.

Reports to Comply with Securities Registration Requirements. Pursuant to the Securities Exchange Act of 1934, as amended, the banking regulatory authorities have issued regulations requiring that banks with 500 or more shareholders of any class of equity securities must register with their appropriate federal banking agency. Registration is accomplished by filing a statement containing detailed information concerning the bank's principal security holders, management, and financial history. Subsequent to this initial registration, other reports are required. The frequency and nature of these additional reports vary according to the federal banking supervisory agency involved.

Of all the agencies, the FDIC requires the most elaborate set of reports under its securities registration regulations.[1] These reports include the following:

1. An initial registration statement.
2. An annual report.
3. A current report, which must be submitted within ten days after the close of any month during which any of a specific number of events occurred that altered or will alter the securities ownership or condition of the bank.
4. A quarterly report.
5. A registration statement for the issuance of an additional class of securities.
6. A report by any person who becomes the beneficial owner (including through tender offers) of more than 5 percent of any class of equity security.

[1]For a description of these reports, see Part 335 of FDIC, *Rules and Regulations*.

7. Reports dealing with proxy statements and solicitations and tender offers.
8. Reports on the securities transactions of "insiders."

Reports to Shareholders

Annual Report

Banks with 500 or more shareholders of any class of equity securities are required under authority of the Securities Exchange Act of 1934, as amended, to mail to each shareholder a written annual report. FDIC regulations require for insured nonmember banks that this report contain (1) comparative statements of condition at the end of each of the last two fiscal years, (2) comparative statements of income in a form providing for the determination of "net income" for each fiscal year and per share earnings data, (3) comparative statements of changes in capital accounts for each fiscal year, and (4) comparative reconciliations of the "Allowance for Possible Loan Losses" account and of the "Reserve on Securities" account. Guides for these first two statements were shown in Tables 3-1 and 3-2.

A suggested format for the "Statement of Changes in Capital Accounts" is illustrated in Table 3-3. This statement shows changes in capital notes and debentures and equity capital. Included in the latter are preferred and common stock, surplus, undivided profits, and contingency reserves.[2] Normally, the principal addition to capital accounts (specifically, undivided profits) is from net income. The primary deductions from capital are for cash dividends and transfers to reserves for loan and security losses.

"Valuation reserves," as they are sometimes called, are established to absorb possible losses on loans and securities. A guide for the reconciliation of the "Allowance for Possible Loan Losses" account is shown in Table 3-4. Transfers from income to the "Allowance for Possible Loan Losses" are listed under operating expenses as "Provision for Loan Losses" and are equal to either actual loan losses (charge-offs less recoveries) or an average percentage of loan losses experienced during the previous five years, applied to average loans outstanding during the current year. Most banks have elected to use the latter or *forward-moving*-average method of calculating the "Provision for Loan Losses." Additional amounts may be transferred from undivided profits to maintain

[2]*Contingency reserves* represent capital reserves or a segregation of undivided profits set aside for possible or unforeseen losses due to shrinkages in book value of assets or for other unforeseen or indeterminate liabilities not otherwise reflected in the bank's books. For example, a contingency reserve might be established as a precautionary measure against an unfavorable lawsuit.

Table 3-3
Statement of Changes in Capital Accounts (Sample)

Year Ended December 31, 1977: Increase (Decrease)	Capital Notes and Debentures	Preferred Stock $10 Par	Common Stock $5 Par	Surplus	Undivided Profits	Contingency Reserve
1. Net income transferred to undivided profits					827,909	
2. Capital notes and debentures and common stock sold (par or face value)	2,317,500					
3. Stock issued incident to merger and acquisitions		60,000				
4. Premium on capital stock sold						
5. Addition to, or reductions in, surplus, undivided profits, and reserves incident to mergers						
6. Transfer to allowance for loan loss, exclusive of portion charged against income, less related income tax effect of $53,910					(65,889)	
7. Cash dividends declared on preferred stock					(2,400)	
8. Cash dividends declared on common stock					(343,850)	
9. Stock issued in payment of stock dividend, shares at par value						
10. All other increases (decreases)						
transfer to reserves on securities					(30,000)	
transfer to surplus				100,000	(100,000)	
11. Net increase (decrease) for the year	2,317,500	60,000		100,000	285,770	
12. Balance at beginning of year			2,477,500	1,357,500	1,224,090	100,000
13. Balance at end of year	$2,317,500	$60,000	$2,477,500	$1,457,500	$1,509,860	$100,000

Table 3-4
Allowance for Possible Loan Losses (Sample)

	1977	1976
Balance at beginning of period	619,915	523,958
Recoveries credit to allowance	14,264	33,631
Additions due to mergers and absorptions	—	—
Transfers to allowance		
From income	63,601	33,426
From undivided profits	119,799	71,895
Total	$817,579	$662,910
Losses charged to allowance	197,664	42,995
Balance at end of period	$619,915	$619,915

the "Allowance for Possible Loan Losses" at the maximum amount permitted by Treasury regulations.[3]

Because banks tend to buy only high-quality securities, there is less need to establish a large "Reserve on Securities." The FDIC's suggested format for changes in this account is shown in Table 3-5. Losses charged to the securities reserve account generally result from a bank's voluntary sale of securities at a price below cost rather than from default by the issuer.

Other Reports

Quarterly Reports. Most banks mail to their shareholders a quarterly report that contains a statement of condition and possibly an income statement. Usually this report is included with any quarterly dividend

Table 3-5
Reserves on Securities (Sample)

	1977	1976
Balance at beginning of period	201,054	185,421
Additions due to mergers and absorptions		
Transfers to reserve		
From income	—	—
From undivided profits	30,000	25,000
Total	$231,054	$210,421
Losses charged to reserve	8,351	9,367
Transfers from reserve	—	—
Balance at end of period	$222,703	$201,054

[3]A discussion of the Treasury limitation on the "Allowance for Possible Loan Losses" is presented in Chapter 6.

payment. Reporting the bank's progress at least quarterly to shareholders helps to maintain their interest in promoting the bank in the community.

Newsletters. One of the best techniques for cultivating shareholders as potential salesmen for the bank is through the use of monthly shareholder newsletters. These communication devices serve to inform shareholders of new services, promotional campaigns, management changes, and other happenings.

Bank Profit Planning

Before proceeding to a discussion of internal bank reports, that is, those reports intended for use only within the bank, it would be helpful to consider the nature, objectives, and steps involved in bank profit planning. This is because most internal bank reports are designed to provide follow-up information for the bank's profit plan.

Nature and Objectives

Bank profit planning is essentially a managerial process designed to achieve a company's profit objectives over a specified period of time. An important part of profit planning is the development of a formal *profit plan,* which is a written statement in both financial and nonfinancial terms of a firm's profit objectives. Usually a bank develops an annual plan and a three- or five-year profit plan.

Profit planning has a variety of objectives. Some are tangible, such as the profit plan, policy statements, and follow-up reports. Others are intangible; that is, they are primarily psychological and are designed to produce a highly motivated group of officers and employees. According to the Bank Administration Institute, major tangible objectives of profit planning are the following:

1. To determine the goals and objectives of the bank, to evaluate the alternatives available, to agree upon a plan of action, and to develop a formal plan for the bank.
2. To develop and communicate the final plan to key officials and employees of the bank.
3. To assign responsibility for its accomplishment.
4. To measure the results achieved.
5. To compare these results with the agreed-on plans and with other standards, to investigate the variations disclosed, to correct the conditions giving rise to unsatisfactory performance, and/or to revise the bank's plans if that is the desirable course of action.

Some principal intangible objectives cited by the Institute are:

1. To develop, as the result of participation in the planning process, a sense of involvement and commitment for achievement among diverse levels of management.
2. To explore alternative goals, methods, and consequences to rationalize conflicting demands and points of view in a way that produces an understanding and cohesive organization, not one that is divided by an inability to meet all desires and demands.
3. To develop the acceptance of responsibility for results.
4. To gain acceptance of the discipline of measuring and reviewing performance.
5. To teach the participants in the overall planning process how to plan in the smaller areas of the bank for which they have responsibility.
6. To weld management together as a team.[4]

A Ten-Step Profit-Planning Program

In spite of the many benefits that can be derived from profit planning, most banks do not have a profit-planning program. A simple ten-step method of profit planning is described below.

Step 1: Prepare Economic and Financial Forecast for National and Local Economics. The planning cycle is begun when the bank's economic staff or consulting economist prepares the economic and financial forecast for the coming year. Included in the financial forecast should be estimates of the potential sources and uses of funds in the various markets in which the bank operates. These forecasts are distributed to the executive group to develop preliminary goals and to the local managers to develop profit plans for the various profit centers, such as the branches and sections.

Step 2: Set Preliminary Goals for Earnings per Share and Return on Capital. With the aid of the economic and financial forecast and the knowledge of the current year's operating results, the executive group of the bank meets during August or early September and sets for the next fiscal year preliminary goals for earnings per share and return on capital. These goals are communicated to each branch and section manager.

[4]Bank Administration Institute, *Successful Profit Planning for Banks* (Park Ridge, Ill.: Bank Administration Institute, 1970), pp. 6–7.

Step 3: Estimate the Demand for Credit, by Types, and for Other Services at Each Branch and Section. On the basis of the preliminary profit goals and the economic and financial forecasts, each branch and section manager has the responsibility to estimate the demand for the various types of credit and services that his unit will face if credit conditions are tight, or that can be generated if the demand for credit is slack.

Step 4: Estimate the Amount and Types of Deposits and Other Funds That Can Be Generated by Each Branch and Section. Given the information provided in Step 1, each branch and section manager must estimate the amount and types of funds that his unit can provide.

Step 5: Each Branch and Section Submits a Profit Plan. Taking into account the estimated sources and uses of funds, each profit unit submits a profit plan for the coming year. Only income and expenses that are controllable at the unit level are included in the profit plan. Besides these quantitative estimates, the plan should contain details on the organizational structure, efficiency improvement, innovation and development, and promotional effort required to achieve the profit objective.

Step 6: Develop Consolidated Profit Plan for the Bank, Estimate Provision for Income Taxes, and Calculate Earnings per Share and Return on Capital. In developing the bank's consolidated profit plan, senior management must take into account expenses such as administrative overhead that cannot be imputed to a branch or section.

Step 7: Compare Earnings per Share and Return on Capital with Preliminary Goals and Critically Review Branch and Unit Profit Plans. As is usually the case, the preliminary earnings per share goal is higher than the projected total based on the consolidated income statement. Senior management then must review each branch and section profit plan to determine the reasonableness of the revenue and expense estimates.

Step 8: Evaluate Alternative Strategies to Increase Bank Profits. If it is decided that individual units must make a greater contribution to bank profits, the executive group must evaluate the impact of alternative strategies, such as a cost-reduction program, or stepping up the acquisition of savings deposits by paying daily interest, or striving to increase the percentage of installment loans in its total portfolio. If top management decides that new programs will be adopted, then these plans are communicated to the branch and section managers, who, in turn, must submit revised profit plans.

Step 9: Draft Final Profit Plan. Based on the revised unit profit plans, the executive group must draft a final profit plan, which should be submitted to the board of directors for review no later than the December meeting. Individual profit centers must be provided a copy of this plan along with their approved unit profit plan.

Step 10: Measure Results over the Year. The final step involves the receipt and analysis of monthly profit center, responsibility, and key item reports, which provide follow-up information as to how well each unit and its manager are performing in relation to its profit objectives. Each manager is required to comment on significant variances in revenue and expenses. Because profit center and responsibility reports are submitted monthly, the manager has ample opportunity to know his unit's status in terms of meeting its objective and to take corrective action if necessary.

Profit Center Report

Reports are submitted monthly by each profit center, which usually is each branch and section. In addition to monthly comparisons, *profit center reports* also provide year-to-date comparisons. The primary purpose of these reports is to indicate the performance of each profit center in relation to its profit objectives.

An example of a profit center report is shown in Table 3-6. The principal headings are for "controllable income" and "controllable expenses." As the terms imply, the individual unit manager has some degree of influence over the amounts under these headings. Under "controllable income" is an item for "transfer fund income," which reflects interest credit (perhaps measured by the average rate on federal funds) for excess reserves that the particular unit generates beyond those equal to loan demand at the unit itself. The branch that is primarily a receiver of deposits is recognized with an income credit just as is the branch that is successful in acquiring loans.

"Controllable income" less "controllable expenses" equals the "net controllable contribution" of the branch or section. To this sum is added "noncontrollable income," which is the amount of income that the branch is responsible for at other sections of the bank, such as in the international or trust departments. For example, the manager of the branch servicing the account of a large corporation may have been responsible for acquiring that company's pension plan for the bank's trust department. In such a case it is reasonable to credit that profit center with part of this income.

"Noncontrollable expenses" would include only that portion of head-office and administrative expenses that logically can be allocated to the profit center. For example, depreciation on the computer, a por-

Table 3-6 A Profit Center Report

April 1977

Branch: Westside
Manager: B. Bucks

Current Month Actual	Current Month Variance	Description	Year-to-Date Actual	Year-to-Date Variance	Year-to-Date Profit Plan
		Controllable income			
$60,000	+4,000	Interest—loans and discounts	236,000	+12,000	224,000
3,000	+ 200	Loan fees	11,750	+ 550	11,200
2,000	—	Other income	7,900	− 100	8,000
5,000	+1,000	Transfer fund income	19,350	+ 3,350	16,000
70,000	+5,200	Total	275,000	+15,800	259,200
		Controllable expenses			
24,500	+1,500	Interest on deposits	96,000	+ 4,000	92,000
10,500	—	Personnel expense	43,000	+ 1,000	42,000
3,750	+ 550	Processing expense	14,000	+ 1,200	12,800
5,250	+1,250	Other direct operating expense	17,150	+ 1,150	16,000
—	—	Transfer fund expense	—	—	—
44,000	+3,300	Total	170,150	+ 7,350	162,800
26,000	+1,900	*Net controllable contribution*	104,850	+ 8,450	96,400
2,000	—	*Noncontrollable income*	8,100	+ 100	8,000
		Noncontrollable expenses			
1,200	—	Depreciation	4,800	—	4,800
2,300	—	Rentals	9,100	− 100	9,200
7,250	− 250	Other fixed expenses	30,200	+ 200	30,000
7,150	+ 150	Applicable income taxes	28,050	+ 50	28,000
17,900	− 100	Total	72,150	− 150	72,000
10,100	+2,000	Net contribution to earnings	40,800	+ 8,400	32,400
8,600	+ 800	*Desired return on equity capital*	38,700	+ 7,500	31,200
+ 1,500	+1,200	Residual earnings	+ 2,100	+ 900	+ 1,200

tion of executive office salaries, directors' fees, and advertising may be allocated to each profit center. These noncontrollable items are deducted from the "net controllable contribution" to derive the unit's "net contribution to earnings."

Finally, an optional step involves the allocation of capital to each unit and the calculation of the "desired return on equity capital" in accordance with the bank's return on capital objective. This sum is subtracted from the unit's "net contribution to earnings" to produce the "residual earnings" of the profit center. This step permits senior management to evaluate better the relative profit contribution of each unit and its manager within the bank. In addition, profit center managers are motivated more to accept proposals that will produce greater residual earnings.

Responsibility Reports

Closely related to profit center reports are *responsibility reports,* which seek to measure the performance of officers responsible for the various profit centers, regions, sections, and departments of the bank's operation. Responsibility reports typically contain a more detailed breakdown of controllable income and expense than do profit center reports and so make it possible to pinpoint the source of variance between actual and planned profits at all levels. A responsibility report for a group of three branches or regions is shown in Table 3-7.

Key Item Reports

As a bank grows and as its officers take on more specialized duties and responsibilities, it becomes increasingly important that information regarding the many phases of the bank's operation flow to the people who need it. On the other hand, as banks adopt more sophisticated accounting and management information systems and make greater use of data-processing equipment, the quantity of information available on the bank's operations grows at an exponential rate. In order not to be inundated with information, most medium-sized and large banks have developed a key item reporting system whereby only essential items are reported to those officers whose responsibilities and duties are affected by the data.

Sample lists of key item reports to (1) the executive group, (2) the funds acquisition group, (3) the funds users group, (4) the servicing group, and (5) the board of directors are shown in Table 3-8. As may be seen, a number of key item reports are common to several groups in order that managers in the various interdependent groups may have access to the same data.

Table 3-7 A Responsibility Report

Region: *Brookville*
Westside, Elm, and
Plaza Branches

Responsibility:
I. M. Profit
Senior Vice-President

April 1977

Current Month Actual	Current Month Variance	Description	Year-to-Date Actual	Year-to-Date Variance	Year-to-Date Profit Plan
		Controllable income			
$ 83,100	+5,600	Commercial loans	325,400	+15,400	310,000
88,600	+1,100	Installment loans	359,350	+ 9,350	350,000
13,600	− 100	Mortgage loans	54,700	− 300	55,000
2,550	+ 50	Charge card	10,300	+ 300	10,000
2,400	− 100	Other loan income	9,750	− 250	10,000
400	—	Safe deposit rentals	1,650	+ 50	1,600
8,550	+ 150	Deposit service charges	34,050	+ 650	33,400
7,600	+ 100	Transfer fund income	31,100	+ 1,100	30,000
206,800	+6,800	Total	826,300	+26,300	800,000
	+3.4%	Percentage variance		+3.3%	
		Controllable expenses			
63,400	+ 900	Interest on deposits	255,300	+ 5,300	250,000
29,300	+ 100	Personnel expense	118,500	+ 1,700	116,800
12,150	+ 325	Processing expense	49,400	+ 2,100	47,300
18,100	+1,625	Other direct operating expense	74,300	+ 8,400	65,900
—	—	Transfer fund expense	—	—	—
122,950	+2,950	Total	497,500	+17,500	480,000
	+2.5%	Percentage variance		+3.6%	

Table 3-8
Key Item Reports (Samples)

A. *To the executive group*

Daily

1. Total assets, loans, investments, and deposits
2. Liquidity position
3. Large, new deposit accounts
4. Large deposit accounts lost
5. Large, new or renewed commercial loans

Weekly

1. Average daily deposits and loans, by type, size, and location
2. Major loan delinquencies

Monthly

1. Income statement
2. Profit center reports
3. Responsibility reports
4. Yields and profit contributions, by types of loans and investments
5. Personnel strength and turnover

Quarterly

1. Share of market
2. Economic forecast

B. *To the funds acquisition group*

Daily

1. Total deposits and loans, by type, size, and location
2. Cumulative reserve status computation
3. Liquidity position
4. Large deposits and withdrawals

Weekly

1. Average daily deposits and loans, by type, size, and location
2. Results of officer call program

Monthly

(Same as to the executive group)

Quarterly

(Same as to the executive group)

C. *To the funds users group*

Daily

1. Total deposits and loans, by type, size, and location; total investments
2. Cumulative reserve status computation
3. Liquidity position
4. Large deposits and withdrawals
5. Large, new and maturing commercial loans

Table 3-8 (continued)

6. New commercial loan commitments
7. New lines of credit approved
8. Portfolio transactions; money market rates and outlook

Weekly

1. Average daily deposits and loans, by type, size, and location
2. Contingent liabilities

Monthly

(Same as to the executive group)
plus

1. Unused lines of credit
2 Loan delinquencies and recoveries

Quarterly

(Same as to the executive group)
plus

1. Loans by type of collateral
2. Loan concentration by SIC code

D. *To the servicing group*

Daily

1. Total deposits and loans, by type, size, and location; total investments
2. Cash letter sendings
3. Unusual deposits and withdrawals
4. Large overdrafts
5. Equipment downtime

Weekly

1. Average daily deposits and loans, by type, size, and location

Monthly

(Same as to the executive group)

Quarterly

(Same as to the executive group)
plus

1. Absences and vacations

E. *To the board of directors*

Monthly

1. Statement of condition
2. Income statement and profit plan comparison
3. Loans and lines of credit
4. Report of past-due loans
5. Report of sales and purchase of securities
6. Report of trust division
7. Report of building committee
8. Report of audit and examining committee

Suggestions for Additional Reading

Adams, E. Sherman. "Bank Planning Activities." In William H. Baughn and Charls E. Walker, eds. *The Banker's Handbook*. Homewood, Ill.: Dow Jones-Irwin, 1966, chap. 67.

Austin, Douglas V., and Booker, Gene S., eds. *Modern Techniques in Bank Management*. Boston: Warren, Gorham and Lamont, 1969, part 2c.

Bank Administration Institute. *Successful Profit Planning for Banks*. Park Ridge, Ill.: Bank Administration Institute, 1970.

Bell, Frederick W., and Murphy, Neil B. *Costs in Commercial Banking: A Quantitative Analysis of Bank Behavior and Its Relation to Bank Regulation*. Research Report No. 41. Boston: Federal Reserve Bank of Boston, April 1968.

Board of Governors of the Federal Reserve System. *Functional Cost Analysis*. Washington, D.C.: Board of Governors of the Federal Reserve System (Annual).

Ellis, Charles C. "Profit Planning For Banks." New York: Irving Trust Company.

Haskins and Sells (Certified Public Accountants). *Bank Costs For Planning and Control*. Park Ridge, Ill.: Bank Administration Institute, 1972.

CHAPTER

4

Income, Expenses, and Profitability of Commercial Banks

As at any profit-seeking business, the income statement is the focal point for commercial bank management. All revenue and explicit costs realized by the bank are reported in this statement. In this chapter we shall (1) analyze briefly each of the principal sources of bank income and each major expense item shown on the income statement that must be submitted to the FDIC, (2) note the various measures of bank income, (3) discuss the trends in allocation of net income, and (4) consider several selected bank financial ratios.

Sources of Bank Income

Interest and Fees on Loans

A principal source of bank income is the interest, fees, and similar charges levied against all assets classified as loans and discounts on condition reports. Included also are interest on acceptances, commercial paper purchased in the open market, and paper sold under resale agreements. In addition, this income category includes investigation and service charges, renewal and past-due charges, commitment fees, and fees charged for the execution of mortgages or agreements securing the bank's loans.

Interest and fees on loans are by far the largest source of operating income to banks. As shown in Table 4-1, income from loans more than quadrupled between 1965 and 1976. There are two primary reasons for this increase. First, the volume of bank loans outstanding rose by 165.5 percent, from $203.1 billion in 1965 to $539.3 billion in 1976. Second, the general level of interest rates and fees charged by banks for loans rose significantly during this period.

Income on Federal Funds and on Securities Purchased Under Resale Agreements

In recent years, most banks have stepped up their activity in *federal funds*, which are defined as excess reserves lent by one bank to another, typically on an overnight basis. For the lending bank, the federal funds market provides an excellent opportunity to employ surplus funds profitably. Another way that some banks invest short-term funds is to enter into an agreement with a securities dealer to purchase a given amount of Treasury obligations and to resell them to the dealer after a specified period of time at a certain price. With this technique, the bank is guaranteed a fixed return, and the dealer acquires funds to make adjustments in his inventory or for other purposes. Income from federal funds transactions and security repurchase agreements, which was reported separately for the first time in 1969, totaled $2.0 billion in 1976, or 2.5 percent of total operating income.

Interest on Treasuries

The majority of the Treasury securities owned by banks are short-term issues and are held primarily for liquidity purposes, that is, to meet possible deposit withdrawals, loan demands, and maturing liabilities. As loan demand increased during the 1960s, banks attempted to economize on their liquidity reserves and, as a result, interest income on Treasuries declined. Between 1965 and 1976, income from this source fell from 13.2 percent to 7.4 percent of total operating income.

Interest and Dividends on Agencies

In recent years, banks have increased their holdings of "agencies," that is, the securities of federal or federally sponsored agencies such as the

Table 4-1
Operating Income of Insured Commercial Banks, Selected Years, 1965–1976 (millions of dollars)

Year	Total	Interest and Fees on Loans[a]		Income on Federal Funds Sold and Securities Purchased under Resale Agreements[a]		Interest on Treasuries		Interest and Dividends on Agencies[b]		Interest on Municipals[b]	
		Amount	Percent	Amount	Percent	Amount	Percent	Amount	Percent	Amount	Percent
1965	16,817	11,205	66.6	—	—	2,225	13.2	—	—	—	—
1970	34,716	22,967	66.2	1,006	2.9	3,079	8.9	688	2.0	2,620	7.6
1971	36,364	23,069	63.4	871	2.4	3,396	9.3	917	2.5	3,127	8.6
1972	40,248	25,630	63.7	1,027	2.6	3,396	8.4	1,145	2.8	3,494	8.7
1973	53,036	35,376	66.7	2,487	4.7	3,465	6.5	1,472	2.8	3,865	7.3
1974	68,161	47,139	69.2	3,712	5.4	3,441	5.0	2,019	3.0	4,454	6.5
1975	66,559	43,380	65.2	2,295	3.4	4,441	6.7	2,349	3.5	4,919	7.4
1976	80,634	51,626	64.0	1,984	2.5	5,975	7.4	2,414	3.0	5,133	6.4

Year	Interest and Dividends on Other Securities[b]		Trust Department Income		Service Charges on Deposit Accounts		Other Service Charges, Commissions and Fees		Other Operating Income	
	Amount	Percent	Amount	Percent	Amount	Percent	Amount	Percent	Amount	Percent
1965	1,285	7.6	690	4.1	843	5.0	304	1.8	266	1.6
1970	152	.4	1,132	3.3	1,178	3.4	842	2.4	1,050	3.0
1971	238	.7	1,258	3.5	1,231	3.4	989	2.7	1,267	3.5
1972	322	.8	1,366	3.4	1,262	3.1	1,083	2.7	1,522	3.8
1973	372	.7	1,460	2.8	1,327	2.5	1,262	2.4	1,961	3.7
1974	468	.7	1,502	2.2	1,460	2.1	1,409	2.1	2,554	3.7
1975	533	.8	1,602	2.4	1,555	2.3	1,654	2.5	3,832	5.8
1976	854	1.1	1,794	2.2	1,635	2.0	2,182	2.7	6,502	8.1

Source: FDIC, *Annual Reports* and unpublished data.
NOTE: Details may not add due to rounding.
[a]"Income on federal funds sold" was included in "Interest and discount on loans" in 1968 and prior years.
[b]"Interest and dividends on agencies" and "Interest on municipals" were included in "Income from other securities" in 1968 and prior years.

Federal Land Banks and the Federal Home Loan Banks. Although agencies are not direct obligations of the federal government, investors consider these securities as virtually free from the risk of default. Besides involving little or no credit risk, agencies also are attractive because they tend to carry a higher yield than Treasuries. During 1976, interest and dividends on agencies amounted to 3.0 percent of total bank operating income.

Interest on Municipals

In the parlance of the investment community, the term "municipals" includes the obligations of states and their political subdivisions, such as cities, counties, school districts, and other public authorities. The principal feature of municipals is that the interest income from these obligations is not subject to federal income taxes or to state income taxes in the state in which they are issued. Banks in the highest corporate tax bracket considerably increased their holdings of municipals during the 1960s because, on an after-tax equivalent basis, municipals tend to yield more than most types of loans and investments they can make. In 1976, interest on municipals comprised 6.3 percent of total bank operating income.

Interest and Dividends on Other Securities

Included under the heading of interest and dividends on other securities is income from holdings of all stocks, bonds, notes, and debentures that have not been reported under other security income categories. Also included is income from shares in savings and loan associations and credit unions. Interest and dividends from other securities constituted only 1.1 percent of total operating income in 1976.

In summary, total investment income from Treasuries, agencies, municipals, and other securities declined from 20.8 percent of total bank operating income in 1965 to 17.9 percent in 1976.

Trust Department Income

Bank trust department income rose between 1965 and 1976. This growth reflects the increase in demand for personal and corporate trust services brought about primarily by the expansion of income and wealth in the nation. Even with the large absolute growth in trust department revenue, this source of income between 1965 and 1976 fell from 4.1 percent to 2.2 percent of total bank operating income.

Service Charges on Deposit Accounts

Banks typically levy a fixed maintenance fee and various activity fees on the personal and business demand deposit accounts they hold. Although bank deposit service charges do not cover fully the expense of providing demand deposit accounts and of deposit transfers, these fees do offset to some degree the large costs incurred. Between 1965 and 1976, service charges more than doubled; however, during this period, these fees fell from 5.0 percent to 2.0 percent of total operating income.

Other Service Charges, Collection and Exchange Charges, Commissions, and Fees

Other service charges, collection and exchange charges, and fees comprised only 2.7 percent of total bank operating income in 1976. A considerable portion of the income in this catchall category consists of exchange charges, which are fees charged by banks on the face amount of checks drawn upon them and presented to them through the mails for collection. These charges range from 1/10 to 1/4 of 1 percent of the face amount. Banks that levy such charges are termed "nonpar banks" and usually are located in rural areas. Over the years, the number of nonpar banks has steadily declined and, at the end of 1976, only 54 nonpar banks remained.[1]

Other sources of income under this heading include commissions on the sale of credit life insurance policies and the collection of premiums; the collection of bills for public utilities and other firms; the sale of bank drafts; the purchase and sale of securities, acceptances, and commercial paper for domestic banks and other customers; the negotiation of loans for customers of correspondents; the underwriting and sale of securities owned by the bank; the servicing of real estate mortgages or other loans held by others; percentage charges to merchants for handling credit-card or charge sales; equipment leasing and rental fees; data-processing services; and reimbursements received for services in redeeming savings bonds.

Other Operating Income

Other operating income consists of the gross income from foreign and other departments; gross rentals from other real estate and safe deposit boxes; interest on time balances with other banks; net trading account income; and regular operating credits such as net teller overages, forgery recoveries, recoveries on payment of checks over stop-payment orders, and similar recurring operating transactions. The two major items in this list are income from foreign departments and net trading account income. These sources of income are significant for a number

[1]National banks and state member banks are prohibited from levying exchange charges. Moreover, checks on nonpar banks may not be processed through the Federal Reserve System.

of money market banks. In 1976, other operating income represented 8.1 percent of total operating income.

Operating Expenses

Salaries, Wages, Pensions, and Other Benefits

Included under this heading is compensation for personal services of all officers and employees, including dining room and cafeteria employees, but exclusive of building department officers and employees; bonuses and extra compensation; and pensions and other benefits.

Between 1965 and 1976, benefits increased 243.8 percent (see Table 4-2), while the number of officers and employees rose only 71.3 percent. The improvement in the average salary during this period reflects both increased productivity and the cost-of-living. Since the end of World War II, virtually all banks made huge investments in data-processing equipment and other labor-saving devices. This capital equipment enabled the average bank clerical employee to become much more productive in terms of number of accounts and items handled. Salaries and wages as a percentage of total bank operating costs also fell as a result of economies of scale resulting from the more efficient use of specialized officer personnel. For example, banks employ specialists in many areas, such as credit analysis, commercial lending, investments, trust, and personnel. As a bank grows and activity increases in each of the various specialized functional areas, average costs decline. As additional banks automate other functions and as more and more banks achieve economies of scale, it is likely that salaries and wages will continue to decline as a percentage of total bank costs.

Pensions and other benefits comprise about one-sixth of total compensation paid. This subcategory of expenses includes a bank's own contribution to its retirement or pension fund; life insurance premiums (net of dividends received) and hospitalization insurance premiums; unemployment and Social Security taxes paid by a bank on its own account; the net cost to the bank for employee dining rooms, restaurants, and cafeterias (exclusive of salaries and wages); the cost of medical or health services (exclusive of salaries and wages); and other fringe benefits for officers and employees. Also included are total expenditures under profit-sharing plans that allow officers and employees an option as to the portion to be received as current compensation or to be held and invested by the bank.

Interest on Deposits

Perhaps the most important development in banking since 1960 has been the dramatic increase in time and savings deposits as a source of

Table 4-2
Operating Expenses of Insured Commercial Banks, Selected Years, 1965–1976 (millions of dollars)

		Salaries, Wages, Pensions, and Other Benefits		Interest on Deposits		Expense of Federal Funds and Securities Sold under Repurchase Agreements[b]		Interest on Other Borrowed Money[b]	
Year	Total[a]	Amount	Percent	Amount	Percent	Amount	Percent	Amount	Percent
1965	12,486	4,288	34.3	5,071	40.6	—	—	190	1.5
1970	27,589	7,717	28.0	10,484	38.0	1,401	5.1	465	1.7
1971	29,651	8,395	28.3	12,218	41.2	1,096	3.7	139	.5
1972	32,996	9,085	27.5	13,844	42.0	1,429	4.3	115	.3
1973	44,330	10,128	22.8	19,835	44.7	3,899	8.8	504	1.1
1974	58,910	11,587	19.7	27,888	47.3	5,986	10.2	918	1.6
1975	57,582	12,686	22.0	26,246	45.6	3,323	5.8	377	.6
1976	70,717	14,743	20.8	34,994	49.5	3,312	4.7	666	.9

	Interest on Capital Notes and Debentures[a]		Net Occupancy Expense		Furniture and Equipment, etc.		Provision for Loan Loses[a]		Other Operating Expense	
Year	Amount	Percent	Amount	Percent	Amount	Percent	Amount	Percent	Amount	Percent
1965	—	—	732	5.9	412	3.3	—	—	1,795	14.4
1970	105	.4	1,255	4.5	909	3.3	703	2.5	4,551	16.5
1971	142	.5	1,410	4.8	1,018	3.4	867	2.9	4,365	14.7
1972	214	.6	1,584	4.8	1,088	3.3	973	2.9	4,665	14.1
1973	254	.6	1,783	4.0	1,201	2.7	1,265	2.9	5,461	12.3
1974	283	.5	2,052	3.5	1,361	2.3	2,286	3.9	6,549	11.1
1975	294	.5	2,325	4.0	1,533	2.7	3,612	6.3	7,185	12.5
1976	344	.5	2,763	3.9	1,720	2.4	3,688	5.2	8,487	12.0

Source: FDIC, *Annual Reports* and unpublished data.
NOTE: Details may not add due to rounding.
[a]"Interest on capital notes and debentures" and "Provision for loan losses" not included in "Operating expense total" in 1968 and prior years.
[b]"Expense of federal funds purchases and securities sold under repurchase agreements" were included in "Interest on borrowed money" in 1968 and prior years.

bank funds. As will be explored in more detail in Chapter 5, banks, beginning in early 1961, began to encourage corporate customers to place surplus cash balances in time certificates of deposits (CDs) instead of purchasing Treasury bills or other money market instruments. Time and savings deposit growth also was stimulated and facilitated by numerous increases in the interest rate payable on these balances over the decade.

Owing both to increases in the volume of time and savings deposits and the interest rate paid on them, "interest on deposits" between 1961 and 1976 rose from 28.3 percent to 49.5 percent of total bank operating expense. This cost is now by far the largest expense item incurred by banks, and it is very likely to remain so over the foreseeable future.

Federal Funds and Securities Sold Under Repurchase Agreements

Banks that experience temporary deficiencies in required reserve balances may borrow federal funds from other banks or sell securities under repurchase agreements. Some large banks incur expense under this heading when they borrow federal funds from several smaller banks and then sell federal funds to other banks at a slightly higher rate. During the tight-money year of 1970, expenses for federal funds purchased and securities sold under repurchase agreements exceeded $1.4 billion, or 5.1 percent of total bank operating expenses. The cost of obtaining funds via these methods declined in 1971, as the Federal Reserve maintained a relatively loose money policy. Between 1972 and 1974, however, the cost of funds raised in the federal funds market and through repurchase agreements rose considerably as monetary conditions tightened. In 1974, this expense item represented 10.2 percent of total bank costs. In 1975 and 1976, interest rates fell, and this item expense element declined significantly in both absolute and relative terms.

Interest on Other Borrowed Money

During the early to mid-1960s, a number of banks began to issue capital notes and debentures as a means of acquiring additional loanable funds. Interest on these securities totaled $344 million, or 0.5 percent of total bank operating costs in 1976.

Net Occupancy Expense

"Net occupancy expense" is equal to "gross occupancy expense" less rental income. "Gross occupancy expense" includes the following: compensation for those officers and employees of a bank and its consolidated bank premises subsidiaries who spend the major part of their working time on bank building and related "housekeeping" functions regardless of whether the bank has a building investment; all supplementary benefits, other than direct compensation, paid or accrued on behalf of building department personnel; normal and recurring depreciation charges; ordinary repairs to bank premises and lease hold improvements; all current expenses such as the cost of heat, light, water, outside janitor services, janitor supplies, fire insurance, and similar expenses; and all rents paid on bank premises and parking lots, interest on liens or other encumbrances on bank premises owned, and all property and other taxes paid or accrued related to bank premises. Many banks construct home office buildings with more space than they currently need. Income derived from rental of this extra space is offset against gross occupancy expense itemized above. During 1976 rental income totaling $497 million was subtracted from gross occupancy expense of $3,260 million to produce a net occupancy expense of $2, 763 million. Although net occupancy expense more than tripled between 1965 and 1976, this cost item fell down 5.9 percent to 3.9 percent of total bank operating expenses.

Furniture and Equipment, Depreciation, Rental Costs, Servicing, and Similar Expenses

Total outlays for furniture and equipment and the like remained between 2.3 and 3.4 percent of total bank operating costs during the period between 1965 and 1976. This expense category includes normal and recurring depreciation; rental costs of office machines and data-processing equipment; ordinary repairs, including servicing costs to furniture and office machines; and taxes on furniture and equipment.

Provision for Loan Losses

Prior to 1969, loan losses for banks that had established loan loss reserves were not charged against operating income or net income but were charged to the loan loss reserve. Transfers to this reserve were included as a charge against net income (but not against operating income). As a result of the Tax Reform Act of 1969, banks are required to report a minimum provision for loan losses as an operating expense. For most banks this provision may be calculated by one of two methods.

Under the *loan loss ratio method,* the bank determines the average net charge-offs (charge-offs less recoveries) for the five most recent calendar years, including the current year. Gross loans as reported in the twenty call statements of condition (see page 44) may be used to derive this average. The bank then derives the average loans outstanding for the same five years. Next, average net charge-offs are divided by average loans to produce the loss experience ratio. This ratio is then multiplied by average loans outstanding during the current year as reported on the four statements of condition. This product represents a minimum provision for loan losses to be included in operating expense for the current year.

Under the *actual net loan loss method,* the bank may use actual net loan losses or recoveries (charge-offs less recoveries) as a minimum provision. Until the severe recession of 1973–75 led to excessive loan losses, the "provision for loan losses" had averaged 2.9 percent or less of operating expenses. In 1975, costs for this item jumped to $3.6 billion or 6.3 percent of operating expenses as banks had to write off loans in significant amounts especially in the real estate area. During 1976, the provision for loan losses rose to $3.7 billion, but declined in relative terms to 5.2 percent of total operating expenses.

Other Operating Expenses

"Other operating expenses" contain many costs for items vital to bank operations. Included are fees paid to directors and members of committees for attendance at board or committee meetings, including travel and expense allowance; interest paid on Eurodollars obtained from foreign branches of the bank; premiums on fidelity insurance; operating expenses (except salaries) connected with holdings of real estate other than bank premises, including interest paid on liens and normal or recurring depreciation charges on "other real estate"; office supplies bought; telephone and telegraph; cost of examinations by supervisory authorities; retainer fees; expenses related to the use of automobiles for bank business; costs of data processing performed by others; losses from counterfeit money, forged checks, net cash shortages, payment of checks over stop-payment orders and similar recurring types of losses; net deposit insurance assessment expenses; advertising costs; and postage. During 1976, these operating expenses comprised 12.0 percent of total bank operating expenses.

Measures of Bank Income

Net Operating Income

As we have seen, several changes were made in 1969 in the reporting of bank income and expenses. These changes led to numerous other modifications in the reporting of net income. Prior to 1969, the two principal measures of bank income were (1) "net operating income" (operating income minus operating expenses) and (2) "net income" (net operating income plus or minus net nonoperating income or losses and minus income taxes.)[2] With the reporting changes in 1969, three

[2]"Net nonoperating income" included net security gains or losses and net recoveries, charge-offs, and transfers from reserves.

measures of bank income are emphasized: (1) "income before income taxes and security gains and losses," which is comparable to "operating income" (on the old basis), except that "interest on capital notes and debentures" and "provision for loan losses" were not included in "operating expenses" for 1968 and prior years; (2) "income before security gains and losses" ("income before income taxes and security gains and losses" minus "applicable income taxes"); and (3) "net income" (income before security gains and losses minus net nonoperating income or losses.)[3]

Although total operating income rose 379.5 percent between 1965 and 1976, net operating income (old basis) or income before income taxes and security gains and losses at insured banks increased only 129.0 percent (Table 4-3). As a consequence, the bank gross profit margin (net operating income over total operating income) fell from 25.8 percent in 1965 to 12.3 percent in 1976. The principal reason for this decline was the sharp rise in interest costs on time and savings deposit.

Net Nonoperating Income or Losses

Nonoperating items include a number of deductions or additions that can have a significant bearing on net income. Primary nonoperating adjustments consist of transfers to reserve accounts for loan losses, gains or losses on securities, extraordinary charges or credits, and deductions for minority interests in consolidated subsidiaries.

In addition to the minimum provision for loan losses, which is an operating expense under the reporting system instituted in 1969, banks also may make additional transfers to reserve accounts for loan losses. This transfer is a nonoperating deduction from "income before security gains and losses" and has the effect of reducing bank income tax liabilities.[4]

Banks incur security losses when the issuer defaults, when securities must be sold below purchase price, or when the book value of securities still held must be written down. Following the banking collapse of 1933, regulations were instituted that limited bank investments to only those of the highest quality. As a consequence, bank losses due to default have become rare. Most of the security losses suffered during recent years occurred when banks were forced to liquidate securities at depressed prices so as to accommodate loan demands. Banks are willing to accept these losses because they are fully deductible for tax purposes and because the banks must meet the legitimate loan demands of valued customers in order to retain them. All insured banks together

[3]"Nonoperating income" here includes net security gains or losses and net extraordinary charges or credits less minority interest in consolidated subsidiaries.

[4]The limitation on this additional transfer is discussed in Chapter 6.

Table 4-3

Income, Expenses, and Profits of Insured Commercial Banks, Selected Years, 1960–1976 (millions of dollars)

Year	Operating Income	Operating Expenses	Net Operating Income	Net Non-operating Income (+) or Losses (−)[a]	Net Income before Taxes	Income Taxes[b]	Net Income	Dividends[c]	Net Addition to Capital
1960	10,724	6,933	3,791	-404	3,387	1,384	2,003	832	1,171
1965	16,817	12,486	4,331	-787	3,544	1,029	2,515	1,202	1,313

Year	Operating Income	Operating Expenses	Income before Income Taxes and Security Gains and Losses	Applicable Income Taxes[d]	Income before Security Gains and Losses	Net Non-operating Income (+) or Losses (−)[e]	Net Income	Dividends	Net Addition to Capital
1970	34,716	27,589	7,128	2,174	4,954	-117	4,837	2,040	2,797
1971	36,364	29,651	6,713	1,689	5,024	212	5,236	2,231	3,005
1972	40,248	32,997	7,251	1,707	5,543	111	5,654	2,197	3,457
1973	53,036	44,330	8,707	2,121	6,585	- 6	6,579	2,429	4,150
1974	68,161	58,910	9,251	2,084	7,167	- 76	7,091	2,768	4,323
1975	66,559	57,582	8,977	1,793	7,184	71	7,255	3,032	4,223
1976	80,634	70,717	9,918	2,291	7,627	220	7,847	3,037	4,810

Source: FDIC, *Annual Reports* and unpublished data.

NOTE: Details may not add due to rounding.

[a]Includes net security gains or losses and net recoveries, charge-offs, and transfers from reserves.

[b]Income taxes were $1,864 million in 1970, $1,652 million in 1971, $1,599 million in 1972, $1,715 million in 1973, $1,760 million in 1974, $1,727 million in 1975 and $2,410 million in 1976.

[c]In 1968 and prior years, "Dividends declared on preferred stock" was reported in combination with "Interest on capital rates and debentures."

[d]"Applicable income taxes" is an estimate of the tax liability that banks would incur if their taxes were based solely on operating income and expenses.

[e]Includes net security gains or losses and net extraordinary charges or credits less minority interest in consolidated subsidiaries.

incurred net security losses every year from 1964 through 1970. During the tight-money year of 1969, insured banks incurred security losses of a record $512 million before taxes, or $238 million after taxes. In 1970, as credit conditions eased, net, after-tax losses on securities fell to $104 million. However, in 1971, banks made a record after-tax gain of $213 million on their security transactions, as they cashed in profits made on obligations purchased largely during the previous two high interest-rate years. In the four-year period from 1972–1975, net security gains about balanced with security losses in the aggregate. In 1976, with interest rates declining during the last half of the year, banks realized net security gains of $194 million.

Extraordinary charges or credits reflect the results of events or transactions occurring in or relating to the current reporting period and of a character significantly different from the customary activities of the bank. Examples of these gains or losses might include those from (1) the sale or abandonment of buildings or premises or a significant activity or portion of the enterprise, (2) gains or losses from a major revaluation of a foreign currency, and (3) significant tax-loss carryforwards when realized in the current period.

Finally, "minority interest in consolidated subsidiaries" must be deducted so that only the net contribution to bank income is shown. Examples of consolidated subsidiaries are those that provide data-processing services or hold bank real estate.

Income Taxes

Bank income is subject to both federal and state corporate income taxes. As shown in Table 4-3, corporate income taxes on bank income totaled $1,029 million in 1965. In 1976, applicable income taxes amounted to $2,291 million. Whereas income taxes took 29.0 percent of net bank income before taxes in 1965, they absorbed 23.1 percent in 1976. The principal reason for this decline in the effective bank income tax rate during this period was that banks increased their investment in state and local government securities from $38.5 billion in 1965 to $103.5 billion in 1976. The interest income on these obligations is not subject to federal income taxes and state income taxes in the state of issuance. Therefore, banks reduced the proportion of total operating income subject to income taxes. It is likely that the effective tax rate on bank income will increase somewhat in the years ahead because the Tax Reform Act of 1969 severely limited future tax-free additions to the loan loss reserve.

Net Income

Although in recent years gains in net income of insured banks did not keep pace with the percentage rise in operating income, nevertheless, the increase was impressive in absolute terms. Net income increased from $2.5 billion in 1965 to $7.8 billion in 1976. In the near future, it is unlikely that percentage gains in net income will match those achieved during the 1960s or early 1970s. This is mainly because time and savings deposits are expected to continue to increase as a proportion of total deposits; hence rising interest costs are likely to take a larger percentage of operating income.

Allocation of Net Income

Because of the relatively lower return on capital earned over the years, many banks have had difficulty raising capital in the open market. Consequently, most banks have tended to retain a majority of their net income. Between 1971 and 1976, banks paid out only 33.9 percent of net income in the form of dividends on common and preferred stock. Dividends on equity capital averaged 4.1 percent during the six-year period. It is significant that this dividend rate exceeded the 3.56 percent average dividend rate on the 500 common stocks in Standard and Poor's industrial average during these years.

Selected Bank Financial Ratios

Trends in a number of selected bank financial ratios are shown in Table 4-4. Owing to rising interest rates on loans and investment, operating income as a percentage of total assets rose sharply between 1965 and 1970. "Income before income taxes and security gains and losses," after peaking in 1970 at 1.31 percent of assets, declined each year except one through 1976. As we have seen, mounting costs on time and savings deposits and larger "provisions for loan losses" were the major factors contributing to this pressure on profits. Net income as a percentage of total equity capital trended downward between 1971 and 1976. It is interesting to note that for banks the average ratio of net income to total equity capital was 12.1 percent for the first period, 1971–1975, whereas the average ratio of profits to stockholders' equity for manufacturing firms in the U.S. was 11.66 percent for the same time span.

Table 4-4
Selected Financial Ratios for Insured Commercial Banks, 1965, 1970–1976

	1965	1970	1971	1972	1973	1974	1975	1976
Amounts per $100 of total assets								
Operating income—total	4.66	6.38	6.03	5.93	6.83	7.82	7.20	7.18
Net operating earnings (old basis)	1.20	—	—	—	—	—	—	—
Income before income taxes and security gains & losses	—	1.31	1.11	1.07	1.12	1.06	.97	.88
Amounts per $100 of total equity capital								
Net income	n.a.	n.a.	12.39	12.25	12.86	12.53	11.75	11.41
Cash dividends declared on common stock	n.a.	n.a.	5.26	4.75	4.74	4.89	4.91	4.41
Net additions to capital from income	n.a.	n.a.	7.11	7.49	8.11	7.64	6.84	7.00
Special ratios								
Income on loans per $100 of loans[a]	5.85	7.95	7.31	7.08	8.35	9.79	8.52	8.48
Income on U.S. Treasury securities per $100 of U.S. Treasury securities	3.74	5.68	5.67	5.48	5.91	6.51	6.73	6.75
Income on municipals per $100 of municipals[b]	—	4.23	4.19	4.15	4.33	4.71	4.97	5.00
Income on other securities per $100 of other securities[b]	3.09	6.55	6.34	6.15	6.28	7.05	7.35	n.a.
Interest paid per $100 of time and savings deposits	3.69	4.95	4.78	4.66	5.71	6.93	5.92	5.53

Source: FDIC, *Annual Reports.*

NOTE: Because of changes in the form of reporting by banks, figures for 1969 and 1975 are not fully comparable with those in 1968 and prior years.
[a]Includes federal funds sold.
[b]"Income on municipals" included in "Income on other securities" in 1968 and prior years.

Suggestions for Additional Reading

Bedford, Margaret E. "Federal Taxation of Financial Institutions." Federal Reserve Bank of Kansas City, *Monthly Review* (June 1976), pp. 3–15.

——— "Income Taxation of Commercial Banks." Federal Reserve Bank of Kansas City, *Monthly Review* (July–August 1975), pp. 3–11.

Board of Governors of the Federal Reserve System. *Annual Report.* Washington, D.C.: Board of Governors of the Federal Reserve System.

Carter H. Golembe Associates, Inc. *The Tax Reform Act of 1969: A Consideration of Provisions Affecting Commercial Banks.* Chicago: Association of Reserve City Bankers, 1969.

The Comptroller of the Currency. *Annual Report.* Washington, D.C.: U.S. Government Printing Office.

Federal Deposit Insurance Corporation. *Annual Report.* Washington, D.C.: Federal Deposit Insurance Corporation.

Hamlin, Melvin L. "Impact of 1969 Tax Reform Act on Financial Institutions." *The Banking Law Journal,* 88 (October 1971), pp. 867–880.

Mullineaux, Donald J. "The Taxman Rebuffed: Income Taxes at Commercial Banks." Federal Reserve Bank of Philadelphia, *Business Review* (May 1974), pp. 11–23.

PART II

Sources of Bank Funds: Deposits, Capital, and Other Liabilities

CHAPTER

5

Deposits

The demand and time deposits of individuals, partnerships, and corporations (IPC), the U.S. government, state and local governments, foreign governments, and other banks are the principal sources of funds to individual commercial banks. At the end of 1976, deposits accounted for 82.2 percent of the funds available to insured banks, while capital accounts and miscellaneous liabilities provided only 7.7 percent and 10.1 percent, respectively, of the funds available for bank asset acquisition.

In this chapter we shall (1) develop the principles of deposit expansion and contraction for one bank and for the entire banking system, (2) examine the trends and factors influencing ownership of demand and time deposits in our banking system, (3) analyze the causes and implications of the changing demand-time deposit mix, and (4) discuss the FDIC deposit insurance program, which has had such an important influence on commercial banking policies and practices in this country.

Principles of Deposit Expansion and Contraction

The manner in which deposits expand and contract within our banking system is a mystery to most people. In Chapter 1 it was stated that commercial banks have the unique ability to create money (demand deposits) as well as credit. In this section we shall explore in more detail the principles of deposit expansion and contraction at one bank and for the banking system as a whole.

Definitions

The following definitions will assist in understanding the principles of deposit expansion and contraction:

1. *Legal reserves*—those assets that may be counted as reserves for purposes of meeting the Federal Reserve or state reserve requirement.
2. *Reserve ratio*—that percentage of a bank's deposits or other liabilities that must be held in the form of legal reserves in order to meet the Federal Reserve or state reserve requirement.
3. *Required reserves*—that portion of a bank's legal reserves that must be held, given the bank's deposits and other liabilities and the applicable Federal Reserve or state reserve requirement.
4. *Excess reserves*—that portion of a bank's legal reserves in excess of its required reserves.
5. *Primary deposits*—deposits made in a bank in the form of currency, coin, or checks drawn on other banks.
6. *Secondary deposits*—deposits that may be created by a bank when it acquires loans or investments.

Deposit Expansion and Contraction at One Bank

In order to obtain earning assets, a commercial bank, like other financial intermediaries, must acquire funds, either by receiving primary deposits, by increasing capital, or by incurring other liabilities. In return for issuing these various types of claims or promises to depositors, shareholders, and other debt holders, the bank receives *cash assets*, such as cash-in-vault, balances in the Federal Reserve Bank, balances in other banks (correspondent balances), or cash items in the process of collection that within a day or two will be one of the first three types of cash assets. Member banks count cash-in-vault and balances in the Federal Reserve Bank as their legal reserves.

Once the funds have been acquired, the bank multiplies the applicable reserve requirement times the designated liabilities, such as demand and time deposits and balances due foreign branches, in order to determine the amount of required reserves. The volume of legal reserves that does not have to be set aside as required reserves, that is, excess reserves, then establishes the limit on the amount of assets, such as loans and investments, that the individual bank can acquire. The bank acquires these assets either (1) by crediting the account of the borrower that surrenders the asset, (2) by issuing a cashier's check (a liability to the bank), or (3) by going to the vault and paying out currency and coin in exchange for the asset. In the first case, the bank expects that the newly created (secondary) deposits probably will be withdrawn shortly by one of two ways: (1) the presentation of a check to the teller in the bank in exchange for cash-in-vault, or (2) the presentation of a check to someone outside the bank, who, in turn, presents it to his bank for collection from the deposit-creating bank. At any rate, unless the check is deposited in the originating bank, the lending bank loses excess reserves, either in the form of cash-in-vault, balances with the Federal Reserve Bank, or, in the case of a state, nonmember bank, perhaps balances at a correspondent bank. Thus the maximum amount of assets that the individual bank can acquire at any point in time is limited to its excess reserves, which is the maximum amount of cash assets that the bank can lose and not be deficient in required reserves.

From the above discussion we can see that if an individual bank wishes to increase its loans and investments, it must acquire legal reserves (part of which will be excess reserves) by attracting deposits or by increasing capital and other liabilities. Once this is done, the only other limit on an individual bank's ability to acquire loans and investments is the reserve ratio, which determines the amount of legal reserves that must be held against the appropriate liability accounts.[1]

Deposit contraction at an individual bank takes place when a borrower uses demand deposits at the bank to repay loans or investment securities. This repayment of bank-held debt with demand deposits reduces required reserves and increases excess reserves. The bank now has the ability to make new loans and investments equal to its newly gained excess reserves. If the loan or investment had been repaid with currency or coin, then total reserves and excess reserves at the recipient bank would have increased.

Deposit Expansion and Contraction for the Banking System

Although the individual bank may only expand its demand deposits by an amount equal to its excess reserves, all banks together may increase their deposits by a multiple of the amount of excess reserves in the

[1]Within the limits set by the volume of legal reserves and the reserve requirement, the actual amount of loans and investments that the bank can acquire depends on the borrowing public's demand for funds.

system.[2] The limits of this expansion are set by (1) the volume of excess reserves and (2) the reserve ratio.[3] The reason all banks can accomplish this multiple expansion of deposit money is the institutional arrangement that requires them to hold only a fraction of their deposits in the form of legal reserves. Hence, when the excess reserves that exist in the banking system are spread among many banks, they can support a multiple amount of deposits.

In algebraic form let

ΔTDD = potential change in total demand deposits at all banks
TER = total excess reserves at all banks
r_d = reserve ratio on demand deposits

Then, for the banking system,

$$\Delta TDD(r_d) = TER$$
$$\Delta TDD(r_d)/r_d = TER/r_d$$
$$\Delta TDD = TER \cdot 1/r_d$$

To illustrate, if there is $100 million in excess reserves in the banking system and $r_d = .10$, then all banks together could expand demand deposits by $1 billion.

If the banking system is "loaned up," that is, there are no excess reserves available, then deposit contraction will occur if (1) the system loses legal reserves (for example, when the public converts a portion of their demand deposits into currency and coin) or (2) the reserve ratio is increased. If the banking system loses cash, then these lost legal reserves are unavailable to support deposits; hence deposits (and loans and investments) must contract. The same is true if the reserve ratio is raised; existing legal reserves will not support the present level of deposits, thus necessitating a decrease in deposits and assets. The extent of the deposit contraction also will be a multiple of the amount of lost reserves, just as deposit expansion reaches a multiple of the available excess reserves. For example, if the public converts $5 million of demand deposits into currency and coin, then with a reserve ratio of .20, the potential amount of deposit money must decline by $25 million. To illustrate, suppose the aggregated balance sheet for all banks is as follows:

[2]This apparent contradiction is known as the *banking paradox*. For a complete discussion of the principles of deposit expansion and contraction, see Federal Reserve Bank of Chicago, *Modern Money Mechanics: A Workbook on Deposits, Currency, and Bank Reserves* (Chicago: Federal Reserve Bank of Chicago, 1975).

[3]To simplify the discussion, assume (1) that no excess reserves will be used to support time or savings deposits, (2) that no reserves will be withdrawn in the form of currency and coin, (3) that there are enough creditworthy borrowers willing to take all the funds that banks will lend or invest, and (4) that all individual banks will lend or invest to their potential, that is, the amount of their excess reserves.

All Banks

Cash	$20M	Demand deposits	$100M
Loans and investments	$80M		

Immediately after the $5 million deposit conversion, the combined balance sheet is

All Banks

Cash	$15M	Demand deposits	$ 95M
Loans and investments	$80M		

Because they are now deficient in required reserves, banks must reduce their lending and investing until their combined balance sheet appears as follows:

All Banks

Cash	$15M	Demand deposits	$ 75M
Loans and investments	$60M		

Sources and Uses of Bank Reserves to the Banking System

Given the reserve requirement, the potential level of bank deposits within the banking system will fluctuate with the supply of legal reserves available to support these deposits. It is important for bankers to understand the factors that supply and absorb legal reserves. These factors are combined to form the *bank reserve equation,* which is the Federal Reserve's principal framework for evaluating the various influences on total legal reserves, including its own.

The bank reserve equation on a daily average for February 1977 is shown in Table 5-1. As seen in this table, the Federal Reserve is the principal source of legal reserves to member banks. The Federal Reserve creates these reserves as it acquires U.S. government securities, federal agency issues, and banker's acceptances[4]; makes a loan to a bank; or gives credit to a bank for checks presented to it before they are collected from other banks (known as *float*). These reserve deposits merely are credit entries made to member banks' accounts at the Federal Reserve.

The purchase and sale of U.S. government securities, federal agency issues, and bank acceptances by the central bank for its own account is

[4]A *banker's acceptance* is a time draft drawn on and accepted by a bank, which in effect substitutes the credit of a bank for the credit of an individual or company. Banker's acceptances, which represent an unqualified promise of the acceptor (bank) to pay at maturity, are used to finance imports, exports, and certain domestic transactions.

Table 5-1

Factors Supplying and Absorbing Member Bank Reserves
Monthly Averages of Daily Figures—February 1977
(millions of dollars)

Factors Supplying Reserve Funds		
1. Federal Reserve bank credit		109,021
U.S. Government securities	95,843	
Federal agency securities	6,846	
Bankers' acceptances	330	
Loans	79	
Float	2,899	
Other F. R. assets	3,024	
2. Gold stock		11,658
3. Special drawing rights certificate account		1,200
4. Treasury currency outstanding		10,930
TOTAL		$132,809
Factors Absorbing Reserve Funds		
5. Currency in circulation		91,753
6. Treasury cash holding		499
7. Deposits at F. R. (other than member bank reserves)		11,608
Treasury	10,698	
Foreign	294	
Other	616	
8. Other F. R. liabilities and capital		3,224
SUBTOTAL		107,084
Reserves at F. R. Banks		25,725
TOTAL		$132,809
Reserves at F. R. banks		25,725
Currency and coin		8,326
Total Member Bank Reserves		$34,051

Source: *Federal Reserve Bulletin.*

known as *open-market operations.* It is the principal means by which the Federal Reserve may influence member bank reserves. The Federal Reserve makes loans to a bank primarily as an accommodation; the impetus for increasing this form of reserve credit rests largely with the banks themselves. The level of float is primarily a function of the schedule with which the Federal Reserve agrees to credit the reserve account for cash items presented for collection and the speed with which the central bank can collect these items. For example, a power failure in New York City would result in a large, involuntary increase in reserves (which the Federal Reserve probably would offset by selling securities).

When the U.S. Treasury purchases gold, it pays for it by writing a check on its account at the Federal Reserve. The seller then presents the check for collection at a bank, which, in turn, forwards it to the Federal Reserve for collection. The central bank credits the bank's reserve account and debits the Treasury's account. The Treasury is also responsible for initiating credits to the Special Drawing Rights (SDR) Certificate Account when it issues them to the Federal Reserve in exchange for an increase in a special Treasury account at the Federal Reserve, which is shown under the "other deposit liabilities" heading.[5] This Treasury transaction does not affect bank reserves directly because they are absorbed simultaneously under "other deposits," as shown in Table 5-1. Finally, when the Treasury issues currency to the Federal Reserve, it also receives a corresponding increase in its deposit account. The Treasury may pay out these funds by checks, which, when the funds are collected by banks, will result in an increase in member bank legal reserves.

The principal factor absorbing reserves on the books of the Federal Reserve is the currency demands of banks and the public. When a bank requests currency from its Federal Reserve Bank, the bank's reserve account is decreased. The bank may pay out this currency in response to its depositors' demands or hold a portion of it in its vault. Cash held in bank vaults, however, counts as legal reserves; hence it is necessary to add this currency to reserves held at the Federal Reserve in order to figure total legal reserves.

Treasury cash holdings represent currency and coin held in the Treasury's vaults. When the Treasury increases its cash holdings, member bank reserves with the Federal Reserve are reduced. In a similar manner, increases in Treasury, foreign, and other deposits at the Federal Reserve lead to a reduction in member bank reserves held at the Federal Reserve. Finally, funds in any other Federal Reserve liability or capital account are unavailable to support deposits and, therefore, represent an absorption of member bank reserves.

To determine the volume of reserves remaining in the Federal Reserve banks, the total amount absorbed is subtracted from the total supplied. As shown in Table 5-1, $25,725 million is in reserve balances at the Federal Reserve. Vault cash of $8,326 million is added to this sum, giving total member bank reserves of $34,051 million.

Given this level of reserves and the applicable reserve ratio, the actual amount of deposits that will exist depends on the amount of loans and investments that banks make. If there is sufficient demand for

[5] *SDRs* or "paper gold" are credits issued by the International Monetary Fund to participating governments and are redeemable or convertible into any world currency that is, in turn, convertible into gold.

funds, the actual level of deposits will tend toward the limits set by total legal reserves and the reserve ratio. If the demand for funds is weak, the central bank or the commercial banks will find it difficult to increase deposits. Thus the central bank sets the upper limit on the money supply, but the public determines the actual amount that exists.

Demand Deposits

After banks initially expand demand deposits in the process of making loans and investments, the deposits will be transferred among many banks and many different owners before they are erased from the books by the repayment of loans and investments. Also, a portion of the expanded demand deposits will be converted into time and savings deposits or into currency. Let us take a closer look at the pattern of ownership of demand deposits, their distribution by size of account, and the service charges that banks receive for holding and transferring demand deposits.

Ownership

The individual commercial bank is interested in knowing the pattern of demand deposit ownership in its market area so that it can formulate an effective marketing strategy for the acquisition of deposits. There are four principal classes of owners of demand deposits: (1) businesses and individuals, (2) governmental units in the United States, (3) domestic banks, and (4) foreign governments and banks.

As of December 31, 1976, IPC deposits comprised 76.5 percent of total domestic demand deposits (Table 5-2). Based on a June 1968 FDIC survey of IPC demand deposit ownership, approximately 59 percent of these deposits are held by businesses and 41 percent are owned by "others" (Table 5-3).[6] Approximately 75 percent of the business deposits in 1968 were held in banks with deposits of $100 million or more. This is primarily because large corporations, which account for the bulk of the business deposits, have to go to the large money market banks to accommodate their credit needs and, as part of the loan agreement, usually agree to keep their corporate deposits at the lending bank. As shown in Table 5-3, there is a direct correlation between size of bank and the percentage of IPC demand deposits held by businesses.

At the close of 1976, certified and officers' checks, cashier's checks, letters of credit, and traveler's checks accounted for 3.5 percent of total demand deposits. A *certified check* is a regular check drawn by a customer on his bank, which, in turn, stamps it "certified" or "guar-

[6]A similar survey in 1961 indicated that 58.9 percent of IPC demand deposits were held by businesses.

Table 5-2

Ownership of Demand Deposits in All Insured Commercial Banks, December 31, 1965, and December 31, 1976
(millions of dollars)

Types of Deposits	1965	Percentage Distribution	1976	Percentage Distribution
Business and Personal Deposits				
Individuals, partnerships, and corporations	139,078	75.7%	255,359	76.5%
Certified and officer's checks, letters of credit, travelers checks, etc.	5,932	3.2	11,560	3.5
Government Deposits				
U.S. Government	5,524	3.0	3,037	0.9
States and subdivisions	14,242	7.7	17,903	5.4
Domestic Interbank Deposits				
U.S. commercial banks	15,779	8.6	35,959	10.8
U.S. mutual savings banks	860	0.5	1,385	0.4
Foreign Government and Bank Deposits				
Foreign governments, central banks, etc.	893	0.5	1,847	0.6
Foreign banks	1,529	0.8	6,767	2.0
Total demand deposits	183,837	100.0%	333,816	100.0%

Source: FDIC, *Annual Reports* and unpublished data.

NOTE: Details may not add due to rounding.

Table 5-3

Distribution of IPC Demand Deposits in Insured Commercial Banks, Grouped by Deposit Size, June 29, 1968
(millions of dollars)

Banks with Total Deposits of	Total	Business	Other	Percentage Distribution	
				Business	Other
All Banks	147.2	86.6	60.6	59%	41%
Less than $5M	6.3	1.5	4.8	24	76
$5–10M	9.1	2.8	6.3	31	69
$10–25M	15.5	6.2	9.3	40	60
$25–100M	21.6	11.1	10.5	51	49
$100M or more	94.7	65.1	29.7	69	31

Source: Mary T. Mitchell, "Business Holdings of Demand Deposits in Insured Commercial Banks, June 1968" (Washington, D.C.: FDIC, 1970), p. 10.

NOTE: Details may not add due to rounding.

anteed." An *officer's check* or *cashier's check* is an order on the bank to pay on demand drawn by a bank officer. A *letter of credit* authorizes specified individuals to draw drafts on the bank payable on demand. A *traveler's check* is an engraved instrument that gives the holder the right to demand money at any time. Banks charge their customers a small fee for selling them any of these instruments. Of course, banks immediately deduct the amount of any of these obligations issued from the customer's account. This is why these liabilities may be classified as demand deposits.

United States government deposits largely represent funds held in Treasury tax and loan accounts in the name of the district Federal Reserve Bank, which is the Treasury's fiscal agent. Any incorporated bank in the country is eligible to receive Treasury deposits if it qualifies through the district Federal Reserve bank.

The primary function of the tax and loan accounts is to permit the Treasury to smooth the flow of funds to and from its accounts at the Federal Reserve banks. As we have seen, increases in these accounts cause a decline in bank reserves. By having a large number of tax and loan accounts in which to channel tax revenue and the proceeds from security sales, the Treasury can reduce the possible destabilizing influence of its activities.

From a bank's point of view, deposits in a tax and loan account represent a source of additional loanable funds and therefore are welcomed. The bank must pledge government and certain other eligible securities as collateral against Treasury deposits held above the amount insured by the FDIC (presently, $40,000). There are at least two other advantages to the bank of having a tax and loan account. First, the bank may pay for its own and its customers' subscriptions to Treasury securities by a credit to the tax and loan account. The Treasury may extend withdrawals from this account over a one- to two-week period, thus giving the bank longer use of the funds. Second, the bank may request that its customers make their tax payments through the bank tax and loan account instead of remitting them directly. This also extends the period that the bank has use of these funds.

States and their subdivisions accounted for 5.4 percent of total demand deposits at the close of 1976. Because of the nature of their revenue sources, these governmental units receive funds at infrequent intervals. For example, local property taxes usually are due on a specific date, but these funds are expended at a fairly uniform rate over the year. The proceeds from bond issues also are not disbursed immediately and, therefore, usually are left on deposit at a bank for some period of time. During recent years, as interest rates were raised on time deposits, public treasurers have tended to place a larger proportion of the total funds available in time deposits. Deposits of state and local governments also are collateralized by appropriate U.S. government and other securities. In spite of this additional requirement, there is intense competition for these deposits. Usually, they are allocated among local banks on the basis of some formula involving the total deposits and capital of the banks involved.

The balances that commercial banks keep with one another comprise the second largest category of demand deposits. These interbank, or correspondent, balances represent an implicit compensation for services performed. Perhaps the principal service performed by most correspondent banks involves check collection. At the end of 1976 there were 8,914 state nonmember banks, most of which must depend on a member bank to collect their checks through the Federal Reserve's clearing system. Other services performed by correspondent banks include portfolio planning, safekeeping of securities, participation in loans, currency and coin shipments, and credit information.

In the recent high-interest-rate periods, correspondent relationships have come under close scrutiny from both sides. Small banks have become more conscious of the opportunity cost of keeping excessive balances, and many city correspondents have requested additional balances as the work load of clearing checks and the demand for other services has increased. With competition for correspondent accounts quite keen among the larger banks, and with size of the compensatory balance negotiable, many city banks, undoubtedly, have a number of unprofitable correspondent banking relationships. One possible solution to the problem would be to establish a fee schedule for various services performed.

Distribution of Accounts and Deposits by Size of Accounts

At the end of June 1972, accounts with $20,000 or more represented only 1.2 percent of the total IPC demand deposit accounts at all insured banks, but these accounts held 57.4 percent of the total funds in this deposit category (Table 5-4). At the lower end of the spectrum, IPC demand accounts with $1,000 or less represented 79.4 percent of the total number of accounts, and held only 9.9 percent of the total balances. A significant portion of a bank's total operating costs is incurred in servicing these small accounts. Banks obviously covet the large accounts because of the greater likelihood of making a profit on them. Morgan Guaranty Trust Co. of New York is known as a "wholesale" bank because it solicits and serves primarily large corporate accounts. On the other hand, Citibank of New York is known as a "retail" bank because it directs its services largely at the individual depositor and borrower. Although they tend to operate at opposite ends of the deposit spectrum, both banks have been highly successful in terms of profitability and deposit acquisition. Most banks across the nation, however, have some

Table 5-4
Distribution of Accounts at Commercial Banks, by Size of Accounts, June 30, 1972 (thousands of dollars)

Type of Deposit	Total	$1,000 or Less	$1,001 to $20,000	$20,001 to $100,000	$100,001 or More
Demand IPC	94,161	74,780	18,250	935	196
Savings	84,440	63,659	20,214	541	26
Other time IPC	29,727	16,333	12,726	574	95
States and political subdivisions	705	228	277	118	83

Distribution of Deposits by Size of Accounts (in billions of dollars)

Type of Deposit	Total	$1,000 or Less	$1,001 to $20,000	$20,001 to $100,000	$100,001 or More
Demand IPC	$191.6	$18.9	$62.8	$36.9	$73.0
Savings	120.1	11.6	85.1	17.0	6.4
Other time IPC	135.5	5.6	68.0	21.9	40.1
States and political subdivisions	51.0	.1	2.0	6.2	42.7

Source: FDIC, *Summary of Accounts and Deposits in All Commercial Banks* (Washington, D.C.: FDIC, 1972).

large, profitable accounts and many small accounts that are only marginally profitable at best. Generally speaking, banks in this country have chosen not to turn small depositors away but to take their accounts and hope that someday the total account relationship will prove profitable.[7] In the interim, these small depositors are subsidized by large depositors.

Service Charges

In addition to holding deposits for the public, banks also provide a means by which these deposits may be transferred among accounts in an individual bank and among accounts in different banks. The function of merely holding deposits does not involve much cost. The act of deposit transfer, however, is a bank's most costly activity, one that involves the employment of a large number of people, the purchase or

[7]We should note that small depositors are the principal users of installment credit, which is highly profitable to the bank.

rental of sophisticated mechanical and electronic equipment, the printing of numerous forms and checks, and the incurring of a large number of other associated expenses. As we saw in Chapter 1, the public has many other alternatives to holding deposits at commercial banks. They could accept claims issued by any of the other nonbank financial intermediaries. However, except for NOW accounts at federally insured commercial banks, savings and loan associations, cooperative banks, and mutual savings banks in six New England states, and savings and loan associations and credit unions that handle preauthorized payments, such as the monthly remittance that an individual makes to his mortgage company or insurance company, nonbank intermediaries do not provide a payments transfer system for the public as do commercial banks. Because they provide this service, banks receive the deposits, which gives them the resources to make loans and investments, and the public benefits by having an efficient means of remitting payments.

Now the question is, who should pay the expense of providing a payments mechanism—the bank or the public? The microeconomist would probably state that efficient resource allocation dictates that the public should be charged an amount that covers the marginal cost of providing such a payments mechanism. This solution is more easily suggested than implemented. Because they have profitable outlets for funds in the form of loans and investments, banks have not worried a great deal about recouping the cost of maintaining the deposit transfer system. They also knew that the public could effect many payments with currency and that prohibitive pricing of the deposit transfer system on their part could bring about a relaxation of regulatory constraints on nonbank intermediaries and hence greater competition for funds. Thus banks generally have made only token attempts to achieve the economist's standard of marginal cost pricing of the deposit holding and transfer functions. As a result, service charges on demand deposit accounts and deposit activity recoup only a fraction of the total cost of providing these services.

Banks have developed many different methods of levying service charges. The method of calculation and the level of bank service charges generally depend on the type of account, personal or business, and the community involved. With respect to charges on personal checking accounts, some banks do not have an account maintenance fee and therefore advertise "free banking." Other banks have a flat service charge depending on the average or minimum balance, while some banks have more elaborate rating schemes involving, perhaps, a deposit maintenance fee, so many "free" checks (depending on the average or minimum balance), and a flat fee for each check written beyond the "free check limit." Many banks attempt to offset costs by selling personalized checks containing the name and address of the depositor.

The pricing of business checking account services has received more attention by banks. Perhaps this is because banks know that business customers are more aware of the costs involved and, therefore, are more willing to pay for service received. Typically, banks attempt to analyze their costs of performing each function involved, for example, receiving a deposit, processing a check, and providing coins and currency. Then, depending on their competition and the communities involved, they set a price for performing each function that they hope will equal the cost plus a profit. Banks also grant a credit allowance against these charges equal to some percentage of the net investable balance left with the bank during the period. The net business service charge, then, is the difference between the gross charges and the credit allowance. Figure 5-1 provides an illustration of a complete business account analysis.

Time Deposits

Deposits that are not payable on demand are classified as time deposits. Regulation Q of the Board of Governors of the Federal Reserve System and corresponding FDIC regulations prohibit the payment of interest on demand deposits and regulate the amount that may be paid on time deposits. Let us note the various types of time deposits, examine the ownership of these deposits, and discuss the regulation of time deposit interest rates.

Types

There are three principal kinds of time deposits: (1) savings deposits; (2) time deposits, open account; and (3) time certificates of deposit.

Savings Deposits. The term *savings deposits* means a deposit

1. Which consists of funds deposited to the credit of one or more individuals, or of a public unit as defined in section 3(m) of the FDIC act, or of a corporation, association, or other organization operated primarily for religious, philanthropic, charitable, educational, fraternal, or other similar purposes and not operated for profit, or in which the entire beneficial interest is held by one or more individuals or public units, or by such a corporation, association, or other organization.
2. Which consists of funds deposited to the credit of, or in which all or part of the beneficial interests is held by a corporation, partnership, association, or other organization which does not come with paragraph (e) (1) (i) of this section but only to the extent that such deposits do not exceed $150,000 for any such corporation, partnership, association, or other organization in any one bank.[8]

[8]FDIC, *Rules and Regulations,* part 329. 1.

ANALYSIS OF EXPENSE				
1.	# 416	Items Deposited to Account @ 3c each	12	48
2.	# 227	Items Charged to Account @ 6c each	13	62
3.				
4.		Non-Cash Collection Items—Outgoing		
	#	a. No Documents Attached @ $1.00 each		
	#	b. With Documents Attached @ $2.50 each		
5.		Cash Collections Items—Outgoing		
	#	a. No Documents Attached @ $1.00 each plus int.		
	#	b. With Documents Attached @ $2.50 each plus int.		
6.	$	Coupons @ 25c per $100		
7.	$	Bonds @ 25c per $100		
8.	# 5	Transfer of Funds @ $2.00 each	10	00
9.	#	Private Wire Messages @ $2.00 each		
10.	#	Payable Thru Drafts @ 6c each		
11.		Stop Payments:		
	# 1	a. Original @ $1.00 each	1	00
	#	b. Renewals @ 50c each		
12.	#	NSF or OD Checks @ $3.50 each		
13.	$	Analysis Overdraft at Prime Interest Rate (%)		
14.	$	Other		
15.				
16.				
17.				
18.				
19.				
20.				
21.				
22.		Maintenance Charge per Month	1	00
23.		TOTAL ANALYSIS EXPENSE	38	10

NON-PAR ITEMS (Actual Charges)				
24.	$	Rate 18c per hundred		
25.	$	Rate 1/4% @ 25c per hundred		
26.	$	Rate 1/5% @ 20c per hundred		
27.	$	Rate 1/8% @ 12.5c per hundred		
28.	$	Rate 1/10% @ 10c per hundred		
29.		TOTAL NON PAR EXCHANGE COSTS		

ANALYSIS OF FUNDS ON DEPOSIT		
30. AVERAGE LEDGER BALANCE	9	650
31. LESS: AVERAGE UNAVAILABLE FUNDS	2	400
32. AVERAGE COLLECTED BALANCE	7	250
33. LESS: FEDERAL REQUIRED RESERVES		979
34. AVERAGE LOANABLE BALANCE	6	271
35.		
36.		
37.		
38.		
39.		
40.		
41.		
42.		
43.		
44.		
45.		

INCOME AND EXPENSE		
46. EARNINGS ON LOANABLE BALANCE		
47.	29	7[illegible]
48.		
49.		
50. LESS: TOTAL ANALYSIS EXPENSE	38	1[illegible]
51.		
52.		
53. ANALYSIS PROFIT OR (LOSS)	(8	31
54. TOTAL NON-PAR EXCHANGE COSTS		
55.		
56.		
57.		
58.		
59.		
60.		
61.		
62.		
63. TOTAL ANALYSIS (LOSS) AND/OR NON PAR EXCHANGE COSTS	(8	31

JHL Corporation
123 Main Street
Columbia, South Carolina 29201

ANALYSIS OF ACCOUNT
FOR MONTH OF June 1977
ANALYSIS DEPARTMENT
THE SOUTH CAROLINA NATIONAL BANK
P. O. Box 345 . **Office** Assembly Street
Telephone No. 765-1234

20-048 (Rev. 10/69)

Figure 5-1 Analysis of Business Account Activity

The bulk of these funds is held by individuals, and, in practice, banks do not require a written notice of redemption. The volume of commercial bank savings deposits depends on (1) the amount of personal savings channeled into financial assets, (2) the proportion of such savings that are placed in financial intermediaries, (3) the proportion of savings placed in financial intermediaries that is placed in deposit and share savings accounts, and (4) the commercial banks' share of the growth in deposit and share savings accounts.

The average and marginal propensities to save in the household sector of the American economy tend to be rather stable. During the recent recessions, however, there was a noticeable increase in the average propensity to save out of disposable income and, significantly, this movement was accompanied by a sharp gain in savings-type deposits at financial intermediaries.

The proportion of savings placed in financial intermediaries as opposed to the organized securities markets depends on expectations regarding the business cycle, price changes, and interest rates, and the aggressiveness of these institutions in seeking funds. In recent years, financial intermediaries have been very successful in increasing their share of the financial savings generated in the economy.

The commercial banks' share of the increase in savings-type accounts rose significantly following the raising of Regulation Q ceilings in 1962 and on subsequent occasions since that time. From the end of World War II until the late 1950s, savings and loan associations, because of a favorable interest-rate differential and because of aggressive promotional policies, far surpassed commercial banks in savings acquisition. The rate of savings growth at savings and loan associations did not taper off until banks began to compete seriously for savings during the 1961–1964 period and until the high rates on money market instruments after 1965 diverted funds from all intermediaries. Since the awakening of commercial banks to the need to compete for savings deposits and other time money, a battle royal has raged among all financial intermediaries for these funds.

Time Deposits, Open Account. The term *time deposit, open account* means a deposit, other than a time certificate of deposit, with respect to which there is in force a written contract with the depositor that neither the whole nor any part of such deposit may be withdrawn, by check or otherwise, prior to the date of maturity, which shall be not less than thirty days after the date of the deposit, or prior to the expiration of the period of notice which must be given by the depositor in writing not less than thirty days in advance of withdrawal. If funds in a time deposit, open account, are withdrawn before maturity, the depositor must forfeit three months' interest payable at the rate on savings deposits and interest on the amount withdrawn is reduced to the rate on savings deposits.

Since banks began to compete actively for time deposits, they have been highly successful in attracting funds into time deposit, open accounts. The "golden passbook savings account," which has been advertised extensively by banks in all parts of the country, is, technically, a time deposit, open account. This type of deposit account has been responsible for attracting large amounts of savings that ordinarily would have gone into regular passbook savings accounts and, possibly, into the organized securities markets.

Time Certificate of Deposit. A *time certificate of deposit* is a deposit evidenced by a negotiable or nonnegotiable instrument (the certificate) that provides on its face that the amount of each deposit is payable (1) on a certain date, specified in the instrument, not less than thirty days after date of deposit; or (2) at the expiration of a specified period, not less than thirty days after the date of the instrument; or (3) upon written notice to be given not less than thirty days before the date of repayment.

In February 1961, metropolitan New York banks began to promote negotiable CDs as a "creative response" to the efforts of corporate cash managers to pare demand balances to a minimum, and to the banks' own need for funds to meet anticipated loan demands. At the end of 1960, negotiable CDs had totaled only slightly in excess of $1 billion. On December 29, 1976, the volume of outstanding negotiable CDs in denominations of $100,000 or more at 160 large weekly reporting banks alone stood at $65.9 billion.

Negotiable CDs usually are denominated in amounts ranging from $100,000 to $10 million, with a $1 million face value as a standard trading unit. The most popular maturities lie in the six-months to one-year range. The principal purchasers of these instruments are large corporations, state and local governments, foreign governments, central banks, official institutions, and wealthy individuals. The main advantage to the holder of negotiable CDs over other money market instruments such as Treasury bills, commercial paper, and banker's acceptances is that the maturity date can be tailored to fit the special needs of the purchaser. For example, most large corporations make quarterly dividend and tax payments. The corporation's cash manager could purchase a negotiable CD that would mature on the date the dividends or taxes were payable, thus permitting the corporation to earn maximum interest income on its funds. If it becomes necessary for a negotiable CD holder to liquidate his certificate before the maturity date, there are a number of dealers who offer a secondary market in negotiable CDs. Dealers prefer negotiable CDs issued by large money market banks because they are more secure and more marketable than those issued by smaller institutions. FDIC insurance covers only up to $40,000 of each negotiable CD.

Nonnegotiable CDs also have been developed extensively during the past decade. These instruments are denominated in amounts ranging from $500 to $100,000, with $5,000 and $10,000 as typical face values. Interest is calculated from day of deposit and may be compounded daily, monthly, or quarterly. The principal purchasers of nonnegotiable CDs are individuals, small to medium-sized businesses, and state and local governments.

Ownership

Ownership of time deposits follows a pattern very similar to that of demand deposits, with businesses and individuals holding the bulk of the funds. As shown in Table 5-5, this category of deposit holders accounted for 86.2 percent of total time deposits at the end of 1976, as compared with 88.2 percent at the close of 1965. The composition of their time deposit holdings, however, has shifted markedly. The 1965 savings deposits represented 62.7 percent of total business and personal deposits; by 1976 this proportion had fallen to 39.8 percent. The promotional efforts behind other kinds of time deposits and the attractive yields and terms available on these balances largely explain their unprecedented growth and why savings deposit growth lagged.

The next largest group of time deposit owners consists of the states and their political subdivisions. These governmental units added $38.0 billion to their time deposit holdings between 1965 and 1976. Tax receipts of state and local governments have risen sharply during the last decade, as a result of an increase in both tax rates and tax bases (property, sales, income, for example). Therefore, the average deposit holdings of these political units rose. With yields on time deposits at an

Table 5-5
Ownership of Time Deposits in All Insured Commercial Banks, December 31, 1965, and December 31, 1976
(millions of dollars)

Types of Deposits	1965	Percentage Distribution	1976	Percentage Distribution
Business and Personal Deposits				
Savings deposits	92,555	62.7%	197,736	39.8%
Deposits accumulated for payment of loans	1,078	0.7	146	[a]
Other IPC	36,562	24.8	230,667	46.4
Government Deposits				
U.S. Government	281	0.2	736	0.1
States and subdivisions	12,170	8.2	50,121	10.1
Domestic Interbank Deposits				
U.S. commercial banks	510	0.3	6,818	1.4
U.S. mutual savings banks	162	0.1	319	0.1
Foreign Government and Bank Deposits				
Foreign governments, central banks, etc.	4,086	2.8	8,585	1.7
Foreign banks	271	0.2	1,779	0.4
Total time deposits	147,676	100.0%	496,908	100.0%

Source: FDIC, *Annual Reports* and unpublished data.

NOTE: Details may not add due to rounding.
[a]Less than 0.1 percent.

attractive level, it is only natural to expect public treasurers to hold a greater proportion of their funds in interest-bearing deposits.

The largest other holders of time deposits are foreign governments and central banks. These institutions have accumulated large dollar holders, owing to the United States' protracted balance of payments deficit. In October 1962, the Federal Reserve removed the ceiling on the maximum interest rate that banks could pay on time deposits held by foreign governments, central banks, and official institutions to encourage them to hold dollars instead of exchanging them for gold.

Interest Paid

Congress first enacted legislation to regulate interest payments on commercial bank deposits in the Banking Act of 1933. This act prohibited interest payments on demand deposits and required the Federal Reserve Board to limit interest paid on time deposits by member banks.[9] The principal argument for a ceiling on time deposit interest rates is that such a ceiling prevents competitive rate increases among commercial banks, thus reducing the need for banks to reach out for lower-quality assets. Also, it is alleged that interest-rate wars among banks lead to lower earnings, which limits the growth of capital.

On the other hand, regulation of time interest rates limits the ability of commercial banks to compete with other financial intermediaries for funds. This ceiling is the principal reason why the rate of growth of savings at savings and loan associations was five times that of commercial banks between 1945 and 1961. Although the Board of Governors raised the ceiling on all or certain types of time deposits nine times between 1965 and 1976, growth of bank IPC time and savings deposits was only $3.5 billion more than the combined increase in savings deposits at mutual savings banks and loan associations. Table 5-6 indicates the Regulation Q ceilings for selected dates in effect on March 31, 1977.

Even though the Federal Reserve Board raised Regulation Q ceilings five times between July 1966 and July 1973, there were several periods during which it appeared that the Reserve Board, in the course of pursuing a tight-money policy, delayed in adjusting bank interest-rate ceilings upward, even though money-market rates were above these ceilings and rising. Under such conditions, banks (as well as other financial intermediaries) were faced with massive withdrawals of time and demand deposits (financial disintermediation). By not adjusting Regulation Q ceilings, the Federal Reserve decreased the net flow of funds to banks, thus causing banks to reduce their loan commitments

[9]The Federal Reserve Board's ceilings on time deposit interest rates are enumerated in its Regulation Q. Since February 1, 1936, maximum rates that may be paid by nonmember insured commercial banks, as established by the FDIC, have been the same as those in effect for member banks.

Table 5-6

Maximum Interest Rates on Commercial Bank Time and Savings Deposits (percentage per annum)

Type and Maturity of Deposit	In effect March 31, 1977 Percent	In effect March 31, 1977 Effective Date	Previous Maximum Percent	Previous Maximum Effective Date
Savings	5	7/1/73	4½	1/21/70
Negotiable order of withdrawal (NOW) accounts[a]	5	1/1/74	—	—
Time (multiple-and single-maturity unless otherwise indicated):				
30–89 days:				
Multiple-maturity	5	7/1/73	4½	1/21/70
Single-maturity			5	9/26/66
90 days to 1 year:				
Multiple-maturity				7/20/66
Single-maturity	5½	7/1/73	5	9/26/66
1 to 2 Years			5½	1/21/70
2 to 2½ Years	6	7/1/73	5¾	1/21/70
2½ to 4 Years	6½	7/1/73	5¾	1/21/70
4 to 6 Years	7¼	11/1/73	[b]	—
6 Years or More	7½	12/23/74	7¼	11/1/73
Governmental units (all maturities)	7¾	12/23/74	7½	11/27/74

Source: *Federal Reserve Bulletin.*

NOTE: The maximum rates on time deposits in denominations of $100,000 or more were suspended in the mid-1973.

[a] For authorized states only. Federally insured commercial banks, savings and loan associations, cooperative banks, and mutual savings banks were first permitted to offer NOW accounts on Jan. 1, 1974. Authorization to issue NOW accounts was extended to similar institutions throughout New England on Feb. 27, 1976.

[b] Between early July 1, 1973, and Oct. 31, 1973, there was no ceiling for certificates maturing in 4 years or more with minimum denominations of $1,000; however, the amount of such certificates that an institution could issue was limited to 5 percent of its total time and savings deposits. Sales in excess of that amount, as well as certificates of less than $1,000, were limited to the 6½ percent ceiling on time deposits maturing in 2½ years or more.

Effective Nov. 1, 1973, the present ceilings were imposed on certificates maturing in 4 years or more with minimum denominations of $1,000. There is no limitation on the amount of these certificates that banks can issue. In December 1975, the Federal regulatory agencies removed the minimum-denomination requirement on time deposits representing funds contributed to an individual retirement account (IRA) established pursuant to the Internal Revenue Code. Similar action was taken for Keogh (H. R. 10) plans in November 1976.

and, in many cases, to sell securities from their permanent investment portfolio. Hence Regulation Q ceilings became an active tool of credit control, just as are open-market operations and changes in the discount rate.

On several occasions during this period, however, the Reserve Board raised Regulation Q ceilings when it appeared that perhaps they might have put excessive pressure on the banks. For example, on January 21, 1970, the board raised the interest ceiling on time deposits of $100,000 or more with a maturity of one year or more from 6.25 to 7.50 percent in an effort to reverse the disintermediation process and to encourage bank credit expansion. On July 1, 1973, it suspended the interest ceiling on CDs of $100,000 or more in order to permit banks to bid for time deposits and make credit extensions to many major corporations that were having difficulty meeting their short-term obligations.

The implications of the Federal Reserve's actions during recent years for bank management are important. If the Federal Reserve plans to make changes in Regulation Q an active part of its monetary policy actions, then bank management must be prepared for periodically large drains and inflows of funds. These possibilities obviously mean that liquidity requirements, loan commitments, and portfolio planning must be monitored more closely in the light of these contingencies. Presently, many banking observers believe that in the near future, the Reserve Board might remove other interest-rate ceilings. Such an action is likely to stimulate further competition among financial intermediaries.

The Changing Deposit Mix

As we have just seen, total time deposits have increased sharply during the last decade in relation to total demand deposits. Time deposits have risen from 33.4 percent of total deposits in 1961 to 59.8 percent of the total in 1976 (Table 5.7). The causes and implications of this shift in the deposit mix will be explored in this section.

Causes

The principal cause of the increase in bank time deposits since 1961 was the increase in interest rates that banks paid for these funds. From January 1, 1936, until January 1, 1957, the maximum rate payable on bank savings deposits was 2.5 percent. From the last date until January 1, 1962, the maximum rate was 3 percent. Actually, between the 1929 and 1961 recessions, the Treasury bill rate, which is the basic indicator of short-term interest rate, never surpassed 3 percent. During the depression decade of the 1930s, banks were flush with excess reserves and had no need to bid for time money. From 1941 until 1951, the Federal Reserve itself pegged interest rates at very low levels to protect the holders of the newly created federal debt from possible losses through interest-rate increases and to mollify those who believed that the nation's economy might slip back into depression. With the famous Federal Reserve-Treasury Accord of March 1951, the Federal Reserve no longer had to peg interest rates. Since that time, interest rates, except for the recession years, have trended upward.

Prior to 1961, banks did not bid for corporate time deposits because they believed the funds would come mainly from corporate demand de-

Table 5-7
Deposit Mix at Insured Commercial Banks, Selected Years, 1965–1976 (billions of dollars)

Year	Demand Deposits	Savings Deposits	Other Time Deposits	Total Time Deposits	Total Deposits
1965	183.8	92.6	55.1	147.7	331.5
1970	246.2	98.2	134.8	233.0	479.2
1971	262.3	112.2	164.7	276.9	539.2
1972	296.4	124.2	196.3	320.5	616.9
1973	309.1	127.8	244.7	372.5	681.6
1974	314.4	136.3	295.7	432.0	746.4
1975	321.4	160.7	298.6	459.3	780.7
1976	333.8	204.0	292.9	496.9	830.7
		Percentage Distribution			
1965	55.4%	27.9%	16.6%	44.6%	100.0%
1970	51.4	20.5	28.1	48.6	100.0
1971	48.6	20.8	30.5	51.4	100.0
1972	48.0	20.1	31.8	52.0	100.0
1973	45.3	18.8	35.9	54.7	100.0
1974	42.1	18.3	39.6	57.9	100.0
1975	41.2	20.6	38.2	58.8	100.0
1976	40.2	24.6	35.3	59.8	100.0

Source: FDIC, *Annual Reports* and unpublished data.

NOTE: Details may not add due to rounding.

posits. Meanwhile, improved methods of cash management began to permit corporate treasurers to reduce their demand balances and to place the newly found excess funds into money market instruments. Some of these cash management techniques were improved billing and bookkeeping systems brought about by the use of computers; lockbox arrangements whereby banks in different parts of the country served as depositories for locally due bills; and the wire transfer of funds whereby balances due in other parts of the country could be transferred immediately, without the delay normally accompanying check transfers. All these techniques enabled corporate treasurers to reduce their cash balance requirements. It was these innovations that prompted the development of CDs.

With rising interest rates, individuals also began to find ways to economize on demand balances and to shift funds into savings and other time deposits. The ubiquitous use of credit cards, in particular, has enabled individuals to reduce the size of the demand deposit holdings. With credit cards, people may purchase just about any item they need and make only one monthly payment. Thus credit cards permit individuals to carry smaller demand balances and larger time and savings deposits.

Implications

A time-honored principle of finance is to match short-term liabilities with short-term assets and long-term liabilities with long-term assets. Historically, most commercial bank liabilities were of a very short-run nature; that is, they were payable on demand. This is why banks, until recent years, primarily made only short-term loans. The large-scale shift in deposits from demand to time and savings deposits has had obvious implications for asset management. For example, with the lengthening of the deposit structure, banks have used this opportunity to make more term loans to business.[10] Whereas before businesses looked to banks primarily for seasonal financing, they now consider banks a primary source of loans with maturities up to ten years and, in some cases, longer. Banks also have used the longer-term nature of their liabilities as a rationale for stepping up their mortgage-lending activities.

The shifting deposit mix also has had important implications for investment management. During the last decade, banks have added sharply to their holdings of municipal securities. Moreover, investment strategy with respect to Treasury securities has changed. Many banks now reach out and purchase higher-yielding Treasury notes and bonds, if investment analysis warrants the move. It should be pointed out, however, that banks have *had* to look for longer-term loans and investments in order to cover the higher interest rates on time deposits. The extension of the maturity of the asset portfolio has been partly out of necessity. As a result of the shifting deposit mix, banks now are more effective competitors with life insurance companies and other suppliers of long-term funds.

Deposit Insurance

Origin, Purpose, and Cost

As a result of the wave of bank failures prior to and during the Great Depression, Congress provided, temporarily, for national deposit insurance in the Banking Act of 1933. A permanent plan of deposit insurance through the Federal Deposit Insurance Corporation was put in operation on January 1, 1934. The initial amount of insurance provided was $2,500, but this coverage was raised to $5,000 in mid-1934. Subsequently, the insurance maximum was increased to $10,000 in 1950, $15,000 in 1966, $20,000 in 1969, and $40,000 in 1974.

[10]*Term loans* are those with an original maturity of one year or longer.

Contrary to popular belief, the FDIC insures depositors, not deposits. The purpose of deposit insurance is to indemnify depositors up to the maximum coverage, if a bank has to suspend its operations. Presently, a husband and wife can maintain separate accounts, and also a joint account in one bank and have deposit insurance on the three separate accounts totaling $120,000. This couple could maintain three separate accounts in any number of insured banks and receive similar coverage in each institution.

Milton Friedman, the eminent monetary economist, has stated that "the most important monetary event after 1933 was the establishment of Federal insurance of bank deposits."[11] Because of the existence of the FDIC, depositors believe that their money is safe and secure. Actually, however, only 66.7 percent of the total bank deposits at the end of 1976 were covered by the $40,000 of insurance coverage, and the amount of the insurance fund ($7.3 billion) constituted only 1.25 percent of these insured deposits. The contribution of the FDIC is, therefore, largely psychological. Be that as it may, the existence of the FDIC reduces greatly the chance of massive bank runs like those that occurred in the Great Depression.

The cost of FDIC insurance coverage is nominal. The statutory annual premium is $\frac{1}{12}$ of 1 percent of total assessable deposits of each insured bank. Because deposit losses have been relatively small, the FDIC now credits each bank's current assessment with $66\frac{2}{3}$ percent of net assessment income (gross assessment income less administrative and operating expenses and net additions to reserve to provide for insurance losses). This credit reduced the net assessment rate to $\frac{1}{27}$ of 1 percent in 1976.

Deposit-Insurance Activities of the FDIC

As the deposit-insurance agency, the FDIC, by law, has an active program of loss prevention. That is, it attempts to minimize deposit losses through its supervisory and examination functions. The FDIC, or the other regulatory agencies, conducts a regular examination of each insured bank. If, through ordinary supervision, examination, and consultation, the FDIC is unsuccessful in getting a bank to correct an unsafe or unsound banking practice or a violation of law or regulation, then it may initiate proceedings to terminate the bank's insured status. Before that happens, however, the bank is given a specified period of time in which to correct the irregularity. If at the end of this period the problem remains, the bank's insured status is terminated.

[11]Milton Friedman, *A Program for Monetary Stability* (New York: Fordham University Press, 1959), p. 20.

In the case of an actual bank failure, the FDIC may either (1) pay off the depositors and attempt to liquidate the assets or (2) have a solvent bank assume all the liabilities and sound assets. The FDIC prefers the second method because it results in continued banking services at the existing locations, and it tends to minimize the FDIC's total payout since another bank exists to collect the loans outstanding. Between 1934 and 1976 the FDIC dealt with 539 bank failures, of which 303 were classified as payoff cases and 232 were assumption cases.

Suggestions for Additional Reading

Basch, Donald. "The Diffusion of NOW Accounts in Massachusetts." Federal Reserve Bank of Boston, *New England Economic Review* (November–December 1976), pp. 20–30.

Bender, Mark G. *EFTS/Electronic Funds Transfer Systems: Elements and Impact.* Port Washington, N.Y.: Kennikat Press, 1975.

Cates, David C. "Bank Capital Management: Paying Interest on Checking Accounts." *The Bankers Magazine* (Spring 1976), pp. 114–118.

Crum, Lawrence L. *Time Deposits in Present-Day Commercial Banking.* Gainesville, Fla.: University of Florida Press, 1964.

Federal Reserve Bank of Boston. *The Economics of a National Electronic Funds Transfer System.* Boston: Federal Reserve Bank of Boston, 1974.

Federal Reserve Bank of Chicago. *Modern Money Mechanics: A Workbook on Deposits, Currency, and Bank Reserves.* Chicago: Federal Reserve Bank of Chicago, 1975.

Gibson, Katharine. "The Early History and Initial Impact of NOW Accounts." Federal Reserve Bank of Boston, *New England Economic Review* (January–February 1975), pp. 17–26.

Haywood, Charles F. *The Pledging of Bank Assets: A Study of the Problem of Security for Public Deposits.* Chicago: Association of Reserve City Bankers, 1967.

———. *Regulation Q and Monetary Policy.* Chicago: Association of Reserve City Bankers, 1971.

Haywood, Charles F., and Linke, Charles M. *The Regulation of Deposit Interest Rates.* Chicago: Association of Reserve City Bankers, 1968.

Herzig-Marx, Chayim. "Advertising for Demand Deposits." Federal Reserve Bank of Chicago, *Business Conditions* (September 1975), pp. 10–14.

Kimball, Ralph C. "Recent Developments in the NOW Account Experiment in New England." Federal Reserve Bank of Boston, *New England Economic Review* (November–December 1976), pp. 3–19.

Knight, Robert E. "Account Analysis in Correspondent Banking." Federal Reserve Bank of Kansas City, *Monthly Review* (March 1976), pp. 11–20.

———. "Correspondent Banking: Parts I–III." Federal Reserve Bank of Kansas City, *Monthly Review* (November 1970), pp. 3–14; (December 1970), pp. 12–24; and (December 1971), pp. 3–17.

Murphy, Neil B. "Removing Deposit Interest Ceilings: An Analysis of Deposit Flows, Portfolio Response and Income Effects in Boston Co-Operative Banks." *Journal of Bank Research* (Winter 1977), pp. 256–265.

Pugh, Olin S., and Wood, Oliver G., Jr. "Bank Service Charges in the South." *National Banking Review* (December 1966), pp. 175–182.

Ruebling, Charlotte C. "The Administration of Regulation Q." St. Louis Federal Reserve Bank, *Review* (February 1970), pp. 29–40.

CHAPTER

6

Bank Capital and Other Liabilities

Although capital and other nondeposit liabilities provide only a small portion of a bank's total investable funds, these accounts perform several important functions and contribute a great deal of flexibility to the institution's successful operation. In this chapter we shall (1) note the various bank capital and reserve accounts, (2) discuss the functions of bank capital, (3) consider the measures of capital adequacy, (4) examine the various nondeposit liabilities, and (5) develop a simple bank capital budgeting model to aid bankers in the management of both the sources and uses of funds sides of their balance sheet.

Capital and Reserve Accounts

Common Stock, Surplus, and Undivided Profits

The capital accounts at most banks consist of common stock (usually termed "capital stock"), surplus, and undivided profits. The sum in the *common stock account* is equal to the number of common shares outstanding times the par value of the stock. The *surplus account* reflects the sale of common stock at a premium over the par value. The *undivided profits* account is similar to the earned surplus account of nonbank businesses. As undivided profits accrue, funds may be shifted from this account to the surplus account.

Preferred Stock

Because many banks in financial difficulty during the Great Depression issued preferred stock to the Reconstruction Finance Corporation as a means of raising needed capital, a stigma was placed upon this form of bank equity capital. The issuance of preferred stock by banks was taken as a sign of weakness. In the late 1960s, however, a number of banks issued preferred stock (convertible and nonconvertible) in connection with mergers with other banks. A peak of $107.3 million was reached in 1970. Since then the amount of preferred stock outstanding has declined markedly, primarily because of exchanges of convertible preferred for common shares.

The principal advantage of preferred stock over alternative means of raising bank capital is that the former has no maturity and carries no voting privilege. On the other hand, dividends paid by the bank on preferred stock are nondeductible for income tax purposes, which makes the cost of capital from this source very high. Moreover, investors are not attracted to preferred stock since its appreciation potential is limited.

Capital Notes and Debentures

Origin and Use. *Capital notes and debentures* are long-term obligations to repay money in the future. They carry fixed interest rates, and their claim for payment is subordinated to that of depositors and other creditors. Capital notes and capital debentures essentially are alike, differing only in their form and issuing procedures. The Commission on Money and Credit, which made the most thorough study of our banking and financial system since the National Monetary Commission of 1908, recommended in 1961 that banks consider seeking authorization to issue debt as a means of augmenting equity capital. In response to this suggestion, the Advisory Committee on Banking to the Comptroller of the Currency issued a report stating that "there is no sound reason why national banks should be deprived of any legitimate capital-raising method that is available to corporations generally." On December 28, 1962, James J. Saxon, then Comptroller of the Currency, published a ruling permitting national banks to issue convertible or noncovertible debentures. He ruled further that capital notes and debentures "shall not exceed an amount equal to 100 percent of the bank's unimpaired paid-in capital stock plus 50 percent of the amount of its unimpaired surplus fund." Since the Comptroller's ruling of 1962, state banking authorities have given their banks authorization to issue capital notes and debentures.

Capital notes and debentures may contribute in several ways to improved capital adequacy. First, because their claim is subordinated to that of depositors and other creditors, capital notes and debentures directly increase the bank's ability to absorb losses. Second, the issuance of capital notes and debentures has a leverage effect, which may lead to an increase in bank earnings and, perhaps, dividends.[1] To the extent that undivided profits are increased, capital adequacy is enhanced. An improved rate of growth in earnings generally leads to a higher price-earnings ratio, which facilitates the acquisition of additional equity capital.

As an alternative means of obtaining operating funds, capital notes and debentures possess several advantages over time deposits and new equity capital. Banks do not have to hold reserves or pay deposit insurance on capital notes and debentures, as they do with time deposits. In addition, the administrative costs associated with these debt instruments are less than on time deposits. Thus the after-tax cost of capital notes and debentures tends to be less than that of time deposits.

Capital notes and debentures usually are a much less expensive source of funds than is common equity capital.[2] The cost of internal equity capital to a bank or any other business essentially is the rate of return that investors expect to receive on the stock. This cost of funds can be estimated by the formula $k = D/P + g$, where D is expected dividends, P is current price, and g is the expected appreciation in the stock price. For example, if the expected dividend is $1, the current price is $25, and the expected appreciation in price is 6 percent, then the cost of equity funds is 10 percent (0.04 + 0.06). If 10 percent was the expected return on a bank's stock and there were alternative investments of similar risk also yielding 10 percent, that is, the opportunity cost of funds invested in the banks is the same, then investors would not hold the bank's stock if it was expected to yield less than 10 percent. Since 1962, banks issuing capital notes and debentures generally have had to pay a coupon rate of between 5 to 9 percent plus underwriting fees and administrative fees. Therefore, given that capital notes and debentures are forms of debt, it is expected that the cost of equity funds, which involve a greater degree of risk, would be higher for the bank.

Banks quickly took advantage of their newly acquired permission to issue capital notes and debentures. At the end of 1962, banks had only

[1]*Financial leverage* is the use of funds with fixed costs such as capital notes and debentures in order to increase earnings on stockholders' equity.

[2]*Equity capital* is defined here to exclude preferred stock. For a bank, equity capital includes common stock, capital surplus, and undivided profits.

$20.5 million of these debt instruments outstanding. By the close of 1965, the total had jumped to $1,652.7 million (Table 6-1). Although the high-interest-rate period of 1966 to 1970 discouraged considerably the issuance of bank capital notes and debentures, by December 31, 1976, the total amount outstanding had climbed to $5,123 million. In retrospect, the Comptroller's 1962 ruling was one of the most significant regulatory steps taken in modern times to improve the operational flexibility of banks as financial intermediaries.

The Use of Convertible Capital Notes and Debentures. Since the Comptroller's 1962 ruling, a number of banks have issued capital notes and debentures convertible into the bank's common stock. The chief advantage of the conversion feature is that it lowers the interest cost by 75 to 125 basis points.[3] An advantage of capital notes and debentures over additional equity capital as an alternative means of raising capital is that the former do not result in the immediate dilution of earnings. Another advantage of convertible notes is that if bank earnings grow and the price of common stock appreciates, the convertible notes will become permanent capital. A disadvantage of convertible over non-convertible notes and debentures is that convertible notes usually carry higher underwriting fees. This is because the underwriter must assume the risk that the price of the common stock might fall prior to the issuance of the convertible securities.

[3]One basis point equals 1/100 of 1 percent.

Table 6-1

Capital Accounts of Insured Commercial Banks, Selected Years, 1960–1976 (millions of dollars)

December	Common Stock	Preferred Stock	Surplus	Undivided Profits	Reserve for Contingencies and Other Capital Reserves	Capital Notes and Debentures	Total Capital
1960	6,170.1	14.6	9,916.2	4,020.9	513.6	23.2	20,658.6
1965	8,507.8	39.9	13,464.8	5,437.6	802.2	1,652.7	29,905.0
1970	11,137.8	107.3	18,072.6	10,145.8	1,311.5	2,091.9	42,886.9
1971	11,811.1	91.9	19,895.8	11,135.1	1,307.0	2,956.2	47,197.1
1972	12,853.7	68.9	21,528.4	13,012.2	1,097.1	4,092.8	52,653.2
1973	13,846.1	65.7	23,593.3	15,361.9	1,136.2	4,117.4	58,120.4
1974	14,789.5	43.5	25,313.3	17,969.8	1,212.0	4,259.5	63,587.5
1975	15,565.0	47.9	26,712.9	21,182.3	1,156.1	4,407.9	69,072.1
1976	16,214.4	47.3	28,883.2	25,267.8	1,830.1	5,123.4	77,366.2

Source: FDIC, *Annual Reports* and unpublished data.

NOTE: Details may not add due to rounding.

Reserves for Contingencies and Other Capital Reserves

Also included in bank capital are *reserves for contingencies* and *other capital reserves,* which merely are funds set aside from undivided profits. An example of a contingency reserve is a reserve established because of a pending lawsuit. Examples of capital reserves are amounts set aside for dividends and for possible retirement of preferred stock. Amounts placed in reserves for contingencies are nondeductible items for income tax purposes.

Reserves for Losses on Loans and Securities

Reserve for Losses on Loans. Banks expect a small percentage of their loans to go into default. Under the Internal Revenue Code, bad debts incurred by a business are fully deductible from ordinary income. These deductions may be taken by a specific charge-off or by setting aside a reserve for loan losses.

There are three tax advantages to the loan-loss reserve method as opposed to the charge-off technique of handling bad debts.[4] First, as long as the debt is shown to be worthless, a bank using the reserve method does not have to tie the loss on a particular loan to a specific year. Second, loan losses tend to increase during periods of recession. The use of the reserve method reduces the possibility that a year's income could be completely offset by an inordinate amount of bad debts. Hence, in good as well as in bad years, the bank may, within limits, make additions to the loan-loss reserve and thereby minimize the impact of large losses on current earnings. A third advantage of the reserve method is that by making deductions in advance of the actual loan losses, current taxes are reduced. The funds generated from this tax reduction may be invested to earn income.

Because of this third advantage, most banks would like to build up a large reserve for loan losses since it would be a tax-free source of operating funds. In recognition of this possibility, the Treasury Department has established certain limitations on tax-free additions to the loan-loss reserve. In 1947, the Treasury issued a statement known as Mimeograph 6209, which permitted banks to maintain bad debt reserves based on a twenty-year moving-average experience factor. Under this regulation, the maximum reserve could equal three times the loss-experience factor times the bank's eligible loans. Some banks that had large loan losses in the Depression took advantage of this ruling and accumulated substantial loan-loss reserves.[5] On March 15,

[4]Ray H. Garrison, "Tax Advantages of the Bad Debt Reserve Technique," *The Bankers Magazine* (Summer 1967), pp. 92–95.

[5]In 1963, a bank in Illinois was found to have a reserve for bad debts equal to 24 percent of its eligible loans.

1965, the Treasury acted to limit such practices and established a uniform 2.4 percent (of eligible loans) ceiling on the bad-debt reserve. The 1969 Tax Reform Act set even lower limits on this reserve. The new ceiling is 1.8 percent for the taxable years beginning before 1976, 1.2 percent for taxable years beginning after 1975, but before 1982, and 0.6 percent for taxable years beginning after 1981. These sharp reductions in the ceiling on reserves for bad-debt losses on loans will limit severely further additions to these reserves. At the end of 1976, insured commercial banks had accumulated $6,180 million in reserve for loan losses (Table 6-2).

Reserve for Losses on Securities. Because virtualy all their security holdings consist either of U.S. government or high-grade municipal issues, most bankers have not been compelled to establish an adequate reserve for losses on securities. In view of the sharp drop in security prices during tight-money periods such as 1970 and 1973–74, it would seem that the need to establish a reserve for losses on securities should be reevaluated. Although net security losses may be charged off against ordinary income, it would appear that, as described above, the first and second advantages for establishing a loan-loss reserve are equally applicable in the case of a security-loss reserve. If some banks had had to liquidate a significant percentage of their security holdings during the near-liquidity crisis that occurred in the recent tight-money periods, a number of these institutions would have impaired capital stock in the process of absorbing security losses. In the short run, interest rates tend to rise when the Federal Reserve pursues a tight-money policy. In managing their investment portfolio, banks should be prepared for periodic declines in security prices and the possibility of having to sell many of these securities at depressed prices to meet deposit withdraw-

Table 6-2

Reserve for Bad Debt Losses at Insured Commercial Banks, Selected Years, 1960–1976 (millions of dollars)

Year Ending	Reserve for Bad Debt Losses
1960	2,573.2
1965	4,011.3
1970	5,998.7
1971	6,151.3
1972	6,623.8
1973	7,526.7
1974	8,376.7
1975	8,654.7
1976	6,180.5

Source: FDIC, *Annual Reports* and unpublished data.

als. One way to minimize the impact of this contingency is to establish a reserve for security losses.

Functions of Bank Capital

Bank capital serves four functions: it (1) demonstrates ability to absorb unanticipated losses, (2) provides operating funds, (3) measures ownership, and (4) facilitates stockholder pressure toward managerial efficiency.

Unanticipated Losses

The primary function of bank capital is to demonstrate to the public and to the supervisory authorities the bank's ability to absorb unanticipated losses.[6] When a loan or investment goes into default, the bank must remove the loan from the asset side of its balance sheet and make a corresponding debt entry in the reserve account for either loan or security losses. If losses are large enough to eliminate the bank's valuation reserves and accumulated undivided profits, the bank is in danger of becoming insolvent; that is, it cannot pay its liabilities. In such a case, banking regulations stipulate that the bank must be closed. Thus capital accounts and valuation reserves protect depositors by serving as cushions for absorbing losses.

Banks expect to suffer periodic losses in their loan portfolio. Relatively small losses essentially are absorbed out of current earnings since that is the source of additions to the valuation reserve accounts. One function of a bank's capital accounts is to absorb large *unanticipated* losses such as might result from legal liability, a sharp drop in the price of investment securities, or excessive loan defaults. The source of these unanticipated losses might be severe business fluctuations, inept public policy, local or industry recession, war, or managerial lapses.[7] Bank capital serves as a financial shield to prevent depositors from losing funds if the bank has to be closed and liquidated.[8]

As a protective cushion, bank capital also has a certain psychological value. If depositors and borrowers are convinced that a bank has adequate capital to weather economic storms, the former are less likely to initiate a bank run, and the latter may be more inclined to repay their obligations on time. The amount of capital that a bank has relative to its

[6]For a discussion of this function of bank capital, see Roland I. Robinson and Richard H. Pettway, *Policies for Optimum Bank Capital* (Chicago: Association of Reserve City Bankers, 1967), chap. 3.

[7]*Ibid.*, pp. 18–19.

[8]Large account holders, in particular, are interested in a bank's capital position. Since only $40,000 in deposit insurance is available on each account, individuals or businesses with more than this sum in their accounts must evaluate the adequacy of a bank's capital to protect their funds.

various types of assets and deposits is an outward demonstration of strength and thereby helps to mitigate the adverse impact that exogenous events might have on the bank. Because of this psychological factor, it seems more accurate to state that the primary function of bank capital is to demonstrate ability to absorb unanticipated losses rather than simply to protect depositors.

Operating Funds

A prerequisite for a bank's opening for business is that it have adequate quarters and equipment. The first use of a bank's permanent capital is to finance these fixed assets.[9] Once a bank has adequate facilities, further allocations of the bank's capital for fixed assets may not be the highest priority and best use for these funds. If the bank can gross 14 percent on installment paper, then it should not place funds in fixed assets that probably yield 10 percent or less. This is why, during recent years, many banks have formed real estate subsidiaries or persuaded individuals and businesses to buy and lease back buildings and equipment to the parent bank. Also, as we have noted, funds raised through the sale of capital notes and debentures may be used to expand loans and investments.

Ownership

One function of capital in any business is to reflect ownership claims, rather than creditor claims, on assets. As we saw earlier, bank shareholders had claims on only 7.1 percent of the assets of insured banks at the end of 1976. The banking system's creditors, that is, depositors and others, held 92.9 percent of the claims on these assets.

Stockholder Pressure Toward Managerial Efficiency

Perhaps an overlooked function of bank capital is that of facilitating stockholder pressure toward managerial efficiency.[10] Unlike all credit unions, mutual savings banks, noninsured private pension funds, and some savings and loan associations and life insurance companies, all banks have shareholders. Because these investor-owners have a vested interest in banks' becoming more profitable, it is possible to say that of all classes of financial intermediaries, banks are under the greatest pressure to operate more efficiently.

[9]Under national banking laws, a national bank's investment in bank premises may not exceed the amount of its capital stock.

[10]George R. Morrison and Richard T. Selden, *Time Deposit Growth and the Employment of Bank Funds* (Chicago: Association of Reserve City Bankers, 1965), p. 66.

Capital Adequacy

If the primary function of bank capital is to demonstrate the ability to absorb unanticipated losses, the logical question to ask is; How much capital is adequate to perform this function? Banking supervisory authorities have wrestled with this problem virtually since the time when banks were first chartered in this country. In recognition of the need to protect depositors and to create a stable banking system, federal and state governments have enacted legal capital requirements to ensure capital adequacy.

Legal Requirements

The national banking laws provide for the chartering of national banks by the federal government. As specified in these acts, no national bank will be organized with capital of less than $100,000, except that national banks with a capital of not less than $50,000 may be formed in communities with a population of 6,000 or less. For cities with a population of 50,000 or more, the minimum capital requirements for a national bank are $200,000. However, in outlying districts of such a city where state laws permit the organization of state banks with a capital of $100,000 or less, national banks now organized or hereafter organized may, with the approval of the Comptroller of the Currency, have capital of not less than $100,000. In addition to these capital stock requirements, national banks are required to begin business with a paid-in surplus equal to 20 percent of its stock in order to cover organizational expenses and any initial operating losses.[11] Most state banking statutes also relate minimum capital requirements to population and have a stipulation that banks begin operating with a minimum amount of capital surplus. Moreover, in order to establish out-of-town branches, national banks and most state banks must satisfy the same minimum capital stock and surplus requirements that would apply if a new unit bank were going to open in the proposed branch office city.

We know that unexpected losses may result from a variety of contingencies. It should be obvious that population is not a satisfactory measure of the risks that banks face. Moreover, except for minor changes, the minimum capital requirements outlined above for national banks were enacted over a century ago. The reason these requirements have not been updated is that the determination of capital adequacy has become a matter of administrative judgment rather than definitive law.

The decisions of the banking supervisory agencies about a bank's capital adequacy are, however, based on legal considerations. The Federal Deposit Insurance Act requires that the Comptroller of the Cur-

[11]This 20 percent capital surplus requirement was added in 1933.

rency, in the case of a national bank; the Board of Governors, in the case of a state member bank; and the FDIC Board of Directors, in the case of a state nonmember bank, certify as to the adequacy of the bank's capital structure as a condition for obtaining federal deposit insurance. Regulation H of the Federal Reserve Board of Governors stipulates that the net capital and surplus of a member bank "shall be adequate in relation to the character and condition of its assets and to its deposit liabilities and other corporate responsibilities." The Code of Federal Regulations requires the Comptroller of the Currency to consider a number of factors in assessing the adequacy of capital at a national bank. Finally, the Bank Merger Act of 1966 requires the appropriate banking supervisory authority to examine capital adequacy as a condition for approval for a proposed bank merger.

The Measurement of Capital Adequacy

Because of the early emphasis on bank capital as a primary means of protecting depositors, it seems only natural that banking supervisory authorities would measure capital adequacy in relation to deposits. California banking law stipulated in 1909, and the Comptroller of the Currency's *Annual Report* in 1914 strongly suggested, that bank capital should not be less than 10 percent of total deposits. Yet the potential sources of loss to the bank, and hence to depositors, do not originate because banks hold deposits; they result primarily because banks accept promises from borrowers to pay money in the future, and because of the risk that the price of securities may fall, thus causing a shrinkage in the market value of the investment portfolio. It should be clear that these contingencies arise because the banks hold assets, not liabilities.

During the 1930s, the misleading nature of the capital-to-deposits ratio became apparent when it fell below 10 percent for a number of banks, even though these banks had large excess reserves. Under such conditions and after the shakeout of the weakest banks during the Great Depression, the risk of loss to depositors had diminished, not increased. Even without these extraordinary conditions, there is nothing magic about a 10 percent capital-to-deposits ratio. Suppose banks A and B each had 10 percent capital-to-deposits ratios, but bank A had a large number of risky loans outstanding, while bank B held only short-term Treasury securities. Obviously, the risk to depositors is greater at bank A than at Bank B.

The rapid growth of bank deposits during World War II, as the banking system acquired billions in government securities, was the *coup de grâce* for the capital-to-deposits ratio as the sole criterion for measuring capital adequacy. As a more meaningful alternative, the Comptroller of the Currency in 1948 began to compute a capital-to-risk assets ratio. Although no uniform definition of risk assets was adopted, the term generally meant all bank assets except cash and U.S. government securities.

At present, the Comptroller of the Currency and the FDIC do not rely on ratios of capital-to-risk assets and to total deposits in assessing the adequacy of capital of national banks and state, nonmember, insured banks, respectively. As stated in Sec. 14.1 of the Comptroller's Regulations, ". . . the capital position of the bank will be analyzed and appraised in relation to the character of its management and its asset and deposit position as a going institution under normal conditions, with due allowance for a reasonable margin of safety, and with due regard to the bank's capacity to furnish the broadest service to the public." The Comptroller considers the following factors in assessing the adequacy of capital:

1. The quality of management.
2. The liquidity of assets.
3. The history of earnings and of the retention thereof.
4. The quality and character of ownership.
5. The burden of meeting occupancy expenses.
6. The potential volatility of deposit structure.
7. The quality of operating procedures.
8. The bank's capacity to meet present and future financial needs of its trade area, considering the competition it faces.

The FDIC's basic approach is quite similar. Its examiners attempt to evaluate, among other things, the quality of a bank's assets, the deposit structure, and the competence of management. The FDIC's examiners do make comparisons of capital-to-assets and capital-to-deposits ratios at a particular bank with the national averages. Like the Comptroller, however, the FDIC gives greater weight to the bank's overall condition than to oversimplified capital ratios.

The Federal Reserve Board of Governors takes a more involved approach to the measurement of capital adequacy for state member banks. On its "Form for Analyzing Bank Capital" (revised in March 1972), assets are classified under six headings: (1) primary reserves (cash assets and federal funds sold), (2) secondary reserves (commercial paper, banker's acceptances, and securities maturing under 1 year), (3) minimum risk assets (securities maturing in 1–5 years), (4) intermediate assets (securities maturing in 5–10 years and loans specially secured or guaranteed), (5) portfolio assets (securities maturing in over 10 years and real estate, consumer installment, and all other loans), and (6) fixed, classified, and other assets. Then a capital charge (percentages) is assessed against each class of assets for the credit risk (the risk of default) and the market risk (the risk of a fall in price associated with a rise in interest rates). For example, a 1 percent capital charge is made for both the credit risk and market risk associated with commercial paper and banker's acceptances. On the other hand, for real estate loans, a 5 percent capital charge is made for the credit risk and a 25 percent capital charge is made for the market risk. The required capital to support the bank's asset structure is totaled and compared with existing capital. If the bank is deficient, it may be directed to eliminate some of its more risky assets or to acquire more capital.

With respect to the problem of measuring capital adequacy, it is significant that the Federal Reserve noted on its "Form for Analyzing Bank Capital" that

> A thorough appraisal of the capital needs of a particular bank must take due account of all relevant factors affecting the bank. These include the characteristics of its assets, its liabilities, its trust or other corporate responsibilities, and its management—as well as the history and prospects of the bank, its customers and its community. The complexity of the problem requires a considerable exercise of judgment. The groupings and percentages suggested in the Form for Analyzing Bank Capital can necessarily be no more than aids to the exercise of judgment.

It should be evident from our discussion that there are no precise methods for measuring capital adequacy. Each of the three federal banking supervisory authorities considers many factors, some of which are nonquantifiable, in evaluating a bank's capital adequacy.

Nondeposit Liabilities

The Concept of Liability Management

Traditionally, banks more or less have accepted their deposits and other liabilities as given and have concentrated on the management of assets in order to achieve certain objectives in terms of liquidity, safety, and income. In tight-money periods, such as 1973–74, banks are faced simultaneously with a short supply of loanable funds and huge demands for credit, primarily from corporate borrowers. This dilemma forces the banks that want to accommodate the credit needs of many of their old and established customers to bid aggressively for deposits and to develop new sources of loanable funds. Beginning with the tight-money period of 1966, the emphasis in bank management seemed to shift from asset management to *liability management,* which is simply the process of locating and acquiring adequate funds from sources with the lowest possible cost.[12] In addition to the traditional sources of deposits and capital, many banks, in practicing liability management, ac-

[12] Coordination of bank assest and liability management is discussed in Chapter 15.

quire the funds to meet their customers' credit needs through one or more of the following nondeposit liability accounts: (1) federal funds purchased, (2) Eurodollar borrowings, (3) borrowing from Federal Reserve Banks, (4) banker's acceptances outstanding, (5) commercial paper sold, (6) loans sold outright or through participation repurchase agreements, and (7) sale-and-leaseback arrangements. Some banks also accommodate their customers' credit demands indirectly by guaranteeing customer paper issued in the money market. These guarantees are contingent liabilities and appear as footnotes to a bank's balance sheet.

Direct Liabilities

Federal Funds. Federal funds are excess reserves that banks lend to each other, usually overnight. Prior to 1966, most banks that purchased federal funds were attempting to make up temporary reserve deficiencies. Perhaps the first sign that banks were practicing liability management was when a number of banks began to use the federal funds market as a continuing source of loanable funds. The primary sources of federal funds were banks located outside of the money market cities of New York, Chicago, and Boston. In 1974, during the peak of the tight-money period, the bid price on federal funds reached 13 percent.

Eurodollars. *Eurodollars* are dollar-denominated deposits held in banks located outside the United States. These deposits may be in foreign commercial banks or in the foreign branches of U.S. commercial banks. The Eurodollar market centers in London, but other cities in Western Europe, Japan, and the Bahamas are included also. Eurodollars may be owned by U.S. or foreign citizens, businesses, or governments. Eurodollars have two basic characteristics: (1) they are short-term obligations to pay dollars, and (2) they are liabilities of banking offices located outside the United States. These deposits may originate in several ways. First, foreign or U.S. citizens may simply transfer dollars from a U.S. bank to a foreign bank or to a branch of a U.S. bank. Second, foreigners may receive checks drawn on U.S. banks and deposit the funds in dollar accounts in their banks. Or, third, foreign central banks and official institutions may place large dollar deposits in local banks in order to stabilize money market conditions. The maturity of Eurodollar deposits ranges from call to over one year, but the majority mature in three months or less.

United States banks first began to borrow significant amounts of Eurodollars in 1966 when a sharp outflow of CDs occurred. As with federal funds, banks turned what ordinarily is a temporary source of liquidity into a source of long-term funds to meet loan demands.

Table 6-3

Selected Liabilities of Banks Reporting Weekly to the Federal Reserve, 1966–1976
(millions of dollars)

Quarter Ended			Large Negotiable CD's[a]	Federal Funds Purchased[b]	Gross Liabilities of Banks to Foreign Branches[c]	Commercial Paper: Placed Through Dealers	Commercial Paper: Placed Directly	Loans Sold Outright[d]
1966	March	30	17,418	—	1,879	—	—	—
	June	29	18,312	—	1,951	—	—	—
	September	28	17,005	—	3,472	—	—	—
	December	28	15,668	—	4,036	—	—	—
1967	March	29	19,299	—	3,412	—	—	—
	June	28	19,135	—	3,166	—	—	—
	September	27	19,897	—	4,059	—	—	—
	December	27	20,330	—	4,241	—	—	—
1968	March	27	20,538	—	4,920	—	—	—
	June	26	19,256	—	6,241	—	—	—
	September	25	22,261	—	7,104	—	—	—
	December	25	23,468	—	6,948	—	—	—
1969	March	26	18,770	—	9,621	—	—	—
	June	25	15,252	12,799	13,269	602	643	—
	September	24	11,732	15,468	14,349	1,000	1,594	3,651
	December	31	10,919	13,472	12,822	1,160	3,134	3,799
1970	March	25	11,820	16,591	12,356	932	5,545	6,682
	June	24	12,976	17,758	12,701	666	6,937	7,858
	September	30	22,240	13,903	9,787	329	4,269	5,037
	December	30	26,075	18,775	7,669	352	1,997	2,735
1971	March	31	27,458	18,854	2,858	354	1,338	2,560
	June	30	28,460	19,048	1,512	432	4,301	3,058
	September	29	32,959	22,989	2,476	504	1,396	2,960
	December	29	33,951	26,046	909	524	1,449	2,840

Between mid-1966 and mid-1969, Eurodollars obtained by U.S. banks solely from their foreign branches increased from $2 billion to over $14 billion (Table 6-3). Besides borrowing Eurodollars directly, U.S. banks also sold loans and other assets to their branches and encouraged their customers to borrow directly from these branches or from foreign banks.

There are several reasons for the sharp growth in Eurodollar borrowings. First, Eurodollar deposits are not subject to Regulation Q ceilings. Second, these deposits are not subject to the FDIC insurance assessment or, until the summer of 1969, reserve requirements. The interest

Table 6-3 (continued)

Selected Liabilities of Banks Reporting Weekly to the Federal Reserve, 1966–1976
(millions of dollars)

Quarter Ended		Large Negotiable CD's[a]	Federal Funds Purchased[b]	Gross Liabilities of Banks to Foreign Branches[c]	Commercial Paper: Placed Through Dealers	Commercial Paper: Placed Directly	Loans Sold Outright[d]
1972 March	29	33,456	28,232	1,532	585	1,587	2,779
June	28	35,846	28,934	1,442	671	1,300	2,296
September	27	41,219	27,735	2,023	829	1,539	2,264
December	27	44,911	31,085	1,400	1,226	1,411	2,598
1973 March	28	54,932	35,693	1,127	1,493	1,963	3,161
June	27	59,258	37,077	1,521	1,849	2,434	3,520
September	26	68,846	38,447	1,731	2,077	3,154	4,637
December	26	64,391	47,759	1,703	1,938	2,943	4,300
1974 March	27	67,815	53,527	2,947	2,137	3,908	4,904
June	26	80,174	51,325	3,388	1,579	5,373	5,372
September	25	89,712	47,705	2,918	2,107	6,525	5,293
December	25	92,830	44,303	3,553	1,800	6,518	4,903
1975 March	26	88,765	49,920	1,922	1,682	7,272	4,692
June	25	81,941	50,141	1,882	1,561	7,230	4,688
September	24	84,180	45,850	2,304	1,482	7,316	4,517
December	31	82,781	44,712	4,081	1,762	6,892	4,375
1976 March	31	72,414	50,371	3,151	1,654	6,773	4,234
June	30	70,555	51,168	3,674	1,710	6,297	4,491
September	29	65,990	62,494	4,684	1,681	6,213	3,920
December	29	65,851	51,520	6,206	1,930	5,928	4,074

Source: Board of Governors of the Federal Reserve System, *Annual Statistical Digest, 1971–1975*, and *Federal Reserve Bulletin*.

[a]Issued in denominations of $100,000 or more.

[b]Includes securities sold under agreements to repurchase.

[c]This is the commonly used measure of Eurodollar borrowings. Eurodollars also may be borrowed from branches in U.S. territories and possessions and from unaffiliated foreign banks.

[d]Amounts sold under repurchase agreement are excluded. After August 28, 1974, this series revised. The new groups exclude domestic banks. Loans sold to nonaffiliated institutions are no longer included as they were before August 28, 1974.

rate on three-month Eurodollar deposits climbed to over 13 percent during the tight-money years of 1969 and 1974.

Federal Reserve Banks. Banks that are members of the Federal Reserve System enjoy the privilege of borrowing from their Federal Reserve Bank. These banks get either direct advances secured by U.S. Government obligations or discount loans to obtain funds to meet deposit withdrawals or the legitimate credit demands of businesses.

Acceptances. A *banker's acceptance* is a draft (written order) drawn by an individual or firm upon a bank ordering it to pay a sum of money on a specified date in the future. When the bank "accepts" the paper drawn by a customer, the bank guarantees to redeem the paper at maturity. Because of this guarantee, the paper is more marketable. In return for this service, the bank receives a small fee and a promise from the customer to provide the bank with funds to redeem the paper at maturity. The bank's books now show an asset (customer's liability on acceptances outstanding) and a liability (acceptance executed for customers). Banker's acceptances arise out of transactions involving the export or import of goods, the warehousing of staple commodities, or the shipment of goods within the United States. Acceptances arising from these transactions are "eligible" to serve as collateral for loans at the Federal Reserve. Acceptances used for other types of loans are termed "ineligible" to serve as collateral at the discount window.[13] During 1969 and 1970, banks began to create more ineligible acceptances as a way to meet their customer's credit needs.

Commercial Paper. In September 1964, the First National Bank of Boston announced it would seek operating funds by issuing short-term promissory notes that were unsecured and negotiable. Several other banks followed suit and issued both negotiable and nonnegotiable notes. Typically, these obligations were in $1 million denominations and matured in one year or less. The principal purchasers of these notes were large corporations, state and local governments, and wealthy individuals. By late 1965, it was estimated that there were $500 million of these issues outstanding. The principal reason promissory notes have not become a significant source of funds is that during mid-1966, subordinated notes with an original maturity of less than two years were made subject to reserve requirements and to interest-rate restrictions on deposits under Regulations D and Q, respectively.

The initial success of promissory notes was an indication that, perhaps, the subsidiaries of bank holding companies or their nonbank affiliates could acquire operating funds through the sale of commercial paper, which is essentially a short-term, unsecured promissory note. When credit conditions tightened in mid-1969, bank-related affiliates moved quickly to tap this source of funds. Commercial paper of bank affiliates of weekly reporting banks rose from $1.2 billion on June 25, 1969, to $7.6 billion on June 24, 1970 (Table 6-3). As credit conditions eased later in 1970, bank-related commercial paper outstanding declined sharply. When credit conditions tightened in 1973–74, bank-related commercial paper again became an important source of loanable funds.

[13] Ineligible acceptances are often called "working capital acceptances" or "finance bills."

Proceeds from the sale of commercial paper by a bank holding company may be used to purchase loans from the bank's portfolio. The bank then has the funds to make new loans. Bank-related affiliates, such as finance or mortgage companies, also may issue commercial paper to finance their activities. Effective September 17, 1970, the Federal Reserve Board of Governors placed a reserve requirement on bank-related commercial paper.

Loan Participations. Another technique to acquire loanable funds is to sell loans outright or participations in pools of loans under repurchase agreements to other banks, corporate customers, and individuals.[14] Although it is an established practice to sell loans or to execute repurchase agreements with other banks, the new aspect of these transactions introduced in 1969 was to sell loans or participations to nonbank customers at rates and maturities not subject to Requlation Q. The volume of repurchase agreements executed by weekly reporting banks with the nonbank public reached $1.3 billion on July 30, 1969, but subsequently fell to $.2 billion on December 31, 1969, as the Board of Governors moved to place repurchase agreements with the nonbank public under reserve-requirement and interest-rate restrictions. Banks may still execute repurchase agreements in U.S. government and agency obligations without restriction.

Sale-and-Leaseback Arrangements. Another technique to acquire loanable funds is for a bank to sell its bank buildings or equipment to a bank subsidiary or to an outside investor, who, in turn, would lease it to the bank. If the bank realizes more than the depreciated book value for the assets, this excess is credited directly to the common equity account.

Guaranteed Customer Paper

During 1969, when banks were unable to satisfy all the demand for loans that they ordinarily could accommodate, several banks issued irrevocable letters of credit guaranteeing payment at maturity for commercial paper issued by some of their customers with less than prime credit ratings. The effect of this guarantee was to enable these cus-

[14] Under *repurchase agreements*, banks sell loans or securities under an agreement to repurchase them at a later date. These agreements usually have a maturity of two months to one year. Under such agreements loans or securities would be offered to holders at interest rates competitive with other money market rates. When a repurchase agreement is executed, the bank increases a liability account, "Loans Sold under Repurchase Agreement," and it receives a corresponding increase in a cash or reserve account.

tomers to issue commercial paper at an interest cost below prevailing market rates. Such a guarantee is a contingent liability of the bank.

A Capital Model for Banks

Capital budgeting for a firm is the process of determining the allocation of scarce financial resources among various investment projects.[15] A *capital budget* is a schedule of rates of return, from highest to lowest, for a series of proposed asset acquisitions. The cost of funds necessary to finance these asset acquisitions is usually termed a firm's *cost of capital.*

Like any profit-seeking enterprise, a commercial bank attempts to allocate scarce resources among a number of competing uses. For a bank, resources are in the form of investable funds acquired from shareholders, depositors, and debt holders. The uses of bank funds, of course, are the many forms of loans, investments, and other assets that the bank may acquire. It is useful, and perhaps imperative, to employ a conceptual framework for balance-sheet management, that is, a capital budgeting model that integrates asset management and liability management.[16]

The various sources of funds have been noted in this and the last chapters. Because of the recent emphasis on liability management, banks have much greater flexibility in selecting the source of their investable funds. The basic principle in liability management is that banks should acquire funds from the least expensive source first, then the second least expensive source, and so on, up to the point where the cost of acquiring the last dollar from that source is equal to the expected return from lending or investing that dollar. This principle is nothing more than the application of the marginal principle in economics to funds acquisition and allocation at a commercial bank.

The Cost of Bank Funds

Demand Deposits. There are many costs associated with the acquisition of demand deposits: for example, the printing of checks and forms, computer and equipment rental, and tellers' and officers' salaries. As a bank's demand deposits grow, the cost per dollar of deposits tends to decline as these costs are spread over a larger volume. After a point, the per unit cost of demand deposits begins to rise, owing to the greater volume of checks and to competition from other banks and financial intermediaries.

[15]This section is based largely on F. Lee Jacquette's excellent article, "A Capital Budgeting Model for Commercial Banks," *The Bankers Magazine* (Autumn 1966), pp. 29–38.

[16]In this discussion "capital" means any investable bank funds, not just equity or debt capital.

Time Deposits and Short-Term Liabilities. Because their net costs tend to be similar, and in order to facilitate the analysis, time deposits and other short-term nondeposit liabilities described earlier in this chapter will be considered together here. The principal costs of these sources of funds are the interest rate and the associated acquisitions and administrative expenses. During periods of credit stringency, it is recognized that the cost of borrowed funds and of funds raised by the creation of other liabilities will tend to rise above that of time deposits, provided these sources are not subject to reserve requirements and interest-rate restrictions as are time deposits. The average cost of these sources of funds will tend to decline slightly with increased volume as administrative costs are spread over more deposits. After a point, however, it is reasonable to expect that the bank would have to pay successively higher interest rates in order to acquire additional funds.

Capital Notes and Debentures. The primary costs involved in the issuance of capital notes and debentures are interest costs, underwriting fees (if the issue is not privately placed), and administrative expenses involved in servicing the debt. More than likely, there will be a tendency for the average cost of funds raised to decline slightly as more debt is issued. Because of the present limitations on the amount of capital notes and debentures that can be issued, it is doubtful that many banks will reach the point where average unit costs begin to rise because of the greater risk involved.

Equity Capital. Because investors will not hold bank stocks unless the return is at least equal to that on other investments of similar risk and because an equity investment involves more risk than other types of claims that banks issue, it is to be expected that the cost of equity funds to a bank would be higher than other sources of funds. For analytical purposes, it may be assumed that the average cost of equity capital is constant. The average cost per unit of acquiring funds from the four sources just described is shown in Figure 6-1.

Weighted Average Cost of Funds versus Return on Invested Assets

As a bank grows, it will tend to finance the acquisition of additional assets with increments from all sources of funds. That is, small increases in equity capital will be combined with funds acquired from deposits, the creation of other liabilities, and from capital notes and debentures to acquire the highest yielding assets currently available. Thus a bank's cost of investable funds is a weighted average of the cost of each source.

For a business, the expected return on invested assets will tend to fall as the firm moves down its capital budget, selecting successively

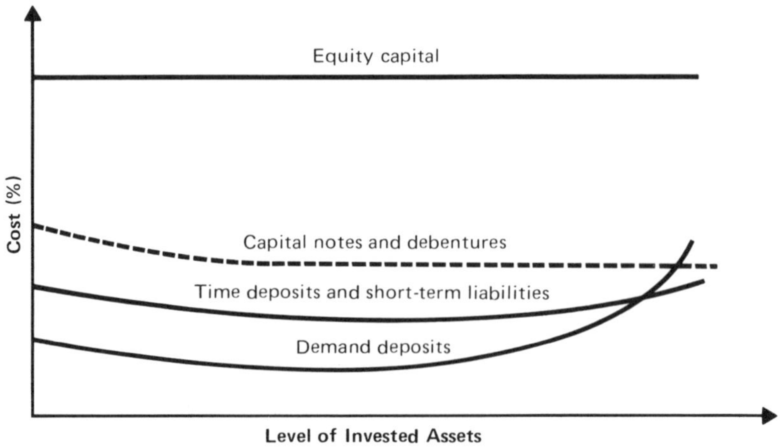

Figure 6-1 Average Cost of Investable Funds for Commercial Banks

lower-yielding investments. Individual banks, however, face a seemingly infinite supply of loans and investments; therefore, it may be assumed that the average and marginal returns on additional assets will not decline noticeably. In other words, an individual bank may continue to acquire additional commercial loans or installment loans or U.S. government securities that have virtually the same net yield. Based on the assumption that a bank always will acquire funds from the least expensive source before moving to its other sources, the equilibrium level of invested assets for a bank can be seen in Figure 6-2. In this diagram, the bank that is coordinating its asset management with liability management will carry asset acquisition up to the point where the marginal return on assets equals the marginal cost of funds.

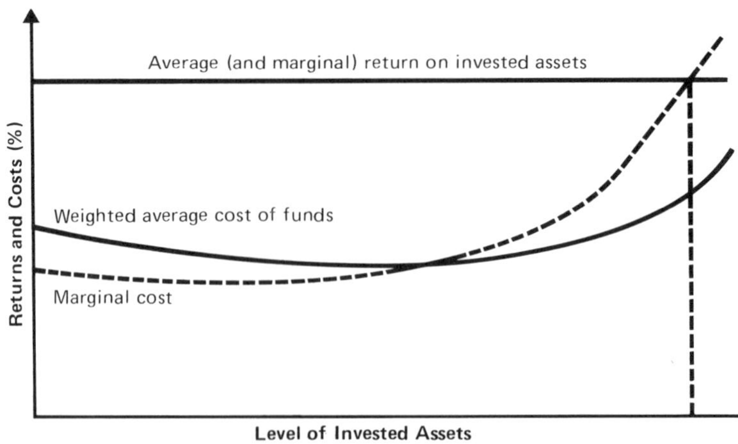

Figure 6-2 Weighted Average Cost of Funds versus Return on Invested Assets

In order to implement the model presented in this section, banks need to have adequate functional cost data. Even though most banks have not developed such data, they should attempt to acquire and to allocate funds based on the conceptual framework outlined above if they seek to maximize profits.

Suggestions for Additional Reading

The American Bankers Association. *Use of Senior Capital by Commercial Banks.* Washington, D.C.: The American Bankers Association, 1967.

Austin, Douglas V. "Senior Debt and Equity Securities." *The Bankers Magazine* (Winter 1974), pp. 73–84.

Carter H. Golembe Associates, Inc. *The Adequacies of Bad Debt Reserves for Banks—A Preliminary Study.* Chicago: Association of Reserve City Bankers, 1972.

Cohen, Kalman J. "Dynamic Balance Sheet Management: A Management Science Approach." *Journal of Bank Research* (Winter 1972), pp. 9–19.

Cohen, Kalman J., and Hammer, Frederick S. "Linear Programming and Optimal Bank Asset Management Decisions." *Journal of Finance* (May 1967), pp. 147–165.

Cohen, Kalman J., and Rutenberg, David P. "Toward a Comprehensive Framework for Bank Financial Planning." *Journal of Bank Research* (Winter 1971), pp. 41–57.

Cohen, Kalman J., and Thore, Sten. "Programming Bank Portfolios under Uncertainty." *Journal of Bank Research* (Spring 1970), pp. 42–61.

DePamphilis, Donald M. "The Application of Econometric Techniques to Commercial Bank Asset and Liability Management." *The Journal of Commercial Bank Lending* (November 1976), pp. 33–40.

———. "The Short-Term Commercial Bank Adjustment Process and Federal Reserve Regulation." Federal Reserve Bank of Boston, *New England Economic Review* (May–June 1974), pp. 14–23.

Dince, Robert R., and Fortson, James C. "The Use of Discriminant Analysis to Predict the Capital Adequacy of Commercial Banks." *Journal of Bank Research* (Spring 1972), pp. 54–62.

Duckworth, S. M. *Problems in Liability Management: Case Studies of Attitudes at Seven Banks.* Research Report No. 56. Boston: Federal Reserve Bank of Boston, October 1974.

Friedman, Milton. "The Eurodollar Market: Some First Principles." Federal Reserve Bank of St. Louis, *Review* (July 1971), pp. 16–24.

Gable, L. G. "Asset and Liability Management—A Supervisor's View." *The Journal of Commercial Bank Lending* (August 1975), pp. 23–40.

Golembe, Carter H. "Capital Adequacy and Bank Losses." *The Journal of Commercial Bank Lending* (August 1975), pp. 11–22.

Hagaman, T. Carter. "Financial Planning for Banks." New York: Irving Trust Company.

Hodgman, Donald R. *Commercial Bank Loan and Investment Policy*. Champaign, Ill.: University of Illinois, Bureau of Economic and Business Research, 1963, chap. 9.

Jacquette, F. Lee. "A Capital Budgeting Model for Commercial Banks." *The Bankers Magazine* (Autumn 1966), pp. 29–38.

Jessup, Paul F., ed. *Innovations in Bank Management: Selected Readings*. New York: Holt, Rinehart and Winston, 1969, part 3.

Johnson, Thomas S. "Capital Planning." *The Journal of Commercial Bank Lending* (July 1976), pp. 24–31.

Pike, William E. "Loan Loss Reserves." *The Journal of Commercial Bank Lending* (June 1977), pp. 3–10.

Robinson, Roland I., and Pettway, Richard H. *Policies for Optimum Bank Capital*. Chicago: Association of Reserve City Bankers, 1967.

Rosenblum, Harvey. "Bank Capital Adequacy." Federal Reserve Bank of Chicago, *Business Conditions* (September 1976), pp. 2–11.

Sealey, Calvin W., Jr. "Commercial Bank Portfolio Management with Multiple Objectives." *The Journal of Commercial Bank Lending* (February 1977), pp 39–48.

Veazey, Edward E. "Federal Funds-Market Expansion Aids Mobilization of Funds." Federal Reserve Bank of Dallas, *Business Review* (January 1975), pp. 1–6.

Vojta, George J. *Bank Capital Adequacy*. New York: Citicorp, 1973.

Watson, Ronald D. "Banking on Debt for Capital Needs." Federal Reserve Bank of Philadelphia, *Business Review* (December 1974), pp. 17–28.

Willis, Parker B. *The Federal Funds Market*. Boston: The Federal Reserve Bank of Boston, 1970.

PART

III

Liquidity Management

CHAPTER

7

Managing the Money Position

In Part II we dealt with the types and nature of the promises that banks make to acquire funds. In Part III (Chapters 7 and 8) we shall be concerned with liquidity management, the primary objectives of which are to enable banks to fulfill their promises to depositors and others, to meet their legal reserve requirements, and to meet the ligitimate loan demands of their customers. In this chapter we shall (1) discuss the dilemma that is created because banks have to make a profit as well as maintain adequate liquidity, (2) note the various forms of cash assets that banks hold to meet their liquidity requirements, (3) outline the cash reserve requirements imposed by law and by banks on themselves in order to meet the claims of depositors and others, and (4) see how banks manage their money position in order to fulfill statutory requirements and their obligations to claimholders.

Introduction to Liquidity Management

The Banker's Dilemma: Liquidity versus Profitability

As we saw in Chapter 1, all financial intermediaries make promises to pay money in the future. Most of these promises stipulate that payment will be made at the end of a certain period of time, as in the case of savings-type deposits. Banks, however, promise to redeem demand deposit liabilities on demand. Banks could prepare for the contingency that holders of demand deposits, currently due time deposits, and other liabilities might all request their funds at the same time by holding cash assets equal to 100 percent of these claims. Because cash assets yield a zero return, however, banks would have to charge demand depositors prohibitively high service fees in order to earn a sufficient income to pay expenses and a fair return on shareholders' capital. Obviously, this course of action would be implausible because other financial intermediaries offer alternative means for storing and transferring funds.

At the other extreme, in an effort to maximize income, banks could acquire only high-yielding, long-term assets and hope that the daily inflow of new funds would be greater than, or equal to, the daily requests for deposit redemption and loans. It is highly unlikely, of course, that the inflows and outflows of funds will always balance. Obviously, the best strategy for banks to follow lies somewhere between the two extremes of holding all cash or all relatively illiquid assets.

Banks strive to find the optimal balance between liquidity and profitability in the management of their assets and liabilities. In the ordering of priorities, however, meeting deposit and other liability claims clearly stands ahead of earning a profit. If depositors and other liability holders do not have confidence that banks can honor their promises, they simply will refuse to place funds in banks. The acquisition of deposits and other funds, of course, is a necessary condition for the expansion of loans and investments beyond the amount permitted by the use of capital only. Maintaining adequate liquidity is perhaps the most important constraint upon bank management's primary objective—maximizing profits.

The Nature of Bank Liquidity and Liquidity Management

An *individual bank's liquidity* is its ability to meet deposit withdrawals, maturing liabilities, and loan requests without delay. A bank is considered "liquid" if (1) it holds cash assets or primary reserves (cash-in-vault, balances at the Federal Reserve Bank, or balances at correspondent banks) equal to its expected liquidity demands, or (2) in the event that it holds less than this amount of cash assets, it also possesses a sufficient amount of other assets that can be exchanged for cash without delay and without undue loss of full market value, or (3) it has the ability to acquire cash through the creation of various liabilities.

Liquidity management involves the continuous estimation of, and provision for, the bank's immediate, short-term or seasonal, and long-term (cyclical and secular) cash requirements. Immediate cash needs or primary reserve requirements are specified by legal reserve requirements and *working reserve requirements,* which involve meeting the day-to-day transaction demands for currency and coin and having sufficient balances on deposit at correspondent banks as compensation for services rendered. *Short-term or seasonal liquidity requirements* are those that vary from month-to-month and that tend to recur regularly from year to year. *Cyclical and secular liquidity requirements* are those that are related to the level of economic and financial activity in the economy and those that stem from the absolute growth in the bank's deposit and loan acitivity over time. Thus, there are three levels of liquidity management: (1) primary reserve or money position management, (2) short-term or seasonal liquidity management, and (3) long-term or cyclical and secular liquidity management. Money position management is the subject of this chapter; short-term and long-term liquidity management will be discussed in Chapter 8.

Cash Assets

There are four types of bank cash assets: (1) cash-in-vault, (2) items in the process of collection, (3) balances at Federal Reserve banks, and (4) balances in correspondent banks.

Cash in Vault

Banks hold cash in vault as an accomodation to their customers. Although the great majority of payments today are effected with checks and credit cards, currency and coin are needed for vending machines and small, day-to-day transactions. Banks replenish their vault cash by requesting it from Federal Reserve banks or correspondent banks.[1] Because currency and coin are nonearning assets and a target of bank robbers and burglars, banks try not to have excess cash balances. Since 1960, vault cash has served as a legal reserve for member banks.

Cash Items in the Process of Collection

Each day, a bank receives deposits of checks and currency and coin. The checks deposited frequently are not payable at the bank where deposited but must be sent to the bank on which they are drawn for payment. These checks sent for payment are referred to as "cash items."

[1]Cash is shipped primarily through the U.S. mail or in armored cars.

Checks drawn on other banks in the city where deposited ordinarily present no problem since they usually are collected through the local clearinghouse the same day they are deposited.[2] Checks drawn on out-of-town banks may be sent directly to the drawee bank or, more typically, to a Federal Reserve or correspondent bank for collection. Cash items sent to a Reserve bank are credited to the individual bank's reserve account based on a predetermined schedule established by the Reserve bank. Some cash items are credited immediately, but others are deferred from one to two days. Cash items sent to a correspondent bank for collection are also usually credited to the transmitting bank's account, based on the time it takes for the correspondent bank to receive credit, although some correspondent arrangements stipulate that an immediate credit will be granted to the remitting bank's account.

Since cash items in the process of collection represent a nonearning asset, banks attempt to use every means possible to speed their collection. Although cash items are subtracted from gross deposits for purposes of reserve computation, banks would prefer to have these items count as deposits and also have the corresponding credit in their reserve account.

Balances at Federal Reserve Banks

The Federal Reserve Act specifies that member banks must keep balances at a Federal Reserve bank or branch. Nonmember banks have the privilege of maintaining a balance at a Reserve bank for purposes of clearing checks. Banks use their Reserve account much like an individual or business uses its demand deposit account. They may write checks on it, make deposits to it, and permit the Reserve bank to debit their account in order to remit funds due other banks or the Treasury. The Federal Reserve also may give member banks loans by crediting funds to their reserve account. In recent years member banks have tended to hold approximately 25–30 percent of their total cash assets in the form of balances at Federal Reserve banks.

Balances in Correspondent Banks

Balances in correspondent banks represent an implicit payment for services performed. Large money market and regional banks are the principal institutions that solicit balances from other banks. Typically, small banks in the hinterland maintain accounts in several regional

[2]It is a common practice for banks in a community to form a clearinghouse for the collection and payment of checks and other cash items originating locally. At a designated time, representatives of all banks in the area meet to exchange these items. Those banks with net clearing obligations usually pay by check on a Federal Reserve or correspondent bank.

banks and an account in the closest national money center, such as New York, Chicago, or San Francisco. Large regional banks would tend to carry balances in most of the other regional centers within their geographic quadrant of the country and in all of the national money centers.[3] The most important service performed by correspondent banks is check clearance. The size of the correspondent balances held will depend largely on the volume of checks remitted for collection and the nature and frequency of other services performed, such as investment counseling, securities trading, and loan participations. During recent years, correspondent balances have come under closer scrutiny by all banks involved. The high opportunity cost of holding excess balances has caused most banks to trim to a minimum the balances held with their city correspondents. As a result, it is believed that most correspondent accounts are only marginally profitable to the holder. At the end of 1976, demand interbank balances represented 25.4 percent of the total cash assets held by insured banks.

Cash Reserve Requirements

Purposes of Legal Reserve Requirements

The practice of requiring banks to hold a certain amount of cash reserves goes back to pre-Civil War days. During this period, several states required banks to hold cash reserves, such as gold, against their note liabilities. Since a bank's ability to expand its assets (loans primarily) through the issuance of more notes was limited by these legal requirements, some degree of prudence was forced upon banks with respect to the maximum amount of credit they could extend. Moreover, since there was a limit to credit expansion, legal cash requirements may have induced banks to select better-quality loans for their portfolio.

Since the time when cash reserve requirements were instituted as a means of limiting the expansion of note issues, the prevailing view of these requirements has been modified twice. At some point in our banking history, it became popular to view cash requirements as a liquidity requirement that guaranteed that depositors could withdraw or transfer their deposit balances at any time. The fallacy in this view is that cash reserve requirements are only a fraction of deposit liabilities; hence depositors are protected only partially by these requirements. To illustrate, if cash reserve requirements are 12.5 percent of demand deposit liabilities, then for each $100 in demand deposit withdrawals, only $12.50 is released from required reserves as a result of the

[3] Current correspondent relationships for banks are listed in *Polk's World Bank Directory* (Nashville, Tenn.: R. L. Polk and Co.).

withdrawal. The bank must obtain $87.50 in cash from other sources in order to meet its obligation.

The modern view of cash reserve requirements is that they are a means of credit control. As we saw in Chapter 5, the limits on bank deposit expansion, and therefore credit expansion, are set by the volume of cash reserves and the legal reserve requirements. Given the latter, the volume of deposit money and credit will tend to rise and fall as cash reserves are expanded and contracted, primarily by Federal Reserve open-market operations. Cash reserve requirements today serve essentially as a lever over the volume of money and credit and only secondarily as a means of protecting deposits.

Present Legal Requirements

All national banks and those state banks that are members of the Federal Reserve System are subjected to reserve requirements as specified by the Federal Reserve Board of Governors. All other state banks must meet the reserve requirements of the state in which they operate.

Federal Reserve Requirements. Reserve requirements on domestic demand and time deposits are set forth in the Reserve Board's Regulation D. Presently, demand deposit reserve requirements are imposed on "net demand deposits." Net demand deposits equals gross demand deposits plus commercial paper with less than thirty days' maturity issued by an affiliate of the bank, such as a holding company, less cash items in the process of collection and balances in domestic banks. Separate reserve requirements are imposed on savings deposits and other time deposits, which include bank-related commercial paper with a maturity of thirty days and longer. Reserve requirements effective March 31, 1977, on domestic deposits are shown in Table 7-1. For member banks, two cash assets count toward meeting these reserve requirements: vault cash and collected balances with a Federal Reserve bank. Banks strive to handle cash items as efficiently as possible in order to receive reserve credit for these funds as soon as possible.

State Requirements. Reserve requirements vary from state to state, but in general they are much lower than Federal Reserve requirements. In addition, state banking statutes have a more liberal definition of what cash assets may serve as legal reserves. In most states vault cash and correspondent balances serve as legal reserves. Moreover, several states permit federal government and state securities to count toward meeting legal reserve requirements.

Table 7-1
Reserve Requirements on Member Bank Domestic Demand and Time Deposits in Effect March 31, 1977

Liability	Reserve Requirement (percentage)
Net demand deposits	
First $2 million or less	7
Over $2 million to $10 million	9.5
Over $10 million to $100 million	11.75
Over $100 million to $400 million	12.75
Over $400 million	16.25
Time deposits	
Savings deposits	3
Other time deposits	
First $5 million, maturing in	
30–179 days	3
180 days to 4 years	2.5
4 years or more	1
Over $5 million, maturing	
30–179 days	6
180 days to 4 years	2.5
4 years or more	1

Source: Federal Reserve Bulletin.

Working Reserve Requirements

Because a bank meets its legal reserve requirements does not guarantee that it can meet all immediate deposit withdrawals and demands for loans from creditworthy borrowers. Banks have a need for *working reserves,* cash assets in excess of the amount required to satisfy legal requirements. Banks hold working reserves (1) to meet deposit withdrawals and loan demands that are very imminent and (2) to compensate correspondent banks for services performed. Because of the opportunity cost of holding cash assets, bank money position managers must estimate working reserve requirements very closely in order to minimize the income lost from holding nonearning funds. An experienced money manager will be familiar with the composition of the money flows for his bank. He knows, for example, when large industries in his community write substantial checks against their accounts, the size of his customers' payroll demands, the expected Treasury calls on the tax and loan account, the expected cash inflow from maturing loans and investments, and the expected cash outflow from his bank's loan and investment commitments. The money manager must project and anticipate both the bank's legal and working reserve needs. There is no simple formula for measuring these requirements.

Calculating the Bank's Reserve and Money Positions

At large money market banks, the net daily change in deposits and loans can amount to several hundred million dollars. Therefore, it is imperative that an experienced officer be given the responsibility of managing the bank's money position. Throughout the day, information on factors affecting the money position is passed to a money position clerk, who continually updates the bank's legal and working reserve requirements. Appropriate action then can be taken by the designated officer to increase or decrease cash assets as the circumstances dictate.

Banks that manage their money position closely have guidelines for the reporting of transactions that affect legal reserves and gross deposits.[4] For example, one large bank requires immediate reporting to the money manager of all transactions of $100,000 or more that result in an immediate debit or credit to the reserve balance. Such transactions might include deposits of Treasury or Federal Reserve checks and daily clearinghouse settlements. Immediate reporting of all transactions of $1 million or more that change gross deposits also must be reported as they occur. Moreover, future transactions of $1 million or more that will affect the reserve position, and those of $5 million or more that will affect gross deposits, must be reported as they become known. At smaller banks, the procedure outlined above would be applicable except that the amounts involved would be smaller, and one of the bank's investment or loan officers would have the responsibility of managing the money position in addition to his other duties.

Required reserves represent the major portion of the bank's money position. Required reserves are determined and maintained as follows:

1. Reserve periods cover one week, beginning on Thursday and ending on Wednesday.
2. Required reserves for a given week are calculated from deposits held two weeks earlier.
3. Reserves maintained during a given week consist of currency and coin held two weeks earlier, together with reserve account balances held at the Federal Reserve bank during the current week.

[4] George W. McKinney, Jr., "Managing the Bank's Money Positon," in William H. Baughn and Charls E. Walker, eds., *The Banker's Handbook* (Homewood, Ill.: Dow Jones-Irwin, 1966), pp. 581–583.

4. Either excess or deficit reserves of up to 2 percent of required reserves will be carried forward to the next reserve week.

As soon as possible after the close of business each Wednesday, member banks submit a "Report of Deposits, Currency and Coin, and Loans, and Securities" to the Federal Reserve bank or branch holding their reserve account (Figure 7-1).[5] This report provides the Reserve bank with the data for computing required reserves. Required reserves are computed on the basis of the member bank's average daily net deposit balances and its average daily currency and coin (using closing balances) during the seven-day computational period. Since these factors are known to both the member bank and the Reserve bank one week ahead of the beginning of the seven-day period during which reserves must be maintained, the minimum required balance at the Reserve bank becomes the focal point for reserve management.

Each Wednesday night the Reserve bank will dispatch to each member bank a "Statement of Required Reserves" for the following week (Figure 7-2). Each day, along with the "Statement of Reserve Account," the Reserve bank sends to each bank a "Cumulative Reserve Status Computation" (Figure 7-3). This statement reflects the daily average reserve balances needed for the remainder of the week. At the close of the computational period, excesses or deficiencies of up to 2 percent of required reserves will be carried forward to the following week but may not be carried forward to additional weeks. The money manager thus has some degree of flexibility within which to plan the bank's reserve position.

Adjusting the Money Position

Ideally, the money manager would like to have zero excess reserves for each reserve computation period and the knowledge that all money demands have been met satisfactorily and efficiently. At the beginning of each reserve period, the money manager knows the volume of required reserves needed at the Reserve bank, but he does not know the actual amount of working reserves that will be needed during the week, even though he attempts to project these requirements. Although the bank holds reserves during any given week for deposits held two weeks previous, a deposit withdrawal or loan demand in the current week usually results in an immediate decrease in legal reserves at the Reserve bank. Since these actual working reserve needs are likely to be

[5] The reserve computational procedures outlined in the accompanying example are those of the Charlotte Branch of the Federal Reserve Bank of Richmond. Procedures at other Federal Reserve banks and branches may tend to vary. For a more detailed explanation of the technical features of reserve computation, consult pertinent operating circulars and instructional booklets available at the nearest Federal Reserve bank or branch.

MAIL to ACCOUNTING DEPARTMENT – CHARLOTTE BRANCH
FEDERAL RESERVE BANK OF RICHMOND
CHARLOTTE, NORTH CAROLINA 28230
on Thursday after the close of the weekly period.

Base period ending Wednesday________________ 19____ ________________ Official Signature

PLEASE REPORT IN NEAREST THOUSANDS AS OF CLOSE OF BUSINESS EACH DAY

			DEMAND DEPOSITS						Deductions From Demand Deposits					
			DEMAND DEPOSITS OF BANKS		U.S. GOV'T. DEMAND DEPOSITS		OTHER DEMAND DEPOSITS		CASH ITEMS IN PROCESS OF COLLECTION		DEMAND BALANCES DUE FROM BANKS		NET DEMAND DEPOSITS Columns 1,2,3, Minus 4 & 5	
DAY	DATE		1		2		3		4		5		6	
			Mil.	Thous.	Mil.	Thous.	Mil.	Thous.	Mil.	Thous.	Mil.	Thous.	Mil.	Thous.
Thurs.	4–28	1		135		199	6	461		191	1	303	5	301
Fri.	4–29	2		105		216	6	465		436	1	262	5	088
Sat.	4–30	3		105		216	6	465		436	1	262	5	088
Sun.	5–01	4		105		216	6	465		436	1	262	5	088
Mon.	5–02	5		146		363	6	809		440	1	403	5	475
Tues.	5–03	6		228		461	6	442		283	1	730	5	118
Wed.	5–04	7		234		340	6	440		218	1	681	5	115
Total		8	1	058	2	011	45	547	2	440	9	903	36	273

LOANS AND SECURITIES

Complete the form below if your bank does not submit Weekly Report of Condition (Form F.R. 416)

CLOSE OF BUSINESS ON May 4 (Wednesday) 19 77

	Mil.	Thous.
1. LOANS AND DISCOUNTS, INCLUDING FEDERAL FUNDS SOLD AND SECURITIES PURCHASED UNDER RESALE AGREEMENTS	12	627
2. UNITED STATES TREASURY SECURITIES – (Include securities sold under repurchase agreements.)	5	368
3. OTHER SECURITIES – (Obligations of States and political subdivisions; securities of Federal agencies and corporations, and other securities and corporate stocks, including Federal Reserve Bank stock. Include securities sold under repurchase agreements)	2	225
4. TOTAL LOANS AND SECURITIES (Total of Items 1,2, and 3 above)	20	220
5. TOTAL ASSETS, EXCLUDING LOAN LOSS RESERVES AND UNEARNED INCOME ON LOANS	23	931

Figure 7-1 Reports of Deposits, Currency and Coin, Federal Funds, Loans and Securities (Sample)

reflected in the bank's reserve position at the Federal Reserve bank, the money manager concentrates his efforts on adjusting this position. The techniques of adjusting the money position of a large bank differ somewhat from those at small banks.

Large Banks

Money managers at large banks may adjust their money positions by a number of different techniques. The primary method employed today

0539-0176-1
REPUBLIC NATIONAL BANK
COLUMBIA, S. C. 67-176

Prepared By

PLEASE REPORT IN NEAREST THOUSANDS AS OF CLOSE OF BUSINESS EACH DAY

TIME DEPOSITS								CURRENCY AND COIN (Including currency and coin in transit with F.R. Bank)		FEDERAL FUNDS SOLD (Including securities purchased under resale agreements)		FEDERAL FUNDS PURCHASED (Including securities sold under repurchase agreements)	
SAVINGS AND CLUB DEPOSITS		OTHER TIME DEPOSITS (Excluding Club Deposits)											
		INITIAL MATURITIES 30 TO 179 DAYS		INITIAL MATURITIES 180 DAYS OR GREATER BUT LESS THAN 4 YRS.		INITIAL MATURITIES 4 YEARS OR MORE							
7		8		9		10		11		12		13	
Mil.	Thous.	Mil.	Thous.	Mil.	Thous.	Mil.	Thous.	Mil.	Thous.	Mil.	Thous.	Mil.	Thous.
1	736		684	8	634	1	273		193	--	350	--	--
1	741		684	8	634	1	273		183	--	150	--	--
1	741		684	8	634	1	273		183	--	150	--	--
1	741		684	8	634	1	273		183	--	150	--	--
1	659		684	8	634	1	273		194	--	375	--	--
1	647		677	8	150	1	665		165	--	--	--	150
1	654		677	8	150	1	665		171	--	--	--	150
11	919	4	774	59	470	9	695	1	272	1	175	--	300

Budget Bureau No. 55 – R171.7

involves the purchase and sale of federal funds. Large banks have officers whose sole task is to buy and sell federal funds for their banks as well as for other medium-sized and small banks located throughout the country. During periods of tight money, large money market banks usually are net buyers of federal funds. It is quite common for large banks to pool relatively small quantities ($100,000) of federal funds from many small and medium-sized banks in order to meet their money requirements. Other methods of adjusting money positions involve the traditional technique of buying or selling secondary reserve assets such

```
                CHARLOTTE BRANCH  - FEDERAL RESERVE BANK OF RICHMOND
0539 0176 1  STATEMENT OF REQUIRED RESERVES - IN THOUSANDS OF DOLLARS

                                     RESERVE PERIOD ENDING 05 18 77
 REPUBLIC NATIONAL BANK                           DATE RUN  05 12 77
 P O BOX 52
 COLUMBIA S C  29202

1. REQUIRED RESERVES                       BASE WEEK ENDING   REQUIRED      REQUIRED
   AGGREGATE DEPOSITS                          05 04 77       PERCENTAGE    RESERVES
  A.  NET DEMAND
      1. BASE $   14MIL                        14,000                          980
     2. REMAINDER                              22,273          9.50          2,116
  B. SAVINGS                                   11,910          3.00            358
  C. OTHER TIME DEPOSITS
     MINIMUM STATUS                            73,939          3.00          2,218


  F. TOTAL REQUIRED RESERVES                                                 5,672
2. EXCESS RESERVES OR DEFICIENCY (-) FROM PREVIOUS WEEK                        15-
3. CURRENCY AND COIN                                                         1,272
4. AGGREGATE RESERVES BALANCES NEEDED WEEK ENDING 05 18 77                   4,415
```

Figure 7-2 Statement of Required Reserves (Sample)

CC 1477

CHARLOTTE BRANCH
FEDERAL RESERVE BANK OF RICHMOND
CUMULATIVE RESERVE STATUS COMPUTATION-IN THOUSANDS OF DOLLARS

0539 0176 1 — RESERVE PERIOD ENDING 05 18 77 — 05 16 77
REPUBLIC NATIONAL BANK — BASE PERIOD ENDING 05 04 77
P O BOX 52
COLUMBIA S C 29202

1. REQUIRED RESERVES-CURRENT WEEK	5,672	
2. CURRENCY AND COIN HELD DURING BASE WEEK		1,272
3. RESERVE BALANCES HELD SO FAR DURING CURRENT WEEK		2,906
4. NET ALLOWANCES AND DEDUCTIONS		
5. CARRY-OVER OF EXCESS OR DEFICIENCY FROM PREVIOUS WEEK		15-
6. CUMULATIVE RESERVES TO MEET REQUIREMENTS - CURRENT WEEK		4,163
7. A. EXCESS RESERVES HELD FOR CURRENT WEEK		
B. AGGREGATE RESERVE DEFICIENCY FOR CURRENT WEEK	1,509	
8. DAILY AVERAGE RESERVE BALANCE NEEDED FOR REST OF WEEK	755	

Figure 7-3 Cumulative Reserve Status Computation (Sample)

as Treasury bills, other U.S. government securities, banker's acceptances, and commercial paper.

Recently, the technique of liability management has played an important part in the management of the money position of large banks. As we saw in Chapter 6, many large banks, especially in tight-money periods, will go into the money market and bid for the funds they need rather than hold what they consider to be excessive amounts of short-term assets that can be readily converted into cash. Banks can raise funds very quickly by purchasing federal funds, borrowing Eurodollars, selling loan participations, or borrowing from the Federal Reserve. Other techniques of liability management, such as the bank holding company's selling commercial paper, take more time to execute.

Small Banks

Money management at small banks is similar to that at large banks, except that the amounts involved at the former are smaller and the techniques available for adjusting the money position are more limited. The payoff from efficient money management in terms of earnings per share, however, is just as significant. Since many large banks recently have become brokers in federal funds, the task of the money manager at most small banks has been simplified greatly. The money manager at a small bank now has a more accessible outlet for the surplus funds that his bank has in correspondent accounts or at a Reserve bank. Through the use of the wire transfer system available at his correspondent bank or the Reserve bank, he can very easily sell (which is the typical case) or buy federal funds to adjust his bank's cash position. Other commonly used alternatives of money position adjustment open to the small bank are borrowing from correspondent banks for short periods of time, borrowing from the Federal Reserve, buying or selling loan participations, and buying or selling Treasury bills or other short-term government securities.

Suggestions for Additional Reading

Cowan, Leon W. "Seasonal Borrowing Privilege Liberalized." Federal Reserve Bank of Dallas, *Business Review* (November 1976), pp. 9–11.

Kaminow, Ira. "The Case Against Uniform Reserves: A Loss of Perspective." Federal Reserve Bank of Philadelphia, *Business Review* (June 1974), pp. 16–21.

Mayne, Lucille S. "Deposit Reserve Requirements: Time for Change." *Journal of Bank Research* (Winter 1976), pp. 268–274.

McKinney, George W., Jr. "Managing the Bank's Money Position." In William H. Baughn and Charls E. Walker, eds. *Banker's Handbook*. Homewood, Ill.: Dow Jones-Irwin, 1966, chap. 44.

"Member Bank Reserve Requirements—Heritage from History." Federal Reserve Bank of Chicago, *Business Conditions* (June 1972), pp. 2–18.

Nichols, Dorothy M. "Toward More Uniform Reserve Requirements." Federal Reserve Bank of Chicago, *Business Conditions* (March 1974), pp. 3–12.

Poole, William. "A Proposal for Reforming Bank Reserve Requirements in the United States." *Journal of Money, Credit and Banking* (May 1976), pp. 137–148.

Waage, Thomas O. "The Need for Uniform Reserve Requirements." Federal Reserve Bank of New York, *Monthly Review* (December 1973), pp. 303–306.

CHAPTER

8

Short-Term and Long-Term Liquidity Management

Chapter 7 focused on the management of a bank's money position. A bank's money position reflects its reserve requirements and the necessity to meet near-term deposit withdrawals, loan demands, and maturing liabilities. After meeting these requirements, a bank must prepare for liquidity needs that result from seasonal or random declines in deposits and increases in loans and from cyclical or secular declines in deposits and increases in loans. *Liquidity management* involves the estimation of, and provision for, these short-term and long-term cash needs. In this chapter we shall (1) discuss the nature of short-term and long-term bank liquidity requirements, (2) develop the techniques to estimate these requirements, and (3) note the various methods banks employ to manage their liquidity position.

The Nature of Bank Liquidity Requirements

Short-Term Liquidity Requirements

A bank's *short-term liquidity needs* may be defined as those that result from seasonal and random fluctuations in the demand for funds by depositors and borrowers over the course of a one-year time horizon. The pattern of these fluctuations tends to vary widely among banks. For example, the demand for funds at a bank in Florida located in the heart of the citrus belt would have a different seasonal profile from that of a bank in Texas located in a ranching community. Large money market banks in New York would not have identical short-term liquidity needs because each bank serves different corporate and individual customers. Every bank has a unique set of factors that determines its short-term liquidity requirements.

Deposit Liquidity. As a rule, small demand and savings deposits held by individuals are quite stable in the aggregate. The primary sources of funds deposited and held in these accounts are wages and salaries, which tend to be paid and deposited on a regular weekly, biweekly, or monthly basis. Although the average balance in these accounts is small, these accounts provide a bedrock of funds to a bank.

The need for deposit liquidity is largely the result of fluctuations in large demand and time deposits held by businesses, governmental units, and wealthy individuals. Major corporations usually make sizable withdrawals in order to remit quarterly tax and dividend payments. For example, on December 10, 1976, General Motors paid a quarterly dividend and extra dividend amounting to $3.00 per share on approximately 287.6 million shares of common stock outstanding, for a total outlay of $862.8 million. Within one week, the bulk of these checks could be expected for presentation for payment at the bank holding the General Motors dividend account. The payment for carload lots of raw material and the subsequent sale of finished products in similar quantities is another illustration of activity that tends to produce large fluctuations in demand and time deposits at individual banks.

With the widescale use of CDs, some of the instability formerly experienced in corporate demand deposits has been shifted to time deposits. It is a practice of many large corporations to invest funds that will be paid out for taxes, dividends, and other large purchases in CDs that mature on the date these payments are due. Many banks experience a sizable runoff of CDs around tax-payment dates and the beginning of a quarter, when many dividends are remitted to shareholders.

Treasury tax and loan deposits in small banks tend to be stable and quite predictable, but Treasury balances in large banks are subject to wide swings on short notice. Banks serving as Treasury depositories are classified as being in Group A, B, or C, based on the total amount of deposits credited during the previous calendar year. These groups and the total deposits credit are as follows:

Group A—$7.5 million or less.

Group B—$7.5–80 million.

Group C—$80 million or more.

Group A banks are subject to 3–4 calls per month for Treasury funds; Group B banks may be called for funds 2–3 times per week and are subject to accelerated calls at the Treasury's discretion. Group C banks are subject to regular and special daily calls in order to bring the balance in the Federal Reserve Banks to a precise level. Clearly, Treasury calls have much greater significance in the short-term liquidity plans of banks in Group C than in those in Groups A and B.

Generally, the demand deposits of state and local governmental units fluctuate rather predictably. The date that tax payments are due is known in advance, and the bulk of the checks written on these accounts represents regular withdrawals for wages and salaries. As we saw in Chapter 5, almost three-fourths of the total state and local government bank balances are in time deposits, primarily CDs.

The demand deposits of wealthy individuals tend to vary widely as these people receive and pay out their incomes and purchase and sell securities, land, and other assets. A bank's liquidity manager cannot predict when these deposits will fall or rise significantly. Moreover, many of these balances are not subject to seasonal changes. Thus a portion of the random element inherent in deposit fluctuations may be due to the actions of large individual account holders.

Deposits "due to banks" also may fluctuate considerably. State nonmember banks that actively use their correspondent accounts as reserve depositories would tend to make large daily deposits to the accounts, but sizable irregular withdrawals as the banks conduct their loan and investment activities. Member banks also make large daily deposits to their correspondent account, but these banks tend to effect immediate transfer of any excess funds to their reserve account at a Federal Reserve bank.

While all the deposit fluctuations just discussed are associated with the activities of large account holders, a considerable part of a bank's seasonal deposit liquidity depends on its location. Banks in Florida expect funds to be drawn down during the citrus-growing season, but they also expect a heavy inflow of funds during the winter, when the fruit is sold. Similarly, banks in South Florida expect an inflow of funds during the winter tourist season and an outflow during the "off season" or summer. Rural banks in the Midwest expect deposit outflows during the spring planting season and deposit inflows in the fall when the crops are sold.

Loan Liquidity. A bank's need for loan liquidity ordinarily parallels its need for deposit liquidity because borrowers usually draw down their deposits before they seek loan accommodations. Thus the same institutional arrangements and seasonal influences that bear on deposit liquidity determine loan liquidity requirements. During recent tight-money periods many corporations had to borrow heavily to meet quarterly tax payments and other cash needs. In fact, the dollar amounts and the number of corporations involved were so large that the financial press started reporting how well banks were able to meet the demand for loans around tax-payment dates.

Besides the need to meet tax payments, each industry has its own special seasonal borrowing needs. Firms in the tobacco industry would tend to increase their borrowing during the late summer and fall when they have to purchase the current year's tobacco crop. Retail businesses typically borrow in the late summer and early fall in order to purchase their Christmas inventory. The seasonal peak in the sales of automobiles, appliances, and television sets during the fall tends to coincide with the seasonal demand for bank loans by sales finance companies, who finance the purchase of a large portion of these items. Construction companies have a great demand for loans during the spring and summer because of the seasonal peak in residential building. The agricultural sector, of course, has its own unique seasonal borrowing needs, depending on the crop. Every bank has customers with seasonal loan demands. To the extent that these loan demands cannot be met from loan repayments and increases in deposits, the bank must have adequate short-term liquidity reserves.

Long-Term Liquidity Requirements

Long-term liquidity requirements have their origin primarily in the cyclical nature of economic activity. There are also secular forces that influence a bank's long-term liquidity requirements, but these influences are so barely discernible that they ordinarily are ignored in liquidity planning. Unlike short-term liquidity requirements, which tend to be repetitive because of the nature of our tax system, quarterly dividend payments patterns, the weather, and the celebration of holidays, cyclical liquidity needs are rather unpredictable. Since World War II, the U.S. economy has experienced six major recessions: (1) 1948–1949, (2) 1953–1954, (3) 1957–1958, (4) 1960–1961, (5) 1969–1970, and (6) 1973–1975. The periods of economic expansion that separated these recessions varied considerably in length and in intensity. Moreover, numerous observers believe that the Federal

Reserve's monetary policy is a contributing factor to both the expansionary and contractionary phases of the business cycle. In planning for cyclical liquidity requirements, a bank's liquidity manager must know the direction and rate of growth in economic activity and the probable course of monetary policy. Large banks maintain a staff of professional economists whose responsibility it is to make financial and economic forecasts and to keep the bank's liquidity manager informed as to current trends and developments in monetary policy and economic activity. Liquidity managers at smaller banks, however, must rely heavily on the forecasts and analysis of economists at large banks, the Federal Reserve, and in the federal government.

Liquidity Needs During Recessions. According to modern liquidity theory, banks do not have to make provision for cyclical liquidity during recessions.[1] This is because banks likely will be surfeited with liquidity during recessions as required reserves fall when loans and deposits decline. There are several reasons why it is unlikely that the banking system will experience another severe liquidity panic like that of the Great Depression and previous economic declines. First, the establishment of the FDIC has increased the public's confidence in banks, thereby greatly precluding the possibility of widespread currency hoarding and bank runs. Second, the Federal Reserve authorities have a greater knowledge of the causes of business fluctuations and the art of central banking. If a recession should occur, banks can rely on the Federal Reserve to increase legal reserves through open-market purchases of securities and to reduce the discount rate so that banks can borrow at a lower cost. Third, because of the Employment Act of 1946, the federal government has accepted the responsibility of maintaining "maximum production, employment, and purchasing power." Through the use of its taxing and spending powers, the federal government has the ability to maintain income and employment at or near the full employment level. Finally, bank lending officers are better trained, and the quality of bank loan portfolios is much higher than during the Great Depression, with the result that banks can expect a substantial flow of funds from loan repayments.

Liquidity Needs during Expansion Periods. Typically, loan demand rises sharply during the expansion phase of the business cycle. Loans to businesses to finance new plant and equipment, inventories, and accounts receivables usually represent the bulk of this increase. Individual banks are more or less committed to accommodate the loan requests of their established customers, or they risk losing their accounts to other banks. Moreover, because the Federal Reserve usually

[1]Much of this discussion is based on G. Walter Woodworth, "Bank Liquidity Management," *The Bankers Magazine* (Autumn 1967), pp. 66–78.

attempts to restrict the growth of deposits during the last phases of an economic expansion, banks ordinarily cannot rely on this source of funds to finance an expansion of loans. In order to meet these loan requests, banks must have enough short-term securities that can be sold with little or no loss or they must have the ability to borrow funds in sufficient volume through various liability management techniques to fulfill their customers' credit needs. During the expansionary phase that preceded the 1969–1970 recession, a number of banks were caught with inadequate loan liquidity and had to sell securities from their permanent investment portfolio. Losses (after taxes) on securities sold by insured banks amounted to $238 million in 1969. Adequate cyclical liquidity reserves would have precluded these heavy losses. As a result of the scramble for liquidity during 1969, most banks were better prepared for the liquidity requirements of the 1971–1973 expansion phase.

Estimating Bank Liquidity Requirements

Because it is impossible to forecast accurately future loan demand, deposit flows, and Federal Reserve monetary policy, no bank liquidity manager is able to estimate precisely either short-term or long-term liquidity requirements. But even though the future is uncertain and the nature of forecasting is inexact, the liquidity manager must attempt to estimate as best he can his bank's future liquidity requirements and not rely on intuitive guesses. The income lost from having excessive liquidity or the embarrassment from having insufficient liquidity are too great for him not to devote considerable effort to the task of estimating future liquidity needs.

Most writers on bank liquidity management agree that any estimate of short- or long-term liquidity needs must be based on an analysis of past experience and trends and a detailed consideration of the factors that might have a bearing on future needs. The forecasting technique suggested below for the estimation of short- and long-term liquidity needs is designed to enable bank liquidity managers to take into account both past and future trends and developments.[2] The basic assumption of this technique is that short- and long-term liquidity needs result primarily from changes in either total deposits or total loans.[3] That is, liquidity needs increase when (1) an increase in loans is not offset by an increase in deposits or (2) a decrease in deposits is not offset by a decrease in loans. Changes in the statistical series "net change in total deposits and total loans" (total deposits minus total loans) are an indication of a bank's total liquidity needs during a given period.

[2]The technique that will be presented in this section is a modified and shortened version of that described by G. Walter Woodworth, "Planning Bank Liquidity Needs," *The Bankers Magazine*, 151 (Summer 1968), pp. 22–32.

[3]A change in legal reserve requirements could also alter liquidity needs.

A Ten-Step Liquidity Forecasting Technique

The liquidity forecasting technique developed below is divided into ten steps.[4] This technique is applied to deposit and loan data obtained from a medium-sized bank (hereafter called Beta Bank). Beta Bank probably is a typical bank because it is faced with increasing liquidity needs during expansionary phases of the cycle and declining liquidity needs during the contractionary phases of the cycle.

Step 1. Tabulate the monthly series for total deposits and total loans for a selected period.[5] The total deposit series should be adjusted downward by an appropriate percentage to allow for legal and working reserves. The size of this adjustment will depend on the applicable legal reserve requirements, the deposit structure of the bank, and the margin of working reserves the bank wishes to hold. For the Beta Bank, total deposits have been adjusted downward by 15 percent to derive "total net deposits" [Table 8-1, column (1)].

Total loans should include those types of customer loans that banks have some obligation to grant, and not loans such as commercial paper, banker's acceptances, and federal funds sold, that the bank can make when funds are available. In Table 8-1, column (2), total loans include all commercial, individual, and charge-card loans.

Step 2. Chart the series for total net deposits and total loans using either a ratio or arithmetic scale (Figure 8-1). The purpose of this step is to aid the liquidity manager in interpreting past changes and to facilitate the forecasting of future changes in loans and deposits.

Step 3. Subtract total loans from total net deposits for each month in the period to derive the difference series [Table 8-1, column (3)]. Express the difference series as a percentage of total net deposits [Table 8-1, column (4)]. The difference series is converted into percentage terms so that changing liquidity needs are comparable even though the bank is growing.

Step 4. Calculate seasonal indices for total net deposits and total loans. This step involves a relatively simple statistical technique that is explained in most elementary textbooks on statistics or quantitative

[4]The 1969–1973 period seems best for purposes of illustration because this time frame included the 1969–1970 recession when liquidity needs receded at most small and medium-sized banks and most of the 1971–1973 expansion phase when liquidity needs increased sharply. The expansion phase following the 1973–1975 recession has been weak; loan demands and hence liquidity needs have been uncharacteristically slow in developing.

[5]Ideally, the monthly series should be an average of the weekly series. In the example shown, however, end-of-month totals were used.

Table 8-1
Estimated Total Liquidity Needs of Beta Bank, January 1969–May 1972 (millions of dollars)

		(1) Total Net Deposits	(2) Total Loans	(3) Difference Series (1) - (2)	(4) Difference Series as a Percentage of Total Net Deposits (3) ÷ (1)
1969	January	361	273	88	24.4%
	February	363	272	91	25.1
	March	378	283	95	25.1
	April	380	288	92	24.2
	May	378	292	86	22.8
	June	397	297	100	25.2
	July	390	291	99	25.4
	August	379	286	93	24.5
	September	388	290	98	25.3
	October	381	293	88	23.1
	November	389	296	93	23.9
	December	412	306	106	25.7
1970	January	392	296	96	24.5
	February	384	296	88	22.9
	March	400	306	94	23.5
	April	397	305	92	23.2
	May	394	305	89	22.6
	June	428	313	115	26.9
	July	406	325	81	20.0
	August	424	318	106	25.0
	September	429	311	118	27.5
	October	429	315	114	26.6
	November	442	319	123	27.8
	December	458	325	133	29.0
1971	January	442	325	117	26.5
	February	466	321	145	31.1
	March	450	326	124	27.6
	April	456	325	131	28.7
	May	477	342	135	28.3
	June	488	342	146	29.9
	July	477	339	138	28.9
	August	490	337	153	31.2
	September	499	335	164	32.9
	October	496	349	147	29.6
	November	496	360	136	27.4
	December	519	363	156	30.1
1972	January	511	362	149	29.2
	February	497	365	132	26.6
	March	486	380	106	21.8
	April	496	391	105	21.2
	May	524	399	125	23.9

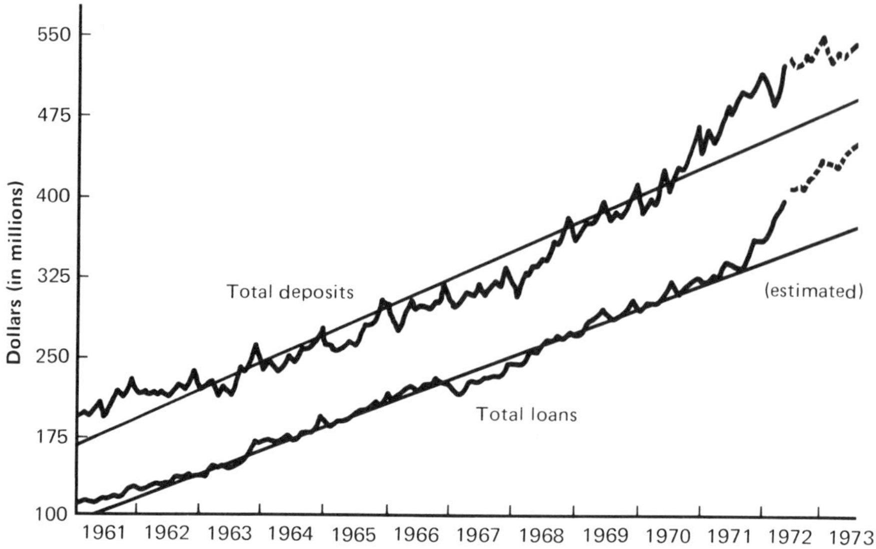

Figure 8-1 Total Net Deposits and Total Loans of Beta Bank, January 1961–May 1973

methods. For those banks with access to a computer, however, there are "canned" programs available that seasonally adjust time-series data. One of the most widely used seasonal adjustment programs (and the one used in this computation) is the Bureau of Census's computer program, "The X-11 Variant of the Census Method II Seasonal Adjustment Program."[6] With the X-11 program, seasonal indices for deposits and loans are calculated for each month in the series and for one year in advance. The seasonal indices for total net deposits and total loans calculated in this step will be used in Steps 8 and 9 to determine changes in the liquidity of the bank.

Step 5. Fit a trend line to the total net deposits series and total loans series and project it over the next twelve months. Trend lines may be in the form of mathematically fitted curves or developed by subjective evaluation. Mathematically fitted trend lines are relatively easy to calculate through the use of canned computer programs. For the Beta Bank the simple linear function was found to provide a satisfactory fit for both series. Except in extreme growth situations, the linear function

[6]A detailed description of this program is contained in U.S. Bureau of the Census, *The X-11 Variant of the Census Method II Seasonal Adjustment Program, Technical Paper No. 15*, 1967 revision (Washington, D.C.: U.S. Government Printing Office, 1967). See also "A Seasonally Adjusted World: The Census Seasonal Adjustment Technique," Federal Reserve Bank of Richmond, *Monthly Review* (August 1970), pp. 2–5, 8.

probably will generate the best approximation of both past and future trends in deposits and loans. However, following careful analysis of expected changes in national and local economic conditions and possible banking and financial developments, it may be necessary to project, by inspection, a trend line that deviates somewhat from the calculated line. Projected trend ordinates for total net deposits and loans are shown in Table 8-2, columns (1) and (5), and are plotted in Figure 8-1.

Step 6. Using the trend ordinates derived in Step 5 as a basic measure of secular trend, estimate the cyclical and secular variations of both total net deposits and total loans for a period such as twelve months [Table 8-2, columns (2) and (6)]. This step entails a forecast of financial and economic conditions and any other relevant factors except seasonal influences that will affect total net deposits and total loans in the selected time horizon. It is important to know whether the economy will be in an expansionary or contractionary phase of the business cycle because during the expansion phase of the cycle, total loans tend to grow more rapidly than total deposits. During the contraction phase, total loans tend to decline faster or grow more slowly than total deposits.

Step 7. Multiply projected total net deposits and total loans by their respective projected seasonal indices as generated by the X-11 program. These products are shown in Table 8-2, columns (4) and (8). The purpose of this step is to introduce seasonal variation into the projected total net deposit and loan data, which, as presented in Table 8-2, columns (2) and (6), reflect only cyclical and secular influences.[7]

Step 8. Subtract projected total loans from projected total net deposits, as calculated in Step 7. This projected difference series is shown in Table 8-2, column (9).

Step 9. Express the projected difference series as a percentage of projected total net deposits [Table 8-2, column (10)].

Step 10. Chart the historical difference series expressed as a percentage of total net deposits [Table 8-1, column (4)] and the projected difference series as a percentage of projected total net deposits [Table 8-2, column (10)]. These series are plotted in Figure 8-2.

[7]The X-11 program projection of the seasonal factors is for only one year. As actual deposit and loan data become available, the X-11 program should be used to update the projected seasonal indices.

Figure 8-2 Total Liquidity Needs of Beta Bank as a Percentage of Total Net Deposits, January 1961–May 1973

Table 8-2

Estimated Total Future Liquidity Needs of Beta Bank, June 1972–May 1973 (millions of dollars)

		(1) Projected Trend for Total Net Deposits	(2) Projected Total Net Deposits	(3) Projected Seasonal Index for Total Net Deposits	(4) Projected Total Net Deposits with Seasonal Variation (2) × (3)
1972	June	$471	$525	101.8	$534.5
	July	473	527	99.3	523.3
	August	475	528	99.7	526.4
	September	477	530	101.1	535.8
	October	479	532	99.3	528.3
	November	482	534	100.3	535.6
	December	484	536	104.2	558.5
1973	January	486	539	99.3	535.2
	February	488	541	97.4	526.9
	March	490	543	99.1	538.1
	April	493	545	98.0	534.1
	May	495	547	100.2	548.1

Interpretation and Implementation

The difference series expressed as a percentage of total net deposits may be used as a measure of a bank's total short-term and long-term liquidity needs. Upward and downward movements in the difference series expressed as a percentage of total net deposits also may be employed to measure changes in a bank's liquidity requirements. In order to use the liquidity measurement technique developed in this chapter, a bank first must project maturing liabilities and attempt to estimate potential deposit drains and loan demands in the light of possible future economic conditions. Based on these considerations, bank management would establish its liquidity requirements in terms of the difference series expressed as a percentage of total deposits. Money market banks and most regional banks with the ability to acquire funds through the various techniques of liability management would tend to establish lower liquidity requirements than smaller banks. As economic and financial conditions change, banks should reevaluate their liquidity requirements and revise them upward or downward as conditions dictate. After the tight-money conditions of 1969 and early 1970 forced many banks to liquidate securities at substantial losses, the Beta Bank's management adopted a policy to maintain a liquidity position equal to approximately 23.5 percent of total net deposits (total deposits minus legal and working reserves). Management of the Beta Bank did not consider this liquidity position as inflexible; that is, it was prepared to operate in the short run with a lower liquidity position in order to accommodate the legitimate loan demands of its customers.

(5) Projected Trend for Total Loans	(6) Projected Total Loans	(7) Projected Seasonal Index for Loans	(8) Projected Total Loans with Seasonal Variation (6) × (7)	(9) Projected Difference Series (4) - (8)	(10) Projected Difference Series as a Percentage of Projected Total Net Deposits (9) ÷ (4)
$357	$403	101.6	$409.4	$125.1	23.4%
359	407	100.8	410.3	113.0	21.6
361	411	100.0	411.0	115.4	21.9
363	415	98.5	408.8	127.0	23.7
365	420	99.7	418.7	109.6	20.7
366	425	100.2	425.9	109.7	20.5
368	430	101.3	435.6	122.9	22.0
369	434	99.2	430.5	104.7	19.6
371	438	98.0	429.2	97.7	18.5
373	442	100.0	442.0	96.1	17.9
375	446	99.8	445.1	89.0	16.7
377	450	100.5	452.3	95.8	17.5

An analysis of Figure 8-2 shows that the Beta Bank gradually reduced its liquidity position from early 1962 through early 1966. During this period, the economy was in a cyclical upturn and loans increased relative to deposits. Following a sharp increase in the bank's liquidity position in late 1966, which was a precautionary reaction to the money crunch of late summer 1966, the bank's liquidity position averaged approximately 23–25 percent of total net deposits through mid-1970. Then, primarily as a result of the weak loan demand associated with the 1969–1970 recession and the subsequent slow economic recovery, the bank's liquidity position increased sharply between mid-1970 and mid-1971. As the pace of economic recovery accelerated in the last half of 1971, the bank's liquidity position dropped rapidly as loan demand increased.

For the twelve months beginning June 1972, the Beta Bank expected a slowdown in the rate of deposit growth and a continued increase in loan demand. As a result of these developments, the projected difference series during this period was expected to decline to 17.5 percent of total net deposits by May 1973. Unless the Beta Bank intentionally decided to reduce its liquidity requirement, the bank would have to acquire additional short-term securities such as Treasury bills, commercial paper, and banker's acceptances, and/or rely on liability management techniques in order to meet anticipated liquidity needs.

An Evaluation

The ten-step liquidity forecasting technique represents an attempt to reduce to quantifiable terms one of the most difficult problems confronting banks. This technique has several merits. First, it is simple and easy to use and to update, especially for banks with access to a computer. Second, it tends to provide a better measure of liquidity needs than an analysis of the potential volatility for individual deposit categories. According to Roger A. Lyon, "the more one subdivides the analysis of deposit performance, the more he reduces the insurance principle of averaging the risk of deposit volatility. A transfer of funds among types of deposits, for instance, requires no liquidity per se, but would show up as a liquidity need on the subdivided deposit basis."[8] Finally, future liquidity estimates should be more credible because they would be linked to the bank's past experience with respect to seasonal, cyclical, and secular liquidity needs.

It is still necessary for the bank liquidity manager to forecast cyclical fluctuations and a secular trend in deposits and loans, and this is not an easy task. The length and amplitude of each cycle in economic activity

[8]Roger A. Lyon, "Establishing Bank Liquidity Policies (Analysis of Basic Determinants);" in William H. Baughn and Charls E. Walker, eds., *The Banker's Handbook* (Homewood, Ill.: Dow Jones-Irwin, 1966), p. 576.

tends to be different. It is important that deposit and loan forecasts be updated at least every month in order to incorporate the latest cyclical and secular movements in these variables.

A bank's first task is to meet deposit withdrawals, loan demands, and maturing liabilities. Once these liquidity needs are known and provided for, the bank may proceed to acquire loans, investments, and other earning assets. The liquidity forecasting technique suggested in this chapter may be of valuable assistance to banks in both loan and investment planning.

Managing the Bank's Liquidity Position

There are two principal ways a bank may meet its positive liquidity needs: (1) by holding *secondary reserves*, which are of short term (usually maturing in one year or less), high credit quality, readily marketable, and open market obligations, or (2) by the techniques of liability management described in Chapter 6.

Secondary Reserve Management

Banks could meet their expected short-term and long-term liquidity needs by holding primary reserves or cash assets equivalent to these requirements. This we know would be costly because cash assets earn no income. Until the time when banks are faced with deposit withdrawals, loan demands, and maturing liabilities, most banks prefer to meet part of their potential liquidity requirements by holding secondary reserves. These assets earn some income until the time when they must be converted into primary reserves to meet imminent liquidity needs. The conversion is accomplished by selling secondary reserve assets in the market. For these assets to be sold quickly and without appreciable loss, they must be open-market obligations that are short term, of the highest credit quality, and readily marketable.

Qualities of Secondary Reserve Assets. Banks are assured of having secondary reserve assets that are of the highest credit quality and readily marketable if they hold only open-market obligations. The term "open market" means that the relationship between borrower and lender is characterized by impersonality; that is, the borrower never meets the lender face to face as in the "closed" or "personal" market, where customers and loan officers sit across the desk from each other. Rather, loan transactions usually are carried out through an intermediary, such as a broker or a dealer. For example, when a bank purchases commercial paper, it usually does so through a commercial paper dealer who may have underwritten the obligations or purchased them from another lender. Banks also acquire U.S. government obligations through a third party, such as a government securities dealer or a Federal Reserve Bank, which handles the original issue of these securities.

By limiting secondary reserve assets to open-market obligations, the bank liquidity manager knows that, because of the impersonality of the open market and because only the highest-rated borrowers can issue open-market obligations, these debts will be repaid at maturity. Moreover, the ready marketability of open-market obligations is assured because there are dealers willing to buy or sell these securities in reasonable amounts. The dealers are willing to "make a market" in open-market obligations because they know that there are enough investors, such as banks, insurance companies, pension and trust funds, college endowment funds, and foreign institutions, who hold and trade in these obligations to create a broad and continuous market.

Finally, secondary reserve assets should be *short term*, meaning one year or less to maturity, to avoid the *money risk*, which is the possibility that the market price of a security will fall before maturity as the market rate of interest rises. If the market price fell and it became necessary for the bank to sell the security to meet liquidity demands, then the bank would suffer a loss. The bank avoids the *credit risk*, the possibility that the obligation will not be repaid at maturity, by purchasing only open-market obligations. Restricting secondary reserve assets to short-term, open-market obligations helps the bank avoid the money risk. This is because when interest rates rise, the price of short-term securities falls less than the price on long-term securities. As an open-market obligation approaches maturity, its price is less susceptible to the influence of rising interest rates. In other words, there is less reason for the market price to deviate from the face value of the obligation if the payment of this sum is within one year.

Types of Secondary Reserve Assets. The most widely used secondary reserve assets are (1) federal funds, (2) short-term U.S. government obligations, (3) short-term federally sponsored agency securities, (4) banker's acceptances, and (5) commercial paper.

As we saw in Chapter 7, transactions in federal funds have become increasingly important in recent years as a method for banks to adjust their cash positions. Many banks, however, now consider federal funds a convenient outlet for secondary reserve funds, which, ordinarily, would have been placed in short-term government obligations. It is not uncommon for banks to have significant amounts continuously invested in the federal funds market for weeks at a time. Like open-market obligations, federal funds sold have virtually no credit risk attached to them because they are the obligation of financially sound banking institutions, and they have no money risk because they have overnight maturities.

Short-term U.S. government obligations include all those (1) with an original maturity of one year or less or (2) with an original maturity of more than one year that are now within a year of maturity. Those in the first group include *Treasury bills*, which are the shortest-term obligation the Treasury issues. Those in the second group consist of *Treasury notes* and *Treasury bonds*.

There are four series of Treasury bills: (1) *3-month bills* and (2) *6-month bills*, which normally are auctioned every Monday for payment and delivery the following Thursday; (3) *12-month bills*, which usually are sold at monthly auctions about one week before the end of each month, most often on a Tuesday; and (4) *tax-anticipation bills*, which are issued irregularly and have maturities that are one week after corporate tax-payment dates. "Tax bills" are acceptable at full maturity value on tax-payment dates or may be redeemed for cash on the maturity date. Bills are issued at a discount; thus the difference between the purchase price and the par value represents the interest earned.

Treasury notes are coupon issues with a maturity of not less than one year or more than seven years. *Treasury bonds* are coupon issues with an original maturity in excess of five years, although legally, Treasury bonds may be of any maturity.

The outstanding issues of certain federal and federally sponsored agencies, chiefly the Banks for Cooperatives, Federal Home Loan Banks, Federal Intermediate Credit Banks, Federal Land Banks, Federal National Mortgage Association (Fannie Mae), Tennessee Valley Authority, the Government National Mortgage Association (Ginnie Mae), and the Public Housing Administration, have become important outlets for liquidity reserves during recent years. These "agency" securities usually yield 10 to 40 basis points more than Treasury securities, and an active secondary market enhances the shiftability of these obligations.

Banker's acceptances were discussed in Chapter 6. At the end of 1976, there were $22.5 billion of these securities outstanding, of which $10.4 billion were held by banks.

Commercial paper consists of short-term promissory notes of prime business corporations. These obligations usually are in standard denominations of $5,000, $10,000, $50,000, and $100,000 and may be sold by the issuing corporation through commerical paper dealers who resell to investors in the open market, or they may be placed directly with banks, life insurance companies, pension funds, and other large lenders. At the end of 1976, the volume of commercial paper outstanding totaled $52 billion.

Liability Management

As we saw in Chapter 6, liability management involves the acquisition of funds through the issuance of CDs, the purchase of federal funds, the borrowing of Eurodollars, borrowing from the Federal Reserve, the sale of commercial paper by a bank-related subsidiary, the issuance of banker's acceptances, the direct sale of loan participations, and the use of loan and security repurchase agreements. The development of liability management as a liquidity management technique has enabled banks to reduce their holdings of secondary reserve assets. Banks, primarily located in money market centers, now count on meeting part of their liquidity needs by bidding for funds in the money market.

Which Approach Is Best?

Given the traditional secondary reserve management approach to providing for liquidity, and the more recent emphasis on the liability management technique, the obvious question is, which approach is best? The approach suggested here for nonmoney market banks is that they hold secondary reserve assets at least equal to expected liquidity needs over the next twelve months. Within this time horizon, a bank has some degree of flexibility as to the type and maturities of secondary reserve assets to hold. If actual liquidity needs prove to be greater than those planned for, the bank can resort to one of the liability management techniques for providing supplementary liquidity, or it may sell securities from its long-term investment portfolio.

Money market banks and aggressive regional banks may deviate somewhat from this rule and rely more on liability management to provide needed liquidity. Too much reliance on liability management as a source of liquidity by too many banks, at the same time that the Federal Reserve is attempting to effect a tight-money policy, however, may lead to liquidity crises.

Liquidity Management in Perspective

During the contractionary phase of the economic cycle, banks tend to be surfeited with liquidity. Even seasonal liquidity needs are swamped by the surplus liquidity created during a cyclical downturn. Therefore, the objective for banks during the contractionary phase is essentially how to employ their excess funds. On the other hand, the liquidity manager's greatest challenge comes in the expansionary phase of the cycle. Experience in recent years has shown that many banks were caught with inadequate liquidity reserves and had to sell securities from their investment portfolio at considerable losses.

Employing the liquidity forecasting technique developed in this chapter, a bank can plan more precisely when to employ excess funds not needed in secondary reserves during a forthcoming economic slowdown. Similarly, the bank using this technique can structure more accurately the amounts and maturities of the secondary reserve assets needed for liquidity during an expected expansionary period. With adequate liquidity planning, the bank's chief loan officer can proceed with more certainty in making loan commitments, and the chief investment officer can employ more effectively funds not needed for loans. Improved liquidity management benefits not only depositors and potential borrowers, but also the bank's shareholders, who stand to receive higher dividends and capital gains if bank earnings increase as the result of more efficient utilization of assets.

Suggestions for Additional Reading

Charnes, A., and Thore, S. "Planning for Liquidity in Financial Institutions." *Journal of Finance* (December 1966), pp. 649–674.

Dill, Arnold. "Liability Management Banking: Its Growth and Impact." Federal Reserve Bank of Atlanta, *Monthly Review* (February 1971), pp. 22–33.

"The Eurodollar Market: The Anatomy of a Deposit and Loan Market." Federal Reserve Bank of Cleveland, *Economic Review* (March 1970), pp. 3–29; (April 1970), pp. 3–28; and (May 1970), pp. 3–14.

Gable, L. G. "Liability Management–An Indictment." *The Journal of Commercial Bank Lending* (August 1974), pp. 2–10.

Klopstock, Fred N. "Euro-Dollars in the Liquidity and Reserve Management of United States Banks." Federal Reserve Bank of New York, *Monthly Review* (July 1968), pp. 130–138.

Knight, Robert E. "An Alternative Approach to Liquidity: Parts I–IV." Federal Reserve Bank of Kansas City, *Monthly Review* (December 1969), pp. 11–21; (February 1970), pp. 11–22; (April 1970), pp. 3–12; (May 1970), pp. 10–18.

Komar, Robert I. "Developing a Liquidity Model." *Journal of Bank Research* (Spring 1970), pp. 38–53.

Lyon, Roger A. "Establishing Bank Liquidity Policies." In William H. Baughn and Charls E. Walker, eds. *The Banker's Handbook*. Homewood, Ill.: Dow Jones-Irwin, 1966, chap. 43.

McKinney, George W., Jr. "Liability Management: Its Cost and Its Uses." *The Bankers Magazine* (Winter 1974), pp. 19–28.

Morrison, George R. *Liquidity Preferences of Commercial Banks*. Chicago: University of Chicago Press, 1968.

Robinson, Roland I. *The Management of Bank Funds*. 2nd ed. New York: McGraw-Hill, 1962, part 2.

Schweitzer, Stuart A. "Bank Liability Management: For Better or For Worse?" Federal Reserve Bank of Philadelphia, *Business Review* (December 1974), pp. 3–12.

———. "Liability Management: Guilty As Charged?" *The Journal of Commerical Bank Lending* (May 1975), pp. 30–36.

Smaistrla, Charles J. "Bank Liquidity—Is the Level Adequate for Future Loan Expansion?" Federal Reserve Bank of Dallas, *Business Review* (May 1976), pp. 7–10.

Throop, Adrian W. "Monetary Policy—A New Emphasis in Regulations Affects Liability Management." Federal Reserve Bank of Dallas, *Business Review* (November 1974), pp. 1–14.

U.S. Bureau of the Census. *The X-11 Variant of the Census Method II Seasonal Adjustment Program.* Technical Paper No. 15, 1967 revision. Washington, D.C.: U.S. Government Printing Office, 1967.

Woodworth, G. Walter, "Bank Liquidity Management." *The Bankers Magazine* (Autumn 1967), pp. 66–78.

———. *The Management of Cyclical Liquidity of Commercial Banks.* Boston: The Bankers Publishing Company, 1967.

———. "Planning Bank Liquidity Need." *The Bankers Magazine* (Summer 1968), pp. 22–32.

PART

IV

Loan Management

CHAPTER

9

Bank Lending: General Considerations

This is the first of six chapters dealing with bank lending. After acquiring adequate fixed assets and meeting their cash or primary reserve requirements, and subject to the constraint of maintaining adequate short-term and long-term liquidity, banks attempt to satisfy the legitimate loan demands in the communities or specialized credit markets that they serve. Any excess funds remaining are placed in investment securities such as Treasuries, agencies, municipals, and corporates. Loans rank ahead of investments in the allocation of assets because they generally have a higher yield and because they facilitate and stimulate local economic development, which enhances the future growth of deposits and loans at the bank.

In this chapter we shall (1) discuss the factors external to a bank that influence the demand for bank loans, (2) consider the basic factors within a bank that determine the size and composition of its loan portfolio, (3) discuss the nature, objectives, and specifications of bank lending policy, and (4) note briefly several of the regulations applicable to bank lending.

Bank Lending: External Considerations

The size and composition of loan demand at an individual bank is a function of many factors external to the bank. These include (1) the size and location of the bank, (2) national economic conditions, (3) local economic conditions, (4) the direction of monetary and fiscal policy, and (5) for some banks, international economic conditions.

Location of the Bank

The location of a bank determines to a great extent the composition of its loan demand. Because large corporations usually are headquartered near money centers and because only large banks have the lending capacity to meet the borrowing needs of these corporate giants, it is expected that the loan portfolios of the money market banks will contain primarily commercial loans. To illustrate, at the end of 1976 commercial and industrial loans at weekly reporting New York banks accounted for 50.2 percent of their total loans outstanding. For regional and small local banks, location also determines to a considerable extent the composition of the commercial loan portfolio. For example, loans to the textile and furniture manufacturing industries comprise a significant part of business loans at the large banks in North Carolina. Similarly, the locational factor also explains why New York banks hold most of the loans outstanding to the securities industry and why loans to farmers constitute most of the credit extended by a rural bank in Kansas.

The character of banking, and hence lending practices, differs among states and within areas in a state. For example, because branch banking is prohibited, Texas banking is characterized by many small- to medium-sized banks. As a result, many large borrowers look to out-of-state banks for their credit requirements. Because many small banks tend to have excess liquidity and many loan demands are met elsewhere, the average loans-to-deposit ratio in Texas is well below the average for the region and nation.

On the other hand, California permits statewide branch banking. With branches in virtually every residential area, California banks have been highly successful in acquiring time and savings deposits from individuals. The banks, in turn, have channeled these stable funds into real estate loans, which, on June 30, 1976, made up 30.5 percent of the total loans outstanding at insured California banks.

Other examples could be cited to substantiate the significance of location for a bank's lending practices. It is important, therefore, that every bank's board of directors recognize and take into account the influence of the locational factor on loan demand and hence the bank's loan portfolio.

National Economic Conditions

The demand for most types of bank loans is related directly to the stage of the business cycle, but with a two- to four-month lag. That is, the demand for bank loans tends to pick up approximately two to four months after the trough in the business cycle and to decline about two to four months after the peak in the cycle. Moreover, the level of interest rates charged for bank loans tends to rise during the expansionary phase and fall during the contractionary phase of the cycle.

The demand for commercial loans is particularly responsive to changes in national economic conditions. If the economy is expected to enter a boom period, then businesses would have a greater demand for funds to finance long-term working capital needs. On the other hand no firm wants to be caught expanding its capacity or increasing production if the economy is heading into a slump. Consequently, commercial loan demand tends to contract during recessions.

Real estate and consumer installment loans also are influenced by national economic conditions. Both commercial and residential construction are stimulated by rising income and employment and are dampened during recessions when growth in these factors abates. Similarly, consumers tend to add to installment debt during economic expansions and reduce this debt when economic activity slows down.

Local Economic Conditions

Sometimes the level of economic activity in the various sections of the country does not parallel that for the nation as a whole. For example, during recent years, the southeastern section of the United States has tended to grow more rapidly than the national average. As a result, banks in this area have experienced a sustained growth in the demand for credit. On the other hand, from time to time in the Pacific Northwest, economic growth has been retarded and unemployment has been higher than the national average primarily because of shutdowns and cutbacks in the aerospace industry. Consequently, the demand for bank credit has reflected this weakness in the local economy.

Direction of Monetary and Fiscal Policy

The demand for bank loans and the willingness of bankers to extend credit is conditioned by expectations with respect to the direction of monetary and fiscal policy. Sophisticated corporate managers know that monetary and fiscal policy are an important determinant of the level of economic activity and hence the demand for their product. If monetary and fiscal policy are expected to be expansionary, then some borrowers would reduce their bank credit requests in anticipation of lower interest rates in the future. On the other hand, the expectation of a tight-money policy would cause some borrowers with pressing credit needs to step up their loan requests in anticipation of higher interest rates and a reduced availability of credit during an impending tight-money period.

Bank lending officers typically become more willing to grant loan requests when the outlook is for an expansionary monetary or fiscal policy and less enthusiastic about granting credit if a counterexpectation prevails. This procyclical reaction on the part of bankers stems largely from their knowledge that there are fewer loan defaults during periods when monetary and fiscal policy are stimulative and more loan defaults during periods of contraction when some businesses and individuals fall into bankruptcy.

International Economic Conditions

International economic conditions have an important bearing on commercial loan demand for those firms with foreign subsidiaries or for whom exports constitute a significant part of output. Frequently, the pace of economic activity in foreign nations differs from that in the United States. Commercial loan demand for American businesses active in foreign markets would reflect these conditions to some extent.

Bank Lending: Internal Considerations

Within a bank, there are a number of factors that determine the size, composition, and maturity of a bank's loan portfolio. These include (1) fixed and other asset requirements; (2) legal and working reserve requirements; (3) size of cash items in the process of collection; (4) short-term and long-term liquidity requirements; (5) capital adequacy; (6) size, maturity, composition, and cost of the various sources of funds; and (7) competency of the bank's staff.

Fixed and Other Asset Requirements

The volume of funds available for the loan portfolio is reduced by the amount of fixed and other assets the bank must hold. The first use of bank funds is to acquire those fixed assets necessary for the conduct of banking. At the end of 1976, 1.7 percent of the assets of insured banks consisted of "bank premises, furniture and fixtures, and other assets representing bank premises." In addition, these banks had "other assets" in addition to cash assets, loans, and securities, comprising 9.3 percent of total assets.

Legal and Working Reserve Requirements

The next constraint on a bank's potential lending ability is the amount of required and working reserves that the bank must hold. The volume of required reserves is determined by the applicable reserve requirements and the composition of deposits and other liabilities subject to reserve requirements. The level of working reserve requirements depends on the amount of deposit withdrawals and loan demands that bank management believes is imminent and on the amount of correspondent balances necessary to compensate other banks for services rendered. At the end of 1976, insured banks held $81.9 billion, or 8.1 percent, of their assets in currency and coin, reserves with Federal Reserve banks, and balances at other U.S. and foreign banks.

Cash Items in Process of Collection

By far the largest nonearning asset that banks have is cash items in the process of collection. At the close of 1976, these items totaled $48.4 billion, or 4.8 percent, of the assets of insured banks. To the extent that a bank can reduce its cash items in the process of collection through efficient handling procedures, more funds are available for allocation to loans and other earning assets.

Short-Term and Long-Term Liquidity Requirements

The next priority in the use of bank funds is to provide for short- and long-term liquidity requirements. As we saw in Chapter 8, most banks hold short-term assets such as Treasury, agency, and municipal securities and federal funds sold to meet the majority of these liquidity requirements and rely only marginally on liability management to satisfy their liquidity needs. At the end of 1976, insured banks held approximately $37.0 billion, or 3.7 percent of their total assets in Treasury issues with one year or less to maturity and approximately $50.4 billion, or 5.0 percent, of their total assets in Treasury securities with maturities of from one to five years.

Capital Adequacy

The primary purpose of a bank's capital is to demonstrate its ability to absorb unanticipated losses on its assets. With a larger cushion of capital, the bank can hold more loans relative to short- and intermediate-term investments or hold more longer-term loans such as commercial loans and mortgages.

As we saw in Chapter 6, only the Federal Reserve examiners emphasize fixed ratios of capital to the various bank assets in their evaluation of capital adequacy for state member banks. In the last analysis, examiners for each of the three federal banking regulatory agencies consider many aspects of a bank's operations in judging its capital adequacy. For those banks examined under the Federal Reserve's fixed capital requirements, the amount of capital places a definite constraint on both the types and maturity of loans in the bank's portfolio. Even without the emphasis on capital ratios by the Federal Reserve examiners, most bankers are quite sensitive about the size of their capital position relative to risk assets.[1]

Size, Cost, and Maturity Composition of the Various Sources of Funds

The size of a bank's loan portfolio is a function of the bank's ability to acquire funds through the various liability management techniques. As we have noted, a bank should attempt to acquire funds up to the point where the marginal cost of the last dollar acquired is equal to the marginal return from the last dollar loaned or invested. Large banks, of course, have greater flexibility in practicing liability management than small banks.

The types and maturities of loans in a bank's portfolio also are determined, in part, by the maturity composition of the bank's deposits and other liabilities. Banks tend to match short-term liabilities with short-term assets and long-term liabilities with long-term assets. Prior to the Great Depression, banks made primarily short-term commercial and agricultural loans because their liabilities consisted largely of demand deposits. Over the years, as time and savings deposits increased as a percentage of total deposits, banks have stepped up their acquisition of longer-term commercial loans, consumer installment loans, and mortgage loans.

The use of asset allocation plans by some banks is a recognition of the relationship between the size, cost, and maturity composition of a bank's liabilities and its assets. Essentially, these programs involve allocating each source of bank funds among the various asset categories. The short-term and volatile sources of funds are matched with cash and short-term loans and securities, while the more stable sources such as long-maturity CDs are allocated to long-term loans and invest-

[1]Donald R. Hodgman, *Commercial Bank Loan and Investment Policy* (Champaign, Ill.: University of Illinois, Bureau of Economic and Business Research, 1963), pp. 93–96.

ments. Some banks have developed elaborate asset allocation models that can be simulated on a computer.[2]

The principal advantage of developing and using a bank asset allocation program is that it provides a useful framework for evaluating the profitability of alternative sources of funds. In addition, some banks use asset allocation models to determine their deposit liquidity requirements. However, liquidity needs for individual categories of deposits vary widely over time; therefore, the estimation of a bank's liquidity requirements perhaps is handled best through the use of the aggregate method suggested in Chapter 8.

Competency of the Bank's Loan Officers

The competency of a bank's loan officers to make and supervise various types of loans is an important determinant of both the size and composition of a bank's loan portfolio. For example, loans comprise a below-average percentage of assets at some banks because they do not have enough experienced officers to develop the potential loan volume in the bank's market area. Other banks have a below-average ratio of commercial or mortgage loans because of a lack of expertise in making these types of loans. If a bank's officers make loans they are not qualified to evaluate or supervise, the bank is exposing itself to unnecessary risk. As an illustration, in the late 1960s, a number of banks suffered significant losses because they rushed into the credit-card business with few, if any, officers experienced in granting this type of consumer credit. Another example would be the large amount of bank losses recently on real estate and construction loans that resulted to a considerable extent from inexperienced officers making these types of loans.

Bank Loan Policy

Nature and Objectives

Given the many external and internal considerations influencing bank lending, it is important that every bank have a *written loan policy*, which serves as a set of guidelines covering every major aspect of the lending function. The primary objective of bank loan policy is to specify the types of loans and the terms on those loans that will benefit both the communities the bank serves and the bank itself.

[2]For a discussion of several of these models, see Kalman J. Cohen and Fredrick S. Hammer, *Analytical Methods in Banking* (Homewood, Ill.: Richard D. Irwin, 1966), chaps. 2–5.

Specifications

Specifications in a typical loan policy include (1) the officer with general supervisory authority over bank lending; (2) the lending limits of individual officers, the officers' loan committee, and the directors' loan committee; (3) the types of loans that are considered desirable and undesirable by the bank; and (4) the interest rate and fee schedule for each type of loan the bank seeks to make.

Steps in Formulation

The first step in formulating a bank's loan policy is for the directors to define the market area the bank should serve and the bank's market share and profit objectives. Second, based on these parameters, the bank's executive officers determine the types of loans that will enable the bank best to serve its customers and achieve its market share and profit objectives. Third, the board of directors must approve the policy. Finally, the policy must be communicated to all loan officers and to those customers that it affects. It is important that a bank's loan policy is reviewed and modified, if necessary, at least every quarter or in response to major changes in economic conditions.

Regulation of Bank Lending

Besides the external and internal considerations that influence the total and composition of a bank's loan portfolio, there are also a plethora of legal restrictions spelled out in law and the regulations of the various banking agencies. In addition, the comments and suggestions of bank examiners play an important role in shaping bank lending policies. There is a need for the regulation of bank lending and it is important that all bankers understand the restrictions imposed by the banking authorities.

Need for Regulation

The need for the regulation of bank lending stems from the concern of Congress and the regulatory authorities for the protection of depositors. The public holds demand and time deposits in banks because it has confidence that their funds are safe. This creates for banks a fiduciary responsibility to these depositors. In addition, banks have a responsibility to their shareholders to earn an adequate return on their equity investment. This dual responsibility requires that bank management balance safety and liquidity against income and risk in making its lending and investment decisions. The principal reasons for the banking collapse during the Great Depression were that many banks had acquired risky loans and investments in striving for higher income and had forgotten about their responsibility to their depositors for maintaining liquidity and safety of funds. The primary aim of the Banking Act of 1933 was to enhance bank liquidity and depositor safety by placing restrictions on the amount and types of loans that banks make.

Some Specific Regulations

Loan regulations applicable to national banks are issued by the Comptroller of the Currency and the Federal Reserve; loan regulations applicable to state member banks are issued by the Federal Reserve and the various states; lending activities of state nonmember insured and noinsured banks are issued by the FDIC and the various states. Several important regulations that apply to national banks and state member banks are shown below.

The 10 Percent Rule. For national banks, one of the most important loan restrictions limits the total credit of a national bank to any person, partnership, association, or corporation to an amount equal to 10 percent of the bank's capital stock and surplus. For purposes of this calculation, undivided profits, reserve for loan losses,[3] valuation reserve for securities, and reserve for contingencies are capital accounts includable under the heading of surplus. There are a large number of detailed interpretations and exceptions to the 10 percent rule. For example, there are exceptions for loans secured by goods in shipment or U.S. obligations.

Loans to Executive Officers. For member banks, the Federal Reserve's Regulation O specifies a $30,000 limitation on loans to executive officers to finance the purchase of a residence.[4] In addition, executive officers also may borrow up to $10,000 to finance the college education of their children. Other extensions of credit to these officers may not exceed $5,000 at any one time.

Interest Regulations

National banking laws limit the interest rate that national banks may charge on loans to the rate permitted by the state in which the bank is located, or to a rate 1 percent in excess of the Federal Reserve discount rate on ninety-day commercial paper, whichever is greater. When no

[3]From the reserve for loan losses is subtracted the amount of tax that would be payable with respect to the tax-free portion of the reserve if such portion were transferred from the reserve.

[4]Executive officers usually include the chairman of the board, the president, every vice-president, the cashier, and secretary of the bank.

rate is fixed by state law, a rate of 7 percent may be substituted in the above general rule.

Suggestions For Additional Reading

The American Bankers Association. *A Guide To Developing a Written Lending Policy*. Washinton, D.C.: American Bankers Association, 1973.

Burns, Joseph E. "Compensation Balance Requirements Integral to Bank Lending." Federal Reserve Bank of Dallas, *Business Review* (February 1972), pp. 1–8.

Cohen, Kalman J., and Hammer, Frederick S. *Analytical Methods in Banking*. Homewood, Ill.: Richard D. Irwin, 1966, part 2.

Eckford, Jason I., Jr. "The Role of the Loan Committee." *Bulletin of the Robert Morris Associates* (June 1967), pp. 32–38.

Flechsig, Theodore G. "Banking Market Structure and Performance: A Statistical Study of Factors Affecting Rates on Bank Loans." Wahington, D.C.: Board of Governors of the Federal Reserve System, 1965.

Hardwick, Leo P. "Does Banking Really Need a Prime Rate?" *The Bankers Magazine* (Winter 1972), pp. 45–51.

Hayes, Douglas A. *Bank Lending Policies: Domestic and International*. Ann Arbor, Mich.: University of Michigan, Bureau of Business Research, 1971, chaps. 1–4 and 10.

Hodgman, Donald R. *Commercial Bank Loan and Investment Policy*. Champaign, Ill.: University of Illinois, Bureau of Economic and Business Research, 1963, chaps. 2–5.

Janssen, Christian T. L. "The Case for the Compensating Fee." *The Bankers Magazine* (Summer 1969), pp. 43–46.

La Porte, Anne Marie. "ABC's of Figuring Interest." Federal Reserve Bank of Chicago, *Business Conditions* (September 1973), pp. 3–11.

Machara, W. F. "The ABC's of the Prime Rate." Federal Reserve Bank of Atlanta, *Monthly Review* (July 1974), pp. 100–105.

Maloane, Robert B. "Written Loan Policies." *The Journal of Commercial Bank Lending* (June 1976), pp. 18–24.

Merris, Randall. "The Prime Rate." Federal Reserve Bank of Chicago, *Business Conditions* (April 1975), pp. 3–12.

Mott, Hubert C. "Establishing Criteria and Concepts for a Written Credit Policy." *The Journal of Commercial Bank Lending* (April 1977), pp. 2–16.

Polakoff, Murray E., and Budin, Morris. *The Prime Rate*. Chicago: Association of Reserve City Bankers, 1973.

Preel, Michael J. "Index-Linked Loans: Parts I–II." Federal Reserve Bank of Kansas City, *Monthly Review* (September–October 1971), pp. 12–19; (November 1971), pp. 9–19.

CHAPTER

10

Credit Analysis

In Chapter 9, some of the important external and internal factors that influence bank lending in general were discussed. It is now appropriate to focus on those considerations that influence the decision to grant credit to a business enterprise.[1] The process of investigating and evaluating the factors that influence the bank's decision to extend credit is termed *credit analysis.*

A firm's application for bank credit is made by its controller or other financial officer. A bank loan officer then will have the responsibility to obtain the necessary statements and most of the information required in the loan application. The application then is forwarded by the loan officer to the bank's credit department for an analysis and recommendation. When this process is completed, it is the responsibility of

[1]The considerations that influence the decision to extend credit to an individual are discussed in Chapter 13.

the loan officer or loan committee (in the case of large loans) to make the final decision whether or not to approve the loan.

In this chapter, we shall (1) explore the nature and sources of the risks faced by business borrowers and hence their creditors; (2) note the relationship between the credit risk and credit analysis; (3) consider some of the important factors relative to the principals, business, and industry that are investigated in connection with a business credit request; (4) look briefly at the techniques involved in the evaluation of financial statements; (5) note some of the principal financial ratios used to measure the liquidity, profitability, and debt-carrying capacity of a firm; (6) consider some of the financial forecasting techniques employed to evaluate a firm's ability to pay its obligations; (7) examine the sources of business credit information at both the firm and industry level; and (8) conclude with the organization and functions of a bank credit department.

Sources and Types of Business Risks

Risk may be defined as the possibility of loss.[2] A loss may take the form of a decrease in income, an increase in expenses, or a reduction in assets. When a loan is made to a firm, the lender, in effect, becomes a "partner" with the company and, as such, is exposed to all the risks to which the company is exposed. Credit analysis involves, in large part, the identification and evaluation of the sources and types of risks that borrowers and hence lenders face.

Sources of Business Risks

Social. A firm may suffer losses and have to default or delay payment on loans because of actions of people that adversely affect it. Theft, vandalism, arson, riots, strikes, and accidents are the principal business contingencies of social origin.

Physical. A firm also may sustain losses from sources that are of a physical origin. These sources of risk include fire, floods, drought, tornadoes, hurricanes, lightning, rain, hail, landslides, and earthquakes.

Economic. Finally, businesses are exposed to the risks that result from fluctuations in economic activity. The ability of most firms to discharge their financial obligations is lessened in one way or another when the economy suffers a recession or depression and income and employ-

[2]A more general definition of risk also includes the possibility of a gain. However, bank credit analysis ordinarily is concerned only with the possibility of loss.

ment decline. Similarly, many firms stand to be affected adversely during periods of inflation.

Types of Business Risks

Personal Risks. A firm may suffer a serious loss through the premature death or disability of a key employee. In addition, a business is exposed to personal risks when it accepts that part of the death or disability risk of other employees transferred to it under workmen's compensation laws or by employment contracts.

Property Risks. Businesses lose billions of dollars' worth of property annually. The sources of these losses are social, physical, or economic. The loss of property may impair the ability of a firm to repay its loans.

Liability Risks. Like individuals, firms are liable to others for bodily injury or property damage. This liability could arise from the activities of employees and agents as well as the products and services the firm sells. Obviously, a large award under a liability suit could undermine the solvency of a business and thus its ability to discharge its financial obligation.

The Credit Risk and Credit Analysis

The Nature and Sources of the Credit Risk

The possibility of loss to a lender through default is termed the *credit risk*. When a lender extends credit, it is giving the borrower money to use now in exchange for the promise to repay money in the future. The lender, of course, expects repayment on schedule unless the borrower is either (1) unable or (2) unwilling to discharge his obligation. These two factors are the sources of the credit risk.

The Nature and Objective of Business Credit Analysis

The objective of business credit analysis is to evaluate the sources of the credit risk that the bank assumes, that is, the firm's willingness and ability to repay a loan in the future. An evaluation of a company's expected willingness to repay debt involves primarily an investigation of its past willingness to repay its obligations. It also entails the investigation of the personal financial condition and business dealings of the firm's principal officers. The basic presumption is that people who have demonstrated a willingness to meet their obligations in the past and who have a history of honesty in dealings will continue to exhibit these characteristics in the future.

The determination of a firm's expected ability to repay a loan entails an evaluation of the possible risks to which it might be exposed, and an analysis of the company's past and *pro forma* statements of income and condition. The techniques of credit analysis are discussed later in this chapter.

Methods of Handling the Credit Risk

Every loan involves credit risk. After the credit analyst has evaluated the magnitude and sources of this risk, the next step is for the bank lending officer to determine the best approach to handling the loan request. The area of risk management affords several methods of dealing with risk that banks may apply to the management of the credit risk. These methods include (1) avoidance, (2) loss prevention and control, and (3) transfer.

Avoidance. The first alternative open to a bank is to avoid the credit risk by declining the loan request. This would come about if, given the interest rate and other fees that may be charged, the chance of loss on the loan is too great to justify assumption of the risk, even after the bank has used every technique to eliminate, control, or transfer the risk.

Loss Prevention and Control. If the bank decides to assume the credit risk (and every loan involves a degree of credit risk), it may be only upon the condition that the firm agrees to certain provisions designed to prevent and control loss to the bank. For example, the bank might specify that the borrower maintain a certain ratio of current assets to liabilities, restrict dividends, and limit additional borrowing. These provisions are designed to enhance the borrower's ability to repay the loan on schedule. Periodic visits with the borrower by the bank lending officer also are an important part of loss prevention and control.

Transfer. Closely associated with loss prevention and control is the technique of risk transfer, which involves, in the case of a lender, shifting all or part of the credit risk to a third party or to the borrower. For example, the requirements that the borrower have a cosigner, purchase credit life insurance, maintain adequate property and casualty insurance or post collateral result in a transfer of all or part of the credit risk from the lender.

Investigation and Analysis of the Principals, Business, and Industry

A significant part of business credit analysis involves the consideration of nonfinancial factors such as the background and experience of the principals, the general image and operation of the business, and the characteristics of the industry with which the business credit is associated.[3]

Background and Experience of the Principals

The credit analyst must determine who owns and operates the business. What are their business reputations? Do they have a record of bankruptcies, fraud, or fires? What are their personal worths, other interests, and habits? The obvious purpose of these questions is to determine the extent of the moral and morale hazards underlying the credit risk associated with a proposed loan.[4]

It is important also to know the age distribution of the principals. This enables the credit analyst to evaluate the business's vulnerability to the risks of death or disability of key personnel. In addition, the age distribution of the principals is an indication of their experience and judgment. Ideally, a business needs a blend of the aggressiveness and energy associated with youthful managers and the wisdom and experience of older managers.

General Image and Operation of the Business

The general image and reputation of a business is an indication of its ability to succeed in the future. In this regard, the credit analyst is interested in how the firm deals with its customers, suppliers, and creditors. Does it stand behind its products and services? Does it engage in misleading advertising? Does it pay its suppliers on time? What is its debt payment record with banks and other lending institutions?

Understanding the nature and method of operation of a business is a preliminary step, of course, to the evaluation of its creditworthiness. Here the credit analyst must determine the basic functions performed by the business. Is it primarily a manufacturer, wholesaler, or retailer? What is the degree of vertical or horizontal integration? What are the markets for the firm's products or services? How does the quality of the company's products or services compare with those of other firms within the industry? What are the firm's normal buying and selling terms? Are there seasonal factors involved on either the buying or selling side of the business? If employees are unionized, what are the terms of the labor contract? What is the company's reputation with its employees? What is the condition of the firm's plant and equipment?

[3]Much of the discussion in this section is based on the The American Bankers Association, "A Banker's Guide to Commercial Loan Analysis" (Washington, D.C.: The American Bankers Association, 1977), chap. 2.

[4]The *moral hazard* results from dishonesty or lack of integrity; the *morale hazard* emanates from an attitude of carelessness and lack of concern.

Industry Characteristics

In order to evaluate properly a company's operations, the credit analyst must become familiar with the characteristics of the industry with which the firm is principally associated. This task has become particularly complicated in recent years as more companies evolve into multiproduct and multinational firms.

The credit analyst should determine whether the demand for the industry's product is increasing, decreasing, or stable in relation to growth in gross national product. To what extent is demand affected by recessions? What is the market structure of the industry? To what extent has the industry been able to pass along cost increases in the form of higher prices? What has been the trend in profits? Have changes in technology had an important impact on the demand for the industry's product or its capital requirements? Once the answer to these and similar questions have been obtained, the credit analyst has a basis for a more meaningful appraisal of the relative strengths and weaknesses of the firm.

Evaluation of Financial Statements

Financial statements are the principal source of financial data and information about a prospective business borrower. A firm is usually required to submit (1) statements of condition, (2) income statements, and (3) sources and uses of funds statements for the last three to five years of its operations.[5]

Because financial statements provide vital information about a firm's expected ability to repay its obligations, both the credit analyst and the loan officer must be confident of their accuracy. Firms generally are required to submit statements prepared by a CPA firm or at least by reliable outside accountants. In addition, credit analysts and loan officers are interested in the accountant's opinion about the reliability of the statements. A typical unqualified accountant's opinion would indicate that the statements "present fairly the consolidated financial position of the XYZ Corporation and its subsidiaries on December 31, 1977, 1976 and 1975, in conformity with generally accepted accounting principles consistently applied." A qualified opinion would be rendered if a firm's statements were prepared from unaudited records or if an audit of the firm's books indicate a departure from generally accepted accounting principles. During recent years, many questionable accounting practices have been devised by firms that wish to make their financial condition or earnings appear better than they really are. Hence credit analysts and loan officers are paying ever closer attention

[5]Detailed discussions of each of these statements are provided in most introductory textbooks on accounting and business finance.

to the accountant's opinion as they evaluate a firm's financial statements.

Statement of Condition

A *statement of condition* (balance sheet) reports the assets, liabilities, and owner's equity of a firm as of a given date. Assets, of course, are what the company owns; liabilities are what the firm owes. Assets minus liabilities equals owner's equity, which measures the "cushion" that creditors rely on to protect their interest in the firm should it fail.

Credit analysts usually begin their appraisal of a firm's statements of condition by evaluating each account listed. On the asset side, the credit analyst needs to determine, in particular, the age and quality of the firm's notes and accounts receivable, inventory, and fixed assets. Are any of these assets pledged to secure notes or accounts payable? Does the firm value its inventory on a "first-in, first-out" (FIFO) or a "last-in, first-out" (LIFO) method? What methods of depreciation does the firm employ? On the liabilities side, the credit analyst's inquiry relates primarily to the firm's notes and accounts payable. He needs to know the terms and to whom these obligations are owed. Are any of these debts past due? The answers to these and many other questions may not be revealed directly in the statement of condition but may be contained in footnotes, supporting schedules, exhibits, or in the firm's records. The firm's controller or accountant usually is called on to provide supplementary information after the credit analyst has made an initial review of the financial statements submitted.

Income Statement

An *income statement* reports a firm's sources of revenue, the expenses incurred in earning that revenue, and net income (revenue less expenses and applicable federal and state income taxes) for a period of time such as a month, quarter, or year. Since a major source of funds to repay long-term debt is a firm's net income, income statements covering several years reveal much about a firm's expected ability to liquidate these obligations. In order to make an accurate appraisal of this ability, the credit analyst prefers to have a detailed listing of the firm's important income and expense items.

A widely used technique to analyze income statements is to convert each revenue source into a percentage of total revenue and each expense and profit margin item into a percentage of net revenue (total revenue less returns, allowances, and discounts). When this is accomplished for income statements covering several periods, the credit analyst is able to analyze the data for trends in the various revenue sources, expense items, and profit margins. This evaluation should provide considerable insight into managerial efficiency and also the firm's expected profitability.

Sources and Uses of Funds Statement

Data from a firm's statements of condition, income statements, and statements of changes in owners' equity may be used to prepare a *statement of the sources and uses of funds* during a particular period. Sources of funds are represented by (1) a decrease in any asset account, (2) an increase in any liability account, and (3) an increase in owners' equity due to retained earnings or from the sale of additional stock. In addition, depreciation, which is a noncash charge to income, is considered as a source of funds. Uses of funds are represented by (1) an increase in any asset account, (2) a decrease in any liability account, and (3) a decrease in owners' equity such as through dividends, capital distributions, or losses.

A sources and uses of funds statement is useful to the credit analyst in several ways. First, it permits him to discern imbalances in the firm's various sources and uses of funds. Potential problems that might result from too great a reliance on short-term financing, an excessive investment in inventory or accounts receivable, or an overgenerous dividend policy may be spotted readily through analysis of a sources and uses of funds statement.

Financial Ratio Analysis

The techniques of credit analysis just described involved absolute, not relative, amounts in the firm's financial statements. *Financial ratio analysis* entails comparisons of relative amounts, such as the ratio of current assets to current liabilities (the current ratio). In this section we shall see how to use financial ratios and note the four principal categories of financial ratios: (1) liquidity ratios, (2) capital ratios, (3) profitability ratios, and (4) interest coverage ratios. (See Table 10-1.)

Use of Financial Ratios

Financial ratios for a firm are used (1) to make interyear comparisons, (2) to make comparisons with those of other firms and industry averages, and (3) as inputs for models to predict business failure and for numerical credit scoring systems for commercial loans.

Interyear Comparisons. Interyear comparisons of financial ratios permit the credit analyst to determine quickly whether a firm's liquidity, profitability, efficiency, or debt-carrying capacity has improved, declined, or remained stable. By analyzing financial ratios

Table 10-1
Summary of Ratios Used in Credit Analysis

A. *Liquidity Ratios*

1. Current Ratio $= \dfrac{\text{current assets}}{\text{current liabilities}}$

2. Acid Test or Quick Ratio $= \dfrac{\text{current assets—inventories}}{\text{current liabilities}}$

3. Average Collection Period Ratio $= \dfrac{\text{receivables} \times 360}{\text{annual credit sales}}$

4. Inventory Turnover Ratio $= \dfrac{\text{cost of goods sold}}{\text{average inventory}}$

B. *Capital Ratios*

1. Debt-to-Equity Ratio $= \dfrac{\text{total debt}}{\text{owners' equity}}$

2. Long-term Debt to Total Capital Ratio $= \dfrac{\text{long-term debt}}{\text{total capital}}$

C. *Profitability Ratios*

1. Gross Profit Margin $= \dfrac{\text{sales} - \text{cost of goods sold}}{\text{sales}}$

2. Net Profit Margin $= \dfrac{\text{net profits}}{\text{sales}}$

3. Rate of Return on Common Equity $= \dfrac{\text{net profits} - \text{preferred stock dividends}}{\text{owners equity} - \text{par value of preferred stock}}$

4. Rate of Return on Assets $= \dfrac{\text{net profits}}{\text{total assets} - \text{intangible assets}}$

D. *Coverage Ratios*

1. Interest Coverage Ratio $= \dfrac{\text{income before interest \& taxes}}{\text{interest charges}}$

2. Total Debt Coverage Ratio $= \dfrac{\text{income before interest \& taxes}}{\text{interest} + \text{principal charges } (1/1 - \text{combined state and federal tax rates})}$

from a number of years, potential problem areas in the firm might be recognized and investigated.

Industry Comparisons. It also is helpful sometimes to compare a firm's financial ratios with those of firms of similar size in the industry and with industry averages. These comparisons should reveal much about the company's relative strengths and weaknesses.

Inputs in Financial Models. Recently, several models have been developed that use financial ratios to predict business failure and hence creditworthiness among samples of firms.[6] In addition, a number of banks use financial ratios as part of numerical credit scoring systems that are employed daily in processing small commercial loan applications.[7] Under a numerical credit scoring system, points are awarded based on credit factors such as age of business, successive years of increased profit, and the level of debt-to-equity ratio. For example, under one bank's credit scoring system, a firm with a 7-to-1 debt-to-equity ratio is assigned 5 points, while a firm with a 2-to-1 debt-to-equity is given 25 points. The points awarded for each ratio or factor evaluated are added up and if the total points exceed a certain standard, the loan is granted with only a minimum of further investigation. If the point totals fall within the "gray area," additional time must be spent investigating the firm's creditworthiness. Finally, for those firms that fail to achieve the minimum number of points under the credit scoring system, the bank loan officer must explain that their applications are unacceptable. An effective credit scoring system for commercial loan applications can save credit analysts and loan officers a considerable amount of time and also reduce losses.

Liquidity Ratios

Liquidity ratios are an indication of a firm's present and expected ability to pay short-term debt from the conversion of short-term assets such as inventory and notes and accounts receivable into cash.

Current Ratio. Perhaps the most commonly used measure of liquidity is the *current ratio* (current assets divided by current liabilities). If a firm's current ratio is below the industry average, this indicates that the firm could experience some difficulty in paying its short-term obligations.

Acid-Test or Quick Ratio. A major shortcoming of the current ratio is that inventory, which in some cases may be rather illiquid, is included in current assets. The *acid-test or quick ratio* (current assets less inventories divided by current liabilities) is a better measure of a firm's ability to cover its current liabilities.

Average Collection Period Ratio. If accounts receivable comprise a significant amount of current assets, the credit analyst will want to calculate the *average collection period ratio* (receivables times 360 days

[6]For a summary of five of these models, see Robert O. Edmister, "Financial Ratios and Credit Scoring for Small Business Loans," *The Journal of Commercial Bank Lending*, 54 (September 1971), pp. 10–23.

[7]For an explanation of one of these systems, see Robert P. Abate, "Numerical Scoring Systems for Commercial Loans," *The Journal of Commercial Bank Lending*, 51 (July 1969), pp. 32–36.

divided by annual credit sales). This ratio shows the average number of days that receivables are outstanding. If, for example, the firm's accounts are ordinarily due within thirty days and the average collection period is fifty-one days, this indicates that the firm has difficulty in collecting its receivables and perhaps its obligations in the future.

Inventory Turnover Ratio. Over the years, excessive investment in inventory has led countless firms into bankruptcy. Therefore, credit analysts must examine closely this portion of the firm's current assets. The *inventory turnover ratio* (cost of goods sold divided by average inventory) is a basic measure of the liquidity of inventory. If a firm's inventory turnover ratio has been declining during recent periods or is below the industry average, this may signal difficulties ahead for the firm in paying its short-term debt.

Capital Ratios

Debt-to-Equity Ratio. The *debt-to-equity ratio* (total debt divided by owners' equity)[8] measures the cushion of equity capital available to protect the firm's creditors and is an indication of the firm's ability to borrow additional short- or long-term funds.

Long-Term Debt to Total Capitalization Ratio. Further insight into a firm's creditworthiness is provided by the *long-term debt to total capitalization* (long-term debt plus owners equity) *ratio*. This ratio is particularly relevant to bank credit analysis when a term loan is under consideration.

Profitability Ratios

Profitability ratios measure the firm's profits in relation to sales, assets, and common equity.

Gross Profit Margin. A firm's *gross profit margin* (sales less cost of goods sold divided by sales) reflects the firm's profit on sales after deducting for cost of goods sold and hence is a general measure of the firm's production efficiency. During inflationary periods, this ratio takes on greater meaning because it is an indication of how well a firm can pass along cost increases by raising its prices.

Net Profit Margin. *Net profit margin* (net profits after taxes divided by sales) is a measure of overall efficiency. To calculate net profits, deduc-

[8]In this ratio, owners' equity is usually net of intangible assets such as goodwill.

tions are made from gross profits for selling, administrative, interest, depreciation, and other expenses as well as for federal and state income taxes. A comparison of the current spread between a firm's gross and net profit margins with that in previous years and with those of other firms in the same industry should reveal much about management's ability to control these types of expenses.

Rate of Return on Common Equity. *Rate of return on common equity* (net profits after taxes less preferred stock dividends divided by owners' equity less the par value of preferred stock) is probably the best measure of a firm's profitability. A firm whose rate of return on common equity is above the industry average usually is more able to repay its credit obligations.

Rate of Return on Assets. The *rate of return on assets* (net profits after taxes divided by total assets less intangible assets such as goodwill) measures how efficiently the firm uses all its resources and as such is an indication of the firm's ability to employ additional borrowed funds.

Coverage Ratios

Interest Coverage Ratio. The *interest coverage ratio* (income before interest and taxes divided by interest charges) is an indication of a firm's ability to meet the interest payments on its obligations.

Total Debt Coverage Ratio. The *total debt coverage ratio* [income before interest and taxes divided by interest plus principal charges times (1/1–the combined federal and state income tax rates)][9] measures a firm's ability to pay both interest and principal payments. By including in the denominator of this ratio the interest and principal payments on a proposed loan, the credit analyst has some insight into the expected margin of protection.

Financial Projections for Credit Analysis

All the techniques of credit analysis discussed thus far in this chapter have involved the evaluation of a firm's present and past financial condition. Although this analysis is important in determining the creditworthiness of a firm, it must be remembered that the funds to repay a loan are generated in the future primarily from operations or the liqui-

[9]Since interest payments are made with before-tax dollars and principal payments are made with after-tax dollars, it is necessary to adjust the dollars intended for principal payments to a before-tax basis. If the firm's income is subject to a 50 percent federal and a 10 percent state income tax, then before-tax earnings of $500,000 are needed to cover $200,000 in annual principal payments.

dations of assets. Therefore, it is important that the credit analyst evaluate the credit applicant's future operations and financial condition. Depending upon the type of firm and the maturity and purpose of the loan under consideration, five financial statements generally are used to analyze a company's expected financial needs and ability to pay its obligations. These are (1) the cash budget, (2) the *pro forma* income statement, (3) the *pro forma* statement of condition, (4) the *pro forma* sources and uses of funds statement, and (5) the projected cash flow statement.[10]

Cash Budget

A *cash budget* is a statement of a firm's projected cash inflows and outflows over various periods of time. The first major step in the preparation of a firm's cash budget is to forecast cash receipts. This involves forecasting cash sales, revenue from the collection of receivables, and other income usually for each month in the budget period. The second major step is to forecast cash disbursements. Major items under this heading include payroll, inventory, selling and administrative expenses, interest and principal payments on debt, capital outlays, income taxes, and dividends. The third step is to derive the firm's monthly net cash inflow by subtracting monthly cash disbursements from cash receipts. Finally, the monthly net cash inflow is subtracted algebraically from beginning monthly cash balances to derive the ending monthly cash balances.

A cash budget is of greatest value in evaluating applications for short-term loans such as to finance investment in accounts receivable or inventory. A cash budget indicates when the firm should borrow, how much it needs, and when funds are available to repay the loan.

A soundly conceived forecast of sales and collections is the key to the preparation of a reasonably accurate cash budget. Therefore, credit analysts should devote some time to investigating the basis for the sales and collection estimates used in the formulation of the cash budget.

Pro Forma Income Statement

Projected or *pro forma income statements* show a firm's estimated income, expenses, and net income over the periods ahead. Most of the information necessary to prepare a *pro forma* income statement is developed in the process of formulating a cash budget. Therefore, it is a relatively simple materr to arrange estimated sales, expenses, and taxes into statement form.

[10]Detailed explanations of these statements are contained in most elementary accounting and business finance textbooks.

Pro forma income statements permit the credit analyst to evaluate the results of a firm's future operations. Since net income is a primary source of funds to repay intermediate and term loans, the credit analyst should check thoroughly the estimates and relationships within the *pro forma* income statement.

Pro Forma Statement of Condition

Much of the information that is developed in the preparation of a cash budget and *pro forma* income statement may be used to prepare a projected or *pro forma statement of condition* for a date in the future. The projected cash balance is available directly from the cash budget. Accounts receivable on the projected statement date is calculated by subtracting estimated credit collections from the sum of the estimated credit sales for the period and the beginning receivables balance. Projected inventory is derived by subtracting the estimated cost of goods sold from the sum of the beginning inventory and estimated purchases during the period. Projected fixed assets is simply the sum of present fixed assets plus planned investments less depreciation.

On the liabilities side, accounts payable are derived by adding estimated purchases to the present level of accounts payable and subtracting payments made during the period. Depending on whether the firm is engaged in manufacturing or nonmanufacturing, accrued expenses are estimated on the basis of projected production or sales. Accrued taxes are calculated by adding estimated taxes on income earned during the period to the amount owed at the beginning of the period and by subtracting any payments that were made. Finally, changes in owners' equity would be equal to the beginning balance plus net income less dividends paid.

Pro forma statements of condition show the combined effects of a firm's anticipated borrowing and operations on its financial condition during the periods under study. For example, if a short-term loan is used to repay long-term debt, analysis of the firm's next *pro forma* statements of condition probably would show a decline in the company's current and acid-test ratios. In such a case, the *pro forma* statement of condition provides a framework for the credit analyst to spot potential weaknesses and for the loan officer to discuss with management possible corrective actions, such as reduced dividends or capital outlays.

Pro Forma Sources and Uses of Funds Statement

A *pro forma sources and uses of funds statement* is prepared from a *pro forma* statement of condition and a *pro forma* statement of income. The primary value of these statements to the credit analyst is that they show clearly whether there are any imbalances in the sources and uses of funds at a firm during future periods. As such, they are used primarily in the analysis of requests for term loan applications.

Projected Cash Flow Statement

A *projected cash flow statement* shows the funds generated within a firm from net income and depreciation. Some credit analysts might contend that this statement is redundant since these two sources of cash are shown on the *pro forma* income statement. In the case of a term loan request, however, this simple statement does reveal for both the lender and borrower the anticipated cash flow of funds that is available for debt retirement.

Sources of Credit Information

In evaluating the willingness and ability of a prospective business borrower to repay debt, the credit department seeks information about the firm as an operating entity, how it compares with other firms in the industry, and the character of its management. These sources may be classified as providing information about (1) the firm or (2) the industry.

For the Firm

The Firm's Officers. Before submitting the loan request to the credit department for investigation, evaluation, and a recommendation, the loan officer should develop as much credit information as possible during his initial interview with the firm's officials. During this interview, the loan officer (if he does not know already) must inquire as to the history of the company and its principal officers, the nature of the business, past and expected profitability, the degree of competition that the company faces, and whether or not the company has had or anticipates any difficulties in acquiring raw materials, labor, and other essential products or services. The loan officer then should discuss with the company's officials the purpose of the loan and the firm's proposed repayment plans. At the conclusion of the interview, the loan officer should outline any additional information and the statements that the firm must provide the bank. This is also an appropriate time to arrange for a visit to the company.

Bank's Credit Files. After the credit department receives the loan request, financial statements, and other information that the loan officer has obtained, the next source of information is the bank's credit files. If these files are maintained properly, they should contain detailed information about the company's past relationship with the bank, items from newspapers and trade journals, and other bits of data about the firm. Even if the firm is not presently a customer of the bank, an aggressive credit department manager will have a file established if the company is important in the bank's market area.

Financial Statements. The statements of condition and income statement are primary source documents for information about the individual firm. Ideally, these statements should be prepared by a CPA in whom the bank has confidence. The firm should provide these statements for at least three years so that the credit analyst may determine the direction of the firm in terms of efficiency, profitability, and liquidity.[11]

Retail Credit Bureau. An important source of credit information on individuals and, to a lesser extent, on local businesses is the retail credit bureau. These agencies typically are owned cooperatively by the various businesses and lending institutions in a community, but some are owned privately. Retail credit bureaus provide written and telephone reports on the creditworthiness of individuals and firms. In addition, these bureaus issue weekly or bimonthly reports containing information about bankruptcies filed, recordings of real estate mortgages, and other significant happenings that might affect the creditworthiness of local citizens and businesses. This agency may be a valuable source of information on a firm's principal officers.

Dun and Bradstreet, Inc. Most banks rely extensively on Dun and Bradstreet, Inc., for credit information on prospective borrowers. The famous Dun and Bradstreet rating on a firm provides, with the aid of a key, both the estimated net worth and a credit appraisal (high, good, fair, or limited) for companies on which Dun and Bradstreet has adequate information. Besides the rating services, Dun and Bradstreet will issue written credit reports that contain a brief history of a company and its principal officers, the nature of the business, certain financial information, and the results of a check with the firm's suppliers as to their experience with the company.

Other Lenders. Although the individual bank competes vigorously with other banks and financial intermediaries, it is to the mutual benefit of these lenders that they share credit information. For example, from another bank the credit analyst can learn very quickly the borrowing record, average and range of deposits maintained, and sometimes other bits of information about financial strengths or weaknesses of a prospective borrower.

[11]Data from these statements are arranged on "spread sheets," by years, in order to facilitate analysis.

The Firm's Suppliers and Customers. When it is feasible, the credit analyst should contact directly several of the prospective business borrower's suppliers and customers. The firm's suppliers can indicate their payment experience with the company. The firm's customers can provide valuable information on the quality of the company's services or products and insight into the honesty and integrity of the company's management.

Public Records. Public records are a vital source of credit information. Courthouse records show recorded mortgages, recorded lease assignments, bankruptcy or default judgment filings, and tax liens. In most states, the Secretary of State's Office contains recordings of security interest under the Uniform Commercial Code.

For the Industry

The next task for the credit analyst is to compare operating and financial data for the firm under consideration with similar data for other major firms in the industry and with industry averages. In addition, the credit analyst must become familiar with new developments and trends in the industry in order to appraise the ability of the firm to compete in the future. The principal sources of information at the industry level are described below.

Robert Morris Associates Annual Statement Studies. One of the most widely used sources of industry data is the Robert Morris Associates *Annual Statement Studies.*[12] This publication shows, for almost 300 lines of business and for several classes of firm size, the average ratios for major asset, liability, income, and expense items. In addition, a number of average operating ratios are presented.

Moody's and Standard and Poor's. Besides providing up-to-date financial information at the firm level, the publications of Moody's Investors Service and Standard and Poor's Corporation are excellent sources of industry data. In addition, the periodic analysis provided by industry specialists at these firms is especially valuable.

Trade Publications and Journals. In order to research developments in a particular industry, the credit analyst must rely considerably on trade publications and journals. The libraries at larger banks subscribe to most of this literature. Credit analysts at other banks usually depend on local public or university libraries for these publications.

[12]Robert Morris Associates is the national association of bank loan and credit officers.

Government Publications. Over the last twenty years, the volume of government publications has mushroomed. Credit analysts should be alert to the wealth of information about American and foreign industry and trade contained in these documents. The monthly index to these publications is a worthwhile addition to any bank library or credit department.

The Credit Department

The establishment in virtually all medium-sized and large banks of a separate department to perform credit analysis and other related tasks stems from the growth in the number and size of firms to be investigated and evaluated, the increased availability of information on these firms, and the greater skill and sophistication required in credit analysis.

Functions

Typically, five functions are performed in a bank credit department. The first three functions are the essential elements in credit analysis. First, personnel in the credit department collect information from various sources on the past, present, and expected willingness and ability of prospective borrowers to repay their loans. Second, this information is evaluated. Third, based on this evaluation, a recommendation is made to the loan officer or committee responsible for approving or disapproving the loan.

A fourth credit department function involves the maintenance of credit files on present and prospective borrowers. Personnel in the credit department continuously are collecting information about the financial affairs and condition of these firms and individuals from trade publications, newspapers, financial statements, suppliers, and numerous other sources. These files provide valuable information for loan officers who have the responsibility to administer existing loans and for analysts who will be called on to evaluate credit requests in the future.

The fifth function performed in a credit department entails answering the many letter and telephone requests from banks, other financial institutions, and trade credit suppliers who seek credit information on a prospective borrower. No bank can expect to receive credit information from other lenders unless it reciprocates.[13]

[13]Some bank credit departments perform another important function, the training of loan officers. Many bankers believe that a prospective commercial loan officer should have one to two years of experience in credit analysis before assuming responsibility for a loan decision.

Organization

At many money market banks, the credit department is organized along industry lines in order to facilitate data collection and analysis. That is, firms are grouped into industries. Then, usually several related industries are grouped under a division, and there are typically seven to ten divisions within the department. For example, the aerospace, electronics, and light metal fabricating industries might comprise one division.

At medium-sized banks, the credit department may only collect information, maintain the credit files, and answer credit inquiries. The evaluation of credit information is performed by the bank's loan officers.

Most small banks do not have a separate credit department. The collection and evaluation of credit information is performed by the loan officers. Usually credit files are maintained on only the largest borrowers. The few credit inquiries that the bank receives would be handled by the loan officer familiar with the firm or individual under investigation.

Suggestions for Additional Reading

Abate, Robert P. "Numerical Scoring Systems for Commercial Loans." *The Journal of Commercial Bank Lending* (July 1969), pp. 32–36.

The American Bankers Association. "A Banker's Guide to Commercial Loan Analysis." Washington, D.C.: The American Bankers Association, 1977.

——. "Fundamental Principles of Sound Bank Credit." Washington, D.C.: The American Bankers Association.

Baughn, William H., and Walker, Charls, E., eds. *The Banker's Handbook*. Homewood, Ill.: Dow Jones-Irwin, 1966, chaps. 19–23.

Bryan, Lowell L., and Clark, Simon G. McH. *Unbundling Full-Service Banking*. Cambridge, Mass.: Harcomm Associates, 1973.

Edmister, Robert O. "Financial Ratios and Credit Scoring for Small Business Loans." *The Journal of Commercial Bank Lending* (September 1971), pp. 10–23.

Graham, Benjamin, and McGolrick, Charles. *The Interpretation of Financial Statements*. 2nd. rev. ed. New York: Harper & Row, 1964.

Hoeven, James A., and Oldham, Jerome S. "Commercial Loan Profitability—Pricing Analysis." *The Journal of Commercial Bank Lending* (June 1976), pp. 44–57.

Neff, Dennis C., and Reich, Kenneth E. *Customer Profitability Analysis: A Tool for Improving Bank Profits*. Philadelphia,: The Robert Morris Associates, 1972.

The Philadelphia National Bank. "Profitability Analysis of Commercial Customers." Philadelphia: The Philadelphia National Bank, 1965.

CHAPTER

11

Short-Term Business Loans

Traditionally, *short-term business loans,* those with an original maturity of one year or less, have comprised a significant percentage of total bank loans. At the end of March 1977, short-term commercial and industrial loans at 160 weekly reporting banks totaled an estimated 71.0 billion and accounted for 60.7 percent of total commercial and industrial loans outstanding at these institutions.[1]

In this chapter, we shall (1) explore why banks have tended to favor short-term business loans as an outlet for their funds, (2) determine the basic reasons why businesses need short-term loans, (3) consider the advantages of a business borrowing from a bank as opposed to other nonbank lenders, (4) note the typical arrangements associated with unsecured business loans from banks, and (5) examine the principal types of secured business loans.

[1]Commercial and industrial loans at these 160 weekly reporting banks represent about 70 percent of this type of credit outstanding at all commercial banks.

The Commercial Loan Theory of Bank Lending

Prior to the 1930s in this country, most bankers were proponents of the *commercial loan* or *productive credit* theory of bank lending.[2] This theory holds that a bank should make only short-term, self-liquidating loans. By "short term," bankers mean a period only long enough to allow, for example, a borrowing manufacturer to produce and sell his product, a retailer to buy and sell an inventory of goods, or a farmer to plant, harvest, and sell his crops. The term "self-liquidating" means that the loan itself generates the means for repayment. That is, with the loan proceeds, the borrower has the financial means to produce or acquire goods which, when sold, provide the funds to repay the loan. Bankers believed also that they should make only short-term, self-liquidating commercial loans in order to have a dependable source of liquidity to supplement primary reserves. Because deposits were largely demand liabilities, bankers felt that they had to match short-term assets with these short-term obligations. Since the notion of holding a separate category of assets (secondary reserves) to meet anticipated liquidity needs did not originate until the 1930s, when the supply of short-term, high-quality securities (Treasury bills) became readily available, the early bankers were correct in attempting to keep loan maturities short.

Although banks today primarily meet their liquidity requirements by holding secondary reserves and employing the various liability management techniques, the commercial loan theory still has an important influence on bank lending practices. Most bankers consider short-term, self-liquidating loans to business as the preferred type of credit to extend. This is because the credit risk involved with these loans is usually less than that on term loans and is easier to evaluate. In addition, bankers know that repayments from short-term commercial loans are a significant source of funds to meet deposit withdrawals, maturing liabilities, and pressing loan demands.

Why Businesses Need Short-Term Loans

Essentially, a business needs short-term loans when the inflow of funds from cash sales and collection of receivables is not large enough to cover outlays for such items as inventory, operating expenses, debt payments, dividends, and income taxes without dipping into the minimum cash balance the firm wants to maintain. These short-term or seasonal loan requirements are shown in the firm's cash budget, which summarizes expected inflows and outflows of cash usually on a month-

[2] In England, the counterpart to this theory was called the *real-bills doctrine*. A real bill is simply a promissory note or evidence of indebtedness that results from the production, movement, or distribution of real goods.

to-month basis for the next twelve to twenty-four months. During those months when cash needs exceed cash inflow, the business requires short-term financing. On the other hand, when the firm has excess cash, these funds may be invested in money market instruments such as CDs, Treasury bills, commercial paper, or banker's acceptances.

Unsecured short-term loans to firms with superior credit ratings usually are called simply *working capital loans*. Loan proceeds are comingled with other funds and used for a variety of purposes. If the firm does not enjoy a superior credit rating, it probably will have to borrow on a secured basis for its working capital needs. If accounts receivable or inventory is used as security, the loan would be called an *accounts receivable loan* or an *inventory loan*, even though the funds are comingled and used for many purposes.

Advantages of Obtaining Working Capital Loans from Commercial Banks

Commercial banks generally offer several advantages over business finance companies as a source of working capital loans. These may include (1) lower interest costs, (2) unsecured loans, (3) larger loans, (4) reliable source of funds during liquidity crises, (5) advice of industry specialists, and (6) availability of other services.

Lower Interest Rates. Bank interest rates typically are lower than those offered by business finance companies. The principal reason for this is that these lenders obtain a large part of their funds from banks and, in turn, must charge the borrower a rate sufficiently high enough to cover the cost of funds and administrative expenses and to produce a profit. It should be noted that large, well-known, creditworthy firms ordinarily may obtain short-term funds at a rate slightly below the bank prime rate by selling commercial paper in the open market. However, the cost of issuing these securities tends to eliminate much of the interest advantage of commercial paper. In addition, commercial paper cannot be renewed as can a bank loan.

Unsecured Loans. An important advantage to creditworthy business of obtaining working capital loans from banks is that the funds usually can be obtained on an unsecured basis. This eliminates the costs involved with posting and accounting for collateral such as inventory and accounts receivable.

Larger Loans. The lending limits of business finance companies generally are not high enough to permit them to meet the working capital needs of most medium-sized and large businesses. Individually or through loan participations, the large regional and money market banks can supply the working capital needs of any business in America.

Reliable Source of Funds During Liquidity Crises. Another important advantage of banks as a source of working capital is their greater reliability during liquidity crises. When there is such a crisis, as occurred during certain months in 1969–1970 and again in 1973 and 1974, some large firms may be unable to obtain sufficient funds by selling commercial paper. In addition, many other small to medium-sized firms may be unable to secure adequate loans from business finance companies, who themselves find it difficult to borrow from banks or in the open market. In a liquidity crisis, banks generally have a great deal more flexibility in obtaining funds and hence are better able to meet the credit needs of their customers. Banks may obtain funds from the Federal Reserve (which, of course, was established primarily to prevent or mitigate liquidity crises), through the issuance of CDs, in the Eurodollar market, or by employing any of the other liability management techniques available to them. Bankers feel an obligation to take care of their good customers during periods of credit tightness and will find a way somehow to obtain the necessary funds.

Advice of Industry Specialists. As we have seen, most medium-sized and large banks have loan officers who specialize in dealing with firms in a particular industry. As a result, these officers become familiar with the developments and problems within the industry and at individual firms and are able to render valuable financial counseling.

Availability of Other Services. Besides access to financial specialists, most firms tend to rely on banks for their working capital requirements because of the ready availability from banks, or perhaps a holding company subsidiary, or a variety of financial services such as checking accounts, CDs, lockbox services, mortgage loans, wire transfers, trust services, and data processing.

Unsecured Business Loans

Firms of the highest creditworthiness are able to obtain short-term loans on an unsecured basis. Let us examine the characteristics of unsecured business loans.

Line of Credit

A *line of credit* is an informal arrangement whereby a bank extends to a customer the privilege to borrow up to some maximum limit at any time during a period such as a year. Although banks are not legally bound to honor such commitments, they usually do so because customers that can obtain a line of credit ordinarily are highly valuable to the bank. The primary advantage of a line of credit to a customer is that he does not have to go down to the bank to negotiate a loan every time funds are needed. The bank benefits because the customer's financial attachment and loyalty are strengthened.

In return for a line of credit, the customer does not pay a fee, but usually agrees to maintain a compensating balance equal to some percentage of the line. By basing credit lines on deposits, the bank not only tends to gain deposits but also to increase their stability as well. Banks ordinarily require borrowers with lines of credit to submit periodic financial statements. Upon review of these statements, credit lines may be renegotiated and set for another period.

Revolving Credit Agreement

A *revolving credit agreement* is a legal commitment by a bank allowing a customer to borrow up to some maximum limit at any time during a period of a year or longer. Whereas a line of credit is an informal arrangement, a revolving credit agreement is formal in nature. For the right to borrow under a revolving credit arrangement, a customer is required to pay a commitment fee of typically 0.5 percent on the unused portion of the revolving credit outstanding. This fee is justified because the bank must maintain more liquidity, which involves a sacrifice of income, or it must be prepared to obtain funds on short notice at perhaps a disadvantageous rate in order to honor its commitment.

Individual Transaction Loans

Sometimes prime customers do not want a line of credit or a revolving credit agreement, but prefer to borrow only on an individual transaction basis or whenever an unusual opportunity presents itself. For example, the owner of a laundromat chain may borrow only when he makes his annual purchase of new washing machines and dryers. If this customer has a superior credit rating, he would receive the loan more than likely on an unsecured basis. As another illustration, a retail furniture dealer might have an opportunity to buy the inventory of a bankrupt store at a greatly reduced price. He might obtain the funds needed to purchase the inventory on a short-term note and, as the furniture is sold, repay the obligation. During the year, the average bank lending officer is approached with many proposals for individual transaction loans, and he must evaluate each one on its merits.

Interest Rates

Determining Factors. The general level of interest rates is determined primarily by Federal Reserve policies, the fiscal policies of Congress and the Administration, and the demand for credit. The specific interest rate charge on short-term business loans depends on a number of factors, including the secured status of the loan, the size of the loan, and the section of the country where the loan is made. For convenience, interest rates on both secured and unsecured loans will be discussed in this section.[3]

As a rule, interest rates on secured loans are higher than on unsecured loans. The basic justification for this is the higher administrative costs associated with secured loans. Another characteristic of short-term business loan rates is that the average interest rate on small business loans is higher than on larger loans. This is essentially because small loans generally go to small firms, who ordinarily represent more credit risk than large firms. In addition, fixed costs are much higher, percentagewise, on a small loan than on a large loan. As shown in Table 11-1, interest costs on short-term business loans in New York City tend to be lower than those on loans of similar size in other sections of the country. The chief explanation for this is that a high proportion of the loans made by banks in New York City are to the largest and most creditworthy businesses in the nation, and the great majority of

[3]In its "Quarterly Survey of Interest Rates Charged by Banks on Business Loans," the Federal Reserve does not obtain interest-rate data by the secured status of loans. Data from these surveys are published in the *Federal Reserve Bulletin*.

Table 11-1

Rates on Short-Term Business Loans of Banks, November 1976

	Size of Loan (thousands of dollars)					
Center	All Sizes	1–9	10–99	100–499	500–999	1,000 and over
35 centers	7.28	8.83	8.18	7.66	7.31	7.02
New York City	6.88	8.56	7.94	7.43	7.24	6.74
7 other Northeast	7.62	9.22	8.34	7.88	7.49	7.34
8 North Central	7.28	8.45	8.12	7.69	7.36	7.03
7 Southeast	7.51	9.13	8.48	7.71	7.04	7.07
8 Southwest	7.33	8.51	7.82	7.39	7.21	7.12
4 West Coast	7.52	8.69	8.46	7.88	7.44	7.34

Source: "Quarterly Survey of Interest Rates Charged by Banks on Business Loans," *Federal Reserve Bulletin*.

these firms merit the prime rate, which, by definition, is the lowest rate on short-term business loans to large and financially sound companies.

The Prime Rate

The *prime rate* is the rate charged by banks for short-term loans to businesses of the highest credit quality. As shown in Table 11-2, the prime rate varied from 1.5 to 12.0 percent between 1929 and 1976. Like any other market-determined rate or price, the prime rate is influenced by supply and demand, which, in this case, is for loanable funds. The data in Table 11-2 reflects clearly the severe supply and demand pressures that characterized the financial markets between 1973 and 1975. Since a large part of the dollar volume of business loans are made at money market banks, changes in the prime rate ordinarily are announced by one of these banks, with most other major banks in the nation following suit in a matter of hours.[4]

On October 21, 1971, Citibank announced that in the future its prime rate will be set at approximately 0.5 to 1 percent above the rate on new commercial paper and will be allowed to fluctuate accordingly. Shortly thereafter, several other large banks announced their intention to let their prime rate "float" in a similar manner. The purpose of tying the prime rate to the rate on commercial paper was to have the prime rate change more frequently in response to the pressures of supply and demand.

With the prime rate as the base rate in the loan interest rate structure, interest rates on loans to customers with less than the highest credit rating often are expressed in terms of a markup above the prime rate. For example, the interest rate on a loan to a borrower with slightly less credit standing might be specified as the "prime rate plus 2.00 percentage points."

Methods of Calculating Interest Costs

The effective interest cost on a loan depends on the method used to calculate the interest charges. Three methods are normally used: (1) the simple interest method, (2) the discount method, and (3) the add-on method.

Simple Interest Method. Under the simple interest method, if a borrower wants to borrow $1,000 for one year and the stated interest rate is

[4]However, when conditions seem conducive for a prime rate change, a large regional bank or a small bank in the hinterland sometimes will announce a prime rate change first, mainly for the publicity value.

Table 11-2
Prime Rate Charged by Banks, 1929–1976 (percent per annum)

In Effect During			Rate
1929			5.5 -6
1930			3.5 -6
1931			2.75-5
1932			3.25-4
1933			1.5 -4
1934-1947 (Nov.)			1.5
Effective Date			
1947	Dec.[a]		1.75
1950	Sept.	22	2.25
1955	Oct.	14	3.5
1960	Aug.	23	4.5
1965	Dec.	6	5
1970	Dec.	22	6.75
1971	Jan.	6	6.5
		15	6.25
		18	6
	Feb.	16	5.75
	Mar.	11	5.25-5.5
		19	5.25
	Apr.	23	5.25-5.5
	May	11	5.5
	July	6	5.5 -6
		7	6
	Oct.	20	5.75
	Nov.	4[b]	5.5 -5.6
	Dec.	31	5.25
1972	Jan.	24	5
		31	4.75
	Apr.	5	5
	June	26	5.25
	Aug.	29	5.5
	Oct.	4	5.75
	Dec.	27	6
1973	Feb.	27	6.25
	Mar.	26	6.5
	Apr.	18[c]	6.75
	May	7	7
		25	7.25
	June	8	7.5
		25	7.75
	July	3	8
		9	8.25
		18	8.56
		30	8.75
	Aug.	6	9
		13	9.25
		22	9.50
		28	9.75
	Sept.	18	10
	Oct.	24	9.75
1974	Jan.	29	9.5
	Feb.	11	9.25
		19	9
		25	8.75
	Mar.	22	9
		29	9.25
	Apr.	3	9.5
		5	9.75
		11	10
		19	10.25
		25	10.5
	May	2	10.75
		6	11
		10	11.25
		17	11.5
	June	26	11.75
	July	5	12
	Oct.	7	11.75
		21	11.5
		28	11.25
	Nov.	4	11
		14	10.75
		25	10.5
1975	Jan.	9	10.25
		15	10
		20	9.75
		28	9.5
	Feb.	3	9.25
		10	9
		18	8.75
		24	8.5
	Mar.	5	8.25
		10	8
		18	7.75
		24	7.5
	May	20	7.25
	June	9	7
	July	18	7.25
	Aug.	12	7.75

In Effect During		Rate
1975 Sept.	15	8
Oct.	27	7.75
Nov.	5	7.5
Dec.	2	7.25
1976 Jan.	12	7
	21	6.75
June	1	7
	7	7.25
Aug.	2	7
Oct.	4	6.75
Nov.	1	6.5
Dec.	13	6.25
1977 May	13	6.5
	31	6.75

Source: Federal Reserve Board of Governors, *Annual Statement Digest, 1971–1975*, and *Federal Reserve Bulletin*.

[a]Date of change not available.

[b]Beginning in November 1971, rates are those in effect at the major commercial banks.

[c]Effective April 16, 1973, the Committee on Interest and Dividends introduced a "two tier" approach to rates on business loans. This system allowed rates on large prime loans to move in concert with advances in market rates, but at the same time limited rate increases on smaller loans. For the duration of the Committee on Interest and Dividends, which was abolished on May 31, 1974, the prime rate shown in the table is that on "large" loans.

7 percent, he signs a note for $1,070. In this case the effective interest cost is 7 percent ($70/$1,000).

Discount Method. It is a common practice for banks to discount loans. That is, a borrower might sign a note for $1,000 for one year with a stated interest rate of 7 percent, but if the bank discounts the note (that is, takes out the $70 interest in advance), the borrower receives only $930. Therefore, the effective interest cost is not 7 percent but 7.53 percent ($70/$930).

Add-on Method. Under the add-on method, the interest charges are added to the principal before dividing the balance by the stipulated number of installment payments. Given the same principal, interest, and maturity assumptions as above, if the interest is added to the principal, the borrower would make twelve monthly installments of $89.17 to retire the $1,070 note. Since he had the use, on the average, of slightly more than $500 of the loan proceeds over the year, the effective interest rate would be 12.68 percent.[5]

Compensating Balances

As we have seen, banks typically require businesses to maintain compensating balances in proportion to the line of credit granted. There are three primary reasons for this request. First, since a business must maintain a certain amount of deposits anyway, bankers believe it is only proper that these funds be held at the bank with which the firm

[5]See Board of Governors of the Federal Reserve System, "Annual Percentage Rate Tables," (Washington, D.C.: Board of Governors of the Federal Reserve System).

has a borrowing relationship. Second, compensating balances serve to raise the effective interest yield on a loan if the balance required is above that which the borrower would otherwise maintain. For example, a $1 million loan carrying an interest rate of 8 percent and a 20 percent compensating balance requirement would have an effective interest rate of 10 percent. This is because the borrower has the use of only $800,000 even though, over a year, he would pay $80,000 in interest. Changes in compensating balance requirements often are raised or lowered to adjust the effective interest cost on a loan. A final reason for compensating balances is that they provide partial security for the loan. This is because banks possess the right to offset balances on deposit against matured and unpaid loans.

Secured Business Loans

Reasons for Requiring Security

Although banks prefer to lend on an unsecured basis, a large percentage of the business loans made by banks is secured. There are at least three reasons for a bank to require security for a business loan. These are (1) to transfer part of the credit risk, (2) because security is readily available, and (3) because complete credit information is unavailable.

The Credit Risk. The major function of security on a loan is to transfer part of the credit risk to the borrower or to a third party. If the borrower pledges inventory, equipment, or other assets or has a cosigner when he obtains a loan, the bank has transferred part of the risk of loss to the borrower or the cosigner, as the case may be. When this is accomplished, the loan is more attractive to the bank. Typically, banks seek to transfer part of the credit risk on loans that they make to small or new businesses. These firms are the most likely ones to have difficulty repaying their obligations if they should suffer losses through one or more of the many risks that businesses face.

Besides serving to transfer part of the risk in order to benefit the bank, the pledging of security sometimes also benefits the borrower by permitting him to obtain a larger loan than his financial position might allow or perhaps to bargain for a lower interest rate or compensating balance. For the bank to make concessions of this sort, the security pledged should be of high quality and involve little administrative handling costs to the bank.

Although the pledging of security may transfer part of the credit risk associated with a loan, there is an old banking adage that "security does not make the loan." That is, the bank should be reasonably sure that a loan can be repaid from the liquidation of current assets or cash flow and should not rely on security for repayment. It is costly to the bank to sell pledged assets or to obtain funds from a cosigner to repay a loan in default.

Available Security. Traditionally, loans to investment bankers, mortgage brokers, and security and commodity dealers have been secured because the security was readily available. Negotiable instruments representing the particular asset that these borrowers regularly finance may be obtained quickly and with relatively little cost to the bank. A survey of bank loan officers indicates that for loans to these borrowers, collateral was automatic even though it may be unnecessary from a credit risk standpoint.[6]

Unavailable Credit Information. Banks ordinarily require collateral when it is impossible to obtain accurate information on a business's true net worth and profitability. This may be because the owner keeps poor records or, for some reason, does not want to reveal certain information about his business. If the loan officer has some indication that the business is creditworthy, then the easiest way to accommodate a loan request in situations of this sort is to require adequate security. In this way the bank is protected, and it retains the deposits and other business of the customer. Sometimes secured loans to farmers and small one-man businesses are made with such a rationale.

Security Interest

Before the adoption of the Uniform Commercial Code (UCC), the procedures for obtaining a satisfactory lien on various types of collateral was complex and expensive and varied from state to state. Article 9 of the UCC deals specifically with secured transactions and contains clear and simple rules governing the security interest of lenders.

In place of the many varied security devices required under the old statutes, Article 9 substitutes a single security device designated as a *security interest,* which is defined as an interest in personal property or fixtures that secures payment or performance of an obligation. The only requirements for a security agreement are that it must be in writing, be signed by the debtor, describe the property, and describe the realty, if the collateral covers crops, oil, gas, or minerals to be extracted or timber to be cut from the land or fixtures. In order to obtain a security interest in collateral, the lender must file a copy of the security agreement or

[6]Douglas A. Hayes, *Bank Lending Policies: Domestic and International* (Ann Arbor, Mich.: University of Michigan, Graduate School of Business Administration, Bureau of Business Research, 1971), p. 130.

financing statement, generally in the office of the Secretary of State.[7] The UCC provides, with certain exceptions, that the first lender to file a financing statement has priority over all others, regardless of who made the first advance. Therefore, it is imperative that lenders search the public notices for prior filings and make their own filing even before the loan has been made.

Accounts Receivable Loans

An accounts receivable loan is simply a loan secured by a firm's accounts receivable. Business finance companies, as well as banks, are very active in this area of lending. Accounts receivable loans are an especially appropriate means of short-term financing for a young company that is outgrowing its working capital. Established companies also are good candidates for an accounts receivable loan if their statements no longer warrant an unsecured loan. This could be because these companies experienced a sharp spurt in sales, converted a portion of working capital into fixed assets, or sustained a substantial loss.[8] It is important to note that accounts receivable loans generally represent a continuous financing arrangement. That is, new receivables are assigned to the lender as old receivables are collected. Therefore, the size of the loan fluctuates according to the volume of receivables outstanding.

Lending Procedure. If a business initially approaches a bank for an accounts receivable loan, the first step in considering such a loan request is for the credit department to perform a thorough analysis of the willingness and ability to pay of the prospective borrower. Generally, however, an accounts receivable loan is an alternative that the loan officer suggests to a firm after an unsecured loan has been ruled out on the basis of the credit department's analysis and recommendations. Since a receivables loan is a short-term obligation, the focal point of credit analysis is on the firm's working capital position. A receivables loan usually is an ideal means for a company having receivables with a maturity of sixty to 120 days and accounts payable with a normal maturity of thirty days to take advantage of trade discounts.

[7]A *financing statement* merely gives notice that secured financing has occurred or may occur in the future with respect to a particular debtor. It must be signed by the debtor and the secured party, show the address of both parties, and contain a statement indicating the type of collateral. In all cases where filing is necessary, a financing statement must be filed. However, a copy of the security agreement may serve as the financing statement if it is signed by both parties and contains the necessary information.

[8]Harry C. Culshaw, "Lending Against Accounts Receivable," in William H. Baughn and Charls E. Walker, eds., *The Banker's Handbook* (Homewood, Ill.: Dow Jones-Irwin, 1966), pp. 336–337.

The second step in making a receivables loan is to analyze the quality and size of the firm's receivables. The primary purpose of this step is to determine the amount that can be advanced against the receivables. According to one expert in receivables lending, the following considerations are important with respect to the quality of the receivables:

1. The type of customers to whom the prospective borrower sells, particularly whether they are well rated and financially strong, or whether they are unlisted and unrated.
2. The average length of time the accounts receivable are outstanding.
3. The amount of returns, rejections, and allowances.
4. The dollar amount of volume of goods sold to well-rated concerns compared to that sold to concerns of lesser rating.
5. That the receivables to be assigned are true accounts, as distinguished from contract rights, where payment has not yet been earned and performance is required. Watch carefully for contra accounts and be alert to consignments, special datings, and guaranteed sales.
6. The certainty, especially if operating under the Uniform Commercial Code, that the accounts receivable are not subject to a continuing lien by reason of a financing statement previously filed against inventory, the sale of which created the receivable.[9]

In addition to evaluating the quality of receivables, the credit analyst must determine the size of the individual receivable accounts. This is because records must be kept on each account pledged to secure the loan, and it costs more proportionately to process a small account than it does a large account. Ordinarily, banks will not make loans on the basis of receivables generated through the sale of low-priced items. However, sometimes banks will extend credit based on the blanket assignment of receivables whereby records are maintained only on the total amount of receivables pledged and not for each individual account. On loans of this type, it is necessary for the bank to examine the firm's receivables records at least every thirty or sixty days. Because of the possibility of fraud, lenders generally advance against the receivables pledged under blanket assignment only about half of the amount they normally would.

If credit analysis of the firm and its receivables indicates that a receivables loan represents the most satisfactory method of meeting a firm's short-term financing needs, the final step in making such a loan is to have the borrower sign a promissory note and a security agreement

[9]*Ibid.*, pp. 325–326.

(which also serves as a financing statement for filing purposes, provided that it contains the necessary information required by the UCC). The amount of the loan will depend on the quality and size of the receivables and will range generally from 50 to 95 percent. A 95 percent advance may be justified in the case of government receivables. Lesser amounts are advanced if the customers are of medium to poor credit quality, if the firm experiences a significant amount of bad debts and returns, and if many of the receivables represent the sale of low-priced items.

In addition to an interest rate above that charged on an unsecured loan, banks also receive a service charge of approximately 1 to 2 percent for handling an accounts receivable loan. Generally, the interest rate and service charge combined will amount to approximately 4 percentage points above that charged on an unsecured loan.

Protecting the Loan. Accounts receivable loans offer an excellent opportunity for the borrower to obtain funds through fraud. Therefore, it is imperative that banks initiate certain protective measures with respect to its receivable loans.

One simple measure is for the bank to require a signed shipping document or the delivery receipt for each receivable generated. In addition, the bank should audit the borrower's receivables and cash ledgers at least every 30 or 60 days to verify that the receivables pledged are, in fact, outstanding and have not been paid. Finally, it is a sound practice for the bank to verify a portion of the receivables with the borrowing firm's customers.

Factoring Receivables

Whereas the typical accounts receivable loan entails the assignment of receivables to the lender with the seller retaining title in the receivables, *factoring* involves the outright sale of commercial receivables to the lender usually without recourse to the seller. Since 1963, when the Comptroller of the Currency ruled that factoring was a legitimate banking activity, many large banks have established factoring departments or purchased factoring companies.[10] Factoring is discussed in this section because of its similarities with receivables lending.

Forms of Factoring. There are three principal forms of factoring: (1) maturity factoring, (2) advance factoring, and (3) drop-shipment factoring. Under *maturity factoring,* the factor purchases the receivables. For bearing the credit risk and processing the receivables, the factor

[10]Actually several large banks, notably First National Bank of Boston and the Trust Company of Georgia, were engaged in factoring long before 1963 by writing their factoring agreements in the form of loan agreements.

charges a commission that ranges from ¾ of 1 percent to 3 percent of the purchased receivables. This fee varies with the quality and volume of recievables and the size of the individual accounts.

Under an *advance factoring* arrangement, the factor credits the selling firm's account before the maturity date of the receivables. For this advance, the factor charges, in addition to commission, an interest rate of about 1 percent per month (usually discounted).

Under *drop-shipment factoring* a client who sells some merchandise writes out a purchase order to his supplier and forwards the order to his factor for credit approval of the buyer. If the buyer's credit is acceptable, the factor forwards the purchase order to the vendor and guarantees payment of the bill upon satisfactory receipt of the goods by the buyer. When the shipping invoices are received by the factor, a bill is submitted to the buyer with instructions that he pay the factor, who, in turn, pays the supplier and remits the "gross profit" to his client.

Advantages of Factoring. The primary advantages of factoring for the client are that he is spared the expense of a credit department and of collecting the accounts. In addition, the client benefits by having access to automatic financing when receivables increase. Receivables from the textile and apparel industries reportedly account for approximately 75 percent of total factoring volume.[11] The remainder is generated primarily by the furniture, leather goods, toy, and electronic industries.

Inventory Loans

An *inventory loan* involves the pledge of all or part of a firm's inventory as security for a loan. For many businesses, inventory usually represents the largest asset available and provides convenient security for a loan.

Lending Procedure. Inventory loans frequently are suggested by the lending officer after a credit analysis of the borrowing firm reveals that it does not qualify for an unsecured loan but is an acceptable risk if the loan is secured. On the other hand, loans secured by inventory are a traditional means of financing for wholesalers, retailers, and commodity and security dealers, although many of these firms may have excellent credit reputations. Even for these firms, however, the first step in making an inventory loan is for the bank credit department to make a thorough analysis of the firm's expected willingness and ability to repay the loan.

[11]Charles Rumbel and George E. Phalen, Jr., "Financing Accounts Receivable and Inventory," *The Journal of Commercial Bank Lending* (February 1969), p. 2.

The second step in making an inventory loan is to determine what percentage of the value of the inventory to advance to the borrower. In making this decision, the relevant considerations are the marketability, perishability, and market-price stability of the goods in inventory. The loan value may range from 50 percent on women's dresses, whose value is subject to the whims of consumer tastes, to 95 percent on U.S. Treasury securities, which are highly marketable and usually quite stable in price.

The third step in lending on inventory is to obtain a security interest in the inventory. The type of security device used depends on the type of goods involved and whether the borrower or a third party has possession of them. For hard-to-identify items such as nondurable consumer goods held by the borrower, the bank may obtain a security interest in the goods by obtaining under the UCC a *floating or blanket lien* that covers the inventory for a specified period of time. The bank's interest in the goods is difficult to protect because the borrower continually is selling from and adding to inventory.

For easily identifiable items such as cars, appliances, and industrial equipment, the bank has the borrower sign a *trust receipt security agreement,* which lists each item by serial number. If this agreement contains all the information required by the UCC, it then serves as the financing statement that is filed with the appropriate state official to obtain the bank's security interest. The borrower then signs a demand note and agrees to pay the bank as each item is sold. Under this type of financing arrangement, which is commonly called "floor planning," the bank will make unannounced, monthly checks of the dealer's inventory to verify that the items listed on the trust agreement are still in inventory.

In some cases the bank may prefer to make an inventory loan only if the goods are in the possession of a third party such as a warehouseman. There are two types of warehouses: (1) terminal or public warehouses and (2) field warehouses. In a *terminal warehouse,* space is rented for the storage of various high-value items such as appliances. Under a typical terminal warehouse arrangement, a firm signs a loan agreement with its bank in order to finance the purchase of some goods. The firm then instructs the manufacturer to ship the goods to a terminal warehouse, which, in turn, will issue a warehouse receipt to the bank giving it a security interest to the goods. With the warehouse receipt in hand, the bank then pays the manufacturer. The warehouse company releases the goods to the dealer as they are sold and funds remitted to the bank.

A *field warehouse* is a designated storage area on the premises of the borrower. Usually it is a screened-in portion of a larger warehouse and is under the control of a field warehouse company. When goods are received, the field warehouse company takes custody of the inventory and issues a warehouse receipt to the bank as security for the borrower's loan. Of course, the use of terminal or field warehouses is expensive for the borrower, but under some circumstances it is the only way lenders will make loans on the value of the inventory.

Other Security

Besides accounts receivable and inventory, many other forms of security are pledged to obtain a business loan. Typically, in the case of a small corporation, the bank will require the personal endorsement of the principals in the firm. This practice tends to discourage dishonest individuals from raiding the corporation of its assets and defaulting on its liabilities. Other securities frequently pledged by the owners of a firm to secure a business loan include real estate, bonds, stocks, and cash surrender value of life insurance policies. The amounts advanced, of course, will be proportional to the quality of the security pledged.

Suggestions for Additional Reading

Abraham, Alfred B. "Factoring—The New Frontier for Commercial Banks." *The Journal of Commercial Bank Lending* (April 1971), pp. 32–43.

Baughn, William H., and Walker, Charls E., eds. *The Banker's Handbook.* Homewood, Ill.: Dow Jones-Irwin, 1966, chaps. 24–26, 31–32, 41.

Boyle, Richard J. "Commercial Bank Revolving Credits." *The Journal of Commercial Bank Lending* (November 1969), pp. 2–14.

Crane, Dwight B. *Managing Credit Lines and Commitments.* Chicago: Association of Reserve City Bankers, 1973.

Naitove, Irwin. *Modern Factoring.* New York: American Management Association, 1969.

Rothschild, Fuller M. "Banks in Factoring—Past, Present and Future." *The Journal of Commercial Bank Lending* (October 1969), pp. 28–36.

Rumble, Charles, and Phalen, George E., Jr. "Financing Accounts Receivable and Inventory." *The Journal of Commercial Bank Lending* (February 1969), pp. 2–9.

Van Horne, James C. *Fundamentals of Financial Management.* 3rd ed. Englewood Cliffs, N.J.: Prentice-Hall, 1977, chaps. 9–10.

CHAPTER

12

Term Loans

Term Loans are business loans with an original maturity of more than one year and all outstanding loans granted under a formal agreement—revolving credit or standby— on which the original maturity of the commitment was in excess of one year. Most term loans have maturities in the three- to five-year range, but some extend to fifteen years. An indication of the importance of bank term lending is shown by the fact that on March 1977, term loans comprised 39.3 percent of the business loans outstanding at 160 weekly reporting banks.

In this chapter we shall (1) discuss the development of bank term lending, (2) explore the purposes of term loans, (3) consider the advantages and disadvantages of obtaining term loans from banks, (4) examine the types of term financing agreements, (5) note the provisions contained in most term loan agreements, and (6) take a look at the principal industries borrowing on a term basis.

Development of Bank Term Lending

Early Development

Prior to the 1930s, bank loan portfolios consisted primarily of short-term loans to businesses. Several developments during the Depression decade, however, prompted banks to begin making business loans with maturities extending beyond one year. First, banks became surfeited with excess reserves as total legal reserves rose in response to the inflows of gold and Federal Reserve purchases of securities. This condition, along with the weak demand for credit, drove interest rates to historically low levels.[1] Faced with a huge surplus of funds and low yields on both loans and investments, banks began to make term loans as a means to increase income.

A second factor contributing to bank entry into term lending was the change in attitude toward term loans by the banking regulatory authorities. Prior to the Great Depression, these authorities discouraged term lending because of the lower liquidity involved with this type of credit. However, the prevailing softness in the credit markets during the mid-1930s persuaded the regulatory agencies to accept term loans as a legitimate outlet for funds.

A third reason why banks began to make term loans was the expected greater stability in deposits brought about by the creation of deposit insurance. With the risk of bank runs diminished, banks could trim their liquidity reserves somewhat and reach for longer-term, higher-yielding loans. Finally, the demand for funds to finance capital expenditures during World War II further accelerated the development of term lending.

Why More Banks Now Actively Seek Term Loans

Unlike the Depression and World War II period, when banks more or less took on term loans out of necessity, most banks today are anxious to make term loans to creditworthy businesses. There are several reasons for this change in viewpoint.[2]

First, the growth of time and savings deposits in recent years has encouraged banks to match these relatively long-term liabilities with long-term assets such as term loans. The stable flow of income from term loans is well suited to meet the interest payments on these deposits.

A second reason why banks now actively solicit term loans is that more banks today have the skilled credit analysts and commercial loan

[1]As shown in Table 11-2, the prime rate at 1.5 percent from 1934 to 1947.

[2]J. William Middleton, "Term Lending—Practical and Profitable," *The Journal of Commercial Bank Lending* (August 1968), p. 42.

officers needed to evaluate and extend term credit. The greater availability of these officers is primarily due to the increase in the number of banks offering special training programs in commercial lending.

Finally, banks view term loans more favorably because, by assisting a firm with its long-term financing, they are in an excellent position to provide many other profitable services to the business.

Extent of Bank Term Lending

In a Federal Reserve Survey made on April 19, 1939, of about 400 weekly reporting banks, term loans accounted for 25.6 percent ($987 million) of the $3,858 million outstanding in commercial, industrial, and agricultural loans.[3] A Federal Reserve Survey on November 20, 1946, revealed that term loans represented 34.5 percent ($4,558 million) of total business loans of $13.2 billion.[4] Another Federal Reserve Survey on October 5, 1955, showed that term loans comprised 33.9 percent ($10,441 million) of $30,820 million business loans outstanding at about 2,000 banks.[5] Finally, in March 1977, term loans at 160 weekly reporting banks amounted to $45.8 billion, or 39.3 percent of the $116.8 billion commercial and industrial loans outstanding. Large New York City banks have been the leader in term lending for many years. This is due to their proximity to the headquarters of the nation's major corporations, their great lending capacity, and their overall expertise in business finance.

Purposes of Term Loans

Business seeks bank term loans for a number of purposes, including (1) to finance capital assets, (2) to finance permanent increases in accounts receivable and inventory, (3) to obtain interim funds pending a public offering, and (4) to acquire other companies.

Capital Assets

Perhaps the principal use of bank term loans is to finance the acquisition of plant and equipment. Based on the principle that long-term assets should be financed with long-term liabilities, firms borrow on a term basis to finance plant and equipment with the anticipation that the projected rate of return on the newly acquired assets will be greater

[3]Cited in George S. Moore, "Term Loans and Interim Financing," in Benjamin H. Beckhart, ed., *Business Loans of American Commercial Banks* (New York: Ronald Press, 1959), p. 213.

[4]*Ibid.*, p. 214.

[5]*Ibid.*

than the cost of financing the new investment. Since term loans are repaid out of net earnings and depreciation allowances generated over the life of the assets, bank credit analysts, in considering a term loan request, pay particular attention to a firm's *pro forma* income statement, *pro forma* cash flow statement, and *pro forma* sources and uses of funds statement.

Permanent Increase in Current Assets

A firm's current assets, such as cash, inventory, and accounts receivable, usually fluctuate considerably during a year. Since these assets never completely disappear from the firm's statement of condition, a portion of current assets may be considered as more or less permanent or fixed, while the remaining segment fluctuates on a seasonal basis. As a firm's sales grow, the permanent portion of the business's current assets tends to increase commensurately. Whereas short-term loans are the recommended way to finance seasonal fluctuations in current assets, bank term loans provide an excellent means to finance the underlying buildup of permanent current assets until internally generated capital is available.

Interim Financing Pending a Public Offering

Term loans are used extensively by firms as interim financing pending a public offering. During periods of high interest rates, firms prefer to finance their long-term capital requirements with term loans in order to avoid issuing debt for which they will be committed to pay high interest charges even after interest rates have declined. Moreover, firms like to avoid equity financing during high-interest-rate periods because the price-earnings ratio of their stock probably will be relatively low during such periods, which means that the cost of equity capital will be high. Public utilities, with their heavy long-term capital requirements, use term loans extensively during high-interest-rate periods and then repay these loans with funds raised with debt or equity issues when conditions are more favorable.

By virtue of their size, small firms have to rely on term loans for a large part of their permanent capital requirements. After a firm has grown and achieved a satisfactory "track record," it then usually has access to the capital markets for its debt or equity issues.

Acquiring Other Companies

During recent years, many of the large number of mergers that took place were financed with bank term loans. The acquiring company usually anticipates using part of the increased cash flow from the acquired company to repay the loan.

Advantages and Disadvantages of Bank Term Loans

Advantages

Flexibility. The principal advantage of a bank term loan over other means of financing is its flexibility. In the first place, the payment terms under a term loan generally are more flexible and convenient for the borrowing firm. For example, the loan agreement might call for small quarterly payments with a large annual payment that can be made at any time during the year. Second, if for some reason the firm was unable to meet its payments on schedule, the bank could revise the payments schedule quite easily. This, of course, could not be done in the case of a debt issue in the hands of the public.

Speed. Unlike a public offering, which often takes many months to arrange, a term loan can be obtained in a matter of several days or a few weeks at the most.

Lower Cost. Given the registration and brokerage fees involved with a public offering, the overall cost of a term loan probably will be lower than that on debt or equity issues floated in the capital market. Moreover, the interest rate on a term loan may be allowed to fluctuate with the prime rate, and this may tend to produce a lower average cost over the life of the loan. Finally, the term loan agreement might permit a prepayment of the loan by the firm, thereby reducing the overall cost of funds.

Financial Counseling. Sometimes one of the overlooked advantages of obtaining funds under a bank term loan is the financial counseling available to the firm from the bank. In the process of analyzing a firm loan request, the bank's credit analysts and loan officers must become familiar with all facets of the firm's operations. Since these officers probably have had broad experience in arranging loans for many other firms, perhaps in the same industry, the firm stands to benefit greatly from the advice, counsel, and independent evaluation of the firm's operations and plans.

Disadvantages

Protective Restrictions. Many firms consider the protective restrictions contained in most bank term loan agreements as a disadvantage of term borrowing.[6] For example, the minimum working capital requirement, and the limitations on dividends, additional debt, and capital expendi-

[6] These restrictions are discussed in the next section.

tures, all inhibit the firm's latitude of operations and hence are considered by most business borrowers as drawbacks to term loans.

Maturity. In some instances, the maturities allowed under term loans may not be as long as some firms might prefer. As we saw earlier, term loan maturities average about three to five years. Occasionally, for prime-rated firms, however, banks will make term loans with maturities of up to fifteen years.

Loan Limit. For some large borrowers, a bank's legal lending limit may be a drawback to term borrowing. However, this handicap is usually overcome through the use of a *participation loan* in which several banks agree to lend various portions of the amount required. On the other hand, some small firms may consider the loan limit placed on them by the bank a disadvantage of term borrowing.

Types of Term Financing Agreements

At the beginning of the chapter, a term loan was defined as a business loan with an original maturity of more than one year and all outstanding loans granted under a formal agreement—revolving credit or standby—on which the original maturity of the commitment was in excess of one year. In this section we shall note the three principal types of term borrowing agreements: (1) revolving credit, (2) revolving credit convertible into a term loan, and (3) regular term loan.

Revolving Credit

A *revolving credit* is a formal commitment by the bank to make funds up to a set amount available at any time over a specified period, usually two or three years. During this time as funds are needed, notes are executed at the bank. In return for the bank's formal commitment to lend, the firm pays a commitment fee of about ½ of 1 percent on the unused portion of the credit. Revolving credit arrangements with a maturity of more than one year are particularly well suited for a firm that is expanding rapidly and is uncertain of its future financing requirements.

Revolving Credit Convertible into a Term Loan

When a firm is unsure of its future funds requirements, the bank could extend to the firm a revolving credit convertible into a regular term loan when the company's requirements are more definitive. This conversion would be at the option of the firm.

Regular Term Loan

A regular term loan is simply a business loan with an original maturity of more than one year and granted under a written agreement. Regular term loans comprise the bulk of all bank term financing agreements.

Principal Elements in a Term Loan Agreement

There are a number of major elements in most term loan agreements.

Amount of the Loan

The amount of the commitment or loan is usually listed in the first paragraph of the loan agreement. This total is determined after thorough analysis of the business's credit needs and its expected ability and willingness to pay.

Security Requirements

Whereas most short-term loans are repaid by the liquidation of assets, term loans tend to be repaid from the borrowing firm's future cash flow. Over the life of a term loan, many different contingencies could occur to prevent a firm from realizing the necessary flow of funds to repay the loan as agreed. Therefore, the standard procedure is to require some form of security on term loans in order to transfer part of the added credit risk to the borrower or a third party. For term loans to small businesses, typical forms of security include the personal guarantees of the principals, equipment, real estate, and securities.

Representations and Warranties

In extending term credit to a firm, the bank must depend on the truth and accuracy of many statements made by the firm concerning its financial condition and operations. If it is revealed later that there were inaccuracies and misrepresentations in these statements, the bank may seek a remedy against the firm under the Default Section of the loan agreement. Below are listed some of the representation and warranties found in most term loan agreements:

1. Borrower's power to execute the agreement.
2. Statement of corporate powers relative to borrowing.
3. Accuracy of financial statements.
4. No adverse change in financial condition since the last statement date.

5. No significant legal or court action pending except as otherwise noted.
6. No taxes are overdue.
7. No liens on property, except as otherwise noted.

Interest Rate and Fees

Generally, the first page of the loan agreement contains a statement of the interest rate and fees that must be paid. Because of the greater credit risk associated with term credit, the interest rate on these loans is usually slightly higher than on short-term loans. Many banks today are expressing the rate on term loans as the prime rate plus a markup, such as 0.25 to 5 percentage points, depending on the creditworthiness of the borrower and market condition. In addition, the agreement might specify a minimum and maximum rate regardless of fluctuations in the prime rate. Besides the basic interest charge and the commitment fee, banks typically charge the borrower an amount to cover unusual legal fees, investigation expenses, and appraisal and recording fees.

Equity Kicker

In recent years, a number of banks have begun to incorporate in some term loan and commercial mortgage agreements a provision that the bank will share in the profit, income, or earnings from the business enterprise.[7] These provisions are popularly known as *equity kickers*. The use of equity kickers was prompted by the tight-money and inflationary conditions that prevailed generally after 1965. Equity kickers permit the banks to protect its real interest return on a loan during an inflationary period and possibly to realize a significant gain if the borrower prospers. For the borrower, the granting of an equity kicker might mean the greater availability of funds at a time when other borrowers are being denied loans.

Equity kickers may take several forms.[8] Banks might accept stock purchase warrants, which they may hold or sell.[9] Since the bank cannot own stock in a corporate enterprise except in subsidiaries that provide

[7] The Comptroller of the Currency has ruled that "A national bank may take as consideration for a loan a share in the profit, income, or earnings from a business enterprise of a borrower. Such share may be in addition to or in lieu of interest. The borrower's obligation to repay principal, however, shall not be conditioned upon the profit, income, or earnings of the business enterprise." *Comptroller's Manual for National Banks*, "Interpretive Rulings," 7.7312. A number of states have passed similar rulings for state banks.

[8] Much of the discussion in this section is based upon J. Frank Holahan, "Is There a Kicker in Your Bank?" *The Journal of Commercial Bank Lending*, 51 (May 1969), pp. 2–7.

[9] A *warrant* is an option to buy a stated number of common shares at a specified price.

international banking services, conduct safe deposit business, or own the bank's real property, the bank could never exercise the warrants.

Another approach is for the firm to grant *shadow warrants* to the bank.[10] With this scheme, the term agreement provides that if the market price of the borrower's stock increases to some maximum figure over the life of the loan, the borrower pays the bank interest above the stipulated rate. With shadow warrants, the bank benefits from an increase in the price of the borrower's stock without holding real warrants. From the borrower's standpoint, the payment to the bank is tax deductible and results in no dilution of ownership.

Other equity-sharing arrangements might involve the bank's receiving a percentage of retail sales or net profits or, in the case of a mortgage loan, a percentage of gross rentals. In the years ahead, imaginative lending officers probably will conceive many other forms of equity kickers.

Repayment Schedule

A typical repayment schedule for a term loan calls for monthly, quarterly, or semiannual payments over the life of the loan. Experienced loan officers caution against reducing these periodic payments in favor of a larger or *balloon payment* at the maturity of the loan. A flexible alternative for some borrowers might be a schedule of small quarterly payments and a large annual payment. Many term agreements call for an acceleration of principal payments if the borrower's earnings exceed projections, especially if a balloon payment is involved.

Prepayment Penalty

Most term agreements call for a prepayment penalty if funds used for repayment are borrowed elsewhere. This penalty may be equal to the unpaid commitment fee, but it can be a flat amount such as 2 to 3 percent of the unpaid balance or scaled downward as the term of the loan diminishes. A justification for the prepayment penalty is that the bank has a sunk cost in the loan in terms of credit investigation and other expenses; the bank's rate of profit on the loan is reduced if the borrower prepays the principal on the obligation.

Participation Provisions

If other banks participate in the loan, several provisions must be included in the agreement to cover the extra details involved. The name of the managing bank, which is often called the *agent* or *lead* bank,

[10]Holahan, pp. 4–5.

must be listed along with each bank's share of the loan. In addition, the procedure for collection and disbursement of principal, interest, and fees must be outlined. Finally, the agreement must contain the procedure that will be followed in case the borrower fails to comply with any of the protective covenants in the agreement or defaults on the loan.

Affirmative Covenants

Included in the loan agreement are *affirmative covenants,* which are promises by the borrowing firm to perform certain actions either automatically or at the request of the bank. The purposes of these affirmative covenants are to ensure that the bank is provided with adequate information over the life of the loan to evaluate the continuing creditworthiness of the firm and to ascertain that the firm's general financial conditions remain at the same level as when the loan was initiated. In a typical term loan agreement, the borrower covenants and agrees as follows:

1. It will continue to maintain, in accordance with generally accepted accounting principles and practices, full records and accounts concerning the conduct of its business and will furnish, promptly after the close of each quarter, balance sheets and earning statements signed by an authorized officer, and annually not later than 90 days after the close of its fiscal year prepared by an independent certified public accountant satisfactory to the bank.
2. It will pay promptly all taxes for which it may be liable except such taxes as it may be contesting in good faith and will give to the bank, immediately upon their becoming overdue, notice of any taxes that it may refrain from paying because the liability of the borrower therefor is being so contested.
3. It will with reasonable promptness make available for inspection to a duly authorized officer of the bank any of its books and records when so requested.
4. It will keep its properties in good repair, working order, and condition and from time to time will make all needful and proper repairs, renewals, replacements, extensions, additions, and improvements thereto so that the business carried on by the borrower may be advantageously conducted at all times in accordance with prudent business management.
5. It will keep all its plants, properties, and inventories which are of an insurable character insured by financially sound and reputable insurance companies or associations satisfactory to the bank against loss or damage by fire or other hazards and risks of a na-

ture usually insured against by companies engaged in the same or a similar business, in amounts that will meet with the bank's approval.

6. It will maintain a minimum net working capital of $______.
7. It will maintain a current ratio of ______.
8. It will maintain net worth of ______.
9. It will maintain a maximum debt-to-worth ratio of ______.
10. It will not expend more than ______ for fixed assets during any one fiscal period or *pro rata* sum for any part thereof.

Negative Covenants

Negative covenants are promises by the borrowing firm that it will not perform certain actions without prior written consent of the bank. The primary puposes of these covenants are to limit the company's uses of its funds and the span of the firm's operations. In the negative covenants section of a typical bank term loan agreement, the borrower agrees that without the prior written consent of the bank it will not:

1. Create against any of its assets now owned or hereinafter acquired any pledge, mortgage, lien, or any other encumbrance.
2. Purchase or retire any of its capital stock.
3. Make any loans to corporations, firms, or individuals or make any investments in any other corporation or business enterprise. (Investments in U.S. Treasury bills, notes, and bonds are excluded from this limitation.)
4. Enter into any merger or consolidation or sell or lease a substantial portion of its assets.
5. Change the general nature of its business.
6. Change its management to any substantial degree.
7. Create or assume any obligation, direct or contingent, for money borrowed by it or another.
8. Guarantee, endorse, or otherwise become surety for or upon the obligation of others.
9. Sell receivables with or without recourse.
10. Transact business with any other bank.
11. Increase the total annual compensation (bonuses, salaries, commissions, etc.) of its management in excess of those figures stipulated in the most recent financial statements.
12. Pay dividends in excess of ______ percent of net after-tax profit. (No payment of dividends may be made that reduces the retained earnings of the company for the latest fiscal period.)

Default

The last section of a term loan agreement usually sets forth the legal procedures that will be followed in case the firm defaults on the note, discontinues its business, files for bankruptcy, or fails to observe any covenant or provision in agreement.

Principal Industries Utilizing Bank Term Loans

Generally, industries with a relatively large investment in fixed assets have the greatest need for bank term loans. As shown in Table 12-1, the transportation, public utilities, mining, and services industries are the largest users of bank term loans.

Table 12-1
Term Commercial and Industrial Loans Outstanding, by Industry, at 160 Weekly Reporting Banks, March 30, 1977 (millions of dollars)

Industry	Amount
Durable goods manufacturing	
Primary metals	1,521
Machinery	2,552
Transportation equipment	1,339
Other fabricated metal products	820
Other durable goods	1,625
Nondurable goods manufacturing	
Food, liquor, and tobacco	1,412
Textiles, apparel, and leather	1,071
Petroleum refining	1,770
Chemicals and rubber	1,547
Other nondurable goods	1,032
Mining, including crude petroleum and natural gas	5,856
Trade	
Commodity dealers	199
Other wholesale	1,478
Retail	2,268
Transportation	3,773
Communication	779
Other public utilities	3,907
Construction	1,661
Services	5,111
All other domestic loans	2,433
Foreign commercial and industrial loans	3,686
TOTAL	45,841

Source: *Federal Reserve Bulletin.*

Suggestions for Addition Reading

Baughn, William H., and Walker, Charls E., eds. *The Banker's Handbook.* Homewood, Ill.: Dow Jones-Irwin, 1966, chaps. 24–26, 28, 31–32.

Budzeika, George. "Lending to Business by New York City Banks." New York University, Graduate School of Business Administration, Institute of Finance, *The Bulletin,* September 1971.

Hayes, Douglas A. *Bank Lending Policies: Domestic and International.* Ann Arbor, Mich.: University of Michigan, Bureau of Business Research, 1971, chaps. 6–7.

Holahan, J. Frank. "Is There a Kicker in Your Bank?" *The Journal of Commercial Bank Lending* (May 1969), pp. 2–7.

Houget, George R. "Techniques of Term Loan Analysis." *The Journal of Commercial Bank Lending* (March 1975), pp. 30–36.

Jilk, Lawrence T., Jr. "Quoting Fixed Rate Term Loans." *The Journal of Commercial Bank Lending* (February 1974), pp. 2–16.

Middleton, J. William. "Term Lending—Practical and Profitable." *The Journal of Commercial Bank Lending* (August, 1968), pp. 31–43.

Moore, George S. "Term Loans and Interim Financing." In Benjamin H. Beckhart, ed. *Business Loans of American Commercial Banks.* New York: Ronald Press, 1959, pp. 208–282.

National Conference of Bankers and Certified Public Accountants. "Financial Statement Provisions in Term-Loan Agreements." New York: The American Bankers Association and American Institute of Certified Public Accountants, September 1968.

Van Horne, James C. *Fundamentals of Financial Management.* 3rd ed. Englewood Cliffs, N.J.: Prentice-Hall, 1977, chap. 11.

CHAPTER

13

Consumer Loans

The term *consumer loans* encompasses all loans to individuals to finance the consumer purchase of goods and services. Over the last fifty years, consumer loans have provided an important stimulus to economic activity by helping to bridge the gap between production and consumption. Consumer credit has permitted and encouraged people to buy "big-ticket" items such as automobiles and consumer durables and to pay for them later in convenient monthly installments out of earned income.

In this chapter we shall (1) examine the growth, sources, and types of consumer credit in the economy; (2) discuss briefly the reasons for bank entry into consumer lending; (3) explore the factors involved in consumer credit analysis; (4) note the various types of bank installment loans, including those under bank check credit and credit card plans; (5) discuss the different types of bank noninstallment loans; (6) look into bank lending to sales and consumer finance companies; and (7) consider some important aspects in the legal regulation of consumer lending.

Growth, Sources, and Types of Consumer Loans

Growth

Between 1945 and 1976, total consumer credit (installment and noninstallment loans) outstanding from all sources has increased from $5.7 billion to $217.8 billion, or over 38-fold. In comparison, during the same period, personal consumption expenditures rose from $121.7 billion to $1,079.7 billion, or almost nine times. The sharp rise in consumer credit outstanding is accounted for mainly by the increases in population, income, and prices; the emphasis on consumer lending by commercial banks; and the willingness of consumers to finance a larger part of their expenditures with credit.

Sources

In 1945, commercial banks held only $1.4 billion, or 24.6 percent, of the total consumer loans outstanding. At that time, retail outlets were the primary source of consumer credit. By 1950, banks had passed retailers as the largest supplier of consumer credit. At the end of 1976, bank consumer credit had risen to $97.6 billion and represented 44.8 percent of the total consumer loans outstanding.

Since the early 1950s "finance companies," which include sales, consumer, and other finance companies, have been the second largest supplier of consumer credit. As will be discussed later, bank loans are an important source of funds to finance companies.

Credit unions are the third largest supplier and fastest growing of consumer credit sources. Between 1965 and 1976, consumer loans at credit unions rose from $7.3 billion to $30.5 billion for a compound annual growth rate of 13.7 percent.

Retail outlets are the fourth largest source of consumer credit. Since 1965 retail credit has continued to grow in spite of the introduction and widespread use of bank credit cards.

Types

Approximately 82 percent of the outstanding consumer credit is payable on an installment basis; the remaining 18 percent is of the noninstallment variety. There are five principal types of installment credit: (1) automobile loans, (2) mobile home loans, (3) home improvement loans, (4) revolving credit, including bank credit cards and bank check credit loans, and (5) other loans, including personal loans. At the end of

1976, commercial banks held 47.8 percent of all consumer installment loans (Table 13-1). Each of these types of loans will be discussed later.

There are three main classes of noninstallment credit: (1) single-payment loans, (2) charge accounts, and (3) service credit. At the end of 1976, banks held 88.4 percent of the single-payment loans outstanding. Banks dominate this area in lending primarily because other financial institutions generally have to lend on an installment basis to obtain a yield high enough to cover the cost of funds, other expenses, and realize a profit.

Bank Entry into Consumer Lending

Early Reluctance

Prior to the Great Depression, few banks made consumer loans. One reason for this is that most bankers believed in the commercial credit theory of bank lending, which held that banks should make only short-term, self-liquidating loans, essentially to businesses and farmers. Short-term implied less than one year, and the term "self-liquidating" meant that the loan itself generated the means for payment. Bankers believed that loans to businesses and farmers led to greater production and therefore benefited the economy. On the other hand, most bankers viewed loans to consumers as "unproductive," because the proceeds were not used to finance the direct production of goods. These bankers generally failed to realize that by financing consumption expenditures consumer loans would indirectly lead to greater production.

Table 13-1
Sources of Consumer Installment Loans, Selected Years, 1960–1976 (millions of dollars)

Year Ending	Total	Commercial Banks	Finance Companies	Credit Unions	Retailers[a]	Others[b]
1960	42,968	16,672	15,435	3,923	6,938	
1965	70,893	28,962	23,851	7,324	10,756	
1970	101,898	45,396	27,514	12,986	13,682	2,320
1971	111,195	51,606	28,417	14,770	13,925	2,477
1972	126,756	60,870	31,396	16,913	14,763	2,814
1973	146,434	71,871	35,404	19,609	16,395	3,155
1974	155,384	75,846	36,208	22,116	17,933	3,281
1975	162,237	78,703	36,695	25,354	18,002	3,483
1976	178,775	85,379	39,642	30,546	19,178	4,030

Source: Board of Governors of the Federal Reserve System, *Banking and Monetary Statistics, 1941–1970; Annual Statistical Digest, 1971–1975; Federal Reserve Bulletin;* and unpublished data.

[a] Excludes thirty-day charge credit held by retailers, oil and gas companies, and travel and entertainment companies.
[b] Mutual savings banks, savings and loan associations, and auto dealers.

Bankers also were reluctant to enter the consumer loan field because they thought this type of lending was not in keeping with the dignified image they were supposed to project. Consumer loans were for finance companies and loan sharks, not banks. Finally, there was no pressing need for banks to make consumer loans in the decade prior to the Great Depression because there was more than adequate demand for business credit and securities loans. In fact, by late 1929 almost 40 percent of member bank loans were considered securities loans. With the interest rate on many of these loans ranging as high as 15 to 18 percent, most banks had no incentive to seek consumer loans.[1]

Reasons for Bank Entry into Consumer Lending

Effective Yield. Banks entered consumer lending in the 1930s for many of the same reasons that they began to make term loans at that time. Because of weak loan demand and an excess of funds, interest rates were at record low levels in the mid-1930s. In addition, there was a paucity of investment securities in which to place surplus funds. As a result of these conditions, banks had to turn to consumer loans as a means to raise revenue to meet expenses and increase profits. By making consumer loans on an installment basis, banks were able almost to double the effective return that they could receive on single-payment business loans.

Home Repair and Modernization. Another stimulus to bank consumer lending in the 1930s was the introduction of home repair and modernization loans by the Federal Housing Authority (FHA) under Title I of the Federal Housing Act of 1934. These loans were made on an installment basis for periods up to five years and were insured by the FHA. Home repair and modernization loans provided the first step for many banks into other forms of consumer lending.

Consumer Credit Analysis

Before proceeding to a discussion of the types of bank consumer loans, it is important to consider the factors that bankers take into account in evaluating the creditworthiness of a consumer loan applicant. Essentially, these factors are the same ones considered for a business loan: (1) the ability and (2) the willingness of the borrower to repay the loan in the future. In addition, security requirements are a common feature of most consumer loans.

[1] For a description of the banking system's role in financing the securities speculation of the 1920s, see John Kenneth Galbraith, *The Great Crash* (Boston: Houghton Mifflin, 1961).

Ability To Pay

An individual's ability to repay his debts is a function primarily of his (1) employment, (2) income, (3) assets, and (4) other debts.

Employment. The first questions the loan officer ordinarily asks the consumer loan applicant are (1) "Where are you employed?" and (2) "How long have you been working there?" Consumer credit ordinarily is repaid out of future income and if the applicant is unemployed, he is generally a poor credit risk.

The nature of the applicant's employment also provides some insight into his expected ability to repay his obligations. If a prospective borrower is employed by a firm where layoffs or strikes occur frequently, the risk of default is greater. When a man is out of work, he ordinarily will use the limited amount that he receives from unemployment compensation, welfare, or the union strike fund and his savings to buy food for his family and to meet his rent or mortgage payment. On the other hand, people employed in service industries, retail and wholesale trade, and in the professions generally enjoy a more stable income and hence are better credit risks.

People who change jobs frequently usually are not the best credit risks. Instability in employment indicates, among other things, an instability in income and hence a greater chance of credit default.

Income. After ascertaining the nature of the prospective borrower's employment, the loan officer must then determine the amount of the applicant's income. The loan officer must evaluate whether this amount is sufficient to provide the necessities for the applicant's family, to repay any other obligations, and then to repay the new loan on schedule.

Assets. Instead of using current income to repay his debts, an individual could liquidate part of his assets to acquire the funds to discharge his obligations. Therefore, in order to determine the potential sources of funds to repay debt from this source, the loan officer should request a current statement of condition from individuals who wish to borrow more than some minimum amount, such as $2,000.

Other Debts. The ability of a person to repay any new credit extended to him is a function of the nature, amount, and payment schedule of his other obligations. It is only natural to expect that if a person becomes unemployed or loses his source of income, he will establish a priority schedule for the use of his income and savings to meet the payments of his obligations. Consumer credit payments, including those on his automobile loan, probably will rank below his mortgage payment in the allocation of his funds. With respect to the amount and payment schedule of the existing obligations, the loan officer should make a rough calculation of the projected sources and uses of the applicant's funds in order to ascertain if the prospective borrower's income and funds from the liquidation of assets will be sufficient to cover existing payments and those on any new loan.

Willingness To Pay

A borrower might have the ability to pay his obligations, yet be unwilling to do so. In such a case, the bank would have to initiate a costly, legal action to collect the debt. Thus the bank loan officer must attempt to judge the consumer loan applicant's expected willingness to pay. The best predictor of this is the potential borrower's past payment record. Most consumer loan applications have space for the potential borrower to list at least three credit references. The usual procedure in most banks with a separate consumer loan department is for a consumer credit analyst in that department to telephone these references and to check the payment record of the applicant. A check also should be made with the local retail credit bureau.

Security Requirements

After evaluating the applicant's expected ability and willingness to pay, the loan officer must decide whether to extend the credit. Unlike business lending, where security requirements are imposed in marginal cases, security is required for all consumer loans except some personal loans to individuals with superior credit ratings. In most instances, the item being financed, such as an autombile, mobile home, or appliance, is used to secure the loan as a matter of course. As a general rule, the consumer credit decision should not be based on whether or not the loan is secured but on whether or not the applicant has the ability and willingness to pay. Because of attorney's fees and other costs, the bank usually suffers a loss when it has to foreclose on a consumer loan.[2]

An Operations Research Approach to Consumer Credit Analysis

Unless an individual is known to the bank, it might take several hours to check his credit references and to process his application for credit. For banks that receive daily a large number of consumer credit applications from people unknown to the bank, the job of evaluating these applications easily could become unmanageable. In order to deal with the

[2]To illustrate, a bank in South Carolina received in the mail the keys to an automobile being financed by that bank and a note from the borrower stating that he did not want the car any longer and that the vehicle was in a parking lot in a certain town in Texas. The bank sent a college student by bus to drive the automobile back to South Carolina.

problem, several banks in recent years have developed operations research techniques using a credit scoring or pointing system for processing consumer credit applications.[3] This approach is very similar to that already being used by a number of banks to evaluate business loan applications.

Essentially, a credit scoring system for consumer credit applications involves, first, the selection of certain attributes of an individual's financial situation, such as his occupation, time on job, income, marital status, number of dependents, housing status (renter or owner), type of neighborhood, and the type and size of his checking or savings account. Within each category, points are assigned. For example, under the heading "occupation," 0 points might be assigned if the individual is unemployed or on welfare; 5 points might be awarded if he is a professional, managerial, or clerical employee; 1 point, if he is a seasonal, semiskilled worker, and so on. Points from each category are added up. If the total number of points is above the "high" limits, then perhaps only an employment check need be made before the credit is approved. If the total score falls below the "low" limit, the consumer credit analyst may reject the application unless additional information can be provided to justify the credit. For those applications whose scores fall between the high and low limits or in the "gray area," the credit analyst must make a more thorough evaluation and review. The chief advantages of the numerical credit scoring systems are that it minimizes credit investigation time and costs, it may help to reduce losses, and it gives the credit analysts time to focus on the marginal credit risks.

Bank Installment Loans

Of the total amount of consumer credit outstanding at banks at the end of 1976, 87.4 percent were on the installment basis and 12.6 percent represented single-payment loans. The four main types of bank installment loans are (1) automobile loans, (2) mobile home loans, (3) home improvement loans, (4) revolving credit (bank credit card and bank check credit loans), and (5) "other" and personal loans.

[3]*Operations research* may be defined as the application of mathematical, statistical, and scientific techniques to business problems. Two excellent articles on the application of operations research to consumer credit analysis are Robert A. Morris, "Credit Analysis: An O. R. Approach," *Management Services*, 34 (March–April 1966), pp. 52–57, and H. Martin Weingartner, "Concepts and Utilization of Credit-Scoring Techniques," *Banking* (February 1966), pp. 51–53. These articles are reprinted in Paul F. Jessup, *Innovations in Bank Management* (New York: Holt, Rinehart and Winston, 1969), pp. 300–315.

Automobile Loans

Indirect Loans. Banks acquire automobile paper either indirectly, by purchasing it from automobile dealers, or directly, by arranging the loans with the borrower. As shown in Table 13-2, at the end of 1976, approximately 55.6 percent of the $35.3 billion in automobile paper held by banks represented indirect lending. During recent years, banks have faced stiffer competition from manufacturer-sponsored finance companies and credit unions for automobile paper.

There are several considerations involved in a bank's making indirect automobile loans that are not present in direct lending.[4] First, high-volume automobile dealers are in a position to demand that the bank take a proportion of the high-risk automobile loans they generate. The bank either must accept the loans or face loss of this source of loans to other lenders, who will accept high-risk business.[5]

Second, many autombile dealers also expect their banks to finance their inventory (known as *floor planning*) at a preferential rate. Given the high cost of servicing these loans, many banks find this type of financing unprofitable.

Finally, it is a practice for many automobile dealers to receive a "kickback" equal to approximately 1 percent of the volume of automo-

[4]Much of this discussion is based on Douglas A. Hayes, *Bank Lending Policies: Domestic and International* (Ann Arbor, Mich: University of Michigan Bureau of Business Research, Graduate School of Business Administration, 1971), pp. 177–182.

[5]Bankers generally expect delinquencies on indirect automobile loans to be about twice that on direct loans.

Table 13-2
Installment Credit Held by Commercial Banks, Selected Dates, 1960–1976 (millions of dollars)

		Automobile Paper					Revolving Credit		
Year Ending	Total	Total	Purchased	Direct	Mobile Homes	Home Improvement	Bank Credit Card	Bank Credit Check	Other and Personal Loans
1960	16,672	8,136	5,316	2,820	—	2,200	—	—	3,577
1965	28,962	15,868	10,209	5,659	—	2,571	—	—	6,357
1970	45,396	20,805	12,918	7,888	2,462	3,071	3,792	1,336	16,393
1971	51,606	23,252	13,908	9,344	4,634	3,231	4,490	1,462	14,538
1972	60,870	27,305	16,323	10,982	6,406	3,601	5,408	1,775	16,373
1973	71,871	31,502	18,997	12,505	8,340	4,083	6,838	2,254	18,854
1974	75,846	30,994	18,687	12,306	8,972	4,694	8,281	2,797	20,108
1975	78,703	31,534	18,353	13,181	8,704	4,965	9,501	2,810	21,188
1976	85,379	35,313	19,642	15,671	8,233	5,381	11,075	3,010	22,368

Source: Board of Governors of the Federal Reserve System, *Annual Statistical Digest, 1971–1975* and *Federal Reserve Bulletin.*

bile paper placed with banks. In effect, the dealer participates in the profits from the loan on a no-risk basis. In summary, these considerations may lessen significantly the overall profitability of indirect automobile lending.

Direct Loans. At the end of 1976, direct automobile loans acccounted for 44.4 percent of total automobile loans held by banks. Banks tend to charge a higher rate on direct automobile loans than on indirect loans. This is because of competitive pressures from dealers for lower rates on indirect loans. Given this fact, and the influence of dealer considerations on indirect lending, direct automobile loans usually are one of the most profitable uses of a bank's funds.

Mobile Home Loans

Annual shipments of mobile homes averaged 380,392 units between 1967 and 1976. The principal reasons for the growing importance of mobile homes in the housing market were the lower initial prices as compared with conventional houses, the growing acceptance of mobile homes as family living accommodations, the introduction of governmental and private insurance for mobile home loans, and the greater willingness by banks, finance companies, and savings and loan associations to make mobile home loans. At the end of 1976 insured banks held $8.3 billion of mobile home paper.

In the past, many bankers were skeptical of making mobile home loans for several reasons. First, it was commonly believed that the delinquency rate on mobile home loans was abnormally high. However, many banks now report that their delinquency rate on mobile home loans is below that on automobile loans. Second, most mobile home loans have an initial maturity of twelve years or more. This consideration, together with the fact that mobile homes depreciate very rapidly, meant that if it were necessary to foreclose, there was a good chance that the mobile home's value would be less than the outstanding loan balance. However, the advent of insurance for mobile homes and the enforcement of minimum down-payment requirements has lessened considerably the chance of loss if it becomes necessary to repossess mobile homes.

Home Improvement

Home improvement loans include both FHA-insured credit and noninsured credit extended to customers to finance the maintenance and improvement of their homes. Also included in this loan category is credit used for the purchase and installation of equipment such as heating and air-conditioning systems, hot-water heaters, and kitchen appliances, and storm windows and insulation as energy-saving measures. At the close of 1976, home improvement loans accounted for only 6.3 percent of total bank installment credit. Between 1965 and 1976, bank home improvement loans increased less percentagewise than any other installment loan category. The most important reason for this was the strong competition for these from savings and loan associations, finance companies, and credit unions.

Revolving Credit

Bank Credit-Card Plans. The use of bank credit cards has grown rapidly in recent years. On September 30, 1967, 290 banks had credit-card plans with outstanding credit under these arrangements of $633 million. By the end of 1975, the number of banks offering credit-card plans had risen to 2,027, while credit-card balances had jumped to $9.5 billion.

Under bank credit-card plans, customers are provided a free plastic credit card and a line of credit that may range from $200 to $5,000, with the average being about $1,000. When the customer signs a sales slip at a store he activates his line of credit. The merchant presents the signed sales slip to the bank and receives immediate payment less a discount, which ranges from 1 to 7 percent, depending on the size of the average sales ticket generated by the store. The discount applicable at any store depends on the total volume of credit-card sales generated by the store, the type of goods or services sold, and competitive conditions among banks in the area. Large discount stores tend to pay lower discounts than small specialty stores. The customer receives a monthly bill from the bank for his purchases. He has the option of paying the full bill within a grace period (typically twenty-five days) without a service charge, or he may repay on revolving credit with interest of usually 1.5 percent per month charged on the unpaid balance. An informal survey of bank credit-card plans showed that interest charges provide about two-thirds of total credit-card income, while approximately one-fourth of the total is generated by merchant discounts.

Under bank credit-card plans, the bank provides the credit and, as long as the merchant follows the terms of his agreement, the bank absorbs the credit and fraud losses. A Federal Reserve survey in August 1971 showed that net charge-offs (credit and fraud losses) in 1970 were 3.17 percent of credit-card balances outstanding on December 31, 1970.[6] Fraud losses comprised about 20 percent of net charge-offs. On their credit-card operations, the surveyed banks showed an average net loss for the year of 1.79 percent on credit-card balances outstanding at

[6] Fraud losses occur primarily from the use of lost or stolen cards, collusion with merchants, and deliberate skips.

the end of 1970. Only 30 percent of the surveyed banks reported a net profit in 1970.

Banks attempt to control credit and fraud losses on their credit-card programs in three ways: (1) by closely screening credit-card applicants, (2) by setting maximum limits on single purchases that can be made from given sellers without bank authorization, and (3) by setting credit limits on individual card holders.[7] It would appear that the most important reason for the high credit and fraud losses experienced to date has been the poor selection of credit-card holders.[8] Since 1970 losses from all sources have diminished as banks gained experience in the selection of credit-card applicants and in all other phases of their credit-card operation. In 1975, 68 banks with deposits of $200 million reported gross earnings on average credit-card balances of 6.28 percent (after deduction for expenses and net credit losses).[9] For these banks net credit losses over the past five years averaged 1.66 percent of average balances outstanding. Today, credit-card loans are the most profitable loan category for the vast majority of the banks offering this type of loan.

Check Credit. In the 1950s, a number of banks introduced a new type of installment credit which became known as *check credit* or *revolving check credit*. Under these plans banks provide qualified individuals with a line of credit of from $300 to $5,000. The individual is given a book of special checks that he may use to purchase items and services. When these written checks are presented to the bank for collection, a loan account is activated for the borrower and the check is paid. Some banks have similar plans whereby an individual may use his regular checks to activate a special loan account.

Payment requirements usually specify that $\frac{1}{12}$ or $\frac{1}{24}$ of the loan be repaid each month. Interest rates usually range from 1 to 1.5 percent per month on the unpaid balance. On plans where funds are advanced only in $100 increments, the interest charges are expressed in terms of a daily rate, such as 5 cents per $100 per day.

On September 30, 1967, the total volume of credit outstanding under check credit plans amounted to $483 million. By the end of 1976, this total had grown to $3,010 million. The rate of increase in check credit has slowed considerably as bank credit-card plans have gained in popularity.

[7] Hayes, p. 184.

[8] Harold S. Taylor, "The Chicago Bank Credit Card Fiasco," *The Bankers Magazine* (Winter 1968), pp. 49–52. In another case, one bank requested from a local credit bureau a list of the "good" credit risks and a list of the "bad" credit risks. Through error, credit cards were mailed initially to everyone on the "bad" list. Needless to say, credit and fraud losses were large until the cards were canceled.

[9] Federal Reserve, *Functional Cost Analysis 1975 Average Banks*.

"Other" and Personal Loans

At the end of 1976, "other" and personal loans comprised 26.2 percent of total bank installment credit outstanding. "Other" loans represent credit to purchase apparel, appliances, furniture, jewelry, and boats. Personal loans are made for virtually every conceivable purpose, such as to finance educational expenditures; medical, dental, and hospital bills; vacations; taxes; insurance premiums; and consolidation of consumer debts. A portion of the funds advanced under the heading of personal loans are used to purchase automobiles and other consumer durables.

Bank Noninstallment Loans

Noninstallment credit consists of those forms of consumer credit that are scheduled to be repaid in a lump sum. At the end of 1976, commercial banks held \$12.3 billion or 31.5 percent of the noninstallment loans outstanding (Table 13-3).

Consumers borrow on a single-payment basis for the same variety of reasons that they borrow on an installment basis. Some credit is used for the purchase of consumer goods, but a significant proportion represents funds advanced to pay personal taxes and life insurance premiums. Because the borrower has the use of the funds for the entire term of the loan, the effective interest rate on single-payment loans is

Table 13-3
Noninstallment Credit, Selected Years, 1960–1976
(millions of dollars)

		Single-Payment Loans		Charge Accounts		
End of Period	Total	Commercial Banks	Other Financial Institutions	Retail Outlets	Credit Cards[a]	Service Credit
1960	13,173	3,884	623	4,893	463	3,337
1965	18,990	6,690	981	5,724	706	4,889
1970	25,099	8,469	1,206	6,163	1,805	7,456
1971	27,099	9,316	1,269	6,397	1,953	8,164
1972	30,232	10,857	1,399	7,055	1,947	8,974
1973	33,049	11,753	1,488	7,783	2,046	9,979
1974	33,997	11,500	1,479	8,012	2,122	10,884
1975	35,039	11,576	1,496	7,735	2,205	12,027
1976	38,998	12,270	1,613	9,470	2,294	13,351

Source: *Federal Reserve Bulletin* and unpublished data.

[a]Service station and miscellaneous credit-card accounts and home-heating oil accounts.

significantly less than that on installment loans. Most bank noninstallment loans are unsecured and maturities typically are less than one year.

Bank Financing of Sales and Consumer Finance Companies

Significance

Besides extending credit directly to consumers and purchasing consumer paper from dealers, banks provide a considerable proportion of the funds advanced by sales and consumer finance companies. Based on the most recent (June 30, 1975) Federal Reserve Survey of Finance Companies, commercial banks supplied $7.9 billion or 11.9 percent of the total short-term finance company debt. By making loans to sales and consumer finance companies, banks are helping indirectly to provide funds for those individuals whose credit standings preclude their borrowing directly from banks.

Credit Analysis of Finance Companies

Finance companies usually obtain funds from banks under lines of credit. Before a line is approved for a company, a thorough credit analysis must be performed. Essentially, the techniques of business credit analysis described in Chapter 10 are used to evaluate finance companies.

The first step in evaluating the creditworthiness of a finance company is to obtain and analyze data on the company's financial condition and profitability. Because of the similar pattern of operations among both the sales finance and consumer finance company groups, ratio analysis provides an excellent tool for evaluating the data. The First National Bank of Chicago has published composite ratios on a semiannual and annual basis for sales finance companies since 1935 and for consumer finance companies since 1949. At present the bank publishes fifty different ratios calculated for sales finance companies, and thirty-four different ratios on consumer finance companies.[10] By comparing the level and trend in the absolute ratios of the company being analyzed with industry averages, the bank credit analyst usually is able

[10]For a detailed discussion of the significant ratios for each group, see Ray H. Matson, "Finance Company Loans," in William H. Baughn and Charls E. Walker, eds., *The Banker's Handbook* (Homewood, Ill: Dow Jones-Irwin, 1966), chap. 29; and J. Russell Hanson, "Key Decisions in Loans to Finance Companies," *The Bankers Magazine* (Summer 1966), pp. 20–35. The July or August issue of *The Journal of Commercial Bank Lending* usually contains an article with an analysis of the previous year's finance company ratios as published by the First National Bank of Chicago.

to obtain considerable insight into the company's relative financial condition, profitability, and operating efficiency.

The second step in analyzing the creditworthiness of a finance company is to evaluate the quality of mangement. Usually, the loan officer will visit the company and talk with and observe its officers. In marginal credit decisions, the quality of a company's management ordinarily will be the determining factor in whether or not credit should be extended.

Terms of Finance Company Loans

Most large finance companies borrow at the prime rate. Typically, however, compensating balance requirements are imposed that increase the effective interest rate on the credit. In addition, finance company loans generally are unsecured.

Consumer Credit Protection

Interest Charged

The maximum interest rate that a bank may charge is specified in the laws of the state, territory, or district where the bank is located. For national banks, the maximum rate that may be charged is that permitted by state law where the bank is located, or a rate of 1 percent above the discount rate on 90-day commercial paper in effect at the Federal Reserve bank in the Federal Reserve district where the bank is located, whichever is the greater.

Truth in Lending

In 1969 Congress passed the Consumer Credit Protection Act (popularly known as the Truth in Lending Act), the purpose of which is "to assure that every borrower and customer who has a need for consumer credit is given meaningful information with respect to the cost of that credit." Details as to the implementation of the Truth in Lending Act are set forth in the Federal Reserve's Regulation Z, which "applies to all persons who in the ordinary course of business regularly extend, or offer to extend, or arrange, or offer to arrange, for the extension of consumer credit."

The two most important disclosures required by Regulation Z are the finance charge and the annual percentage rate. The *finance charge* is the total of all costs that the customer must pay, directly or indirectly, for credit. Some of the more common items that must be included in the finance charge are (1) interest; (2) loan fee; (3) finder's fee or similar charge; (4) time price differential; (5) amount paid as a discount; (6)

service, transaction, or carrying charge; (7) points; (8) appraisal fee (except in real estate transactions); (9) premium for credit life or other insurance, if this is a condition for granting credit; and (10) investigation or credit report fee (except in real estate transactions).

The *annual percentage rate* is the relative or effective cost of credit in percentage terms. For example, the typical charge on credit-card balances is 1.5 percent per month on the unpaid balance. The annual percentage rate would be 12 times 1.5 percent, or 18 percent. Other important requirements are that the annual percentage rate must be accurate to the nearest ¼ of 1 percent, and that the words "finance charge" and "annual percentage rate" must stand out especially clearly on the cost disclosure statement that must be provided each customer.

Equal Credit Opportunity Act

In 1974 Congress enacted the Equal Credit Opportunity Act, which forbids discrimination by creditors on the basis of sex or marital status. The Act went into effect October 28, 1975. It covers all who regularly extend credit, including banks, finance companies, department stores, and credit card issuers. In 1976 Congress broadened the scope of the Act to forbid discrimination in credit transactions based on race, color, religion, national origin, age, receipt of income from public assistance programs, and good faith exercise of rights under the Consumer Protection Act of 1968 (which includes the Truth in Lending, Fair Credit Billing, Equal Credit Opportunity, Fair Credit Reporting and Consumer Leasing Acts). The revised act became effective March 23, 1977. Any creditor who fails to comply with the requirements of the Equal Credit Opportunity Act shall be liable to the aggrieved individual for any actual damages sustained and possible punitive damages up to $10,000.

Fair Credit Billing Act

A primary purpose of the Fair Credit Billing Act, which became effective in October 1975, is to help consumers resolve credit billing disputes promptly and fairly. A billing error is any mistake made by a creditor in billing or identifying a transaction on a periodic statement, or it may be a creditor's failure to send a periodic statement to the customer's correct address. In the case of billing errors or complaints, the creditor, not later than thirty days after the receipt of the notice of error or complaint, must send a written acknowledgment to the obligor, unless appropriate corrective action is taken within the thirty-day period. After this acknowledgment, the creditor has an additional ninety days to resolve the dispute. Any creditor who fails to comply with the requirements involving the correction of billing errors forfeits any right to collect from the obligor the amount cited in the notice and any finance charges not to exceed $50.

The Fair Credit Billing Act also overturned the *holder in due course* doctrine. This doctrine required a consumer to continue making payments to a third party creditor even though the goods turned out to be defective. Typically, sellers arrange financing of consumer purchases with third parties, or they finance the goods themselves and then sell the contract to a third-party creditor. If the seller later went out of business, the purchaser would usually be "out of luck" if he attempted recourse against the creditor. The Fair Credit Billing Act has changed all this. For purchases in excess of $50 made within the consumer's state or 100 miles from his address (whichever is farther), a consumer may refuse to continue paying for faulty items until the complaint is resolved. The implication of this act for banks is profound. Now banks are at risk for unsatisfactory goods and services financed by them, but sold or offered by an unrelated seller. Excluded from the new law are purchases made with credit cards or cases where the consumer has arranged financing independently.

Fair Credit Reporting Act

Purpose. The Fair Credit Reporting Act of 1971 requires that consumer reporting agencies "adopt reasonable procedures for meeting the needs of commerce for consumer credit, personnel, insurance and other information in a manner which is fair and equitable to the consumer, with regard to confidentiality, accuracy, relevancy, and proper utilization of such information." With this Act, Congress recognized the need to ensure that any individual or firm that develops credit information "exercise their responsibilities with fairness, impartiality, and a respect for the consumer's right to privacy."

Permissible Purposes of Reports. Under the act, a consumer reporting agency may furnish a consumer report under the following circumstances and no other:

(1) in response to the order of a court having jurisdiction to issue such an order.
(2) in accordance with the written instructions of the consumer to whom it relates.
(3) to a person which it has reason to believe—
  (A) intends to use the information with a credit transaction involving the consumer on whom the information is to be furnished and involving the extension of credit to, or review or collection of an account of, the consumer: or
  (B) intends to use the information for employment purposes; or
  (C) intends to use the information in connection with the underwriting of insurance involving the consumer; or

(D) intends to use the information in connection with a determination of the consumer's eligibility for a license or other benefit granted by a governmental instrumentality required by law to consider an applicant's financial responsibility or status; or

(E) otherwise has a legitimate business need for the information in connection with a business transaction involving the consumer.

Obsolete Information. Except as authorized in the section above under "Permissible purposes of reports," no consumer reporting agency may make any consumer report containing any of the following items of information:

(1) bankruptcies which, from date of adjudication of most recent bankruptcy, antedate the report by more than fourteen years.
(2) suits and judgments which, from date of entry, antedate the report by more than seven years or until the governing statute of limitations has expired, whichever is the longer period.
(3) paid tax liens which, from day of payment, antedate the report by more than seven years.
(4) accounts placed for collection or charged to profit and loss which antedate the report by more than seven years.
(5) records of arrest, indictment, or conviction of crime which, from date of disposition, release, or parole, antedate the report by more than seven years.
(6) any other adverse item of information which antedates the report by more than seven years.

These restrictions are not applicable in the case of any consumer credit report to be used in connection with

(1) a credit transaction involving a principal amount of $50,000 or more;
(2) the underwriting of life insurance involving $50,000 or more; or
(3) the employment of any individual at an annual salary of $20,000 or more.

Civil Liability for Negligent Noncompliance. The Fair Credit Reporting Act provides that any consumer reporting agency or user of information that is negligent in failing to comply with any requirement imposed under this title with respect to any consumer is liable to that consumer in an amount equal to the sum of

(1) any actual damages sustained by the consumer as a result of the failure;
(2) in the case of any successful action to enforce any liability under this act, the costs of the action together with reasonable attorney's fees as determined by the court.

Conclusion

Congress has enacted several complex laws designed to protect consumers. The benefits to consumers are obvious; however, there are significant costs involved to lenders to train personnel and to generate the paperwork to effect compliance. The potential liability for violations of the law makes it mandatory that bank consumer loan officers become familiar with the detailed regulations handed down by government authorities designated to enforce the laws.

Suggestions for Additional Reading

"Bank Credit Cards." Federal Reserve Bank of Chicago, *Business Conditions* (July 1972), pp. 8–16.

"Bank Financing of Mobile Homes." *Federal Reserve Bulletin* (March 1971), pp. 179–182.

Board of Governors of the Federal Reserve System. *Bank Credit-Card and Check-Credit Plans.* Washington, D.C.: Board of Governors of the Federal Reserve System, July 1968.

Brimmer, Andrew F. "Growth and Profitability of Credit Card Banking." Paper presented at the National Credit Card Conference of The American Bankers Association, New Orleans, October 27, 1971.

Edwards, Richard. "The 'Friendly Revolver'—A Method of Financing the Finance Company Industry." *The Journal of Commercial Bank Lending* (July 1976), pp. 9–17.

Fitzpatrick, Dennis B. "An Analysis of Bank Credit Card Profits." *Journal of Bank Research* (Autumn 1976), pp. 199–205.

Gibson, Donald M. T. *The Strategic and Operational Significance of the Credit Card for Commercial Banks.* Research Report No. 42. Boston: Federal Reserve Bank of Boston, 1968.

Godfrey, John M. "Cut-Back in Mobile Home Loans." Federal Reserve Bank of Atlanta, *Monthly Review* (November 1974), pp. 176–177.

Hayes, Douglas A. *Bank Lending Policies: Domestic and International.* Ann Arbor, Mich.: University of Michigan, Bureau of Business Research, 1971, chap. 9.

Matson, Ray H. "Finance Company Loans." In William H. Baughn and Charls E. Walker, eds. *The Banker's Handbook.* Homewood, Ill.: Dow Jones-Irwin, 1966, chap. 28.

Morris, Robert A. "Credit Analysis: An O. R. Approach." *Management Services* (March–April 1966), pp. 53–57.

Orgler, Yair E. "Evaluation of Bank Consumer Loans with Credit Scoring Models." *Journal of Bank Research* (Spring 1971), pp. 31–37.

Taylor, Harold S. "The Chicago Bank Credit Card Fiasco." *The Bankers Magazine* (Winter 1968), pp. 49–52.

CHAPTER

14

Real Estate Loans

Although it is well known that commercial banks are the primary source of short-term credit, many people are unaware that these institutions allocate a significant portion of their funds for real estate loans, some of which have maturities ranging up to thirty years. At the end of 1976, real estate loans comprised 28.1 percent of bank loans outstanding. Of total bank mortgage loans outstanding, 56.8 percent were on residential property. Nationally, residential construction accounts for 20–25 percent of the total gross private domestic investment each year. It is apparent that banks have made a large contribution toward financing one of the important income creating sectors in the economy.

In this chapter we shall (1) examine the growth and sources of real estate loans, (2) note some of the considerations influencing bank real estate lending, (3) determine the types of direct bank real estate loans, (4) discuss the procedures involved in residential real estate lending, (5) consider briefly the provisions and terms of residential real estate loans, (6) discuss the types of indirect bank real estate loans, and (7) note some other important bank real estate activities.

Growth and Sources of Real Estate Loans

Between 1960 and 1976, total mortgage debt in the United States rose from $207.1 billion to $884.2 billion, or more than 4-fold (Table 14-1). At the end of 1976 savings and loan associations held 36.5 percent of the total mortgage debt outstanding. This share was 2.2 times that held by commercial banks and more than 3.5 times that held by life insurance companies.

Between 1960 and 1976, U.S. agencies and mortgage pools and trust of U.S. agencies increased their holdings from $13.2 billion to $116.6 billion. The primary reason for this sharp increase in mortgage credit provided by U.S. agencies was the creation of many federal programs toward the end of the 1960s to finance housing construction. During the tight-money year of 1970, U.S. agencies provided 23.9 percent of the net increase in mortage credit.

Commercial Banks and Real Estate Lending

Reasons for Bank Entry into Real Estate Lending

National Bank Regulations Liberalized. Under the National Banking Acts of 1863 and 1864, national banks were prohibited from making loans on urban real estate. This restriction was liberalized, in part, in 1916 and even more so in 1927. The rationale for this prohibition was that banks could not afford to allocate funds to long-term and illiquid assets such as real estate loans since their liabilities consisted primarily of demand deposits. In other words, it was against the tenets of sound banking "to borrow short and to lend long."

Creation of Government Housing Programs. After restrictions on real estate lending by national banks were lifted, the next significant impetus to bank real estate lending was the creation of government housing programs to insure and guarantee real estate loans and to provide a secondary market for mortgages. The National Housing Act of June 27, 1934, established the Federal Housing Administration (FHA) to insure loans for repairs to real property and mortgages on homes and rental housing and to create privately owned national mortgage associations in order to establish a secondary market for mortgages. A secondary market under government sponsorship was not established until 1938, when the Federal National Mortgage Association (FNMA) was set up with Reconstruction Finance Corporation (REC) capital. The FHA program also established minimum property standards through its in-

Table 14-1

Total Mortgage Debt Outstanding, By Holder, Selected Years, 1960–1976 (billions of dollars)

End of Period	Total	Savings and Loan Associations	Commercial Banks	Life Insurance Companies	Mutual Savings Banks	Federal and Related Agencies	Mortgage Pools and Trusts	Individuals and Others
1960	207.5	60.0	28.8	41.8	26.9	11.3	2.0	38.4
1965	333.3	110.3	49.7	60.0	44.6	12.7	8.7	55.1
1970	474.2	150.3	73.3	74.4	57.9	33.6	4.8	79.9
1971	526.5	174.2	82.5	75.5	62.0	36.8	9.5	85.9
1972	603.4	206.2	99.3	76.9	67.6	40.2	14.4	98.9
1973	682.3	231.7	119.1	81.4	73.2	46.7	18.0	112.2
1974	742.5	249.3	132.1	86.2	74.9	58.3	23.8	117.8
1975	801.6	278.7	136.2	89.2	77.2	56.9	34.1	119.3
1976	889.5	323.1	150.9	91.6	81.7	56.8	49.8	125.6

Source: *Federal Reserve Bulletin* and unpublished data.

spection system. By improving the quality of the security behind mortgage loans, the national marketability of these loans was enhanced.

Another major stimulus to bank real estate lending was the introduction of the VA loan. Under the Servicemen's Readjustment Act of 1944, the Veterans Adminstration agreed to guarantee mortgage loans made by private lenders to veterans for the purchase of homes.

Increased Use of Amortization. Prior to the Great Depression, the majority of mortgage loans were made with the principal due at maturity. An important part of the FHA program was the amortization feature, usually with monthly payments. The use of this feature greatly enhanced the liquidity of real estate loans, lessened the chance of default, and therefore made mortgage loans much more attractive to banks.

Current Rationale for Bank Real Estate Lending

The reasons cited above account largely for the initial stimulus to bank real estate lending, but they do not provide a satisfactory explanation of the sharp increase since 1960 in mortgage debt held by banks.

Growth in Time and Savings Deposits. Perhaps the primary reason for this recent expansion of bank real estate lending was the rapid growth in time and savings deposits relative to demand deposits. As we saw earlier, this major shift in the composition of deposits encouraged banks to match these long-term sources of funds with long-term assets such as mortgage loans, term loans, and municipal securities. The stable flow of monthly income from mortgage loans is particularly well suited for meeting the interest expense of time and savings deposits.

Moderately Good Yield. A second reason for the recent increase in bank real estate lending is that mortgage yields have been at historically high levels. Yields on conventional mortgages on new homes have averaged 8.12 percent for the 1969 to 1976 period. On an after-tax basis, however, these yields generally would rank below those available on municipals, consumer loans, and most business term loans.

Increase in Deposits and Sale of Other Services. Another reason why banks make real estate loans is that such actions may lead, in turn, to an increase in deposits and the sale of other services. In its dealings with an individual mortgagee, the bank has an excellent opportunity to ask for his demand and savings deposits and to provide him with other services, such as a safe deposit box, traveler's checks, installment loans, trust services, and so forth. On the other hand, when a bank accommodates a business's real estate credit needs, it usually is in a position to suggest that the firm maintain a deposit with the bank and utilize other bank services.

Constraints upon Bank Real Estate Lending

In contrast to the above motives for banks' increasing real estate lending, there are several practical and legal constraints on bank mortgage activity.

High Cost of Origination. In comparison with other loans and investments, mortgage loans are relatively expensive to acquire. The property to be mortgaged must be appraised and inspected, and detailed and complex forms must be prepared. Many banks offset a substantial portion of these costs by charging an "origination fee." In most cases, however, competitive conditions limit the size of this charge, and the bank must be prepared to absorb the initial cost of putting the loan on the books.

Relatively Illiquid Asset. In spite of the expanding national secondary market, enhanced even further by the 1970 Housing Act, which empowered the FNMA to purchase conventional mortgages in addition to FHA and VA mortgages, the fact remains that a real estate loan is a relatively illiquid asset. It cannot be sold with the same swiftness as a Treasury security or a municipal obligation, nor can it be sold as readily to another bank as can a business loan to a prime customer.

Legal Limitations. National bank laws limit a national bank's overall holdings of real estate mortgages to an amount equal to the unimpaired capital and surplus of the bank or 70 percent of the amount of time and savings deposits, whichever is greater. There are similar restrictions applicable to state-chartered banks. For most banks, however, these legal limitations have not been an effective restraint on mortgage acquisitions. National bank laws also contain a number of other stipulations with respect to real estate lending.

Types of Direct Bank Real Estate Loans

For purposes of analysis, bank real estate lending activities may be classified under three headings: (1) direct and (2) indirect bank real estate lending, and (3) other bank real estate lending activities. *Direct* bank real estate loans are those made by the bank "directly" to final purchasers for the permanent financing of real estate. *Indirect* bank real estate loans are those not made directly to final purchasers; they include construction loans, loans to mortgage bankers, loans to land developers, and the purchase of the securities of U.S. housing agencies. Other bank real estate lending activities include the origination, sale, and servicing of mortgages; the organization of real estate investment trusts (REITs); and bank trust department mortgage lending. Seven categories of direct real estate loans are discussed below.

FHA Residential Loans

FHA loans are loans insured by the Federal Housing Administration. For this insurance, the borrower pays a premium of ½ of 1 percent of the average unpaid balance of the loan during the year. These premiums are paid into a mutual mortgage insurance fund. If an FHA-insured loan goes into default, the holder conveys it to the FHA and receives, in exchange, debentures of the mutual mortgage insurance fund or cash in an amount equal to the unpaid principal, payments made by the lender for taxes, insurance premiums, special assessments, and foreclosure costs up to $75.

Bank holdings of FHA mortgages have increased very little in recent years. There are several reasons for this. First, because of the ceiling placed on the FHA interest rates, yields on these mortgages frequently have been below the yields on conventional mortgages and most other bank-eligible assets. Second, when FHA interest rates are below conventional mortgage yields, property sellers frequently are unwilling to pay the required "points" or discount on the mortgage needed to make the yield on the FHA mortgage equal to the yield on conventional mortgages. Potential buyers must obtain a conventional mortgage rather than an FHA mortgage. Third, because FHA mortgages on property with an appraised value of over $35,000 require a down payment of 20 percent on the amount above $35,000 up to a maximum loan amount of $45,000, many home buyers in this price range have sought to reduce their down payment by borrowing under conventional mortgage arrangements instead of seeking FHA loans. Fourth, many banks do not prefer to make FHA loans because of the longer processing time involved. Finally, the high foreclosure rate on FHA mortgages in recent years has caused many banks to eschew FHA loans.

VA Residential Loans

VA loans are loans guaranteed by the Veterans Administration. Under the VA guarantee program, a qualified veteran may have his mortgage loan guaranteed up to $17,500 for a single-family home. The Veterans Administration has another program whereby a lender may be reimbursed for losses of up to 15 percent of the total loans made to eligible veterans. Lenders who incur losses under either the guarantee or insurance program are paid in cash.

Table 14-2
Mortgage Loans Held by Commercial Banks, Selected Years, 1960–1976 (millions of dollars)

		Residential					
End of Period	Total	Total	FHA Insured	VA Guaranteed	Conventional	Other Nonfarm	Farm
1960	28,806	20,362	5,851	2,859	11,652	6,796	1,648
1965	49,675	32,387	7,702	2,688	21,997	14,377	2,911
1970	73,275	45,640	7,919	2,589	35,131	23,284	4,351
1971	82,515	52,004	8,310	2,980	40,714	26,306	4,205
1972	99,314	62,782	8,495	3,203	51,084	31,751	4,781
1973	119,068	74,930	8,234	3,297	63,399	38,696	5,442
1974	132,105	82,377	7,155	3,238	71,984	43,679	6,049
1975	136,187	83,237	6,767	3,254	73,216	45,737	6,351
1976	150,810	85,593	8,627		76,966	58,502	6,715

Source: *Federal Reserve Bulletin* and unpublished data.

As may be seen in Table 14-2, during recent years banks have stabilized their holdings of VA loans. Like FHA loans, VA loans generally have been unattractive to banks because their yields were restricted by statutory ceiling and hence were unattractive when compared with the yields on conventional mortgages and most other types of loans and investments.

Conventional Residential Loans

Conventional residential loans are mortgage loans that are neither insured or guaranteed. As shown in Table 14-2, conventional mortgages accounted for practically all of the growth in bank holdings of residential mortgages since 1965. The principal advantages of conventional loans over FHA and VA mortgages are that (1) the interest rate is free to move in response to supply and demand pressures instead of being pegged by regulation or Presidential decree, (2) there is less red tape, (3) servicing costs are lower, and (4) the processing time is faster.

Commercial Real Estate Loans

Commercial real estate loans are loans on business property such as apartments, stores, office buildings, restaurants, motels, and hotels. Because of the greater risks involved with loans on business property, banks normally are reluctant to lend more than 70 percent of the cost or appraised value of the property. In a study of bank commercial real estate loans, it was found that interest rates on these loans were usually

1 to 3 percentage points above the prime rate and that these loans typically were fully amortized over a maturity of fiteen years or less.[1]

Banks make commercial mortgage loans not so much for their yield but as an accommodation to their good business customers. As may be seen in Table 14-2, "other nonfarm" mortgage loans, which include those on commercial, industrial, and specialized property such as churches, rose slightly more than fourfold between 1965 and 1976 and represented 38.8 percent of their total mortgage holdings at the end of 1976.

Industrial Real Estate Loans

Mortgages on industrial property such as manufacturing facilities and warehouses involve a greater risk than those on commercial property. One reason for this is that industrial property is designed for specific types of manufacturing operations, while commercial property can be adapted more readily to a variety of uses. The banks making loans on industrial property must consider very carefully the expected ability of the firm to succeed and hence its ability to meet its mortgage payments. In many cases, banks are obligated to make loans on industrial property for their important customers in order to retain their business.

Loans on Church Property

Loans on church property usually comprise a very small percentage of a bank's mortgage portfolio. As a rule there is little credit risk involved with these loans. Banks usually are obligated to make such loans because the church carries a substantial balance with the bank, or the church's leaders are important businessmen in the community.

Farm Real Estate Loans

At the end of 1976, loans on farm real estate constituted only 4.5 percent of total bank mortgage holdings (Table 14-2). The bulk of these loans were held by small banks in rural communities. Most banks do not solicit farm real estate loans because of the greater risks and relatively low yields involved. The bulk of the farm real estate loans are made by the Federal Land Banks and Production Credit Associations, both of which were established primarily to serve the credit needs of farmers.

[1]Douglas A. Hayes, *Bank Lending Policies: Domestic and International* (Ann Arbor, Mich.: University of Michigan, Graduate School of Business Administration, Bureau of Business Research, 1971), p. 154.

Procedures for Making Residential Real Estate Loans

Each type of real estate lending involves specialized knowledge and techniques. There are a number of basic steps, which we shall consider in detail. These steps are (1) receiving the application, (2) credit analysis of the applicant, (3) inspection and appraisal of the property, (4) preparation of the documents, (5) loan closing, and (6) recording the mortgage or deed of trust. Although procedures involved in making commercial and industrial permanent loans and construction loans are somewhat similar to those required in making residential loans, they do differ in many important respects.

Receiving the Application

A residential real estate loan originates when the prospective borrower submits a written application to the bank. Usually, this application is completed during an initital interview between the customer and a bank real estate loan officer. The first purpose of the application is to provide information about the customer's previous rental and home ownership experience, employment record, income, and financial condition. This information, along with the applicant's credit report, will assist the loan officer in his evaluation of the customer's expected ability and willingness to repay the loan. The second purpose of the application is to obtain a description and location of the property offered as security for the loan.

During this initial interview, it is important that the loan officer explain clearly the mechanics, costs, terms, and legal requirements involved in closing the loan if the credit is approved. Ideally, the customer should be provided with a statement of the estimated closing costs and the mortgage payments.

If the customer wishes the loan to be insured by the FHA, the loan officer at the initial interview usually will assist the applicant in completing the necessary forms and documents that must be submitted to the local FHA office to obtain an insurance commitment. Banks usually have the authority to process loans that are to be guaranteed by the VA, without prior approval from the VA. However, at this time, the lender must submit documents to the VA to request an independent appraisal of the property. The veteran also must certify his intention to occupy the property and obtain a Veteran's VA Certificate of Eligibility for such a loan.

Credit Analysis

The next step in the lending process is to obtain a credit report on the applicant from the local credit bureau. This report should confirm much of the information provided by the applicant in the initial interview. In cases where the credit report reveals discrepancies in information provided by the applicant or several slow accounts, the loan officer must spend additional time investigating the applicant's creditworthiness.

An important part of the credit analysis involved with residential real estate lending is the determination of the applicant's ability to make the required payments. This is a function of expected income and outflow of funds. Also, many rules of thumb have been developed to assist the loan officer. One rule is that the total monthly mortgage payment should not exceed 25 percent of the family's gross monthly income. Another rule is that a family should not spend more than 2.5 times its annual income on a home. Of course, there are no foolproof rules available to the real estate lending officer in determining the applicant's expected ability to service a loan. However, most experienced lending officers will attest that when the standards contained in these rules of thumb are exceeded to any significant extent, the chances are good that, at one time or another, the applicant will be slow in making a payment or, eventually, will default on the loan.

Inspection and Appraisal of the Property

In view of the recent liberalization of real estate loan ratios authorized by the banking regulatory authorities, it is especially important that an accurate inspection and appraisal be made of the property involved. Banks with large real estate loan departments usually have full-time appraisers on their staff to perform this function.

Some of the important general factors influencing the value of a piece of residential property are the economic and social characteristics of the neighborhood; its proximity to schools, shopping centers, and main traffic arteries; and the availability of water, sewerage facilities, garbage collection, and fire and police protection. Some of the important specific features of the property bearing on its value are its physical size and layout; exterior facing; quality and condition of foundation, framing, wiring, roofing, weather-stripping, and caulking; and the availability and condition of its appliances, carpet, drapes, and shrubbery.

Preparation of Documents

The fourth major step in making a residential real estate loan is the preparation of certain documents including (1) the commitment letter, (2) the evidence of title, (3) the mortgage or deed of trust, (4) the note, and (5) a fire- and extended-coverage insurance policy.

Commitment Letter. Following approval of a residential real estate loan by the bank's real estate loan committee, it is a good practice for the bank to send a formal commitment letter to the applicant that specifies the terms and conditions of the loan agreement. In addition, the bank should request that the applicant sign and return a copy of the commitment later in order to preclude any later misunderstandings between both parties to the loan.

Evidence of Title. Following receipt of the signed copy of the letter of commitment, the next step in the lending procedure is for the bank to request its attorney to search the title of the property involved. The attorney will then prepare an "abstract of title," which is a commonly used form evidencing title in property, and an "attorney's opinion" with respect to the validity of the title. Some lenders may require the borrower to purchase a title insurance policy to insure against any defects in the title that might be discovered later.

Mortgage or Deed of Trust. The next step is for the bank to obtain a security interest in the property. This is accomplished by preparing a mortgage or, in some states, a deed of trust and recording it in the local registry office.

Note. A note evidencing the debt and specifying the terms of the loan must be prepared. The mortgage or deed of trust is the security for the note.

Fire and Extended-Coverage Insurance Policy. Finally, the borrower is required to purchase an insurance policy with fire and extended coverage on the property. The premiums may be paid as a part of the mortgage payment to the bank, which, in turn, forwards the amount to the insurance company, or the borrower may purchase and pay for the insurance himself. In a number of cases, the borrower may be required to have a survey made and to add the title insurance policy.

Loan Closing

The next step in making the loan is the *loan closing*, which involves the signing of the documents by all parties concerned in order to convey the lien on the property and to execute the loan. In addition, at the closing, the borrower remits the required down-payment, and the lender pays the loan proceeds to the seller of the property. Typically, loan closings are held at the bank.

Recording

The final step in completing the loan transaction is for the bank's attorney to record the mortgage or deed of trust at the local registry office.

This recording serves to notify all concerned that the property is pledged to secure a debt.

Terms of Residential Real Estate Loans

The three principal factors determining the size of the payment on a residential real estate loan are (1) the loan-to-value ratio, (2) the maturity, and (3) the interest rate and other fees.

Loan-to-Value Ratio

The amount that a state bank may lend on the appraised value of real estate is limited by state laws and regulations; national banks are limited in this regard by the National Banking Act, the Federal Reserve Act, and regulations of the Comptroller of the Currency. National banking laws specify that a national bank may make unamortized loans of up to 50 percent of the appraised value of the property for a term not to exceed five years. A national bank also may lend up to $66\frac{2}{3}$ percent of the appraised value of real estate for a term of up to ten years, provided the installments are sufficient to amortize 40 percent of the principal. In addition, a national bank may lend up to $66\frac{2}{3}$ percent of the appraised value of the property for a term of up to twenty years, if the payments are sufficient to amortize the entire principal within the twenty-year period. Finally, a national bank may advance up to 90 percent of the appraised value for a term not to exceed thirty years, provided the principal is fully amortized within the thirty-year period. These loan-to-value limitations do not apply to FHA-insured or VA-guaranteed loans or to loans insured or guaranteed by a private mortgage company. The purpose of these restrictions is to limit the risk taken by banks. The borrower who has a substantial equity in his home has a greater incentive not to let his loan go into default. Also, the increased equity provides greater protection to the lender in case of a decline in property values. Finally, by making a larger down-payment, the borrower reduces the size of the installments needed to amortize the loan as well as the interest charges over the life of the loan.

A survey in the early 1970s showed that banks generally were more conservative in their loan-to-value requirements than the law permits. A majority of the respondent banks indicated that they limited the amount extended on conventional residential loans to 75 percent or less of appraised value.[2] With savings and loan associations currently permitted to make loans up to 95 percent of appraised value, it is likely that, in order to remain reasonably competitive in residential lending,

[2]Hayes, p, 161.

banks in the near future will have to increase the percentage they are willing to lend on appraised value.

Maturity

The longer the maturity on a real estate loan, the smaller will be the installments required to amortize the principal. Although national banks are permitted to extend 90 percent, fully amortized loans for maturities of up to thirty years, in the survey cited above, three-fourths of the respondent banks indicated that they limited maturities to twenty-five years, while the remainder restricted maturities to twenty years.[3]

Interest Rate and Other Fees

The contract interest rate on conventional mortgages is established by competitive conditions in each local market; rates on FHA and VA mortgages are set by regulations. In addition to the basic interest cost on the loan, the borrower must pay for the cost of surveying and appraising the property and searching and recording the title. In addition, most bank and mortgage lenders levy an origination fee, which tends to average about 1 percent of the amount financed.

On FHA-insured mortgages, the borrower is required to pay an insurance premium of ½ of 1 percent of the unpaid principal. In addition, during high-interest-rate periods, it usually is necessary for the seller to pay a discount charge (also known as "points"), which might range up

[3]*Ibid.*

Table 14-3

Terms on Conventional First Mortgages on New Homes, Selected Years, 1960–1976[a]

Period	Contract Rate (percentage)	Fees and Charges (percentage)[b]	Maturity (years)	Loan/Price Ratio (percentage)	Purchase Price (thousands of dollars)	Loan Amount (thousands of dollars)
1965	5.74	0.49	25.0	73.9	25.1	18.3
1970	8.27	1.03	25.1	71.7	35.5	25.2
1971	7.60	0.87	26.2	74.3	36.3	26.5
1972	7.45	0.88	27.2	76.8	37.3	28.1
1973	7.78	1.11	26.3	77.3	37.1	28.1
1974	8.71	1.30	26.3	74.3	40.1	29.8
1975	8.75	1.54	26.8	74.7	44.6	33.3
1976	8.76	1.44	27.2	74.2	48.4	35.9

Source: *Federal Reserve Bulletin.*

[a]Based on a sample survey of mortgages originated by major institutional lender groups.
[b]Fees and charges—related to principal mortgage amount—include loan commissions, fees, discounts, and other charges, which provide added income to the lender and are paid by the borrower. These exclude any closing costs related solely to transfer of property ownership.

to 13 percent of the principal. For example, suppose a borrower wanted to purchase a $30,000 home and finance $24,000 or 80 percent of the principal. If the bank required that the loan be discounted at 3 percent (or 3 points), the *seller* would have to pay $720 to the lender even though the amount financed would remain at $24,000. This fee is necessitated because the ceiling on the contract interest rate charge on FHA and VA mortgages is less than the rate that lenders may earn on conventional loans. Therefore, the payment of the discount raises the effective yield to the lender.

As shown in Table 14-3, the contract interest rate on conventional mortgages on new homes reached an average of 8.76 percent in 1976. It is important to note also that the average purchase price and the loan amount almost doubled between 1965 and 1976.

Types of Indirect Bank Real Estate Loans

Construction Loans

Construction loans are loans secured by a first mortgage on the property under contruction. Although historical data are unavailable on the annual volume of construction lending, a recent survey shows that in 1974 commercial banks accounted for $17.1 billion of the estimated $42.8 billion extended in construction loans (Table 14-4). Commercial banks typically like to make construction loans because of their high yield and because they generally provide good leads for banks to acquire permanent real estate loans, deposits, and customers for other services.

The first step in making a construction loan is to receive the application. At this point the bank also generally requires evidence that the borrower has a permanent or "takeout" commitment to finance the project. This is important because long-term funds are used to repay the

Table 14-4
Construction Lending by Major Construction Lenders—1974
(billions of dollars)

Lending Institutions	Estimated Dollars Advanced on Construction Loans
Commercial banks	17.1
Savings and loan associations	9.0
Mutual savings banks	1.0
Life insurance companies	.4
Other lenders	15.3
	42.8

Source: *U.S. Factbook.*

construction loan. The second step is to analyze the expected ability and willingness of the borrower to repay the loan. Construction loans generally involve above-average risk because of several contingencies.[4] Bad weather, strikes, and other problems could delay construction and cause the borrower to be unable to repay the loan. Moreover, an engineering error, poor management, or thefts could cause a project to fail. Unpaid workmen and suppliers might find it necessary to record liens on the property, which are sometimes senior to that for the construction loan. Finally, in the case of "speculative" building, the borrower may be unable to sell his finished product, thus necessitating foreclosure by the construction lender.

The third step in construction lending is to issue a letter of commitment to the borrower. The fourth step is to search the title and prepare the necessary documents such as the mortgage or deed of trust, the note, and the construction loan agreement. Fifth, after all documents are signed, the security agreement must be recorded to obtain the lien. Finally, the funds are disbursed according to a schedule set forth in the loan agreement. For example, in the case of a residence, 20 percent might be advanced when the basement, floor joists, and subfloors are in place; 20 percent when the framing and exterior are completed; 20 percent when the plastering, heating, and plumbing are roughed in; 20 percent when the interior and exterior painting is completed and all electrical, heating, and plumbing fixtures are in place; and 20 percent after inspection and a waiver of liens is accepted.[5]

The state interest rate on construction loans has ranged up to 5 percentage points above the prime rate. In addition, the bank will charge an origination fee that ranges from 1 to 2 percent. This fee is justified by the extra expense involved in checking the credit, appraising the property, and preparing the necessary documents associated with construction lending. Although the return on construction loans is attractive, no bank should enter this area of lending without experienced personnel.

Loans to Mortgage Bankers

Commercial banks provide funds to mortgage bankers to finance the warehousing of mortgages until the mortgages can be sold in meaningful blocks to large permanent investors such as life insurance companies, savings and loan associations, or pension funds. *Mortgage warehouse loans,* as they are called, always are secured by the mortgages themselves. In addition, the bank ordinarily requires the mortgage banker to have a purchase commitment from the permanent

[4]Peter A. Schulkin, "Construction Lending at Large Commercial Banks," Federal Reserve Banks of Boston, *New England Economic Review* (July/August 1970), pp. 3–4.

[5]Bruce T. Hughes, "Construction Lending: A Checklist for Construction Loans," *The Journal of Commercial Bank Lending*, 51 (November 1968), pp. 21–22.

investor. Banks usually are willing to lend 90 to 100 percent of the committed amount. Because of the below-average risk involved, rates on these loans generally are at the prime rate or slightly above.

Purchase of Housing Agency Issues

Commercial banks indirectly make real estate loans by purchasing the securities of federal and government sponsored agencies, which, in turn, use the funds to purchase mortgages. U.S. agencies involved in one way or another with real estate lending include (1) the Federal Land Banks, (2) the Federal National Mortgage Association (FNMA), (3) the Federal Home Loan Bank, (4) the Government National Mortgage Association (GNMA), (5) the Federal Home Loan Mortgage Corporation, and (6) the Department of Housing and Urban Development (HUD).

Other Bank Real Estate Activities

Broker and Other Services

Many banks function as mortgage bankers; that is, they originate, sell, and service mortgage loans for other lenders. Today, the total dollar amount of mortgages serviced by commercial banks exceeds by a wide margin their total holding of permanent mortgages.

In recent years, a number of bank holding companies have purchased mortgage banking companies. In some of these cases, some or all of the mortgage banking services performed by the commerical bank in the holding company arrangement have been transferred to the mortgage banking subsidiary.

Sponsorship and Management of REITs

During the early 1970s, a number of banks formed *real estate investment trusts* (REITs), financial institutions that provide funds for construction loans and permanent real estate loans and take equity positions in apartment projects, condominiums, commercial buildings, and other real estate.[6] Bank involvement with the REITs has been

[6]Under 1960 legislation, an REIT is exempt from federal corporate income tax if it meets the following principal requirements: (1) The REIT must be a passive investor rather than an active participant in the operation of its properties, but the active manager of an REIT's properties can give up to 35 percent of the REIT's stock; (2) at the end of each quarter 75 percent of the value of the REIT's total assets must consist of real estate, mortgages, cash, cash items, and government securities; (3) at least 100 people must own shares, and five or fewer persons cannot own more than 50 percent of the shares during the last half of any tax year; (4) at least 75 percent of the gross income of the REIT must be derived from rents, mortgage interest, and gains from the sale of real estate; and (5) at least 90 percent of the REIT's ordinary income must be distributed to the shareholders within one year after the close of the taxable year.

mainly in the role of organizer, manager, provider of loans, and participant in the loan portfolio of the trust. At the close of 1975, thirty-seven commercial banks were acting as "advisers" to an REIT.[7] The primary function of the adviser is to manage the day-to-day operations connected with the trust's investments. Assets of the REIT industry have grown from $1 billion in 1968 to $19.4 billion in 1975, having reached a peak of $21.2 billion in 1974. The 1973–1975 recession and the attendant, well-known "shake-out" in the real estate industry curtailed sharply the growth of REITs. A significant percentage of the REIT loans went into default. As a result most REITs could not meet all their principal and interest payments to their lenders—primarily banks. At the end of 1975, bank loans accounted for approximately half of the total sources of funds to the REITs.[8] To relieve themselves of some of the burden for past-due loans, many REITs have executed "asset swaps" with their bank creditors. Under this arrangement, the REIT gives mortgages or property acquired through foreclosure to the bank in exchange for a reduction in the outstanding loan.

Today, at a number of major banks, "problem loans" to REITs occupy a significant portion of management's time. It will be years before the exact losses on bank REIT loans are known.

Trust Department Activity

Banks also are involved in financing real estate through the activities of their trust departments. At the end of 1975 bank trust departments held $7.1 billion in real estate mortgage loans and $13.4 billion in actual real estate holdings. In addition, trust departments make substantial investments in the securities of federal- and government-sponsored housing agencies.

Suggestions for Additional Reading

The American Bankers Association. *Real Estate Activities of Commercial Banks: A Survey Report.* Washington, D.C.: The American Bankers Association, 1970.

Baughn, William H., and Walker, Charls E., eds. *The Banker's Handbook.* Homewood, Ill.: Dow Jones-Irwin, 1966, chaps. 33–34.

Cook, Timothy Q. "The Residential Mortgage Market in Recent Years." Federal Reserve Bank of Richmond, *Economic Review* (September–October 1974), pp. 3–18.

Erdevig, Eleanor. "Commercial Banks and Mortgages." Federal Reserve Bank of Chicago, *Business Conditions* (September 1974), pp. 3–12.

[7] *REIT Fact Book*, 1976, p. 7.
[8] *Ibid.*, p. 39.

———. "Is There a Future for Variable Rate Mortgages?" Federal Reserve Bank of Chicago, *Business Conditions* (November 1975), pp. 3–11.

Hayes, Douglas A. *Bank Lending Policies: Domestic and International.* Ann Arbor, Mich.: The University of Michigan, Bureau of Business Research, 1971, chap. 8.

Hughes, Bruce T. "Construction Lending: A Checklist for Construction Loans." *The Journal of Commercial Bank Lending* (November 1968), pp. 21–22.

Kaufman, George G. "Variable Rate Residential Mortgages: The Early Experience from California." Federal Reserve Bank of San Francisco, *Economic Review* (Summer 1976), pp. 5–16.

Schulkin, Peter A. "Construction Lending at Large Commercial Banks." Federal Reserve Bank of Boston, *New England Economic Review* (July–August 1970), pp. 3–11.

———. "Real Estate Investment Trusts: A New Financial Indermediary." Federal Reserve Bank of Boston, *New England Economic Review* (November–December 1970), pp. 2–12.

Tockarshewsky, Joseph B. "Reducing the Risks in Construction Lending." *The Journal of Commercial Bank Lending* (May 1976), pp. 10–18.

PART

V

Investment Management

CHAPTER

15

Bank Investments: Some General Considerations

A bank's *investment portfolio* may be defined as those securities not held as secondary reserves. Therefore, it generally encompasses all securities with a maturity of one year or longer. Before a bank allocates funds to loans and investments, it must have sufficient fixed assets such as buildings and equipment to attract and efficiently serve customers. Second, the bank must have adequate secondary reserves to meet its expected liquidity needs, except to the extent that it can rely on the various liability management techniques to acquire funds. After these needs are met, banks allocate funds to meet all legitimate loan demands in their market area. Residual funds are available for acquisition of investment securities.

In this chapter we shall (1) develop the organizational framework for investment portfolio management, (2) consider the objectives of portfolio selections, (4) note the securities eligible for bank purchase, and (5) discuss briefly the bank underwriting function.

Organization for Portfolio Management

The ultimate responsibility for portfolio management at any bank rests with its board of directors. At large and most medium-sized banks, the delegation of authority and responsibility runs from the board to the chief executive officer to the investment policy committee to the head of the investment department (Figure 15-1).

The Investment Policy Committee: The Focal Point for Asset and Liability Management

The size, maturity composition, and quality of the bank's investment portfolio depends to a large extent on loan demand, the availability and cost of funds, and liquidity considerations. Therefore, it follows that at large and medium-sized banks the investment policy committee should

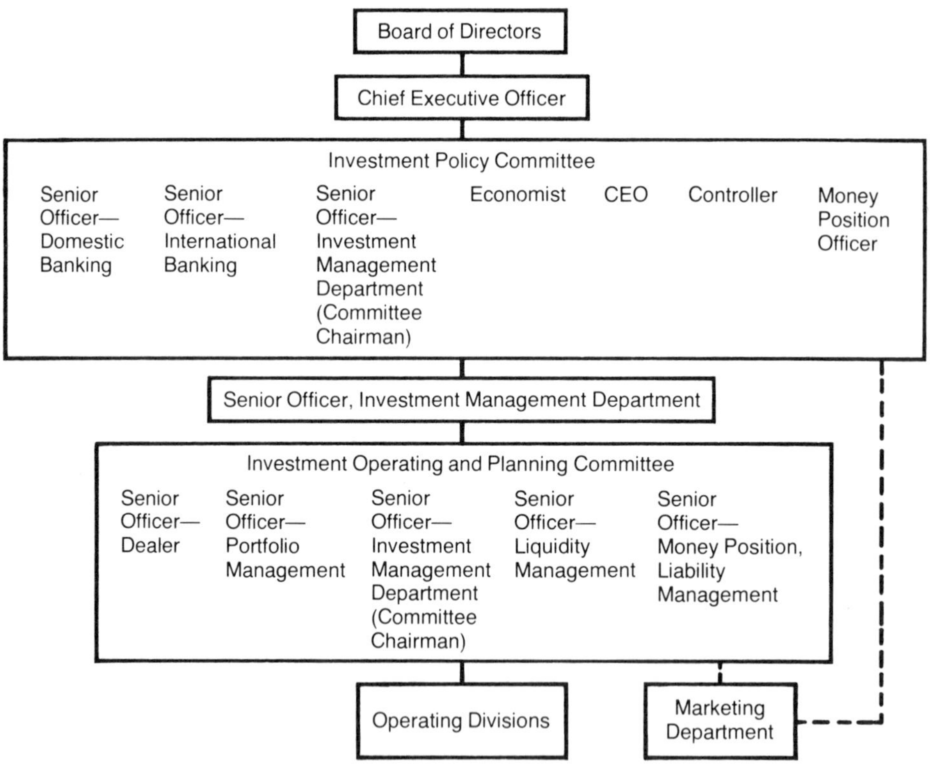

Figure 15-1 Organization Chart for Portfolio, Asset, and Liability Management at Large Banks

Source: The American Bankers Association, *The Role of Investments in Bank Asset Management*, "Study 6: Organization for Portfolio Management" (Washington, D. C.: The American Bankers Association, 1974), page 27. Copyright 1974. The American Bankers Association. All rights reserved. Reprinted by permission.

include senior officers responsible for funds acquisition, loan management, and liquidity management (see Figure 15-1). The chief function of this committee is to formulate portfolio strategy utilizing information about trends and developments from each of these management areas. Because every major funds management area is represented on this committee, it becomes the focal point for bank asset and liability management. Within this committee, decisions can be reached with respect to size and composition of the bank's loan and investment portfolios given the expected availability and cost of the various sources of funds. At small banks the president usually will assume responsibilities for formulating and executing portfolio policy. Therefore, he becomes the focal point for asset and liability management.

The Investment Department

In most large banks the officer in charge of the investment department has overall responsibility for money position management; liquidity management; portfolio management; the *dealer* function, which involves retailing securities to individuals, businesses, and other financial institutions; and the *underwriting* function, which essentially involves the initial purchase of U.S. Treasury obligations, agencies, and general obligation municipals for resale. Specific responsibility for each function is delegated to specialists. However, because these areas are interrelated, communication among the functional specialists is very important.

The Investment Policy Statement

Every bank board of directors should formulate an investment policy statement. The primary purposes of this statement are (1) to define the objectives of the bank's liquidity management and investment portfolio and (2) to define the limits of authority for the portfolio manager. For example, at a medium-sized bank the policy statement might stipulate that the bank must hold secondary reserves equal to 90 percent of the bank's anticipated maximum liquidity needs projected over the next twelve months; that the investment reserves account should contain Treasury and agency securities with one- to five-year maturities equal to 10 percent of net deposits; that municipals purchased for the investment account must be in the top four grades as listed by two rating services; that no securities purchased for the investment account will have maturities beyond fifteen years; and that $10 million be set aside in a special trading account. The idea of the policy statement is not to hamstring the portfolio manager, but to outline for him the necessary guidelines so that he may discharge his responsibilities effectively. Furthermore, a well-defined policy statement provides benchmarks for the evaluation and possible revision of portfolio policies. Finally, a well-planned and up-to-date policy statement eliminates much uncertainty for every bank official with responsibilities in the investment area. As a result, these officers are free to concentrate on other objectives in the bank.

Objectives of the Investment Portfolio

The primary objectives of a bank's investment portfolio are (1) to provide supplementary income and (2) to provide supplementary liquidity.

Supplementary Income

Banks usually have residual funds that can be invested in Treasury obligations, agencies, municipals, and corporates to provide supplementary income, except during the last phases of an economic expansion, when most large and medium-sized banks and some local banks have more loan requests than they can fulfill. Income from investments (including securities held as secondary reserve assets but excluding income from federal funds sold and securities held under repurchase agreements) accounted for 17.8 percent of total income for insured banks in 1976. Although funds allocated for investments tend to be residual in nature, the performance of the investment portfolio often is the difference between a bank's being either average or above average in profitability.

A bank's investments are limited by law to debt obligations. These securities yield income in the form of (1) interest and (2) capital gains, which represents an appreciation of market price over the purchase price.[1] Debt obligations yield interest income from the date of purchase. Capital gains accrue either when the general level of market interest rates falls or when a security (other than a Treasury bill) approaches maturity and its price increases as some investors are willing to accept a lower yield in return for the more liquid asset. On the other hand, the level of market interest rates may rise, thus causing banks to have securities in their portfolio with losses. Some banks ignore these losses and hold their investments primarily for the interest income. Other banks, in addition to trying to earn a satisfactory interest income on their portfolio, seek to avoid such losses and attempt to realize capital gains by buying securities if there is an expectation of a fall in the market interest rate, or even by selling securities short if there is an

[1]Treasury bills are purchased at a discount from par. The difference between the purchase price and the sale price or par, if held to maturity, is treated as ordinary interest income.

expectation of a rise in money market rates.[2] The techniques of portfolio management are discussed in Chapter 16.

Supplementary Liquidity

The second objective of portfolio management is to provide supplementary liquidity. Although a bank liquidity manager attempts to forecast his organization's expected liquidity requirements over the next twelve months and the bank may hold secondary reserves equal to some percentage of these requirements, there always is the possibility that deposits will not grow as rapidly as planned or that loan demand will exceed the forecast. Moreover, something unforeseen, such as a hurricane, tornado, drought, or plant closing, might occur in the area, thus causing deposits to decline and loan repayments to be delayed. Obviously, such contingencies could play havoc with the best-laid liquidity plans. A bank confronted with abnormal liquidity demands may be forced to sell securities from its investment portfolio to supplement funds raised from the sale of secondary reserves and borrowing.

Factors Influencing Bank Portfolio Selections

Many factors determine a bank's investment selections. Some of the most important considerations are (1) quality, (2) maturity, (3) capital adequacy, and (4) tax laws.

Quality

The first criterion for selecting bank investments is quality. With respect to quality, the general legal limitation on national banks is that they may deal only in "investment securities," which are defined as "marketable obligations evidencing indebtedness of any person, copartnership, association, or corporation in the form of bonds, notes and/or debentures commonly known as investment securities . . ." Specific limitations are then set forth for three types of securities. Type I securities are those "which a bank may deal in, underwrite, purchase and sell for its own account without limitation. These include obligations of the United States, general obligations of any State of the United States or any political subdivision, and those of certain federally sponsored corporations and agencies." Type II securities are those "which a bank may deal in, underwrite, or purchase and sell for its own account subject to a 10 percent capital and surplus limitation." These securities include obligations of the International Bank for Re-

[2] *Selling short* involves borrowing securities (usually from a dealer) and selling them with the intention of buying them back later at a lower price, whereupon the securities are then returned to the lender.

construction and Development (World Bank), the Inter-American Development Bank, the Asian Development Bank, and the Tennessee Valley Authority, and obligations issued by any state or political subdivision or any agency of a state or a political subdivision for housing, university, or dormitory purposes. Type III securities include those securities "which a bank may purchase and sell for its own account, subject to a 10 percent limitation, but may neither deal in nor underwrite."

Comptroller's regulations require that "every bank maintain in its files credit information adequate to demonstrate that it has exercised prudence" in making its investment determination. Generally, any security listed in the top four grades by Moody's Investors Service, Inc., and Standard and Poor's Corporation is considered of investment quality. The investment classifications of these services are[3]

	Moody's	*S & P*
Prime	Aaa	AAA
Excellent	Aa	AA
Upper medium	A, A-1	A
Lower medium	Baa, Baa-1	BBB
Marginal speculative	BA	BB
Very speculative	B, Caa	B
Default	Ca, C	D

In addition, the Comptroller, upon request, will rule on the eligibility of specific bond issues for bank purchase. These rulings are listed in the *Comptroller's Manual*.

Through emphasis on quality in portfolio selections, banks minimize their exposure to both the credit and the money risk. Since the investment portfolio provides supplementary liquidity, banks cannot afford to risk default on this group of assets. During the Great Depression, the prices of Treasury issues rose; however, the prices of high-grade corporates declined, in reflection of the increasing credit risk associated with private debt. Moreover, when the general level of interest rates rises, as during the recent liquidity crises of 1966, 1970, and 1974, the prices of Treasury obligations tend to fall less than those of lesser-quality issues. It is because of these considerations that the banking regulatory authorities impose qualitative restrictions on bank investments.

Maturity

One of the most fundamental factors influencing a bank's portfolio selections is the maturity. The longer the time period that a municipal or

[3]Because approximately 87 percent of all municipals fall within the A and Baa categories, Moody's added the A-1 and Baa-1 ratings to differentiate those securities with the best investment qualities of the A and Baa rating categories. Standard and Poor's attaches a plus or minus sign to a S&P rating to indicate a credit in the upper or lower segment of the rating category.

corporate security is outstanding, the greater the opportunity for the credit quality of the issue to deteriorate. In the case of a municipal security, the community issuing the obligations could suffer a natural disaster, lose its most important local industry, or become so top heavy with debt that prompt payment of principal and interest would be endangered. If there were a significant change in a security's credit quality as the result of such developments, the investments rating services probably would lower the issue's quality rating, thereby reducing its marketability and hence attractiveness as an investment.

The most important aspect about maturity for the portfolio manager is that the money risk is directly related to maturity. The longer the maturity of an issue, the greater the impact that a given change in interest rates has on the price of the security. As shown in Table 15-1, if the market yield on a 4 percent security with a one-year maturity increases from 4 percent to 5 percent, the price of the issue declines only $9.60. On the other hand, a similar increase in market yield on a 4 percent, twenty-year bond would result in a $125.50 drop in market price. The investment manager must be aware of the relationship between maturity and potential price fluctuations as he selects securities for the portfolio.

Capital Adequacy

The primary function of bank capital, as we have seen, is to demonstrate to the public and to the supervisory authorities a bank's ability to absorb unanticipated losses. Although banks invest only in high-quality issues, there is always some credit risk associated with municipals and corporates, and there is a money-rate risk inherent in any intermediate to long-term obligation. The extent to which a bank can invest in such securities is therefore a function of its capital position.

Table 15-1

Relative Prices and Price Changes for 4 Percent Coupon Issues with Different Maturities Reflecting a Market Yield Change from 4 Percent to 5 Percent

Maturities	Prices	Price Changes
1 year	$990.40	$-9.60
2 years	981.20	-18.80
5 years	956.20	-43.80
10 years	922.10	-77.90
20 years	874.50	-125.50
30 years	845.50	-154.50

Tax Laws

Bank investment portfolio selections are influenced importantly by two features of our tax laws: (1) the exemption of coupon income on municipals from federal income taxes and (2) the change in the Tax Reform Act of 1969, which made the gain or loss on security holdings includable in, or deductible from, ordinary income with limitation.

Banks are subject to the same corporate income tax rates as industrial firms. That is, the first $25,000 of net income is taxed at a rate of 20 percent; the second $25,000 of net income is taxed at 22 percent; net income above $50,000 is subject to a tax of 48 percent. Because the interest on municipals is exempt from income taxes, these yields usually will be 22 to 48 percent below the yields on taxable issues of comparable quality and maturity. During those times when the calendar of municipal offerings is particularly heavy, and during periods of tight money, the yield differential between taxable and municipal issues will narrow, thereby increasing the attractiveness of municipals as bank investments. For example, at the height of the liquidity crisis in 1974, many A-rated municipals were priced to yield 7.5 percent or more. For a bank in the 48 percent marginal tax bracket, this was equivalent to a before-tax yield of 14.42 percent. It should be evident that banks with income subject to the surtax benefit most from investment in municipals.

Prior to 1969, net security losses for banks were fully deductible from ordinary income, but net profits realized from the sale or exchange of a debt obligation were treated as long-term capital gains, which, of course, are taxed at lower rates. Because of the favorable tax treatment afforded losses, banks were ill-advised to offset these losses against capital gains. Banks would designate certain years as "loss years" and others as "profit years." The Tax Reform Act of 1969 eliminated this practice and made all gains and losses includable in, or deductible from, ordinary income. Since long-term capital gains realized by banks no longer receive preferential treatment, portfolio policy at a number of banks has been altered to emphasize short-term gains.

Bank Eligible Investments

There are four principal categories of bank eligible investments: (1) Treasury obligations, (2) agencies, (3) municipals, and (4) corporates.

Treasury Obligations

Types. As discussed in Chapter 8, there are four issues of Treasury bills: (1) three-month bills, (2) six-month bills, (3) twelve-month bills, and (4) tax-anticipation bills. These issues ordinarily comprise a significant part of the secondary reserve account, but, if interest rates are expected to rise, much of the funds slated for the investment account may be placed in bills.[4]

Treasury notes are coupon issues that pay interest semiannually and have initial maturities ranging from one to seven years.[5] *Treasury bonds* are issued with a maturity of five years or longer and ordinarily are available in either registered or coupon form.[6]

Investment Characteristics. *Safety* of principal and interest is the most distinguishing characteristic of Treasury obligations. Investors know that the federal government has never repudiated or defaulted on its obligations and that it can raise large sums to meet future interest payments through its vast powers of taxation.

Treasury obligations are readily marketable because approximately twenty government securities' dealers, including several money market banks, stand ready "to make a market" in these obligations. Moreover, the market for Treasuries generally has the desirable characteristics of *breadth*, that is, there are many buyers and sellers in the market daily, and *depth*, that is, any significant price movements in either direction will attract sufficient buying or selling interest to keep the market relatively stable. Because of this breadth and depth, the maximum spread between the bid and asked prices typically is only $^4/_{32}$ on one- to three-year maturities and $^8/_{32}$ on longer-term obligations. A typical quotation sheet published by a bank dealing in government obligations is shown in Figure 15-2.

Bank Holdings. As shown in Table 15-2, bank holdings of Treasury obligations as a percentage of total investments have declined from 73.7 percent in 1961 to 40.0 percent in 1976. During periods of easy credit conditions, banks tend to add to their holdings of Treasuries. Conversely, during periods of tight money, banks tend to sell Treasuries to meet loan demands. As shown in Table 15-3, since the mid-1960s banks have shortened considerably their maturity holdings of Treasury obligations. At the end of 1976, only 8.9 percent of the Treasury debt held by banks had a maturity of five years or more.

[4]Treasury bills are quoted on a discounted basis from par ($1,000). The discount formula is discount in dollars = days to maturity/360 × discount basis. For example, the price of a bill with sixty days to maturity and quoted at a discount basis of 4.80 percent would be $992.00

[5]Treasury notes and bonds are quoted in $^1/_{32}$ of a point, where 1 point equals $10. A price of 76.4 equals $76^4/_{32}$ or $761.25. Dealers post both bid and asked prices. The *bid price* is the highest price that they will pay a potential seller; the *asked price* is the lowest price that they will charge a potential buyer.

[6]*Registered bonds* are bonds whose principal is payable only to the named owner. These securities may or may not have coupons, depending on whether they are registered as to principal only or to both principal and interest.

Prices and yields Quoted at 3 p.m. **June 24, 1977**. For delivery **June 28, 1977**.

U.S. Treasury notes and bonds

Minimum denomination $1,000, except (F) denotes $5,000 minimum and (T) denotes $10,000 minimum.
# denotes issues redeemable at par, under certain circumstances, in payment of federal estate taxes.

Bond or note	In millions $ Outstdg	Publicly held[1]	Coupon rate		Maturity	Bid	Asked	Change	Change for week	Current markets	Yield[2] To maturity	Value of 1/32	After 48% tax	Corp tax equiv[4]	Days interest = 1/32	1977 range High	Low
N	3156	2919	7 1/2	F	10/31/77	100.22	100.24	...	...		5.19	.0919	2.70	5.19	1.53	4.77	5.56
N	3630	2357	7 3/4	F	11/15/77	100.27	100.29	...	- 1		5.27	.0823	2.74	5.27	1.46	4.82	5.59
N	2628	2532	6 5/8	F	11/30/77	100.15	100.17	+ 1	...		5.32	.0747	2.76	5.32	1.72	4.87	5.70
N	2765	2443	7 1/4	F	12/31/77	100.28	100.30	+ 1	...		5.34	.0629	2.78	5.34	1.56	4.92	5.74
N	2511	2234	6 3/8	F	1/31/78	100.15	100.17	+ 1	...		5.44	.0541	2.83	5.44	1.77	4.96	5.80
N	8389	5027	6 1/4		2/15/78	100.13	100.15	+ 1	...		5.47	.0506	2.85	5.47	1.81	5.04	5.84
N	2115	2014	8.00	F	2/28/78	101.18	101.20	...	- 1		5.49	.0470	2.86	5.49	1.43	5.11	5.88
N	3162	2871	6 3/4	F	3/31/78	100.26	100.28	+ 1	+ 1		5.54	.0423	2.88	5.54	1.69	5.12	5.90
N	2574	2198	6 1/2	F	4/30/78	100.21	100.23	+ 1	+ 1		5.60	.0383	2.91	5.60	1.76	5.22	5.90
N	3960	3000	7 1/8		5/15/78	101.7	101.9	+ 1	+ 1		5.60	.0364	2.91	5.60	1.61	5.25	5.96
N	4423	2897	7 7/8	F	5/15/78	101.27	101.29	+ 1	...		5.61	.0363	2.92	5.61	1.46	5.25	5.97
N	2567	2396	7 1/8	F	5/31/78	101.8	101.10	+ 1	...		5.64	.0348	2.93	5.64	1.60	5.09	6.00
N	3331	2584	6 7/8	F	6/30/78	101.3	101.7	+ 1	+ 1		5.61	.0320	2.92	5.61	1.65	102.20	99.22
N	2855	2637	6 7/8	F	7/31/78	101.5	101.9	+ 1	+ 1		5.64	.0296	2.93	5.64	1.64	102.21	99.28
N	2462	1820	8 3/4	T	8/15/78	103.13	103.17	+ 1	...		5.48	.0281	2.85	5.48	1.29	105.24	102.20
N	5155	2598	7 5/8	F	8/15/78	102.0	102.4	+ 1	+ 2		5.65	.0284	2.94	5.65	1.48	103.27	100.13
N	2949	2762	6 5/8	F	8/31/78	100.29	101.1	+ 1	+ 2		5.69	.0278	2.96	5.69	1.70	102.11	99.27
N	3195	2779	6 1/4	F	9/30/78	100.15	100.19	+ 1	+ 2		5.74	.0260	2.99	5.74	1.84	101.25	99.20
N	2921	2711	5 7/8	F	10/31/78	99.31	100.3	+ 1	+ 1		5.79	.0246	3.01	5.79	1.94	101.6	99.13
N	8207	4620	6.00		11/15/78	100.3	100.7	+ 1	...		5.83	.0238	3.03	5.83	1.91	101.28	96.28
N	2941	2709	5 3/4	F	11/30/78	99.24	99.28	+ 1	+ 1		5.84	.0232	3.05	5.87	2.00	101.0	99.4
N	2517	2370	8 1/8	F	12/31/78	103.3	103.7	+ 1	...		5.86	.0215	3.05	5.86	1.39	105.14	101.14
N	3377	2953	5 1/4	F	12/31/78	99.0	99.4	+ 2	+ 3		5.87	.0221	3.16	6.08	2.15	99.30	98.8
N	2855	2746	5 7/8	F	1/31/79	99.26	99.30	+ 1	...		5.91	.0209	3.08	5.93	1.92	100.14	99.7
N	4692	2981	7.00	F	2/15/79	101.18	101.22	+ 1	...		5.89	.0201	3.06	5.89	1.61	103.14	98.24
N	2842	2692	5 7/8	F	2/28/79	99.25	99.29	+ 2	+ 1		5.93	.0199	3.09	5.95	1.95	100.13	99.7
N	3507	2504	6.00	F	3/31/79	99.31	100.3	+ 2	+ 1		5.94	.0190	3.09	5.94	1.90	100.20	99.13
N	1981	1471	5 7/8	F	4/30/79	99.24	99.26	+ 2	+ 3		5.96	.0182	3.13	6.01	1.95	99.30	99.5
N	2269	1756	7 7/8		5/15/79	103.6	103.10	+ 1	...		5.98	.0174	3.11	5.98	1.46	105.17	100.26
N	2071	1501	6 1/8	F	5/31/79	100.4	100.6	+ 2	+ 2		6.02	.0174	3.13	6.02	1.86	100.7	99.14
N	1782	1673	7 3/4	F	6/30/79	103.6	103.10	+ 2	+ 3		5.97	.0164	3.11	5.97	1.46	105.16	100.12
▶N	WI		6 1/8	F	6/30/79	100.2	100.4	+ 2	+ 7		6.06	.0168	3.15	6.06	1.87	100.4	99.28
N	4559	2772	6 1/4		8/15/79	100.9	100.13	+ 3	+ 1		6.04	.0158	3.14	6.04	1.81	102.2	96.16
N	2989	2169	6 7/8	F	8/15/79	101.16	101.20	+ 3	+ 2		6.05	.0157	3.14	6.05	1.64	103.15	99.26
N	2081	1864	8 1/2		9/30/79	104.30	105.2	+ 3	+ 2		6.06	.0145	3.15	6.06	1.35	107.20	102.12
N	1604	472	6 5/8		11/15/79	101.1	101.5	+ 3	+ 3		6.09	.0142	3.17	6.09	1.73	103.20	97.16
N	2241	1796	7.00		11/15/79	101.27	101.31	+ 3	+ 3		6.09	.0141	3.17	6.09	1.64	104.21	98.14
N	3376	3105	6 1/4	F	11/15/79	100.6	100.10	+ 2	+ 3		6.10	.0143	3.17	6.10	1.84	102.10	99.5
N	2006	1904	7 1/2		12/31/79	103.1	103.5	+ 2	+ 3		6.12	.0134	3.18	6.12	1.50	105.8	99.14
B	2506	1577	4.00	#	2/15/80	95.4	95.20	+ 6	+ 6		5.81	.0133	3.35	6.44	2.82	95.28	88.20
N	4608	3183	6 1/2	F	2/15/80	100.21	100.25	+ 2	+ 3		6.17	.0130	3.21	6.17	1.74	101.13	99.17
N	2069	1922	7 1/2		3/31/80	103.4	103.8	+ 2	+ 3		6.19	.0122	3.22	6.19	1.52	105.10	99.10
N	7265	1703	6 7/8		5/15/80	101.21	101.25	+ 2	+ 2		6.19	.0119	3.22	6.19	1.67	105.30	97.6
N	2185	1904	7 5/8		6/30/80	103.21	103.25	+ 3	+ 4		6.23	.0113	3.24	6.23	1.49	105.28	100.3
N	4296	1616	9.00		8/15/80	107.21	107.25	...	+ 3		6.22	.0106	3.24	6.22	1.25	110.8	104.10
N	2141	2008	6 7/8		9/30/80	101.16	101.20	+ 2	+ 4		6.31	.0106	3.28	6.31	1.67	103.24	99.21
B	1758	1137	3 1/2	#	11/15/80	92.16	93.0	+ 4	...		5.81	.0108	3.44	6.61	3.28	93.0	84.24
N	2692	2471	5 7/8		12/31/80	98.14	98.18	+ 3	+ 8		6.34	.0102	3.38	6.50	1.92	100.14	96.24
N	1842	1288	7.00		2/15/81	101.24	101.28	+ 4	+ 7		6.41	.0097	3.33	6.41	1.61	104.4	97.0
N	4796	3841	7 3/8		2/15/81	102.27	102.31	+ 4	+ 6		6.44	.0096	3.35	6.44	1.53	105.16	98.10
N	2800	2250	6 7/8		3/31/81	101.9	101.13	+ 6	+10		6.44	.0094	3.35	6.44	1.66	102.0	99.27
N	2020	1866	7 3/8		5/15/81	102.28	103.0	+ 4	+ 6		6.48	.0091	3.37	6.48	1.55	105.14	98.10

▶N	2501	2001	6 3/4		6/30/81	100.27	100.29	+ 5	+ 9	6.49	.0089	3.37	6.49	1.68	100.29	99.29
B	807	399	7.00		8/15/81	101.8	102.8	...	...	6.37	.0086	3.31	6.37	1.61	105.8	96.28
N	2586	2394	7 5/8		8/15/81	103.24	103.28	+ 7	+12	6.54	.0085	3.40	6.54	1.48	106.16	100.0
N	4477	2636	7 3/4		11/15/81	104.8	104.12	+ 7	+10	6.58	.0081	3.42	6.58	1.48	107.6	99.22
N	2543	2507	7.00		11/15/81	101.16	101.20	+ 6	+12	6.56	.0082	3.41	6.56	1.64	104.16	99.18
B	2702	1647	6 3/8		2/15/82	99.0	99.16	+ 4	+ 4	6.50	.0079	3.40	6.54	1.77	101.20	93.24
N	2697	2697	6 1/8		2/15/82	98.0	98.4	+ 9	+12	6.60	.0080	3.52	6.76	1.84	100.0	96.8
N	2747	1312	8.00		5/15/82	105.18	105.22	+ 7	+11	6.61	.0073	3.44	6.61	1.43	108.6	100.18
N	2607	2257	7.00		5/15/82	101.17	101.21	+11	+19	6.60	.0075	3.43	6.60	1.64	101.30	99.31
N	2918	1840	8 1/8		8/15/82	106.3	106.7	+ 9	+16	6.67	.0070	3.47	6.67	1.39	108.28	101.0
N	2902	2206	7 7/8		11/15/82	105.0	105.4	+10	+14	6.72	.0068	3.50	6.72	1.46	107.28	99.28
N	7958	5882	8.00		2/15/83	105.22	105.26	+12	+18	6.74	.0065	3.50	6.74	1.41	108.16	100.14
B	1315	1088	3 1/4	#	6/15/83.78	84.8	85.8	...	...	6.25	.0070	3.79	7.29	3.51	87.0	78.8
N	2309	2223	7.00		11/15/83	101.1	101.5	+11	+16	6.77	.0061	3.52	6.77	1.64	104.14	98.24
▶N	8378	4731	7 1/4		2/15/84	101.27	101.31	+13	+19	6.87	.0059	3.57	6.87	1.56	102.0	99.20
B	2353	950	6 3/8		8/15/84	97.10	97.26	+ 2	- 2	6.76	.0057	3.59	6.90	1.77	100.24	92.16
B	803	624	3 1/4	#	5/15/85	79.24	80.24	...	+12	6.40	.0058	3.89	7.49	3.53	86.16	76.16
B	1063	668	4 1/4	#	5/15/85.78	84.12	85.12	...	...	6.66	.0057	3.90	7.50	2.70	87.16	79.8
N	5219	4449	7 7/8		5/15/86	104.26	104.30	+15	+23	7.11	.0047	3.70	7.11	1.46	107.26	99.7
N	9515	7668	8.00		8/15/86	105.22	105.26	+16	+22	7.12	.0045	3.70	7.12	1.41	108.26	101.2
B	1216	313	6 1/8		11/15/86	93.24	94.24	+ 4	+12	6.89	.0047	3.72	7.16	1.87	98.16	89.4
B	3034	2141	3 1/2	#	2/15/90	75.28	76.28	+ 4	+24	6.16	.0042	3.68	7.08	3.23	86.16	70.0
B	1247	930	8 1/4		5/15/90	107.14	107.22	+ 8	+ 6	7.32	.0036	3.80	7.32	1.39	111.24	101.12
B	3004	1876	4 1/4	#	8/15/92.87	76.28	77.28	...	+12	6.58	.0039	3.84	7.39	2.66	87.20	72.0
B	190	137	4.00	#	2/15/93.88	76.28	77.28	+ 8	+20	6.24	.0037	3.64	7.01	2.82	87.20	71.0
B	627	418	6 3/4		2/15/93	96.28	97.28	...	+ 8	6.97	.0034	3.67	7.05	1.67	99.24	88.12
B	1914	624	7 1/2		8/15/93.88	101.8	101.24	+ 4	+12	7.27	.0041	3.78	7.27	1.50	105.8	94.4
B	1132	676	4 1/8	#	5/15/94.89	76.28	77.28	+12	+40	6.27	.0036	3.64	7.01	2.78	87.12	71.16
B	616	488	3.00	#	2/15/95	75.28	76.28	+ 4	+20	4.99	.0032	2.95	5.67	3.77	86.24	70.0
B	692	364	7.00		5/15/98.93	97.24	98.24	...	+ 8	7.11	.0029	3.72	7.15	1.64	100.16	89.12
B	2205	1491	3 1/2	#	11/15/98	75.24	76.24	+ 4	+16	5.34	.0029	3.11	5.97	3.28	86.20	70.6
B	2414	837	8 1/2		5/15/99.94	108.22	108.30	+10	+16	7.55	.0031	3.93	7.55	1.35	113.0	102.4
B	2771	2278	7 7/8		2/15/00.95	103.10	103.14	+14	+20	7.52	.0032	3.91	7.52	1.43	107.16	96.16
B	2265	1334	8 3/8		8/15/00.95	107.20	107.28	+10	+16	7.57	.0030	3.94	7.57	1.35	112.0	101.4
B	1575	841	8.00		8/15/01.96	104.8	104.16	+12	+18	7.55	.0030	3.93	7.55	1.41	108.24	99.28
B	2221	986	8 1/4		5/15/05.00	106.28	107.4	+10	+14	7.59	.0027	3.95	7.59	1.39	111.8	100.3
▶B	3044	1729	7 5/8		2/15/07.02	100.20	100.24	+16	+24	7.56	.0028	3.93	7.56	1.48	100.26	97.20

U.S. Treasury bills Minimum denomination $10,000

Mil $ outstdg	Days to mat	Maturity	Discount Bid	Discount Asked	$ equiv	Bond equiv yield
5700	2	6/30/77	5.05	4.75	99.974	4.82
6000	9	7/ 7/77	4.95	4.75	99.881	4.82
5900	16	7/14/77	4.95	4.75	99.789	4.83
5900	23	7/21/77	4.95	4.75	99.697	4.83
2967	28	7/26/77	4.95	4.75	99.631	4.83
5900	30	7/28/77	4.95	4.75	99.604	4.84
6000	37	8/ 4/77	4.95	4.80	99.507	4.89
5900	44	8/11/77	4.95	4.80	99.413	4.90
5700	51	8/18/77	4.95	4.85	99.313	4.95
2953	56	8/23/77	5.05	4.85	99.246	4.95
5700	58	8/25/77	4.95	4.85	99.219	4.96
5600	65	9/ 1/77	5.05	4.95	99.106	5.06
5400	72	9/ 8/77	5.00	4.90	99.020	5.02

Mil $ outstdg	Days to mat	Maturity	Discount Bid	Discount Asked	$ equiv	Bond equiv yield
5100	79	9/15/77	5.00	4.90	98.925	5.02
2867	84	9/20/77	5.05	4.90	98.857	5.03
▶5100	86	9/22/77	5.00	4.96	98.815	5.09
3400	93	9/29/77	5.10	4.95	98.721	5.08
3500	100	10/ 6/77	5.10	4.95	98.625	5.09
3500	107	10/13/77	5.10	4.95	98.529	5.09
3095	112	10/18/77	5.15	5.00	98.444	5.15
3400	114	10/20/77	5.10	5.00	98.417	5.15
3300	121	10/27/77	5.10	5.00	98.319	5.16
3300	128	11/ 3/77	5.15	5.05	98.204	5.21
3300	135	11/10/77	5.15	5.05	98.106	5.22
3396	140	11/15/77	5.15	5.05	98.036	5.22
3200	142	11/17/77	5.15	5.05	98.008	5.22

Mil $ outstdg	Days to mat	Maturity	Discount Bid	Discount Asked	$ equiv	Bond equiv yield
3200	150	11/25/77	5.20	5.10	97.875	5.28
3100	156	12/ 1/77	5.20	5.10	97.790	5.29
3000	163	12/ 8/77	5.20	5.10	97.691	5.29
3504	168	12/13/77	5.20	5.10	97.620	5.30
3000	170	12/15/77	5.20	5.10	97.592	5.30
▶3000	177	12/22/77	5.19	5.15	97.468	5.36
3070	196	1/10/78	5.30	5.15	97.196	5.36
2930	224	2/ 7/78	5.30	5.20	96.764	5.42
3105	252	3/ 7/78	5.35	5.25	96.325	5.48
3203	280	4/ 4/78	5.40	5.30	95.878	5.55
2835	308	5/ 2/78	5.40	5.30	95.466	5.57
2400	336	5/30/78	5.40	5.30	95.053	5.58
▶2200	364	6/27/78	5.39	5.35	94.591	5.65

▶ denotes especially active issue. Other footnotes on reverse side.

Date: **June 27, 1977.**

Figure 15-2 Quotation Sheet for U.S. Treasury Securities

Table 15-2
Investments at Insured Banks, Selected Dates, 1961–1976
(millions of dollars)

Year Ending	Total Assets	Total Investments	Treasury Obligations	U. S. Government Agencies and Corps	State and Political Sub-divisions	Other Securities
1961	227,374	89,662	66,091	2,112	20,104	1,355
1965	379,405	103,651	59,210	4,513	38,480	1,447
1970	576,351	141,555	58,880	12,481	67,414	2,779
1971	639,903	163,860	62,697	17,072	80,135	3,956
1972	737,699	178,633	64,710	21,157	87,419	5,348
1973	832,658	179,575	55,293	27,538	91,228	5,515
1974	912,529	185,919	51,874	31,087	96,791	6,166
1975	952,451	222,515	81,011	33,299	100,801	7,404
1976	1,011,053	242,017	96,866	34,306	103,486	7,359

Percentage Distribution

Year Ending	Investment as a Percentage of Total Assets	Total Investments	Treasury Obligations	U. S. Government Agencies and Corps	State and Political Sub-divisions	Other Securities
1961	32.3	100.0	73.7	2.4	22.4	1.5
1965	27.3	100.0	57.1	4.4	37.1	1.4
1970	24.6	100.0	41.6	8.8	47.6	2.0
1971	25.6	100.0	38.3	10.4	48.9	2.4
1972	24.2	100.0	36.2	11.8	48.9	3.0
1973	21.6	100.0	30.8	15.3	50.8	3.1
1974	20.4	100.0	27.9	16.7	52.1	3.3
1975	23.4	100.0	36.4	15.0	45.3	3.3
1976	23.9	100.0	40.0	14.2	42.8	3.0

Source: FDIC, *Annual Reports* and unpublished data.

Agencies

Issuing Institutions. In the financial markets, "agencies" are the obligations of government-sponsored enterprises, federal agencies, and certain international institutions. *Government-sponsored enterprises* issuing securities include (1) the Bank for Cooperatives, (2) Federal Home Loan Banks, (3) Federal Intermediate Credit Banks, (4) Federal Land Banks, (5) the Federal National Mortgage Association (Fanny

Mae), (6) the Federal Home Loan Mortgage Corporation,[7] (7) the Student Loan Marketing Association, and (8) the United States Postal Service. *Federal Agencies* with outstanding obligations include (1) the Federal Housing Administration, (2) the Government National Mortgage Association (Ginnie Mae), (3) the District of Columbia Armory Board, (4) the Export–Import Bank of the United States, (5) the Farmers Home Administration, (6) the General Services Administra-

[7]The Bank for Cooperatives and the Federal Intermediate Credit Banks in December 1968, and the Federal National Mortgage Association in September 1968, converted to private ownership.

Table 15-3

Commercial Bank Ownership of Treasury Securities, by Maturity, Selected Years, 1960–1976
(millions of dollars)

		Within 1 Year						
Year Ending	Total	Total	Bills	Other	1–5 Years	5–10 Years	10–20 Years	Over 20 Years
1960	54,260	14,697	6,976	7,721	31,596	5,654	1,775	538
1965	50,325	18,003	10,156	7,847	19,676	11,640	334	671
1970	50,917	19,208	10,314	8,894	26,609	4,474	367	260
1971	51,363	14,920	8,287	6,633	28,823	6,847	555	217
1972	52,440	18,077	10,289	7,788	27,765	5,654	864	80
1973	45,737	17,499	7,901	9,598	22,878	4,022	1,065	272
1974	42,755	14,873	6,952	7,921	22,717	4,151	733	280
1975	64,398	29,875	17,481	12,394	29,629	4,071	552	271
1976	78,262	31,213	17,303	13,910	40,005	6,278	339	427

Percentage Distribution

		Within 1 Year						
Year Ending	Total	Total	Bills	Other	1–5 Years	5–10 Years	10–20 Years	Over 20 Years
1960	100.0	27.1	12.9	14.2	58.2	10.4	3.3	1.0
1965	100.0	35.8	20.2	15.6	39.1	23.1	0.7	1.3
1970	100.0	37.7	20.3	17.5	52.3	8.8	0.7	0.5
1971	100.0	29.0	16.1	12.9	56.1	13.3	1.1	0.4
1972	100.0	34.5	19.6	14.9	52.9	10.8	1.6	0.2
1973	100.0	38.3	17.3	21.0	50.0	8.8	2.3	0.6
1974	100.0	34.8	16.3	18.5	53.1	9.7	1.7	0.7
1975	100.0	46.4	27.1	19.2	46.0	6.3	0.9	0.4
1976	100.0	39.9	22.1	17.8	51.1	8.0	0.4	0.5

Source: *Federal Reserve Bulletin.*

NOTE: Based on Treasury Survey of Ownership from *Treasury Bulletin*. This survey presently covers 5,499 banks, which hold about 90 percent of the bank-owned Treasury debt.

tion, (7) the Maritime Administration, (8) the Small Business Administration, (9) the Tennessee Valley Authority, (10) the Washington Metropolitan Area Transit Authority, and (11) the Department of Housing and Urban Development. *International institutions* that issue bank-eligible debts include (1) the International Bank for Reconstruction and Development (World Bank), (2) the Inter-American Development Bank, and (3) the Asian Development Bank.[8] Between 1965 and 1976, the outstanding obligations of government-sponsored enterprises and federal agencies increased from $8.9 to $103.3 billion.

Special mention should be made of the *Federal Financing Bank* (FFB), an instrumentality of the U.S. Treasury established in May 1974 to consolidate the financing of a variety of federal agencies and other borrowers whose obligations are guaranteed by the federal government. The FFB's objective is to reduce the cost of borrowing and to smooth the flow of funds to governmental agencies. The FFB is authorized to borrow from the U.S. Treasury and to borrow from the public by the issuance of obligations of the U.S. government just as are Treasury obligations. To date, with the exception of one issue of eight-month bills, the FFB has financed itself by borrowing from the U.S Treasury. Since its inception, the FFB has financed a number of agencies through loans and purchases of obligations.

Investment Characteristics. Although agencies are not direct obligations of the Treasury, they do, in one way or another, involve federal sponsorship or guarantees. Thus agencies are considered virtually free from the credit risk. Agencies have initital maturities ranging from thirty days to over twenty years; however, the bulk of these obligations mature within five years, which increases their attractiveness to banks.

The secondary market for agencies is not quite as active as that for Treasuries and, as a result, the spread between the bid and asked prices tends to be slightly wider. Typically, the spread on agencies ranges from 2/32 on nine-month to two-year issues to 8/32 for obligations beyond this maturity. In addition, it is sometimes difficult to sell longer-term agencies without accepting some reduction in price, especially during periods of tight money. Because agencies may involve some slight credit risk and are not quite as marketable, they usually yield 20–40 basis points more than Treasuries. Most agencies are noncallable prior to maturity, so investors can be assured that their holdings will not be disturbed if interest rates should decline. Finally, interest income on agencies is subject to regular federal income taxes; however, with the exception of Fannie Mae and Ginny Mae obligations issued since

[8]An excellent, concise description of each of these agencies is contained in the First Boston Corporation, *Handbook of Securities of the United States Government and Federal Agencies and Related Money Market Instruments*, 27th ed. (Boston: The First Boston Corporation, 1976), pp. 75–123.

August 2, 1954, agencies are exempt from state and local income of property taxes.

Bank Holdings. Bank holdings of agencies increased from $2.1 billion in 1961 to $34.3 billion in 1976. The primary attraction of agencies over Treasuries, of course, is their yield. In addition, most agencies are accepted as security for fiduciary, trust, and public deposits under the control of the Treasury.

Municipals

The term "municipals" encompasses all securities issued by states and their political subdivisions. Between 1965 and 1976, total state and local debt outstanding increased from $99.5 to $221.2 billion. Funds raised by the sale of these obligations were used to finance the myriad of capital projects, such as schools, roads, hospitals, and bridges, demanded by a growing and more affluent population.

Types. There are two general types of municipal securities: (1) general obligation bonds and (2) revenue bonds. *General obligation bonds* are backed by the taxing power and full faith and credit of the issuing governmental unit. *Revenue bonds* ordinarily are issued by public authorities, such as the Port of New York Authority, to erect public facilities such as bridges, airports, and tunnels. The sources of funds to pay the principal and interest on bonds generally depend on the nature of the project being financed. Typical sources of revenue include (1) user charges on utilities; (2) tolls, commissions, and fees; (3) special taxes; and (4) rental payments.

There are two special types of municipal bonds—public housing bonds and notes and industrial revenue bonds—which deserve separate mention. *Public housing bonds and notes* are created by various states and localities jointly with the federal government. The proceeds are used for slum clearance and for the construction of low-rent public housing. Each issue is secured by the pledge of net rental revenues from the projects and by an annual contributions contract between the Public Housing Administration (PHA) and the local authority, which stipulates that the PHA will make payments to the local authority sufficient to service the debt if revenues are inadequate to meet principal and interest payments. Thus PHAs, as these securities are called, are the highest-grade municipal available.

Industrial revenue bonds are issued by communities to purchase land and to finance construction of factories, plants, and warehouses for prospective new industries. Lease payments from the private corporation are used to amortize the debt.

Investment Characteristics. As we have noted, banks usually invest in the four top grades of municipals. Only the largest and most credit-worthy municipal issues enjoy a national market. Most tax exempt securities trade only on a local or regional basis. As a result, the market for these issues is quite thin. The spread between the bid and asked prices on local issues is ordinarily 1.5 points, but it may be as much as 3 points during tight-money periods. Municipals are traded in the over-the-counter market with approximately 750 investment dealers and most large banks making a market for one or more of the various obligations outstanding. Dealer offerings of municipals are published daily in the *Blue List*.

The great attraction of municipals, of course, is that their interest income is exempt from federal income taxes. In addition, most states exempt bonds issued within the state from property taxation and its own income taxes. However, under the Tax Reform Act of 1969, interest income on industrial development bonds issued since January 1969 will be taxed unless (1) the issue is below $1 million, or (2) the total of the bond issue plus any capital expenditures for the benefiting firm for three years after the issue is under $5 million, or (3) the issue is used to finance housing, convention and transportation facilities, or air- and water-pollution control devices.

Most municipal bonds are issued in "serial" form. That is, a portion of the obligation is scheduled to mature each year over the life of the issue. Coupon rates are lowest on the shorter-term obligations and gradually increase over longer maturities. Investors may select those maturities and yields that best suit their needs.

Bank Holdings. Bank investments in municipals increased from $20.1 billion in 1961 to $103. 5 billion in 1976. During the same period, municipals as a percentage of total bank investments rose from 22.4 percent to 42.8 percent. The primary reason usually cited for the greater emphasis on municipals in bank investment portfolios is the increasing importance of time deposits as a source of funds. Banks have tended to match this longer-term source of funds with longer-term assets, such as municipals, mortgages, and term loans. Also during recent years, banks, with the declining importance of Treasuries in their portfolios, have relied increasingly on long-term municipals to meet the collateral requirements for fiduciary, trust, and public funds. Given the expected capital needs of state and local governments, it is very likely that municipals will increase both absolutely and relatively in bank portfolios.

Corporates

Although corporate bonds carrying the top four quality ratings are bank-eligible investments, banks have shown little interest in them because of three considerations: (1) yield, (2) marketability, and (3) maturity.[9] Because the after-tax yield on corporates is ordinarily below the yield on municipals of similar quality, banks obviously prefer to invest in the latter. In addition, corporates are sometimes difficult to liquidate in volume, especially in a declining market. Finally, because most corporate issues have long-term maturities, they involve more credit and money risk.

Large money market banks, however, do invest considerable sums in *equipment trust certificates*. These securities are used to finance the purchase of rolling stock, airplanes, and trucks. For example, under a typical arrangement, an airliner will contract for the purchase of airplanes and arrange with a group of banks for the creation of an equipment trust to hold title to the airplanes. The banks then will issue trust certificates to investors or hold them themselves until the airline pays the final installment on the certificates.

The Bank Underwriting Function

As we have seen, commercial banks may underwrite without limitation the obligations of the U.S. government, its agencies and instrumentalities thereof, and the general obligations of state and local governments. In addition, banks may underwrite, subject to a 10 percent limitation, the obligations of the International Bank for Reconstruction and Development, the Inter-American Development Bank, the Asian Development Bank, and the Tennessee Valley Authority, and obligations issued by any state or political subdivision or any agency of a state or a political subdivision for housing, university, or dormitory purposes.

A glance at the issue notices in the *Wall Street Journal* will reveal the great extent to which banks participate in underwritings. Banks engage in underwriting for these reasons: (1) profit motive gained from the purchase and sale of bonds; (2) collateral benefits derived from financing in the area of the bank's operation, such as public deposits, public relations, and participation in area development; and (3) in order to obtain bonds at wholesale prices and concessions for their own investment portfolio. Originally, the underwriting function was confined to money market and regional banks. However, recently many medium-sized banks have opened underwriting departments.

Suggestions for Additional Reading

The American Bankers Association. *The Role of Investments in Bank Asset Management.* Six Studies. Washington, D.C.: The American Bankers Association, 1974.

[9]The Amercian Bankers Association, *The Role of Investments in Bank Asset Management*, Study 3: "Characteristics of Securities for Bank Investments," (Washington, D.C.: The American Bankers Association, 1974), pp. 36–37.

Clark, John C. "The Underwriting Function in Commercial Banks." In William N. Baughn and Charls E. Walker, eds. *The Banker's Handbook.* Homewood, Ill.: Dow Jones-Irwin, 1966, chap. 51.

The First Boston Corporation. *Handbook of Securities of the United States Government and Federal Agencies and Related Money Market Instruments.* 27th ed. Boston: The First Boston Corporation, 1976.

Friedman, Benjamin M. "The Determination of Long-Term Interest Rates: Why Were Bond Yields So High in 1974?" Federal Reserve Bank of Boston, *New England Economic Review* (May–June 1975), pp. 35–56.

Homer, Sidney, and Johannesen, Richard I. *The Price of Money 1946 to 1969: An Analytical Study of United States and Foreign Interest Rates.* New Brunswick, N.J.: Rutgers University Press, 1969.

Horton, Joseph J., Jr. "Statistical Classification of Municipal Bonds." *Journal of Bank Research* (Autumn 1970), pp. 29–40.

Johnson, Rodney. "A Fresh Look at the Municipal Bond Market." Federal Reserve Bank of Philadelphia, *Business Review* (July–August 1976), pp. 11–22.

Kaufman, Henry. "Commercial Bank Investments in the New Environment." New York: Salomon Brothers and Hutzler, 1965.

Monhollon, Jimmie R. *Instruments of the Money Market.* Richmond, Va.: Federal Reserve Bank of Richmond, 1970.

Smith, William Paul. "Commercial Bank Entry into Revenue Bond Underwriting: Competitive Impact and Public Benefit." Washington, D.C. Office of the Comptroller of the Currency, 1968.

CHAPTER

16

Executing Investment Policy

Chapter 15 was concerned with the general considerations involved in bank investment management. It is the task of the board of directors and senior management to translate these general considerations into specific guidelines for inclusion in the written investment policy statement. These guidelines must be broad enough to allow the investment manager adequate flexibility in his portfolio decisions. The general purpose of this chapter is to discuss the problems and considerations that confront the investment manager as he makes his portfolio selections. In this chapter we shall (1) examine decisions made by the portfolio manager, (2) note the cycles in interest rates, (3) discuss yield-curve analysis as a basis for portfolio selections, (4) consider the spaced maturities approach to portfolio selections, (5) note the interim investment decisions made between major portfolio moves, and (6) explore the "new environment" for bank investments.

Decisions Made by the Portfolio Manager

The principal decisions of the portfolio manager are made within the guidelines established in the investment policy statement. These decisions relate to (1) quality and diversification, (2) maturity distribution, and (3) timing of major portfolio changes.

Quality and Diversification

If a bank's investment policy statement specifies that 10 percent of net deposits will be held in Treasury and agency securities within a one- to five-year maturity range, the question of quality pertains to the remainder of the portfolio. The extent to which the portfolio manager should reach for the lower-quality issues permitted by the policy statement is determined by a number of factors, including the bank's capital adequacy, loan structure, tax position, and trading philosophy. If the bank's capital position is only marginally adequate, or if the bank has an above-average percentage of term loans, or if the portfolio manager desires the most marketable and highly liquid securities as trading vehicles, the investment manager should emphasize quality in the bank's portfolio by holding Treasuries, agencies, and municipals that carry the top three ratings.

With respect to diversification, the portfolio manager must decide on the geographic dispersion of his municipal holdings, regardless of quality. The policy statement more than likely will stipulate that the portfolio manager will acquire local municipals first, but there is a limit imposed by the need for diversification on the amount that can be purchased.

Maturity Distribution

One of the most difficult decisions the investment manager must make is the maturity distribution of the portfolio. Considerations influencing maturity include the bank's capital adequacy, loan structure, deposit structure, and trading philosophy. Banks that are thinly capitalized or that have an above-average amount of term loans should have a portfolio weighted toward the short-term end. On the other hand, if the bank has a large amount of time and savings deposits, it may want to match these deposits with long-term securities. Finally, those banks that have personnel skilled in trading will emphasize short-term securities if there is a strong expectation that long-term interest rates are going to rise, and long-term securities if long-term rates are expected to fall. As will be discussed below, many banks without investment officers trained in securities trading prefer to space their securities evenly over some designated maturity range, whereas others adopt some more elaborate scheme with, perhaps, Treasuries and agencies in the one- to five-year range and municipals in the predominantly five- to twelve-year range.

Timing Major Portfolio Changes

An important responsibility of every portfolio manager is that of timing major portfolio changes, such as when the portfolio manager is attempting to avoid the impact of expected increases in market yields or to take advantage of expected declines in market yields. Every portfolio manager, at one time or another, has wished that he had bought a little earlier or sold a little later. No portfolio manager possesses that degree of clairvoyance which permits him always to buy at the bottom and to sell at the top. In order not to miss any major move in interest rates, the skilled manager relies heavily upon yield-curve analysis to time his portfolio changes.[1] In addition, he takes cognizance of changes in the money supply, the direction of fiscal policy, and the stage of the business cycle.

Cycles in Interest Rates

J. P. Morgan, the great bank-financier, supposedly was asked once whether or not the stock market was going to rise or fall. His cryptic and sage reply was, "The market will fluctuate." And so it is with interest rates, which tend to fluctuate over a wide range during a complete business cycle. The portfolio manager interested in maximizing income from his investments is vitally concerned with these movements in interest rates.

Historical Movements in Interest Rates

Figure 16-1 depicts the movement of long-term, high-grade, American bonds since 1799. From its first days until 1965, interest rates in the United States followed a cyclical pattern with the basic secular trend downward. These cylical movements occurred within a rather well-defined channel.

The historical low point for interest rates was in 1946, when seasoned prime long corporates were 2.37 percent, long governments were 2.17 percent, and long municipals were 1.00 percent. Since 1946, there has been a secular rise in bond yields, which was interrupted by declines in interest rates during the following periods: 1948–1949, 1953–1954, 1957–1958, 1959–1961, 1970–1971, and 1974–1976. Each of these rallies was associated with recession in general economic activity or the period of slow to moderate growth following a recession. These

[1]Yield-curve analysis will be discussed below.

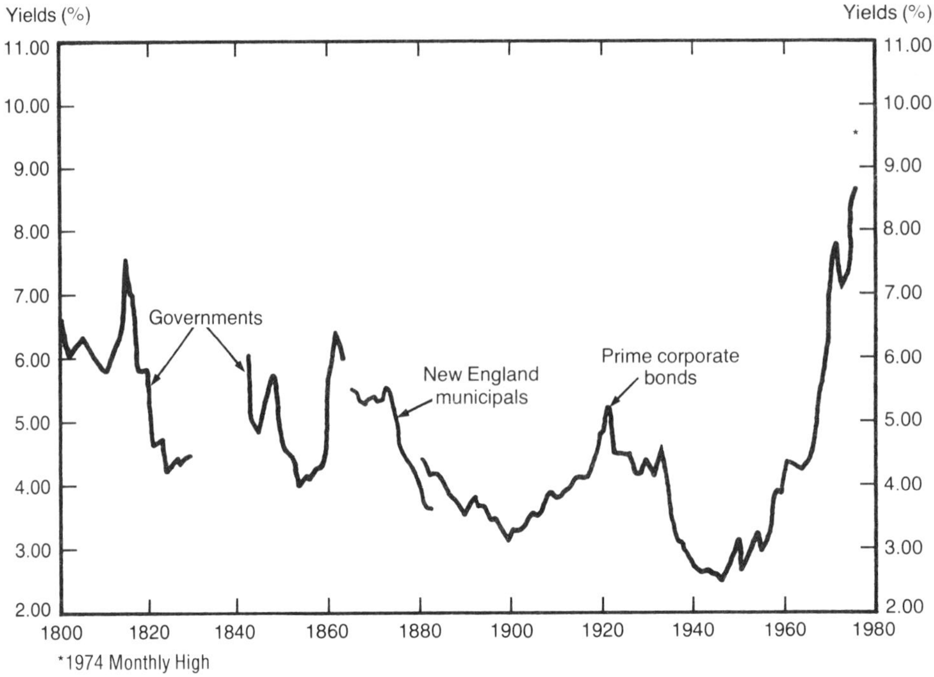

Figure 16-1 Yields of Long-Term High Grade American Bonds Since 1799

Source: Salomon Brothers. Reprinted by permission.

rallies are shown in Figure 16–2, which depicts movements in yields of long-term, high-grade corporate, U.S. Treasury, and prime municipal bonds since 1946.

It is important also to know how yields on securities with different maturities and credit risks have reacted during the long, postwar bear market. As shown in Figures 16-3 and 16-4, yields on Treasury bills and bonds essentially moved in the same direction both secularly and cyclically. However, bill rates move further and faster than yields on bonds. As was shown in Table 15-1, it takes a price change of only $9.60 for the market yield on a 4 percent, one-year issue to move from 4 percent to 5 percent, while a price change of $125.50 is required for the market yield on a 4 percent, twenty-year obligation to move from 4 percent to 5 percent. Pronounced downward movements of bill rates occur during recessions as banks and other investors seek a haven for excess funds. Bill rates usually move sharply upward during expansionary periods as banks and other investors tend to sell bills when loan and other investment opportunities become more available.

Figure 16-4 shows the relationship between bond yields on securities with different credit risks since the 1920s. During the entire period, movements in yields (from highest to lowest) on corporate Baa, corporate Aaa, U.S. government bonds, and high-grade municipals usually have paralleled each other quite closely. The yield relationships shown in Figure 16-4 also indicate that municipal yields have not fully discounted their exemption from federal income taxes because the spread between yields on municipal and Treasury bonds has tended to be much less than 48 percent of the yield on the latter, especially during periods of tight money.

The Four Phases of the Interest-Rate Cycle

A bank must attempt to adapt its portfolio to the cyclical and secular movements in interest rates and business activity.[2] The costs of not doing so may be large losses during upswings or foregone profits during downswings. For purposes of analysis, the cycle in interest rates, as depicted in Figure 16-5, may be divided into four phases:

[2]Much of the discussion in this section is based on The American Bankers Association, *The Role of Investments in Bank Asset Management*, "Study 6: Adapting the Portfolio to Changing Conditions" (Washington, D.C.: The American Bankers Association, 1974), pp.12–17.

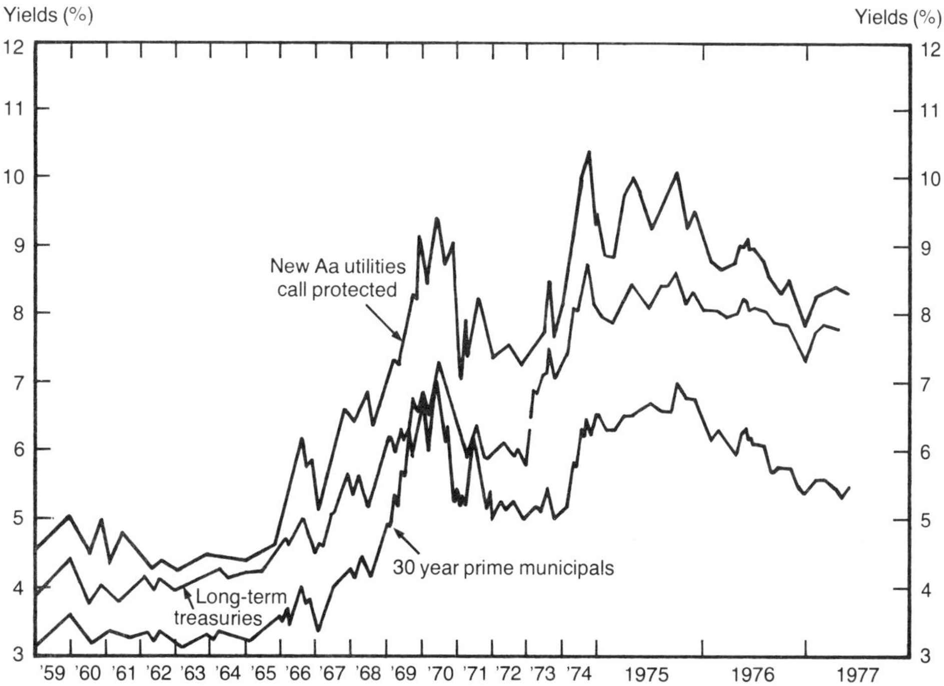

Figure 16-2 Yields of Long-Term High Grade Corporate, U.S. Treasury, and Prime Municipal Bonds

Source: Salomon Brothers. Reprinted by permission.

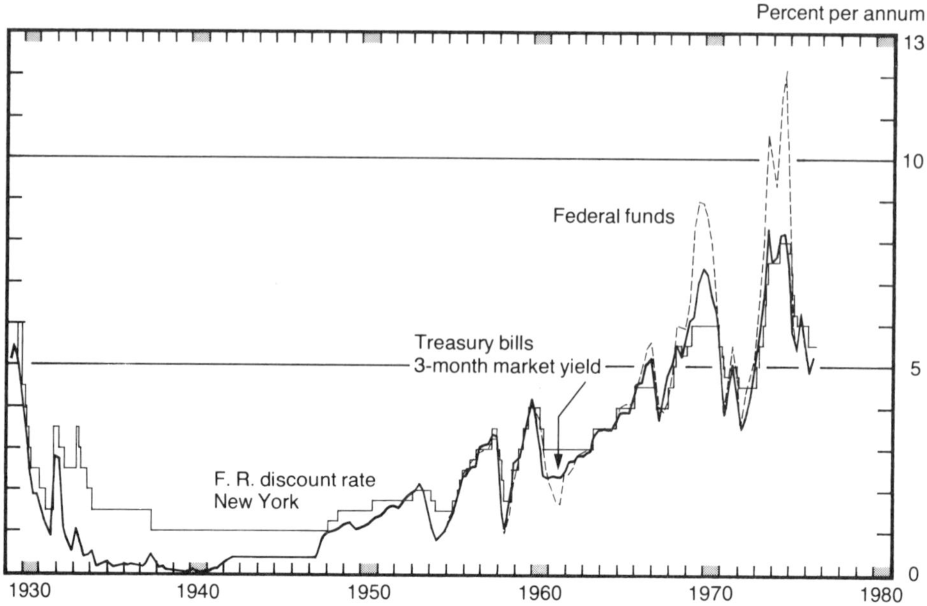

Figure 16-3 Short-Term Interest Rates

Source: Board of Governors of the Federal Reserve System, *Historical Chartbook*.

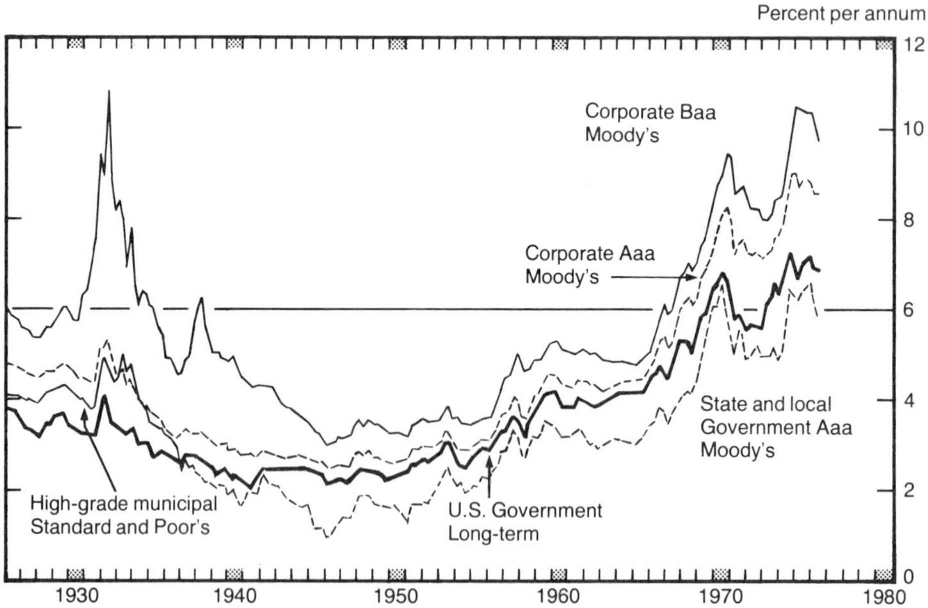

Figure 16-4 Long-Term Bond Yields

Source: Board of Governors of the Federal Reserve System, *Historical Chartbook*.

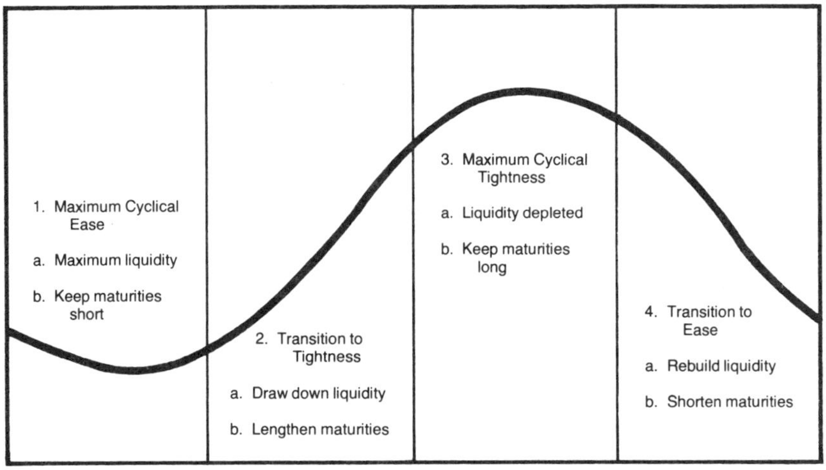

Figure 16-5 The Four Phases of the Interest-Rate Cycle

Source: The American Bankers Association, *The Role of Investments in Bank Asset Management*, "Study 5: Adapting the Portfolio to Changing Conditions" (Washington, D. C.: The American Bankers Association, 1974), page 13.

1. *Maximum cyclical ease.* This is the trough of the cycle. Interest rates are at their lowest levels, the demand for loans is weak, and monetary policy is expansionary. Since 1946, these conditions have been found on seven occasions: late 1946, mid-1954, mid-1958, most of 1961, late 1966, early 1971, and late 1976. The portfolio strategy to adopt during such a period is to complete taking capital gains on long-term securities purchased earlier and to reinvest funds in securities with maturities that coincide roughly with anticipated increases in loan demands. The bank's liquidity position is at a maximum.

2. *Transition to tightness.* As the economy proceeds out of a recession, the demand for loans picks up, monetary policy usually turns less expansionary, and as a result, interest rates begin to rise. Banks draw down their liquid assets to meet loan demand.

3. *Maximum cyclical tightness.* Economic indicators show new highs, the demand for loans is great, monetary policy is probably contractionary, and interest rates are high. During the postwar period, cyclical peaks occurred at the following times: mid-1953, fall 1957, late 1959, late 1966, late 1969, mid-1974. Aggressive banks would shift part of their investment portfolio into long maturities, particularly Treasuries and agencies. However, some medium-quality municipals and high-grade corporates may be purchased because of the tendency for prices of these issues to rise proportionately more during rallies.

4. *Transition to ease.* Following the cyclical peak, the demand for loans weakens, monetary policy becomes more expansionary, and interest rates begin to retreat from their high levels. Portfolio managers must be alert for the time to start taking capital gains and to shorten maturities.

Yield-Curve Analysis

As the investment manager attempts to adapt his portfolio to cycles in interest rates and business activity, perhaps the most useful predictive device available is the *yield curve,* which is simply a freehand line fitted to the maturity distribution of yields on securities with equal credit risks. Yield curves for Treasury issues are published every month in the *Treasury Bulletin,* but they can be derived daily by plotting the schedule of yields shown in *The Wall Street Journal.* Yield curves for agencies and for various grades of corporates and municipals are published regularly by several of the major investment bankers.

Let us note how the portfolio manager can use yield-curve analysis to time his purchases and sales and to determine the maturity distribution of the bank's portfolio. For purposes of discussion, yield curves may be classified as either (1) upward sloping, (2) flat, (3) downward sloping, or (4) humped.

Upward-Sloping Curves

Upward-sloping yield curves with short-term rates below long-term rates ordinarily appear during periods of maximum cyclical ease. In addition, the entire curve usually is at a lower level than at other times. As shown in Figure 16-6, the yield curve for November 26, 1976, is upward sloping. Short-term rates tend to be below long-term rates during periods of recession or slack loan demand (as in November 1976) because banks and other investors have placed their excess funds in short-term securities in anticipation of loan and investment opportunities in the forthcoming expansionary phase of the cycle.

The general expectation surrounding an upward-sloping yield curve is that long-term interest rates will rise. Most banks have learned through experience to resist the temptation to raise current income by lengthening maturities when the yield curve is upward sloping. It makes little sense to buy long-term securities and to watch them fall in price as the level of interest rates rises during an upcoming economic expansion. The best strategy for aggressive bank portfolio managers to follow when the yield curve is upward sloping is to invest in short-term securities that will mature as loan demand picks up during the expansionary phase of the cycle.

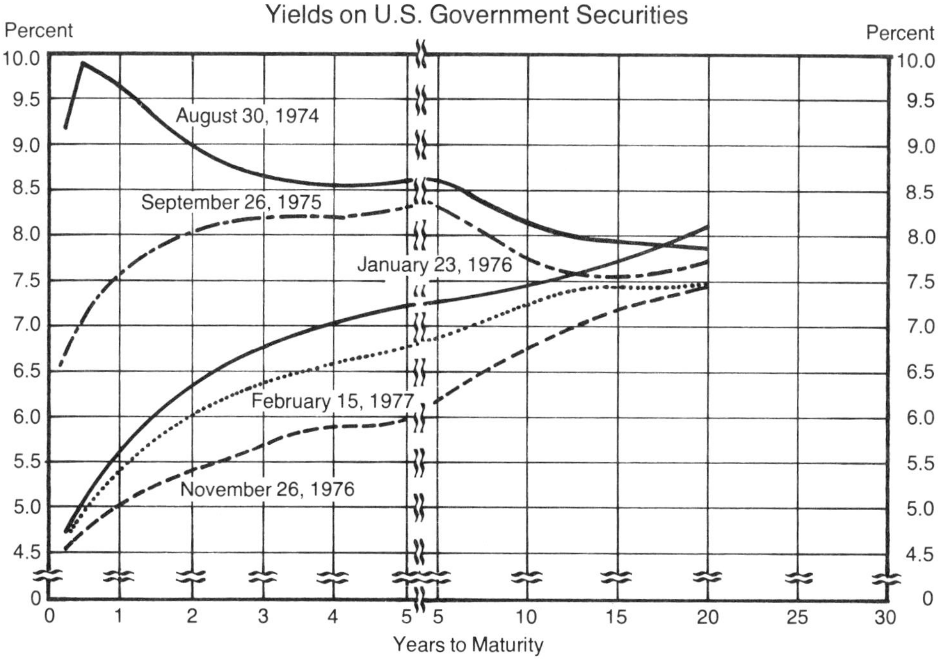

Figure 16-6 Yields on U.S. Government Securities

Source: Federal Reserve Bank of St. Louis.

Flat Yield Curves

Flat yield curves generally signify a period of transition, either from the contractionary phase to the expansionary phase of the cycle or vice versa. Generally, the investment manager does not make any major portfolio moves during periods when the yield curve is flat. During such times he is closely analyzing other financial and economic indicators for signs of upcoming turning points in both the business and interest-rate cycles.

Downward-Sloping Yield Curves

The yield curve typically becomes negatively sloped during periods of maximum cyclical tightness in interest rates, such as August 1974. Short-term rates are driven above long-term rates by a combination of factors. During a cyclical upswing, banks and other investors turn from active buyers to active sellers of short-term securities. This selling pressure, in conjunction with a tight-money policy, works to push short-term rates above long-term rates, even though there is upward pressure on the latter. Moreover, the entire yield curve will have upward pressure on it, if there is a general expectation of inflation.

Nominal interest rates tend to rise when there is an expectation of inflation as investors attempt to keep the "real" return on their portfolio from declining.

The general expectation surrounding a negatively sloped yield curve is that interest rates are going to decline. Therefore, when a downward-sloping curve occurs, the portfolio manager should begin to reach out for longer-term securities, which are the vehicles to reap capital gains. The manger's task is complicated, however, because the bank's liquidity holdings are probably at the minimum level, and he must wait until loan repayments and lessened liquidity needs free the necessary funds to permit an extension of maturities. Usually, there is ample opportunity to acquire longer-term securities because the yield curve typically remains downward sloping for several months. For example, the yield curve was downward sloping throughout much of 1973 and 1974. In order not to commit funds prematurely, the portfolio manager must wait for a confirming signal such as (1) an increase in rate of growth of bank reserves, (2) an increase in the rate of growth of the money supply, (3) a reduction in bank borrowings from the Federal Reserve, or (4) a sharp drop in short-term interest rates. After receiving such a signal, he then must try to gauge when these changes will begin to have an impact. Bank reserves began to turn upward during the second and third quarters of 1974. However, the liquidity positions of banks and other investors were reduced so drastically during the previous expansion that it was evident that long-term rates would not fall until liquidity holdings had been restored to more conservative levels. The patient portfolio manager would have not begun his program of reaching out for longer-term securities until several months after the rates of growth in bank reserves and the money supply had turned upward. The bond market actually bottomed out in October, but bond purchases between July and October 1974 would have proved extremely profitable. For example, the $7\frac{1}{2}$ percent 8/15/93-88 Treasury bond could have been purchased for as low as $90\frac{1}{2}$ in early fall 1974 and sold at $98\frac{1}{4}$ about 4 months later for a profit of $77.50 plus interest per $905 invested.

Humped Yield Curves

A "humped" yield curve occurs when rates on maturities in the three- to seven-year range are the highest available. In other words, there is a hump in the yield curve in the intermediate-term range. Humped yield curves typically occur during the expansionary phase of the business cycle and as the shape of the yield curve is changing from flat to downward sloping.

There are at least two reasons why the yield curve might have a hump in it. First, the hump might be due partially to heavy selling of intermediate maturities by banks, in particular, and other investors. Banks that have underestimated their liquidity needs during the expansion phase of the cycle may resort to selling intermediate-term securities from their investment portfolio. Another contributing cause of the hump is the 4.25 percent legal interest-rate ceiling on Treasury bonds, which forces the Treasury at times to have to finance much of its cash needs by issuing a large volume of notes in the intermediate-term range.[3] This increased effective supply of intermediate-term securities adds upward pressure to yields in this maturity range.

Conclusion

Yield-curve analysis is an invaluable tool for the bank portfolio manager. It can assist him in determining the maturity distribution of the bank's portfolio and in timing purchases and sales. However, as shown by experience, it cannot be used in a vacuum. The portfolio manager must supplement the predictive value of yield-curve analysis with a careful study of other relevant financial and economic indicators and a good intuition.

The Spaced Maturities Approach

Many small banks do not have the skilled investment managers to employ yield-curve analysis in portfolio management. These banks could request the investment department of a regional or money market bank to assist them in portfolio planning, but some choose not to do so. Other small bank officers, perhaps out of ignorance, view yield-curve analysis as being too risky. Most bank managers who share these objections tend to use a spaced maturities approach to portfolio selection. With this method, the investment manager first determines the maximum maturity that he desires to hold, say five years in Treasury and agency securities and twelve years in the municipal portfolio. Second, he determines how he is going to divide the investment portfolio among Treasuries, agencies, and municipals. Many small banks tend to follow a rather conservative policy and hold, maybe, $2 in Treasuries and agencies for every $1 invested in municipals. Third, in the Treasury and agency portfolio, funds would be divided approximately equally among all maturities in the two- to five-year range and, in the municipal portfolio, perhaps equally in the six- to twelve-year maturity range.

One advantage of the spaced maturities approach to portfolio management is that it is simple and easy to administer. In addition, such an approach would tend to guarantee at least average results over

[3]On March 17, 1971, Congress authorized the Treasury to issue up to $10 billion in bonds at rates exceeding 4.25 percent.

the interest-rate cycle. At times, funds would be rolled over into high-yielding maturities and on other occasions into low-yielding maturities. On the other hand, the spaced maturities approach will not tend to outperform a skilled and experienced portfolio manager who takes advantage of interest-rate movements in both directions. The Tax Reform Act of 1969 also is an encouragement to banks to adopt a flexible portfolio policy because they no longer have a tax advantage from waiting 6 months to take any capital gains on their security holdings.

Medium-sized banks tend to use a combination approach to portfolio management. That is, part of the portfolio is shifted to take advantage of expected major movements in interest rates, while perhaps most of the portfolio is divided among various maturities. For both small and medium-sized banks, this more-or-less hedged approach to portfolio management may be the most satisfactory alternative, given the resources that these institutions devote to this portion of asset management.

Interim Investment Decisions

So far we have focused on investment management at cyclical turning points. Between these peaks and troughs in the interest-rate cycle, the portfolio manager is confronted continually with opportunities to adjust the portfolio so as to enhance earnings.

Riding the Yield Curve

Between cyclical turning points, many portfolio managers "ride the yield curve" in order to improve earnings. Riding the yield curve involves purchasing short- and intermediate-term securities and riding them into the very short-term sector of the yield curve. This practice takes advantage of the fact that prices rise (yields fall) as the security approaches the short-term sector, as there are many investors willing to accept a lower yield (pay a high price) for the more liquid security. In its simplest form, riding the yield curve involves purchasing three-month Treasury bills at the auction and selling them when the yield falls enough to make reinvestment worthwhile, which may be anywhere from seven to sixty days. For example, if a three-month Treasury bill is purchased at $988.83 to yield 4.42 percent and thirty days later it is quoted at 4.28 percent or $993.10, the bill could be sold for a profit of $4.27. Assuming that the same yield relationships hold for the next eleven consecutive thirty-day periods, the before-tax profit would be $51.24 from twelve bill roll-overs. Another way to ride the yield curve is to purchase notes and bonds in the one- to three-year range and to hold them until they fall in price as their maturity shortens and liquidity rises. Riding the yield curve is most profitable when the curve is upward sloping; there is a slight dropoff in the very shortest term rates that makes riding the yield curve profitable.

Participation in Treasury Offerings and Refundings

The Treasury makes weekly offerings of three- and six-month bills, monthly offerings of twelve-month bills, and periodic offerings of other securities. Although the Treasury does not permit payment for weekly bills by credit to Treasury tax and loan accounts, it usually does for other issues. Because the Treasury often delays calling funds credited to tax and loan accounts for periods ranging from several days to several weeks, there is an added incentive for banks to participate in Treasury offerings.

Several times a year the Treasury must refund Treasury notes and bonds that are maturing or raise new funds. During recent years, the Treasury has offered holders of maturing issues and other investors a choice between a note maturing in about two years and one maturing in approximately four to seven years, with the shorter-term issue yielding slightly less than the longer-term security. Which option to take would depend to a large extent on the portfolio manager's expectations with respect to future interest rates. Since the yield curve was negatively sloped during most of the period and hence long-term interest rates were expected to fall sooner or later, one strategy for banks with investable funds would have been to reach for the longer-term issue. Such an investment would have proved very profitable because the longer-term notes eventually went to premium prices.[4] An alternative strategy would have been to take the shorter-term note and switch to the longer-term note for its greater appreciation potential when it became clearer that interest rates were going to turn downward.

Taking Advantage of "Out-of-Line" Issues

Sometimes, yields on particular Treasury or agency issues temporarily exceed yields on other issues in roughly the same maturity range. This issue may have gotten "out of line" through heavy selling pressure from several large investors or new issues coming out in the same maturity range. It is sometimes to the portfolio manager's advantage to purchase the out-of-line issue and hold it for a short time until it is bid back into line with yields on comparable maturities.

Similarly, sometimes what appear to be excessive gaps will open up between Treasury and agency issues, with roughly equal maturities. The portfolio manager might purchase the agency issue and hold it until the yield premium is eliminated.

[4]Some large-term Treasury notes issued in the 1969–1970 high period of maximum cyclical tightness went to premiums ranging from 7–14 points in the subsequent bond market rally between mid-1970 and early 1971.

It should be obvious that the decisions we have noted cannot be made without years of study and observation of the market. A good portfolio manager is a valuable asset to any bank because he can contribute substantially to bank income by taking advantage of the many day-to-day trading opportunities.

Influences on Bank Portfolio Management in the Future

Bank portfolio management in the future will be influenced importantly by three factors. These include (1) the 1965–1970 and 1973–1974 bear markets, (2) inflationary expectations, and (3) the stability of monetary management.

The 1965–1970 and 1973–1974 Bear Markets

The 1965–1970 and 1973–1974 bear markets in bonds made an indelible impact on the minds of every portfolio manager. Few experts, if any, expected interest rates to rise as far and fast as they did in each case. During the years ahead, portfolio managers who experienced these bond market collapses will be more cautious about their long positions. As a result, they probably will tend to emphasize short-term securities even more than in the past, except, of course, when there are excellent prospects for major rallies.

Inflationary Expectations

Market interest rates rise and fall, in large part, because of the waxing and waning of inflationary expectations, which, in turn, are influenced by prospects for war or peace, the degree of monetary stimulation, the strength of cost-push forces in the economy, and the relative importance assigned to full employment vis-à-vis price stability in our national priorities. As we proceed through the remainder of the 1970s and into the 1980s, the prospects for peace seem to be improved; the Federal Reserve still seems prone from time to time to permit the money supply to expand at an uneven rate; cost-push forces appear to be having an important influence; and some economists advocate a policy of "full employment at all costs." Except for the improved prospects of peace, all other influences portend of continued inflation and hence high levels of interest rates with, perhaps, periodic wide fluctuations as the central bank switches between tight- and easy-money policies. The expected fluctuations in interest rates will provide important trading opportunities for the experienced portfolio manager.

The Stability of Monetary Management

If the Federal Reserve practices countercyclical monetary policy as opposed to stable monetary growth, the monetary sector probably will continue to contribute to instability in both the interest-rate and business cycles. Therefore, portfolio managers in the late 1970s and 1980s probably will continue to witness periods in which the impact of prior monetary excesses still will be felt as monetary policy is shifted to a restrictive posture, and, of course, the converse should occur too. Policy reversals will make interest-rate forecasting, and hence portfolio management, more difficult.

Suggestions for Additional Reading

Association of Reserve City Bankers. *Investment Policies and Practices of Reserve City Banks.* Chicago: Association of Reserve City Bankers, April 1966.

Board of Governors of the Federal Reserve System. *Historical Chart Book.* Washington, D.C.: Board of Governors of the Federal Reserve System (Annual).

Bradley, Stephen P., and Crane, Dwight B. *Management of Bank Portfolios.* New York: John Wiley, 1975.

"Government Securities—Large Banks Employ Flexible Maturity Structures." Federal Reserve Bank of Dallas, *Business Review* (February 1975), pp. 10–14.

Homer, Sidney, "Bond Investment in the 1970s." New York: Salomon Brothers, November 1970.

Kane, Edward J. "Bonds and Balance-Sheet Cosmetics: Tax Swapping Then and Now." Federal Reserve Bank of Boston, *New England Economic Review* (May–June 1973), pp. 33–38.

Kasriel, Paul L. "Hedging Interest Rate Fluctuations." Federal Reserve Bank of Chicago, *Business Conditions* (April 1976), pp. 3–10.

Scott, Ira O. *The Government Securities Market.* New York: McGraw-Hill, 1965.

Watson, Ronald D. "Bank Bond Management: The Maturity Dilemma." Federal Reserve Bank of Philadelphia, *Monthly Review* (March 1972), pp. 23–29.

PART

VI

Regulation of the Banking Structure

CHAPTER

17

Banking Entry and Branching

This is the first of three chapters concerned with regulation of the banking structure. These chapters will encompass the regulation of banking entry (chartering), branch banking, bank mergers, and bank holding companies. During the 1960s, these areas of inquiry were the objects of a great deal of research and study by the banking regulatory authorities and academicians. The principal reasons for this increased interest were (1) the dramatic changes in the banking structure brought about by the Comptroller of the Currency's more liberal attitude toward chartering national banks, (2) the sharp increase in the number of branches, (3) a continuation of the post-World War II merger movement, (4) the application of the antitrust laws to banking, and (5) the formation of holding companies by virtually all major banks.

In this chapter we shall (1) note the changes in the banking structure over the years, (2) examine the regulation of banking entry and branch banking, and (3) discuss the continuing issue of branch banking versus unit banking as a means of providing for the expansion of banking services.

The Banking Structure in Transition

Changes in the Number of Banks

During the first two decades of the 1900s the number of banks in the United States increased almost 2.5 times, from 12,427 in 1900 to 30,456 in the peak year of 1921 (see Figure 17-1). This sharp rise in banking institutions stemmed largely from the "free banking" policies of both the Comptroller of the Currency and the various state chartering authorities. Virtually every group that applied for a bank charter received one. As a result of this "overchartering," the banking industry became replete with weak institutions that could not weather the impending economic storms.

Between 1921 and 1929, there was a net reduction of 5,486 banks. Most of these had capital of $25,000 or less and were located in agricultural communities which suffered from several adverse developments during the 1920s. First, following the end of World War I, prices for farm products declined sharply, which made it difficult for many farmers to repay loans. Second, land prices fell with farm prices, causing the collateral value of many mortgages held by banks to decline below the amount of the debt they supported. Third, the migration of people toward the cities left many "country-store" banks with insufficient customers to operate profitably. Finally, the increased demand for banking services that could be provided only by large institutions led to the absorption of many banks.

The real "shake-out" in the banking industry occurred between 1930 and 1933. During this four-year period, 10,763 banks either failed or were merged with strong banks. The banking collapse during the early Depression years was the result of many factors, including (1) the Federal Reserve's failure to provide adequate liquidity for the banking system, (2) inadequate control by the banking regulatory authorities over the quality of bank credit extended, (3) a paucity of capable banking executives, and (4) too many undercapitalized banks.

To weed out weak banks and restore the public's confidence, President Roosevelt, by executive proclamation, declared a Banking Holiday on March 6, 1933, and closed all banks. Within ten days, most of the sound banks had reopened, and by June 30, 1933, there were 14, 207 banks in operation.

As shown in Figure 17-1, the number of banks has declined slowly since 1933, except for a slight increase between 1963 and 1965. During the latter period, Comptroller of the Currency James J. Saxon encouraged the chartering of new banks, both national and state, in order

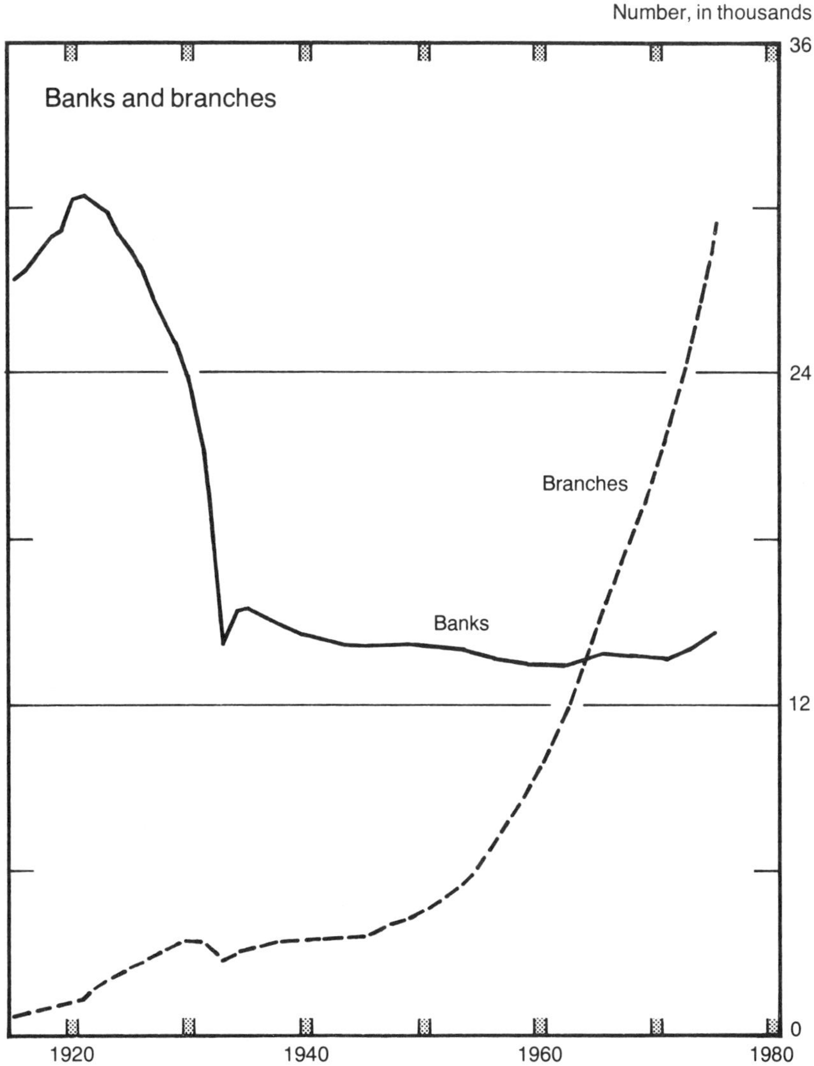

Figure 17-1 Commercial Banks and Branch Offices in the United States

Source: Board of Governors of the Federal Reserve System, *Historical Chartbook*.

to provide a stimulus to banking competition. At the close of 1976, there were 14,618 banks in operation.

Changes in the Number of Branches

A *unit bank* operates from only one location. A *branch bank* operates from two or more locations. The real impetus to branch banking in this country occurred in 1909, when California moved to permit statewide branch banking. Other states followed this precedent and relaxed their branching restrictions. The number of branches rose from less than 100 in 1910, to 150 in 1920, and 375 at the end of 1929. After the reorganization of the banking industry in 1933, the number of branches rose only slightly until the end of World War II. Between 1947 and 1976, the number of branches increased from 3,007 to 31,110. In spite of this rapid expansion in branch banking, 8,886 banks at the end of 1976 did not operate branches.

Banking Entry: The Regulatory Framework

Origin and Evaluation of the Dual Banking System

The United States is said to have a *dual banking system;* that is, there are two levels of government—national and state—that may charter commercial banks. Prior to 1863, and with the exception of the charters granted to the First and Second Banks of the United States in 1791 and 1816, only state legislatures had the right to charter banks. With the passage of the National Banking Acts of 1863 and 1864, provision was made for the granting of national bank charters through the office of the Comptroller of the Currency in the Treasury Department. Under the National Banking Acts, minimum capital and reserve requirements were established, and a number of restrictions were placed on lending activities. By specifying a set of statutory requirements for the chartering of national banks, the National Banking Acts also incorporated the principle of "free banking," which had originated in Michigan in 1837 and in New York in 1838 and which meant that theoretically any group meeting the minimum requirements could receive a bank charter. In practice, however, the Comptroller exercised much discretionary authority in his decisions to approve or deny charter applications.

The concept of a dual banking system with its separate entry routes into banking was altered considerably with the permanent provision for federal deposit insurance through the FDIC in the Banking Act of 1935. This act requires that the Comptroller of the Currency (for prospective national banks) and the Federal Reserve (for prospective state member banks) certify to the FDIC that certain criteria have been evaluated in approving the charter. In addition, the FDIC must consider these criteria before insuring the deposits of a state nonmember bank. Because of the attractiveness of federal deposit insurance, the FDIC acquired, in effect, a veto power over charters granted to state nonmember banks.[1] Thus, the federal level of government has effective control over banking entry, even though states retain the right to issue charters.

[1]Some states stipulate that deposits must be insured by the FDIC before a charter can be issued.

Although the states no longer have effective control of state bank entry standards, two important aspects of the dual banking system remain. First, because a proposed bank organizing group has the right to petition two different levels of government for a charter, there is greater likelihood that the application will be reviewed and acted upon in a fair and nondiscriminatory manner. Second, new charter applicants still retain, under the concept of a dual banking system, the right to choose the supervisory framework under which they will operate. Therefore, although banking entry is effectively under federal control, the continued states' right to charter banks provides a system of checks and balances in our bank chartering arrangements.[2]

Federal Criteria for a New Bank

The considerations that the Banking Act of 1935 required to be evaluated before a proposed bank can receive a national charter, join the Federal Reserve System, or be issued deposit insurance are as follows:

1. The financial history and condition of the bank.
2. The adequacy of its capital structure.
3. Its future earnings prospects.
4. The general character of management.
5. The convenience and needs of the community to be served by the bank.
6. Whether or not its corporate powers are consistent with the purposes of this act.

The typical first step taken by a group that wished to form a bank and satisfy these criteria is to have an economic feasibility study performed by a professor of finance or economics or by a consulting firm. A determination of feasibility involves consideration of the adequacy of existing banking and financial facilities and services in the community, whether or not the economic and financial resources of the community are growing rapidly enough to support the entry of a new bank without causing any other bank or financial institution to become unprofitable of illiquid, and whether or not the proposed directors and management have the necessary experience and financial acumen to operate the bank profitably. Besides satisfying the organizers that a need exists and that the bank can be a profitable venture, the study should aim also to convince the bank chartering agencies and the FDIC that a need exists.

[2]For a good discussion of these and other aspects of our dual banking system, see William J. Brown, *The Dual Banking System in the United States* (Washington, D.C.: The American Bankers Association, 1968).

Therefore, the study should be organized in such a way that it provides extensive information and answers to satisfy the federal criteria (and state, if applicable) and the many detailed questions in the charter application.

Following submission of the feasibility study and the application for a charter and deposit insurance (if the bank is to be a state nonmember insured bank), the appropriate regulatory authorities then conduct an intensive survey to determine if the proposed bank meets the criteria. The survey team talks with bankers and citizens in the community and makes an extensive background investigation of the financial affairs and business dealings of the proposed directors and management. In effect, the survey team subjects the proposed bank and its organizers to a "worthiness" test that attempts to ensure that the public interest will be served if the bank is allowed to open.[3]

Rationale for the Regulation of Banking Entry

Entry into the banking industry is regulated primarily because of the strategic place that banks occupy in our economic and financial system. As we noted in Chapter 1, banks hold deposits and provide the nation with an efficient payments transfer mechanism. When a bank fails, its depositors usually are denied use of their funds temporarily, and some account holders eventually may even lose a portion of their uninsured deposits. Moreover, the general public's confidence in the banking system is shaken in various degrees by bank failures, which always seem to be well publicized.

The banking regulatory authorities probably could reduce the failure rate of existing banks, which, in recent years, has been less than ten banks a year, by declaring a moratorium on bank charters. This approach, however, would deny the public the benefits that accrue from the periodic entry into the market of another competitor. A new bank causes every other bank to reevaluate both the quality and the quantity of its services. Each bank is an alternative source of credit, and this is important, especially for small businesses. Usually, a new bank also offers some services or conveniences that are not otherwise being provided. In general, a newcomer increases the "vigor of competition."

The bulk of the initial deposits and capital for a new bank usually will come from the established banks and other financial institutions in the community. The task of the banking regulatory authorities is to weigh the positive benefits of the new bank against the possibility that

[3]For a discussion of public control over banking entry, see David C. Motter, "Bank Formation and the Public Interest"; Sam Peltzman, "Bank Entry Regulation: Its Impact and Purpose"; and Donald Jacobs, "The Framework of Commercial Bank Regulation: An Appraisal," in The Administrator of National Banks, *Studies in Banking Competition and the Bank Structure* (Washington, D.C.: 1966), pp. 233–299, 337–351.

existing banks and financial institutions will be placed in jeopardy. This is why it is very important to estimate carefully the future growth in financial resources in the community where the new bank is to locate. The economy and deposits in the community should be growing fast enough to permit the new bank to enter without causing any other bank of financial institution to become unprofitable or illiquid.

Branch Banking: The Regulatory Framework

Federal Regulation

The present federal regulatory framework for branch banking is contained in the Banking Act of 1933 and its subsequent amendments. The major provisions of this act are discussed below.

First, a state's branching limitations on its own state banks apply to national banks located within its boundaries. In other words, a national bank may only branch within a state to the extent that the banks are permitted, and no state permits its banks to branch across state lines. For example, in Texas a national bank may not establish branches because state banks are not allowed to do so, but a national bank in California may establish branches in any part of that state.

Second, regardless of state law, permission to branch must be received by national banks from the Comptroller of the Currency, by state member banks from the Federal Reserve Board of Governors, and by state nonmember insured banks from the FDIC. Other than the relevant state limitations and certain minimum capital requirements mentioned below, there are no specific criteria imposed by law on the Comptroller in considering a proposed national bank branch. In contrast, the Board of Governors and the FDIC must take into account the same factors as those required for deposit insurance certification.

Third, for out-of-town branches, national banks must have minimum aggregate capital equal to (1) that required to establish an equal number of separate national banks or (2) that required by state law to establish state bank branches, whichever is greater. No additional capital is required to establish in-town branches, if they are permitted.

Fourth, national and state member banks may establish seasonal agencies in resort areas for the receipt and payment of deposits without an additional capital requirement, but only if the area is without banking facilities, if at least countywide branching is permitted, and if the area is within the head-office county of the national bank concerned.

State Regulation

Most states place restrictions on branch banking. As shown in Table 17-1, only twenty-one states and the District of Columbia permit statewide

Table 17-1
Summary of State Branch Banking Statutes

Statewide Branch Banking	Limited Branch Banking	Unit Banking
Alaska	Alabama	Colorado
Arizona	Arkansas	Illinois
California	Florida	Kansas
Connecticut	Georgia	Minnesota
Delaware	Indiana	Missouri
District of Columbia	Iowa	Montana
Hawaii	Kentucky	Nebraska
Idaho	Louisiana	North Dakota
Maine	Massachusetts	Oklahoma
Maryland	Michigan	Texas
Nevada	Mississippi	West Virginia
New Jersey	New Hampshire	Wyoming
New York	New Mexico	
North Carolina	Ohio	
Oregon	Pennsylvania	
Rhode Island	Tennessee	
South Carolina	Wisconsin	
South Dakota		
Utah		
Vermont		
Virginia		
Washington		

Source: Adapted from compilations of the Board of Governors of the Federal Reserve System.

branching; seventeen states have limited branch banking; and twelve states prohibit branching.

Branch Banking versus Unit Banking

Since the time when state bankers objected to the location of branches of the First Bank of the United States in the communities, the relative merits of branch banking have been the subject of considerable debate. In most of the states in which branching is limited or prohibited, the question of whether or not to liberalize branching laws is a subject of an annual debate in the state legislature. During recent years, a number of studies of the relationship between the banking structure and banking performance have provided important new findings on some of the key issues in the branching versus unit banking debate.[4] The purpose of

[4]An excellent summary of many of these studies is contained in Jack M. Guttentag and Edward S. Herman, "Banking Structure and Performance," New York University Graduate School of Business Administration, *The Bulletin*, 41–43 (February 1967).

this section is to consider some of these issues and the results of recent research on the branch banking controversy.

Competition

One of the important questions has been the impact of branching on banking competition. Competition, in this sense, refers to how banks react to the price and nonprice moves of their rivals. Generally, banks attempt to avoid price competition. They prefer, instead, to engage in nonprice competitive activities that attempt to gain customers with elaborate advertising campaigns, catchy slogans, pretty tellers, friendly service, and similar endeavors. However, nonprice competition in banking is costly, and it involves a waste of resources if it does not result in a wider range of services or more efficient operations. The authors of the study just noted found "some limited and inconclusive evidence that nonprice competition is more intense under branch than under unit banking.[5]

Banks do tend to engage in price competition with nonbank intermediaries. Since 1966 banks have reacted quickly, within the limits permitted by Regulation Q, to interest-rate increases on savings deposits in those areas in which savings and loan associations are important competitors. Moreover, most banks respond to rate changes on consumer credit by the large finance companies and credit unions. There is probably no significant difference between branch banking and unit banking structures as to the speed and intensity of the reaction to price changes on those services offered by nonbank intermediaries that are sufficiently close substitutes for those provided by banks.

The Price of Banking Services

It is virtually impossible to generalize about whether branch banking leads to higher or lower prices for banking services. There is some evidence that branching into nonmetropolitan areas may place some downward pressure on rates for small business loans and mortgage loans. On the other hand, rates on savings deposits and service charges tend to rise in a nonmetropolitan area following the entrance of another bank via merger.[6]

Operational Efficiency

One of the key issues in the debate is whether branch banks are more efficient to operate than unit banks. Proponents of branch banking

[5]*Ibid.*, p. 17.

[6]*Ibid.*, pp. 21–22. As an illustration of why it is difficult to generalize on this topic, service charges have tended to fall in small South Carolina communities whenever a large branch bank entered either through merger or on a *de novo* basis.

frequently argue that branching enables banks to grow larger and to achieve economies of scale, that is, reductions in long-run average costs. There are two possible sources of these economies. First, banks should benefit greatly from labor specialization. Because banks provide such a wide range of services and employ so many highly skilled personnel to provide these services, operations must reach a comparatively large size before maximum proficiency is attained. Second, economies tend to accrue as banks achieve greater diversification in their loan portfolio, which, in turn, should lead to fewer defaults.[7]

There is some evidence that there are economies of scale in banking.[8] These cost savings appear to be greatest for banks up to $10 million level and then taper off in the intermediate range ($10–200 million). Not much is known about economies of scale for banks larger than this.

On the other hand, it has been found that branch banks tend to have higher costs than unit banks in the same size category.[9] The conclusion is that "economies of scale in banking do exist, but they are relatively small and are actually less important than the diseconomies of branch structure."[10] However, branch systems in given size classes should be expected to have higher expense ratios because branch offices provide additional convenience, which tends to inflate costs.[11] On the basis of the studies cited in this section, it cannot be stated conclusively that branch banking promotes operational efficiency.

Allocational Efficiency

Another issue in the branch banking debate relates to allocational efficiency, that is, the extent to which loanable funds are made available to the highest and best use in the economy. Branch banks, through their offices, have a ready mechanism for the transfer of loanable funds to the most creditworthy borrowers within the bank's market area. Some branches in slow-growth areas might be principally receivers of deposits and have a loans-to-deposits ratio of 20 percent; branches in areas with a great demand for loans might have a loans-to-deposits ratio of 150 percent or more and hence primarily be users of funds. Branch banking systems tend to have a higher loans-to-assets ratio than unit banks, which would indicate that branch banks may have an edge over unit banks in promoting allocational efficiency. There seems to be no support for the criticism that is sometimes made that branch banks

[7]Lyle E. Gramley, *A Study of Scale Economies in Banking* (Kansas City, Mo.: Federal Reserve Bank of Kansas City, 1962), pp. 4–5.

[8]Guttentag and Herman, chap. 5.

[9]Paul M. Horvitz, "Economies of Scale in Banking," in The Commission on Money and Credit, *Private Financial Institutions* (Englewood Cliffs, N.J.: Prentice-Hall, 1963), pp. 28–33.

[10]*Ibid.*, p. 52.

[11]Guttentag and Herman, p. 25.

tend to lend a disproportionate amount of funds through their head-office city branches to the detriment of borrowers served by branches elsewhere in the system. Loans-to-deposits ratios at branches in these outlying areas frequently exceed those at branches in the head-office city.[12]

Another question under the heading of allocational efficiency is whether branch banks or unit banks provide a larger number of office facilities in their respective areas served. One study found that metropolitan areas with branch banking had considerably more offices than did areas with unit banking.[13]

Finally, with respect to the range of auxiliary services, such as trust services, payroll accounting, and foreign exchange, it was found that large banks, which usually are branch banks, tend to offer a wider range of services than do smaller banks.[14]

Other Issues

Several other issues in the branch banking debate deserve consideration. First, sometimes it is charged that branch banking personnel are more impersonal than unit banking employees. There is evidence that this may be true because frequently branch offices serve as training facilities for new employees who do not remain at an office long enough to establish a continuing relationship with customers. On the other hand, many branch banks make a great effort to staff their various offices with employees and officers recruited from the local area to be served who are familiar with the people and the economy of that community.

Another criticism frequently made of branch banks is that branch loan officers are so restricted by managerial rules and limitations that they can make only small loans and are not in a position to assist and advise large borrowers effectively. Again, there is an element of truth in this assertion because branch systems do tend to place low lending limits on branch officers, and large loan requests must be referred to senior management at the head office for approval. Delays at branches in approving loan requests may be one of the disadvantages of branch operations, but submission of the larger loan requests to a group of officers who may not know the borrowers personally would tend to benefit both the borrower and the bank, if loans of doubtful quality are weeded out by the application of uniform credit standards. Thus a more objective appraisal of loan requests may be one of the virtues of branch banking.

[12] *Ibid.*, pp. 26–27.
[13] *Ibid.*, p. 28.
[14] *Ibid.*, p. 29.

Finally, proponents of branch banking sometimes claim that branch banks are safer than unit banks. They point out that most of the bank failures in recent years have been unit banks. This is true, but it should be remembered that almost all banks have federal deposit insurance, and actual deposit losses have been insignificant in recent years.

Conclusions

It should be evident that there are advantages to both branch and unit banking. Branch banking tends to lead to a greater concentration of banking resources at the state level, but there is a need also for large banks that can meet the financial demands of large firms. On the other hand, there are vast numbers of individuals and small businesses that prefer to do business with small unit banks, and they should not be denied this privilege. Thus, to assure that there will be a viable banking structure that meets the financial needs of all segments of the economy, the banking regulatory authorities should strive to ensure that the benefits of both large and small banks are available to the public.

Suggestions for Additional Reading

The Administrator of National Banks. *Studies in Banking Competition and the Banking Structure*. Washington, D.C.: Office of the Comptroller of the Currency, 1966, parts 2, 3.

Baker, Donald I. "Competition's Role in the Regulation of Banking." *The Bankers Magazine* (Summer 1971), pp. 75–82.

Brown, William J. *The Dual Banking System in the United States*. Washington, D.C.: The American Bankers Assoication, 1968.

Fischer, Gerald C. *American Banking Structure*. New York: Columbia University Press, 1968, chaps. 2, 5.

Gilbert, R. Alton. "Bank Failures and Public Policy." Federal Reserve Board of St. Louis, *Review* (November 1975), pp. 7–15.

Golbar, Alfred J. "Site Location Analysis for Branch Banking." *The Bankers Magazine* (Winter 1972), pp. 67–70.

Golembe, Carter H., and Hengren, Raymond E. *Federal Regulation of Banking*. Washington, D.C.: American Institute of Banking, American Bankers Association, 1975.

Gup, Benton E. "The Big Debate: Branch Versus Unit Banking." *The Bankers Magazine* (Autumn 1972), pp. 89–93.

Irons, Edward D. *Organizing A New Community Bank*. Studies in Banking and Finance No. 6. Austin, Tex.: University of Texas, Bureau of Business Research, 1965.

Marshall, Robert H. "Competition in Banking." *The Bankers Magazine* (Winter 1973), pp. 81–86.

Mote, Larry R. "The Perennial Issue: Branch Banking." Federal Reserve Bank of Chicago, *Business Conditions* (February 1974), pp. 3–23.

Robertson, Ross M. *The Comptroller and Bank Supervision: A Historical Appraisal.* Washington, D.C.: Office of the Comptroller of the Currency, 1968.

Spofford, Gavin. *Guideposts for Banking Expansion.* New Brunswick, N.J.: Rutgers University Press, 1961.

CHAPTER

18

Bank Mergers

Although the branch banking issue has stirred considerable debate for many years, the most important controversy in the banking industry recently has concerned the regulation of bank mergers.[1] Congress established a framework for such regulation in the Bank Merger Act of 1960, but subsequent application of Sec. 7 of the Clayton Act and Sec. 1 of the Sherman Act to banking by the Supreme Court in 1963 and 1964, respectively, made it necessary for Congress to pass another Bank Merger Act in 1966. Since that time, several Supreme Court and lower court decisions have yielded numerous interpretations and points of law with respect to the regulation of these mergers.

[1]A *merger* occurs when one bank absorbs another bank and operates it under its own charter. A *consolidation* occurs when a newly chartered bank absorbs two or more existing banks and operates them under its own charter. In this discussion, the term "merger" includes mergers and consolidations.

As we shall see, there are many reasons why banks merge. In spite of the stated circumstances, however, the principal motive behind most mergers is to enhance stockholder wealth in both the acquiring and the acquired bank. But what may benefit the acquiring bank may not be good for society, if the merger eliminates an effective present or potential competitor. This concern for maintaining banking competition and an adequate number of alternative sources of banking services is what prompted Congress and the courts to place more stringent requirements on bank mergers.

In this chapter we shall (1) discuss the bank merger movement, (2) note some of the results of recent research on the impact of mergers on competition in the various banking markets, and (3) examine the background and present status of federal regulation of bank mergers.

The Bank Merger Movement

Number of Banks and Resources Involved

The propensity for banks to merge is not a new phenomenon in American banking. Bank mergers totaled 4,732 between 1921 and 1930, 2,618 between 1931 and 1940, and 814 between 1941 and 1950.[2] Between 1950 and 1975, 3,641 banks with resources of $86.9 billion were absorbed by other banking institutions (see Table 18-1).

The wave of mergers during the 1920s and 1930s served to strengthen the banking system because most of the absorbed banks were extremely small and weak. Many of these banks were near failure, and merger provided a graceful exit. Following World War II, the number of mergers did not approach these earlier levels until the mid-1950s. Although the great majority of the banks absorbed during this postwar period were small, most of the merged institutions were not weak or in danger of closing, as during the 1920s and 1930s, but were going concerns capable of operating indefinitely. It was this loss of independent banking entities that caused Congress, in 1955, to begin an investigation of the merger movement with the aim of preventing excessive concentration of banking resources.

Reasons for Bank Mergers

Essentially, banks merge because the management and stockholders of the combining institutions believe that the transaction will enhance their long-run financial positions. Some mergers, however, are encouraged by the regulatory authorities when one of the banks is in danger of failing or has a management succession problem that cannot

[2]House Committee on Banking and Currency, *Hearings on Conflict of Federal and State Banking Laws* (Washington, D.C.: U.S. Government Printing Office, 1963), p. 435.

Table 18-1
Mergers of Commercial Banks, 1950–1975
(resources in millions of dollars)

	Banks Absorbed	
Year	Number	Resources
1950	91	1,129
1951	84	1,778
1952	99	820
1953	115	1,200
1954	216	4,064
1955	225	9,615
1956	186	2,964
1957	165	2,303
1958	151	2,559
1959	171	3,688
1960	136	2,795
1961	133	5,995
1962	193	2,207
1963	151	3,519
1964	139	2,238
1965	167	2,096
1966	136	1,640
1967	122	2,889
1968	130	2,185
1969	155	3,986
1970	154	5,130
1971	118	4,262
1972	112	3,043
1973	101	3,251
1974	124	6,532
1975	67	4,974
	3,641	86,862

Source: House Committee on Banking and Currency, *Hearings Before Subcommittee No. 2 on Regulation of Bank Mergers* (Washington, D.C.: U.S. Government Printing Office, 1960), p. 19; and *Annual Reports* of the Comptroller of the Currency and the Federal Deposit Insurance Corporation.

be resolved in any other way. It is important to note at this point that, presently, the banking regulatory authorities and the courts do not approve mergers based on the benefits to be derived by the banks, but on the basis of a comparison of the effect of the transaction on meeting the convenience and needs of the community with any anticompetitive effects that the merger might produce. Some of the basic motives behind bank mergers are discussed below.

Additional Funds. A fundamental reason for bank mergers is that the acquiring bank desires to gain additional funds. Quite often the acquired bank, for one reason or another, has an excessive liquidity position, a low loans-to-deposits ratio, and a relatively large portfolio of Treasury, agency, and municipal securities. The acquiring bank usually can convert a portion of the funds invested in securities into more portfolio loans.

Capital and Lending Limits. Closely related to the first motive is the desire to expand capital and lending limits. The acquiring bank usually issues common, but sometimes preferred, stock in exchange for the stock of the acquired bank. After the exchange, the acquiring bank would receive all the capital in the acquired bank. As a result, the former's lending limit to an individual borrower would be increased since the limit is a function of bank capital.

Population Shifts. One aim behind many mergers is to compensate for shifts in population to the suburbs and, in some states, from rural to urban areas. In order to retain customers involved in these population movements and to gain new ones, many banks in the declining areas have merged with banks in the expanding areas.

Economies of Scale. A basic principle of economics is that as a firm expands in size, average costs decline. Banks can expand, expecting to achieve economies through internal growth or through external growth (mergers). As a bank increases in size, it should benefit from specialization in such functions as loans, investments, trust, purchasing, personnel, and credit analysis. However, as we saw in Chapter 17, empirical evidence of economies of scale in banking is scattered and inconclusive.

Diversification. Mergers also provide opportunities for banks to obtain diversification in their loan portfolios. By acquiring banks in other communities, not dependent on the same sources on income, a bank is able to hedge against possible loan losses originating from a local economic decline. Moreover, the easiest eay to enter the trust business is to acquire a bank with an established trust department.

Failing or Floundering Banks. Sometimes management ineptness, a crop failure, a natural disaster, or the closing of an important local industry will place a bank in jeopardy. The bank may be in danger of failing because of insufficient liquidity or the prospect of excessive loan losses. In such cases the regulatory authorities encourage merger with another bank. This ensures that banking services will not be interrupted for the customers involved.

Management Succession Problems. It is surprising how many small banks have not provided for the succession of management. In many cases, the top two or three men in a small bank are about the same age, and they all will retire within a few years of each other. Often, in such situations, younger managers have not been brought into the bank with the idea of some day taking over the senior management positions. Small banks are unattractive sometimes to alert young officers because the opportunity for advancement is contingent upon the death or retirement of senior management. Sometimes a merger provides a convenient way for the management team to retire and for the community involved to continue to receive banking services.

Inducements to Management and Shareholders. Merger is usually a very attractive proposition for most acquired banks. Senior management, who typically own a significant percentage of the outstanding shares, often are offered positions with the resulting bank at salaries and benefits exceeding those they are currently receiving.[3] Shareholders are induced to approve the merger with offers to exchange shares in the acquired bank for shares in the resulting bank at a substantial premium above present market values. Often the shares of the resulting bank are more marketable and command a higher price multiple than those of the acquired bank.

Defensive Expansion. A number of mergers have been motivated by the acquiring bank's efforts to keep up with a major competitor in size and earnings growth. It is questionable whether the public benefits when several large banks in a state are permitted to eliminate a large number of small banks just to retain their relative market position.

Possible Social Benefits from Mergers

Most of the benefits from bank mergers cited above accrue to the banks involved and not necessarily to the communities affected. However, there are several possible social benefits from bank mergers. First, the public benefits if it is spared the disruptive effects from a bank failure or the inefficiency of a floundering bank. Second, if a management succession problem could result in the loss of banking services to a community, then, obviously, the public stands to benefit from a merger. Third, mergers frequently result in an expansion in the range and quality of banking services in a community. For example, many small banks are not large enough to offer trust services, investment advisory services, and mortgage loans on a profitable basis. There is good

[3]Sometimes senior management at the acquired banks are assigned duties so undemanding that they are free to spend their afternoons as they wish.

chance that a large bank could offer these and other services at the newly acquired bank with little or no expansion in staff or costs. Fourth, it is sometimes argued that mergers are needed to build bigger banks to provide larger lines of credit. A few big banks are needed in our banking system to meet the credit needs of large businesses, and mergers have helped many of our banking giants to attain their present size. However, capital is free to flow across state lines even though banks are not permitted to branch across state lines. Small banks very readily can get their correspondent banks to participate with them in loans to meet credit demands that are beyond their lending limits. There is a point when the benefits from permitting large banks to become bigger may not outweigh the loss of a small, but independent, source of bank credit.

Concentration and Competition in Banking

The Impact of Concentration on Competition

Clearly, there are strong motives for banks to merge. Mergers between banks in the same market tend to increase the concentration of banking resources, that is, the degree to which bank assets or deposits are controlled by the largest bank or banks in the relevant market area. Concentration usually is measured by the *concentration ratio,* which is the percentage of assets or deposits held by the largest, the three largest, or the five largest banks in an area. Generally the higher the degree of concentration, the less vigorous will be the competition. In the Philadelphia Case, to be discussed further below, the Supreme Court held that

> . . . we think that a merger which produces a firm controlling an undue percentage share of the relevant market, and results in a significant increase in the concentration of firms in that market, is so inherently likely to lessen competition substantially that it must be enjoined in the absence of evidence clearly showing that the merger is not likely to have such anticompetitive effects.[4]

The Supreme Court's analysis is based on several basic tenets of economic theory. Economists state that *perfect competition* exists in a market when four criteria are met: (1) there are many independent buyers and sellers, none of whom are large enough to influence the price of the product or service, (2) there is freedom of entry and exit

[4] 374 U.S. 321 (1963), p. 363.

from the industry, (3) there is reasonably perfect knowledge of market conditions, and (4) the product or service sold is homogeneous. Under conditions of perfect competition, the public obtains the maximum output of the good or service at the lowest possible price, and optimum allocation of resources is obtained. Only the "efficient" firms are allowed to remain in the industry. "Inefficient" firms are driven from the market by the forces of competition because they cannot raise their prices high enough to cover their costs.

Under conditions of "imperfect competition," (1) there are only a few sellers, some of whom may be large enough to influence the price of the product or service; (2) there is only limited entry into the industry; (3) buyers and sellers do not have perfect knowledge of market conditions; and (4) the product or service sold by each firm is heterogeneous, that is, it is differentiated by form, manner of presentation, location, or in other ways. In imperfectly competitive markets, there is a suboptimum level of output, prices tend to be higher, and some resources may not be in their highest and best uses. In other words, "fewness," that is, the absence of some competitive pressure from potential entrants into the industry, and some degree of attachment between sellers and buyers because of differentiated products, tend to yield less than optimum results for the public in terms of output, price, and resource allocation. It follows that if a merger of two banks results in an undue amount of concentration of assets held by one bank, or significantly raises the market share held by the top two or three banks, then competition will tend to be lessened to the detriment of the public interest. However, it should be recognized that competition in some banking markets might be enhanced by greater concentration of banking resources.

Concentration in Banking

The bank merger movement takes on added economic significance when it is realized that most banking markets already are highly concentrated. As shown in Table 18-2, the percentage of deposits held by the top three banks in selected standard metropolitan statistical areas (SMSAs) listed range from 30.9 to 86.6 percent. It is interesting to note that the concentration ratio appears to be related to the state branching laws. Cities in states with state-wide or limited-area branching tend to have higher concentration ratios. Mergers in these areas involving the larger banks would tend to increase concentration and perhaps reduce competition.

A large percentage of the bank mergers do not have significant anti-competitive effects. Many mergers involve a large bank's taking over a small bank in a market area where the acquiring bank is not presently located, or two smaller banks' combining in an area dominated by larger banks.

Table 18-2
Percentage of Total Deposits Held by the Largest Bank, Largest Three Banks, and Largest Five Banks, Selected Standard Metropolitan Statistical Areas, June 30, 1976

SMSAs	Number of Banks	Total Deposits (millions of dollars)	Percentage Held: Largest Bank	Largest Three Banks	Largest Five Banks
In states with state-wide branching prevalent					
Baltimore	38	4,672	29.3	64.9	83.8
Los Angeles–Long Beach	79	27,500	31.1	65.5	79.8
New York	137	112,329	16.4	45.6	64.2
Phoenix	12	3,974	42.7	86.6	95.8
San Francisco–Oakland	46	25,632	43.9	80.1	86.0
In states with limited-area branching prevalent					
Atlanta	78	5,810	21.4	55.5	70.1
Detroit	77	16,984	29.2	58.8	69.1
Indianapolis	41	4,536	29.4	74.2	78.3
Milwaukee	92	5,359	28.0	47.1	55.4
Pittsburgh	41	9,806	46.1	80.6	90.0
In states with unit banking prevalent					
Chicago	409	45,234	20.2	45.7	52.9
Dallas–Fort Worth	215	12,388	17.2	42.3	53.9
Denver	136	4,873	16.5	40.0	53.1
Minneapolis–St. Paul	183	7,425	15.5	43.0	48.2
St. Louis	188	8,722	13.9	30.9	35.4

Source: FDIC, *Summary of Accounts and Deposits in All Commercial Banks* (June 30, 1976).

Federal Regulation of Bank Mergers

Background

Prior to the passage of the Bank Merger Act of 1960, the banking regulatory agencies had little power to disapprove bank mergers. Under the National Banking Act, the Comptroller was required to approve mergers in which the surviving bank was a national bank, but he had no specific authority to disapprove mergers that would lessen competition or promote monopoly. In addition, the FDIC Act required approval of certain mergers by the FDIC, the Comptroller, or the Federal Reserve

Board, as the case might be, but only if the capital and surplus of the surviving institution was less than that of the separate institutions prior to merger. Also, the FDIC was required to approve mergers between insured and uninsured banks. The Federal Reserve Board had authority under Sec. 7 of the Clayton Act to forbid mergers through stock acquisition "where in any line of commerce in any section of the country, the effect of such acquisition may be substantially to lessen competition, or to tend to create a monopoly." However, most bank mergers are accomplished through asset acquisition, that is, through the purchase of net assets and the assumption of liabilities of the absorbed bank. The Celler–Kefauver Act of 1950 closed the asset acquisition loophole but only for corporations subject to the jurisdiction of the Federal Trade Commission (FTC). Banks, of course, are excluded from FTC jurisdiction. For these reasons, banking regulatory authorities lacked the power to prevent mergers that might be detrimental to competition and to the public interest.

The Bank Merger Act of 1960

Beginning in 1955, bills were introduced in both houses of Congress to create a framework for the regulation of bank mergers that had anticompetitive effects. Finally, after numerous failures to get both Senate and House approval, a similar bill (S. 1062) passed the Senate in late 1959 and the House in the spring of 1960 and was signed into law on May 13, 1960, by President Eisenhower as the Bank Merger Act of 1960. The principal provisions of this act, which was an amendment to the FDIC Act, were as follows:

1. Responsibility for approval of bank merger applications depended upon the classification of the resulting bank. The Comptroller of the Currency had jurisdiction if the surviving bank was a national bank; the Federal Reserve Board, for a state member bank; and FDIC, for an insured nonmember bank.
2. In passing upon a merger application, the cognizant authority had to consider the following factors:
   (a) Financial history and condition of the banks involved.
   (b) Adequacy of the resulting bank's capital structure.
   (c) Future earnings prospects of the resulting bank.
   (d) General character of the resulting bank's management.
   (e) Convenience and needs of the community to be served.
   (f) Assurance that the resulting bank's corporate powers are consistent with the Bank Merger Act.
   (g) Evaluation of the probable effects of the merger on competition.
3. Moreover, in considering a merger application, the cognizant regulatory authority had to request an opinion on the probable effects of the merger on competition from the other two regulatory authorities and the Attorney General.

Passage of the Bank Merger Act did little to slow down the number of mergers. Between May 15, 1960, and May 12, 1965, the ratio of approvals to denials by the various regulatory authorities was as follows: Federal Reserve Board, 142/17; Comptroller, 450/12; and the FDIC, 173/2. Under his newly created authority to report on the competitive factor in bank mergers, the Attorney General, between May 13, 1960, and June 30, 1965, reported "adverse competitive effects" on 527 merger applications and "no adverse competitive effects" on 327 applications.

The Philadelphia Case

The Attorney General did not wait long to test in the courts the regulatory framework provided by the Bank Merger Act. On February 25, 1961, he moved to enjoin a proposed consolidation between The Philadelphia National Bank and Girard Trust Corn Exchange Bank, the second and third largest of forty-two commercial banks in the metropolitan area of Philadelphia and its three contiguous counties. The complaint charged violation of Sec. 1 of the Sherman Act and Sec. 7 of the Clayton Act, as amended in 1950 by the Celler–Kefauver Act. The pertinent part of these acts are as follows:

> Sec. 1. Every contract, combination in the form of trust or otherwise, or conspiracy, in restraint of trade or commerce among the several States, or with foreign nations, is hereby declared to be illegal. . . .
>
> Sec. 7. No corporation engaged in commerce shall acquire, directly or indirectly, the whole or any part of the stock or other share capital and no corporation shall acquire the whole or any part of the assets of another corporation engaged also in commerce, where in any line of commerce in any section of the country, the effect of such acquisition may be substantially to lessen competition, or to tend to create a monopoly.

The resulting bank would have been the largest in the four-county area, with approximately 36 percent of the area banks' assets, 36 percent of their deposits, and 34 percent of their net loans. After the merger, the resulting bank and the second largest bank would have had 58 percent of the deposits in the area; the four largest banks would have had 77 percent of the deposits.

On February 24, 1961, the Comptroller approved the consolidation even though the other two banking agencies and the Attorney General advised that the proposed merger would have substantial anticompetitive effects in the Philadelphia metropolitan area. In explaining his decision, the Comptroller stated with respect to the competitive factor that "since there will remain an adequate number of alternative sources of banking service in Philadelphia, and in view of the beneficial effects of this consolidation upon international and national competition it was concluded that the overall effect upon competition would not be unfavorable." In addition, the consolidated bank "would be far better able to serve the convenience and needs of this community by being of material assistance to its city and state in their efforts to attract new industry and to retain existing industry." On the day after the approval, the Attorney General took action to prevent the merger.

The merger was upheld in U.S. District Court. In his opinion Judge Clary stated that the merger did not violate either Sec. 7 of the Clayton Act or Sec. 1 of the Sherman Act and that it would benefit the Philadelphia metropolitan area economically. The Attorney General appealed this decision to the U.S. Supreme Court. On June 17, 1963, the high court ruled that the proposed consolidation would violate Sec. 7 of the Clayton Act, and therefore, that it must be enjoined.

The principal findings in the landmark *Philadelphia Case* are as follows:

1. That Sec. 7 of the Clayton Act applied to banking.
2. That the cluster of products and services offered by "banks make commercial banking a unique line of commerce." The court rejected the idea that the products and services offered by nonbank financial intermediaries are sufficiently close substitutes for those provided by banks.
3. That the "section of the country" which is relevant was the four-county Philadelphia area. The court rejected the bank's contention that the entire northeastern United States was the relevant market.

The Philadelphia decision came as a shock to most bankers. As a result, many potential bank merger partners abandoned their plans in view of the contingency that the Attorney General would challenge other mergers and hence involve the banks in costly and protracted court battles.

The Lexington Case

The banking industry did not have long to wait for its next surprise in the merger field. On April 6, 1964, the Supreme Court ruled that a proposed merger between First National Bank and Trust Co. and Security Trust Co. of Lexington, Kentucky, consituted a violation of Sec. 1 of the Sherman Act.

First National, with 40.06 percent of the deposits, and Security Trust, with 11.88 percent of the deposits, were the largest and fourth largest banks, respectively, of the six banks in Fayette County. The resulting bank would have been more than three times larger than the second largest bank in the county. Prior to the merger, both banks were close competitors for trust business. Security Trust had 50.55 percent and First National had 44.27 percent of the trust assets in the county. The resulting bank would have controlled 94.82 percent of all trust assets in the county.

The Comptroller approved the merger on February 27, 1961, in spite of reports from the other two banking agencies that the proposed consolidation would adversely affect competition in the county. The merger was effected on March 1, and the Attorney General filed a suit on the same day which alleged it to be in violation of Secs. 1 and 2 of the Sherman Act.[5]

The merger was upheld in District Court, and the Attorney General appealed to the Supreme Court. The high court made the following determinations:

1. That "the elimination of significant competition between the parties to the consolidation, which were major competitive factors in the relevant market, of itself constitutes an unreasonable restraint of trade in violation of Sec. 1 of the [Sherman] Act."
2. That "commercial banking is one relevant product market to judge the effect of the consolidation on competition."
3. That "the consolidation should be judged by its effect on competition in Fayette County, the geographical market."
4. That "the new bank controls over half of the relevant market and by its disparity of size, as attested by three of the four remaining banks, will seriously affect the long-range ability to compete despite the absence of any 'predatory' purpose."

The application of both antitrust laws to banking as a result of the *Philadelphia* and *Lexington* decisions led to great confusion and uncertainty in the industry. Approval of a merger by the regulatory authorities was no assurance that the merger would go through. There was also the status of the Bank Merger Act of 1960 and the relative importance of the so-called "banking" and "convenience and needs" considerations. Congress once again tackled the complex problem of bank merger regulation.

The Bank Merger Act of 1966

After lengthy hearings and debates, Congress passed the Bank Merger Act of 1966. Essentially, this act was a combination of the 1960 merger act and the antitrust law. This new act went a long way toward

[5]Section 2 of the Sherman Act states that "Every person who shall monopolize, or attempt to monopolize, or combine or conspire with any other person or persons, to monopolize any part of the trade or commerce among the several States, or with foreign nations, shall be deemed guilty of a misdemeanor. . . ."

eliminating some of the uncertainty and confusion by requiring each of the banking regulatory authorities, the Attorney General, and the courts to consider the same factors when evaluating a proposed bank merger. Other pertinent provisions of the new act were as follows:

1. The responsible agency shall not approve
   (A) any proposed merger which would result in a monopoly, or which would be in furtherance of any combination or conspiracy to monopolize the business of banking in any part of the United States, or
   (B) any other proposed merger transaction whose effect in any section of the country may be substantially to lessen competition, or tend to create a monopoly, or which in any other manner would be in restraint of trade, *unless it finds that the anticompetitive effects of the proposed transaction are clearly outweighed in the public interest by the probable effect of the transaction in meeting the convenience and needs of the community to be served. (Italics added.)*

   In every case, the responsible agency shall take into consideration the financial and managerial resources of the existing and proposed institutions and the convenience and needs of the community to be served.
2. Ordinarily, a merger cannot be consummated until 30 days after approval. If a failure is imminent, the merger can take place immediately, or after 5 days if some other emergency exists.
3. The Attorney General has 30 days after approval within which to initiate litigation against the proposed merger. After this period has expired, the merger may not be challenged for any violation of antitrust law, with the exception of Sec. 2 of the Sherman Act.

Sections (A) and (B) contain identical or nearly identical standards of illegality as specified in Sec. 1 and 2 of the Sherman Act and Sec. 7 of the Clayton Act. It seems clear that Congress intended the new merger act to have the same standards as the antitrust laws.

Recent Supreme Court Decisions

In its first decision under the new bank merger act, *U.S.* v. *First City National Bank of Houston,* the Supreme Court in 1967 made several important determinations. First, in spite of the new merger act, suits may still be brought under the antitrust statutes. Second, the "convenience and needs" argument provides a public interest defense, but the burden of proof is on the merger's defenders. Third, the Comptroller's determination carries no presumptive weight: the courts, and not the banking regulatory authorities, have primary jurisdiction over bank merger litigation.

In *U.S.* v. *Third National Bank in Nashville* in 1968, the Supreme Court reaffirmed its earlier decisions under the Bank Merger Act of 1966. It held that the merger defenders must not only show that the merger will provide such benefits as greater lending limits, better management, and better banking services, but they also must establish clearly how the community will benefit from these changes. Second, the high court ruled that the defendants must show that the merger is "essential" to secure these net gains in the public interest. In other words, they must establish that no course of action, short of merger, could bring these benefits to the community.[6]

In *U.S. v. Crocker-Anglo National Bank*, in a district court decision that was not appealed by the Attorney General, Judge Zirpoli commented on five categories of benefits that would be realized under the "convenience and needs" heading: (1) the resulting bank would be another statewide banking system, thus offering more competition for the Bank of America; (2) the larger bank would take on riskier loans; (3) another underwriter would be provided for municipals; (4) another bank would be available to handle foreign trade transactions; and (5) the statewide flow of funds would be facilitated. The Crocker case affirms that a merger may be saved with a strong showing under the convenience and needs defense.

Conclusion

The Bank Merger Act of 1966 and the recent court decisions have provided the regulatory agencies, the Attorney General, and the courts with what appears to be a reasonable framework for the regulation of mergers. It is clear that the standards of competition under the new merger act and antitrust laws are the same. However, the door is left open for approval of mergers that violate these standards, provided the anticompetitive effects of the transaction are clearly outweighed by the probable effects of the transaction in meeting the convenience and needs of the community served.

Suggestions for Additional Reading

The Adminstrator of National Banks. *Studies in Banking Competition and the Banking Structure*. Washington, D.C.: Office of the Comptroller of the Currency, 1966, parts 1, 2, 5.

Bell, Frederick W., and Murphy, Neil B. *Economies of Scale in Commercial Banking*. Boston: Federal Reserve Bank of Boston, 1976.

Edwards, Franklin R. "Bank Mergers and the Public Interest: A Legal and Economic Analysis of the 1966 Bank Merger Act." *The Banking Law Journal* (September 1968), pp. 753–796.

[6]One of the banks in the Nashville case was a "struggling" bank with a serious management succession problem. In the opinion of many students of banking, showing that any other action short of merger could have solved this bank's many problems would have bordered on speculation.

Fischer, Gerald C. *American Banking Structure*. New York: Columbia University Press, 1968, chaps. 4, 6–8.

Goodman, Oscar. "Judicial Decisions and Litigation Affecting Competition in Banking." In *Proceedings of a Conference on Bank Structure and Competition, 1970*. Chicago: Federal Reserve Bank of Chicago, 1970, pp. 1–26.

Guttentag, Jack M., and Herman, Edward S. "Banking Structure and Performance." New York University Graduate School of Business Administration, Institute of Finance, *The Bulletin*, 41–43 (February 1967).

Hall, George R., and Phillips, Charles F., Jr. *Bank Mergers and the Regulatory Agencies: Application of the Bank Merger Act of 1960*. Washington, D.C.: Board of Governors of the Federal Reserve System, 1964.

Haywood, Charles F. *The Potential Competition Doctrine*. Washington, D.C.: Association of Registered Bank Holding Companies, 1972.

Horvitz, Paul M. *Concentration and Competition in New England Banking*. Research Report No. 2. Boston: Federal Reserve Bank of Boston, 1958.

Solomon, Elinor H. "Bank Merger Policy and Problems: A Linkage Theory of Oligopoly." *Journal of Money, Credit and Banking* (August 1970), pp. 323–336.

Whitesell, William E. "Potential Competition and Bank Mergers." *The Banking Law Journal* (May 1971), pp. 387–408.

CHAPTER

19

Bank Holding Companies

A *bank holding company* is any company that owns or controls the voting stock of one or more banks. There are *one-bank holding companies,* which own or control a single bank, and *multibank holding companies,* which own or control two or more separately incorporated banks. The operation of two or more banks under a holding company is also called *group banking.* Since the last half of the 1960s, the rush to form one-bank holding companies and, to a lesser extent, multibank holding companies has raised sharply the percentage of banking assets under holding company control. Some banks operating under one-bank holding company arrangements become part of a *conglomerate,* that is, a group of companies dealing in diverse activities, some of which may not be related to banking or finance. Other banks become a part of a *congenerics,* that is, a group of companies providing similar services, all of which in this case are related to the banking and finance areas. For the foreseeable future, it appears that more and more banks will become part of either a one-bank or a multibank holding company arrangement.

In this chapter we shall (1) trace the bank holding company movement, (2) examine the present regulatory framework for bank holding companies, and (3) discuss the economics of multibank and one-bank holding companies.

The Bank Holding Company Movement

Origin

The bank holding company movement originated around the turn of the century. One of the first bank holding company applications was for the Adam Hannah Company in Minnesota in 1900 to hold the stock of country banks.[1] Another early holding company was the present Northwest Bancorporation, which was organized in 1903 and which by 1908 held an interest in thirty-one banks.[2] In addition, the predecessors to Atlantic Bancorporation of Jacksonville and Washington Bancshares, Inc., of Spokane had their origin in the first decade of this century.[3]

The main thrust of the early bank holding company movement, however, came in the period immediately preceding the Depression. Between 1925 and 1930, seven of the present top fifteen multibank holding companies were formed. Although the holding company movement occurred predominantly in the Midwest and Northwest, present-day giants were formed in the South, East, and West as well. By the end of 1931, there were 97 bank holding companies with 978 banks and 1,219 branches in the United States.[4]

There were several reasons for the great expansion of bank holding companies toward the close of the 1920s.[5] First, following its success as a device to control large numbers of companies in other industries, the holding company seemed like an ideal means to reap the financial advantage of common ownership of several banks. Often, this advantage was the ready access to funds for the holding company's financial and nonfinancial affiliates.[6] Second, holding companies offered a means to

[1]Gaines T. Cartinhour, *Branch, Group, and Chain Banking* (New York: Macmillan, 1931), p. 90, cited in W. Ralph Lamb, *Group Banking* (New Brunswick, N.J.: Rutgers University Press, 1961), p. 81.

[2]Charles S. Popple, *Development of Two Bank Groups in the Central Northwest* (Cambridge, Mass.: Harvard University Press, 1944), p. 68, cited in Lamb, p. 82.

[3]Lamb, p. 82.

[4]C. E. Cagle, "Branch, Chain, and Group Banking," in *Banking Studies* (Washington, D.C.: Board of Governors of the Federal Reserve System, 1941), pp. 134, 136.

[5]For more extensive comments on the holding company movement in the 1920s, see Marcus Nadler and Jules I. Bogen, *The Bank Holding Company* (New York: Graduate School of Business Administration, New York University, 1959), p. 10.

[6]As defined in the Banking Act of 1933, a bank *affiliate* is an organization owned or controlled by a bank or its stockholders or its executive officers serving as directors.

have multiple-office banking systems in areas where branching was restricted. Third, holding companies provided a means to expand across state lines. In fact, the founders of the Transamerica Corporation, in 1928, envisioned eventually controlling banks across the nation through six regional holding companies.[7] Finally, the large number of failures in the 1920s caused many small banks on the brink of disaster to affiliate with a holding company.

The Great Depression

According to Lamb, "the depression was a sobering and maturing experience for bank holding companies."[8] Management at many of the newly formed companies did not have enough time to work out all their organizational problems before they had to concern themselves with protecting the solvency of their affiliate banks. With respect to solvency, a number of holding companies distinguished themselves. In fact, it has been pointed out that "in areas where failures among unit banks were particularly common, like the Northwest and Far West, the fact that none of the banks affiliated with the leading companies were suspended proved quite helpful to the communities, businesses, and the individual depositors during that difficult period."[9] Close supervision and counsel and contributions of funds to prevent impairment of capital were the principal means used to keep individual banks from failing. Nevertheless, by 1936, there were only 52 holding companies with 479 banks, 847 branches, and $6.8 billion in deposits. The sharp decline from the 1931 totals was largely the result of dissolutions of holding companies because of bank suspensions and the conversion of holding company banks into branches as several states relaxed their restrictions on branches.

Postwar Resurgence

At the end of 1945, there were 33 holding companies with 387 banks, 861 branches, and $18.1 billion in deposits. Since World War II, bank holding companies have enjoyed considerable growth. Between 1949 and mid-1956, the growth rate of deposits of the fifteen largest banking groups was about twice that of all banks.[10] A large part of this growth was accomplished by acquisitions between 1954 and mid-1956. During this period, many holding companies moved swiftly to expand their holdings out of fear that restrictive congressional legislation dealing

[7] Palmer T. Hogenson, *The Economics of Group Banking* (Washington, D.C.: Public Affairs Press, 1955), p. 4.

[8] Lamb, p. 94.

[9] Nadler and Bogen, p. 11.

[10] Gerald C. Fischer, "Market Extension by Bank Holding Companies: History, Economic Implications, and Current Issues," *Proceedings of a Conference on Bank Structure and Competition*, Federal Reserve Bank of Chicago (Chicago: 1969), p.45.

with bank holding companies was forthcoming. A second impetus to deposit growth in group systems was the rebuilding of Transamerica Corporation's bank stock portfolio after its divestment of Bank of America.[11]

Registered Bank Holding Companies

Multibank Holding Companies. Congress moved to limit the activities of bank holding companies through passage of the Bank Holding Company Act of 1956. This act required all bank holding companies owning or controlling 25 percent or more of the voting shares of each of two or more banks, or controlling in any manner the election of a majority of the directors of each of two or more banks, to register with, and be regulated by, the Board of Governors. Companies owning or controlling only one bank were exempt from these requirements. At the end of 1956, there were 53 multibank companies holding 428 banks, 783 branches, and $14.8 billion in deposits registered with the Board of Governors (Table 19-1). From this point until 1965, the percentage of

[11] *Ibid.*, pp. 45–46.

Table 19-1

Registered Bank Holding Companies, Selected Years, 1956–1975

Year Ending	Number of Companies	Banking Offices: Banks	Banking Offices: Branches	Total Deposits (billions of dollars)	Total Deposits Percentage of All Bank Deposits
1956	53	428	783	$14.8	7.5%
1960	47	426	1,037	18.3	8.0
1962	49	442	1,215	21.2	8.1
1965	53	468	1,486	27.6	8.3
1966	65	561	1,802	41.1	11.6
1967	74	603	2,085	49.8	12.6
1968	80	629	2,262	57.6	13.2
1969	97	723	2,674	62.6	14.3
1970	121	895	3,260	78.1	15.5
1971	1,567	2,420	10,832	297.1	55.3
1972	1,607	2,720	13,441	379.4	61.5
1973	1,677	3,097	15,374	446.6	65.4
1974	1,752	3,462	17,131	509.7	68.1
1975	1,821	3,674	18,382	527.5	67.1

Source: Board of Governors of the Federal Reserve System, *Banking and Monetary Statistics, 1941–1970*, and *Annual Statistical Digest, 1971–1975*.

NOTE: Holding Companies listed for the 1956–1970 period are multibank holding companies as defined in the Bank Holding Company Act of 1956, as amended. Data for 1971 and subsequent years include companies that had reported to the board under the Bank Holding Company Act Amendments of 1970 and, therefore, include multibank and one-bank holding companies.

total deposits held by multibank holding companies increased only slightly. However, between 1966 and 1970, the number of multibank holding companies more than doubled, and the percentage of total deposits held increased from 11.6 to 15.5 percent. Concern over possible future restrictions on holding company activities was the primary motivating factor behind many of the holding company formations during this period.

Since 1970 the number of multibank holding companies has risen sharply. By the end of 1975, there were 289 multibank holding companies controlling 2,264 banks with 9,896 branches for a total of 12,160 banking offices. Banks in these multibank holding companies held deposits of $297.5 billion or 37.8 percent of the total in the nation.

One-Bank Holding Companies. Encouraged, in part, by the loophole in the Bank Holding Company Act of 1956, the growth of one-bank holding companies was phenomenal, especially after 1965. As shown in Table 19-2, between the end of 1965 and the end of 1968, the number of one-bank holding companies increased from 550 to 783, and the share of total deposits held by these companies rose from 4.5 to 24.9 percent. By the end of 1970, there were 1,318 one-bank holding companies with 39.7 percent of total deposits controlled by these companies. As a result of the December 31, 1970, amendments to the Bank Holding Company Act, one-bank holding companies were required to register with the Board of Governors of the Federal Reserve System. As may be seen in Table 19-2, the number of one-bank holding companies stabilized after the requirement to register was instituted. One-bank holding companies continued to be formed, but a number of previously formed one-bank holding companies acquired stock in other banks, thereby

Table 19-2

One-Bank Holding Companies, Selected Years, 1955–1975

Year Ending	Number of One-Bank Holding Companies	Holding Company Deposits (billions of dollars)	Percentage of All Bank Deposits
1955	117	11.6	1.7%
1965	550	15.1	4.5
1968	783	108.2	24.9
1970	1,318	191.0	39.7
1973	1,282	207.4	30.4
1974	1,340	222.4	29.7
1975	1,419	230.0	29.2

Source: U.S. Congress, House Committee on Banking and Currency, *The Growth of Unregistered Bank Holding Companies—Problems and Prospects*, Committee Print, 91st Congress, 1st session, 1969, p. 5; *Federal Reserve Bulletin*; Board of Governors of the Federal Reserve System, *Annual Statistical Digest, 1971–1975*.

converting to multibank holding company status. By the end of 1975, there were 1,419 one-bank holding companies controlling 8,486 branches for a total of 9,896 offices. These banks held deposits of $230.0 billion or 29.2 percent of the total for the nation. Thus, at the close of 1975, multi- and one-bank holding companies held 67.1 percent of the nation's bank deposits.

Federal Regulation of Bank Holding Companies

A brief review of past federal regulation of bank holding companies would be helpful in understanding the present regulatory framework.

Banking Act of 1933

Prior to the Great Depression, the Federal Reserve was concerned with the holding company movement primarily because of the growing concentration of banking resources under common ownership. However, in 1931, investigations by a subcommittee of the Senate Banking and Currency Committee and a 1932 Federal Reserve study revealed that banks and their securities affiliates had played major roles in the speculative excesses of the 1920s. Many of the securities affiliates were engaged in underwriting operations, in stock speculation, and in maintaining markets in the bank's own stock, often with funds borrowed from the parent bank. Moreover, the Federal Reserve study revealed that nearly one-half of the known bank holding companies had affiliates engaged in various nonbanking activities. National banks alone had 192 securities affiliates in 1932.[12]

After two years of Senate investigations and hearings, Congress passed the Banking Act of 1933. This act required member banks to divest themselves of their directly owned securities affiliates, but it placed no such restrictions on their other, nonbank businesses. The Banking Act of 1933 also limited loans by member banks to holding company affiliates and to all affiliates to 10 and 20 percent, respectively, of aggregate capital stock and surplus. Holding companies were required to obtain a permit from the Federal Reserve Board to vote the stock of a member bank they controlled. In order to acquire a voting permit, the holding company had to agree to a number of conditions, including severing all connections with their securities affiliates and permitting examinations of the books and affairs of all banks and affiliates under their control. The voting permit device proved to be unsuccessful because a number of holding companies found other means to control their affiliates and, therefore, escaped Federal Reserve regulation just by not applying for the voting permit.

[12] William F. Upshaw, "Federal Regulation of Bank Holding Companies: Part I," Federal Reserve Bank of Richmond, *Monthly Review* (October 1968), p. 3.

Bank Holding Company Act of 1956

The 1933 legislation left many loopholes. As a result, a number of large holding companies continued to acquire banks and branches and to expand into nonbanking activities. The most notable of the companies was the Transamerica Corporation, which, between 1933 and 1946, acquired 126 banks, established 74 branches, and built up nonbanking interests in real estate, insurance, manufacturing, and the fish and seafood industries.[13] In 1948, the Federal Reserve Board instituted antitrust proceedings against Transamerica and, although the corporation successfully defended the action in 1953, the *Transamerica Case* led to the enactment of the Bank Holding Company Act of 1956.[14]

This act had three principal purposes: (1) to define a bank holding company, (2) to control the formation and expansion of bank holding companies, and (3) to require divestment of certain nonbanking interests. A bank holding company was defined as any corporation, business trust, association, or similar organization owning or controlling 25 percent or more of the voting shares of each of *two or more banks*, or controlling in any manner the election of a majority of the directors of each of two or more banks, or acting as trustee for shareholders or members who control 25 percent or more of the voting shares of each of two or more banks.[15]

Holding company expansion was restricted by the requirement that the Federal Reserve Board's approval must be received before a bank holding company could be formed, before a bank holding company could acquire over 5 percent of the voting stock of any bank,[16] or before two bank holding companies could merge. In reviewing holding company applications for the above, the board had to consider five factors:

1. The financial history and condition of the company or companies and banks concerned.
2. Their prospects.
3. The character of their management.
4. The convenience, needs, and welfare of the communities and areas concerned.
5. Whether or not the effect of the acquistion of merger or consolidation would be to expand the size or extent of the bank holding company system involved beyond the limits consistent

[13] *Ibid*., p. 4.

[14] William F. Upshaw, "Antitrust and the New Bank Holding Company Act: Part I," Federal Reserve Bank of Richmond, *Monthly Review* (February 1971), p. 2.

[15] Excluded from this definition were cases in which two or more banks were held by individuals, partnerships, and nonprofit organizations, including testamentary trusts.

[16] Board approval was not required in instances where the company already controlled a majority of bank's voting shares.

with adequate and sound banking, the public interest, and the preservation of competition in the field of banking.

The first three factors are often termed the "banking factors" and essentially are used to evaluate the solvency of the company or companies and the banks involved. The "convenience and needs" factor and the "competitive" factor bring into consideration the possible public benefits from the transaction and the possible antitrust aspects involving competition.

With respect to nonbanking businesses, the 1956 act stipulated that registered companies could not engage in any business other than banking, managing banks, or providing certain services to subsidiary banks. Under the act, registered bank holding companies specifically were authorized to acquire and own voting shares of any company engaged solely in (1) holding or operating properties used wholly or substantially by any banking subsidiary of a bank holding company in the operations of the banking subsidiary, or acquired for its future use; (2) conducting a safe deposit business; (3) furnishing services to, or performing services for, the parent bank holding company and its subsidiaries; and (4) liquidating assets acquired from the parent bank holding company and its banking subsidiaries. In addition, registered holding companies could own shares of any company if all its activities were of a financial, fiduciary, or insurance nature, provided the Board of Governors determined such activities to be so closely related to the business of banking as to be a proper incident thereto and as to make it unnecessary for the prohibitions of the act to apply in order to carry out the act's purposes.

Another important provision of the 1956 act was that a bank holding company could not acquire a bank located outside the state in which it conducted its principal operations unless such an acquisition was specifically permitted by state law where the acquired bank was situated. Thus far, no state has enacted such enabling legislation.

The 1966 Amendments

In 1966, Congress amended both the Bank Holding Company Act of 1956 and the Bank Merger Act of 1960 so that both acts contain uniform standards for evaluating proposed merger and holding company applications. The 1956 holding company act now stipulates that the Board of Governors shall not approve:

1. Any acquistion . . . which would result in a monopoly, or which would be in furtherance of any combination or conspiracy to monopolize or attempt to monopolize the business of banking in any part of the United States, or

2. Any other proposed acquisition . . . whose effect in any section of the country may be substantially to lessen competition, or to tend to create a monopoly, or which in any other manner would be in restraint of trade, *unless it finds that the anti-competitive effects of the proposed transaction are clearly outweighed in meeting the convenience and needs of the community to be served.* [Italics added.]

In every case, the board shall take into consideration the financial and managerial resources and future prospects of the company or companies and banks concerned, and the convenience and needs of the community to be served.

The 1970 Amendments

According to Upshaw, Congress excluded one-bank holding companies from regulation prior to 1970 for three reasons.

> First, since only one bank was involved, the holding company could not be used to evade Federal and State branch banking legislation. Second, most of the banks owned by one-bank holding companies were small. And third, the nonbanking activities of these companies were for the most part quite limited involving primarily, local real estate and insurance agency operations.[17]

On December 31, 1970, President Nixon signed a bill to bring one-bank holding companies under the coverage of the Bank Holding Company Act of 1956. Under this amendment, unlike the separate jurisdictions created for merger approvals, the Federal Reserve Board of Governors was given responsibility for regulating holding companies.

The amended act defines a bank holding company as any company that has control over any bank or over any bank holding company. A company is defined as any corporation, partnership, business trust, association, or similar organization, or any other long-term trust.[18] A company is considered to have control if it, directly or indirectly, or acting through one or more persons, controls 25 percent or more of any class of the voting shares. There is a presumption, however, that a company that owns less than 5 percent of the voting shares does not have control. Sole administrative jurisdiction is vested with the Federal Reserve Board in making a determination as to whether a company exercises controlling influence.

[17] William F. Upshaw, "Antitrust and the New Bank Holding Company Act: Part III," Federal Reserve Bank of Richmond, *Monthly Review* (April 1971), p. 3.

[18] Long-term trusts are those extending beyond twenty-five years or twenty-one years, ten months after the death of the individuals living on the date that the trust was created.

Other major provisions of the 1970 legislation are as follows:

1. A "grandfather clause" date of June 30, 1968, is established, and companies may continue activities engaged in continuously since then. The board has discretion to require divestment of these grandfathered activities if it determines that they are contrary to the public interest. Moreover, the board must review within 2 years the nonbanking activities of all holding companies controlling banks of over $60 million to determine whether or not divestment of such activities is required.
2. Banks are prohibited from extending services to a customer under conditions commonly described as tie-in arrangements. That is, banks may not package their services so as to require a customer to purchase a service from one affiliate as a condition for receiving a service from another.
3. Bank holding companies may acquire interests in nonbanking activities only if they are determined by the board to be *so closely related to banking or managing or controlling banks as to be a proper incident thereto.* In making these determinations, the board must consider *whether the activities can be reasonably expected to produce benefits to the public, such as greater convenience, increased competition, or gains in efficiency, that outweigh possible adverse effects, such as undue concentration of resources, decreased or unfair competition, conflicts of interest, or unsound banking practices.*

Activities determined by the Federal Reserve Board as of March 11, 1977, to meet these criteria and those denied and pending before the Board are shown in Table 19-3.

Whereas the list of approved nonbanking activities of bank holding companies in Table 19-3 is extensive, holding companies have entered predominantly three areas: (1) consumer and commercial finance, (2) mortgage banking, and (3) insurance (underwriting and broker or agency). These areas offer the greatest opportunity for the application of banking expertise.

It would appear that the list of permissible nonbanking activities is close to being exhausted. In 1975 the United States Court of Appeals for The District of Columbia commented in its decision in *National Courier Association* v. *Board*[19] that in order for an activity to be "closely related to banking," one of the following connections must be made:

1. that banks generally have in fact provided the proposed service;

[19] 516 F. 2d 1229, 1237 (1975).

Table 19-3
Status of Bank Holding Company Nonbanking Activities Under Section 4(c)(8) (as of March 11, 1977)

Activities approved by the Board	Activities denied by the Board
1. Dealer in banker's acceptances	1. Equity funding (combined sale of mutual funds & insurance)
2. Mortgage banking	2. Underwriting general life insurance
3. Finance companies a. consumer b. sales c. commercial	3. Real estate brokerage
4. Credit card issuance	4. Land development
5. Factoring company	5. Real estate syndication
6. Industrial banking	6. General management counsulting
7. Servicing loans	7. Property management
8. Trust company	8. Nonfull-payout leasing
9. Investment advising	9. Commodity trading
10. General economic information	10. Issuance and sale of short-term debt obligations ("thrift notes")
11. Portfolio investment advice	11. Travel agency
12. Full payout leasing a. personal property b. real property	12. Savings and loan associations
13. Community welfare investments	
14. Bookkeeping & data processing services	
15. Insurance agent or broker—credit extensions	**Activities pending before the Board**
16. Underwriting credit life & credit accident & health insurance	1. Armored car services
17. Courier service	2. Underwriting mortgage guarantee insurance
18. Management consulting to non-affiliate banks	3. Underwriting & dealing in U.S. Government and certain municipal securities
19. Issuance of traveler's checks	4. Underwriting the deductible part of bankers' blanket bond insurance (withdrawn)
20. Bullion broker	5. Management consulting to non-affiliated depository type, financial institutions
21. Land escrow services	
22. Issuing money orders and variable denominated payment instruments[a]	

Source: Dale S. Drum, "Nonbanking Activities of Bank Holding Companies," in Federal Reserve Bank of Chicago, *Economic Perspectives* (March–April 1977), p. 14.

[a]To be decided on a case-by-case basis.

2. that banks generally provide services that are operationally or functionally so similar to the proposed services as to equip them particularly well to provide the proposed service;
3. that banks generally provide services that are so integrally related to the proposed services as to require their provision in a specialized form.[20]

Given these connection requirements, it is difficult to conceive of services that meet one of these tests yet are not on the approved list.

The Economics of Multibank Holding Companies

Multibank holding companies are in an excellent position to organize the production of banking services for the mutual benefit of the holding company, the affiliate banks, and the public. These benefits include (1) improved operating results, (2) strengthened capital structure, (3) additional banking services to the community, and (4) a better allocation of bank credit.[21]

Improved Operating Results

Banks in a holding company group may enjoy improved operating results through cost savings and possible increases in revenue. On the cost side, banks produce themselves, or purchase from a correspondent bank, many services necessary for the conduct of banking. Usually, it is much more efficient for the lead or dominant bank in the group, or the holding company, or a holding company subsidiary to supply the service to all affiliate banks. Perhaps the most notable example is the check clearing and collection service. All affiliated banks could have their cash items processed and forwarded for collection from a central data point, most probably at a considerable savings for the bank involved. Other services provided by the lead bank, the holding company, or a holding company subsidiary might include investment portfolio advice or management, purchasing of supplies and equipment, advertising and public relations, personnel records, management recruiting, employee-benefit programs, large-loan reviews, risk and insurance programs, tax planning and returns, and audit and examination. Subsidiary banks ordinarily pay for these specialized services through assessments or fees. There is no uniform pattern of organiza-

[20] *Federal Reserve Bulletin* (February 1976), p. 149.

[21] Much of the discussion in this section is based on Robert J. Lawrence, "The Performance of Banking Companies" (Washington, D.C.: Board of Governors of the Federal Reserve System, 1967), pp. 5-10. See also Robert J. Lawrence, "Operating Policies of Bank Holding Companies, Part I, "Staff Economic Studies No. 59 (Washington, D.C.: Board of Governors of the Federal Reserve System, 1971).

tion among holding companies for providing or costing services to affiliated banks.

The holding company arrangement also provides a number of opportunities for banks to increase their operating revenue. First, since many services that typically would be purchased are provided within the holding company organization, subsidiary banks may reduce their correspondent balances held outside the system and perhaps place a higher proportion of their assets in loans or investments. In addition, through advice and counsel from holding company specialists, the affiliated banks may improve earnings on their loan and investment portfolios. Finally, the subsidiary banks may have a better access to loan participations through the network of banks than through their correspondent banks.

Strengthened Capital Structure

A holding company usually can raise capital for its subsidiary banks much more easily than the banks themselves. Because the holding company is better known and perhaps even has its shares listed on a national exchange, it can issue stock or capital notes and debentures at a lower cost and, in turn, purchase stocks or capital notes from the subsidiary banks. If the holding company's securities are sold outside its market area, the region benefits from the importation of additional capital. In addition, if the holding company has virtually complete control over the subsidiary banks, it could vary the dividend policies of the affiliated banks to achieve a more optimum distribution of retained earnings. That is, banks in capital-surplus areas might pay a higher percentage of their net income as dividends to the holding company than banks in capital-poor areas.

Additional Banking Services

A holding company typically is able to provide more and better banking services in the communities they serve than would independent banks. Because of its size, the holding company can employ specialists in such areas as trust, international banking, and financial counseling. Customers at subsidiary banks would have access to these services perhaps more readily than customers who have to rely on an independent bank's correspondent bank.

Better Allocation of Credit

A holding company has several opportunities to improve the allocation of credit in the region that it serves. As we have seen, if correspondent balances of subsidiary banks can be reduced, then perhaps certain types of loans can be increased. For example, subsidiary banks may be able to increase agricultural credit, term loans, mortgage loans, and their holdings of municipals. In addition, holding company subsidiaries may purchase loan paper from another subsidiary without recourse, or engage in loan participations with other subsidiaries. These loan techniques tend to facilitate the interregional mobility of bank credit and hence benefit the public.

The Economics of One-Bank Holding Companies

There are a number of economic benefits to be derived from the formation of a one-bank holding company and the subsequent entry into selected nonbanking activities. These include (1) diversification of revenue sources, (2) economies of scale, and (3) strengthened capital structure.

Diversification of Revenue Sources

One of the primary motives behind the one-bank holding movement was the desire on the part of banks to find new and more lucrative sources of revenue to offset rising costs. As banks became increasingly dependent on time and savings deposits as sources of funds, bank costs rose sharply. By forming holding companies they hoped could acquire a finance company, a data-processing company, a mortgage company, or a factoring company, banks would have a ready and sometimes more profitable outlet for funds.

Another important advantage for a bank's being under a one-bank holding company arrangement is that the entire range of financial services provided by the holding company would attract additional customers to the bank. For example, if a firm has its financial accounting performed by the holding company's data-processing subsidiary, it should be easier for the bank's commercial accounts officers to acquire the firm's deposit and loan business.

Economies of Scale

There should be some economies of operation achieved within the holding company. For example, consolidation of purchasing, personnel administration, advertising and public relations, risk and insurance programs, management recruiting, employee-benefit programs, audit and examination, and tax planning and returns should result in worthwhile cost savings for the various holding company subsidiaries.

Strengthened Capital Structure

An important advantage of forming a one-bank holding company is that the holding company can be a separate source of capital to the bank and the subsidiary companies. By issuing stock, capital notes, or debentures, the holding company could channel capital to the holding company subsidiary that has the most productive use of the funds.

Bank Holding Companies: An Evaluation

Multibank Holding Companies

Multibank holding companies have increased in size to the point that they hold 37.8 percent of the nation's deposits. Growth of these companies has been to a large extent in states that have limited branch banking or unit banking. In evaluating multibank holding companies, one conclusion was that they have had a "slightly favorable" impact on the banking system.[22] On the positive side, multibank holding companies seem to offer a slightly wider range of services and increased consumer and business credit; affiliate banks tend to charge slightly less on loans and pay higher interest rates on time and savings deposits. On the negative side, affiliate banks tend to be not as well capitalized as independent banks; moreover, affiliate banks tend to have higher risk, higher return assets. These negative factors point to the need for monitoring of multibank holding company expansion.

One-Bank Holding Companies

Companies or banks originating one-bank holding companies generally do so with the primary motive of entry into nonbanking activities. The theory is that diversification of revenue sources will stabilize income and will lower the overall level of risk for a given level of return. However, the 1973–75 recession and financial fallout left many one-bank holding companies convinced that "it wasn't too bad to be only in the banking business." As the cost of funds rose, most finance company subsidiaries had profit margins squeezed to the point that funds employed received a lower return than in the bank. The collapse of the real estate market left many holding company mortgage subsidiaries "in the red." The sum and substance of the 1973–1975 experience is that holding companies have adopted a "go slow" policy toward further expansion.

[22] Dale S. Drum, "MBHCs: Evidence After Two Decades of Regulation," Federal Reserve Bank of Chicago, *Business Conditions* (December 1976), pp. 14–15.

The one-bank holding company with its ability to provide a variety of related services is now firmly entrenched in our financial system. However, the management of these financial congenerics and the Board of Governors of the Federal Reserve System must ensure that the quest for diversification and profits is not achieved at a cost of more risk to the banking system or the public.

Suggestions for Additional Reading

Association of Registered Bank Holding Companies. *The Registered Bank Holding Company. Its History and Significance in Modern America.* Washington, D.C.: Association of Registered Holding Companies, February 1969.

Beighley, H. Prescott; Boyd, John H.; and Jacobs, Donald P. *The Financial Structure of Bank Holding Companies.* Chicago: Association of Reserve City Bankers, 1975.

Chase, Samuel B., Jr. "The Bank Holding Company as a Device for Sheltering Banks from Risk." In *Proceedings of a Conference on Bank Structure and Competition, 1971.* Chicago: Federal Reserve Bank of Chicago, 1971, pp. 38–54.

Drum, Dale S. "MBHCs: Evidence After Two Decades of Regulation." Federal Reserve Bank of Chicago, *Business Conditions* (December 1976), pp. 3–15.

———"Nonbanking Activities of Bank Holding Companies." Federal Reserve Bank of Chicago, *Economic Perspectives* (March–April 1977), pp. 12–22.

Eisemann, Peter C. "Diversification and the Congeneric Bank Holding Company." *Journal of Bank Research* (Spring 1976), pp. 68–77.

Fischer, Gerald C. *Banking Holding Companies.* New York: Columbia University Press, 1961.

Hoffman, Stuart G. "The Impact of Holding Company Affiliation on Bank Performance: A Case Study of Two Florida Multibank Holding Companies." Atlanta: Federal Reserve Bank of Atlanta, "Working Paper Series," January 1976.

Jessee, Michael A., and Seelig, Steven A. "An Analysis of the Public Benefits Test of the Bank Holding Company Act." Federal Reserve Bank of New York, *Monthly Review* (June 1974), pp. 151–162.

Kohn, Donald L., and Zoellmer, John F. "The Amended Bank Holding Company Act." Federal Reserve Bank of Kansas City, *Monthly Review* (May 1971), pp. 11–20.

Lamb, W. Ralph. *Group Banking.* New Brunswick, N.J.: Rutgers University Press, 1961.

Lawrence, Robert J. "Operating Policies of Bank Holding Companies, Part I." In *Staff Economic Studies,* No. 59. Washington, D.C.: Board of Governors of the Federal Reserve System, 1971.

Mayo, Robert P. "The 1970 Amendments to the Bank Holding Company Act: One Year Later." Federal Reserve Bank of Chicago, *Business Conditions* (December 1971), pp. 2–11.

"The One-Bank Holding Company—History, Issues, and Pending Legislation." Federal Reserve Bank of Chicago, *Business Conditions* (July 1970), pp. 2–16.

Piper, Thomas R. *The Economics of Bank Acquisitions by Registered Bank Holding Companies.* Research Report No. 48. Boston: Federal Reserve Bank of Boston, 1971.

Prochnow, Herbert V., ed. *The One-Bank Holding Company.* Chicago: Rand NcNally, 1969.

Rose, Peter S. "How the Holding Companies Are Doing." *The Bankers Magazine* (Spring 1977), pp. 88–94.

Rosenblum, Harvey. "Bank Holding Companies: Part I–II." Federal Reserve Bank of Chicago, *Business Conditions* (February 1975), pp. 3–10; (April 1975), pp. 13–15.

———. "Bank Holding Companies: An Overview." Federal Reserve Bank of Chicago, *Business Conditions* (August 1973), pp. 3–13.

Talley, Samuel H. "The Effect of Holding Company Acquistitions on Bank Performance." *Staff Economic Studies,* No. 69. Washington, D.C.: Board of Governors of the Federal Reserve System, 1972.

Upshaw, William F. "Bank Affiliates and Their Regulation." Federal Reserve Bank of Richmond, *Monthly Review* (March 1973), pp. 14–20; (April 1973), pp. 3–9; (May 1973), pp. 3–10.

Upson, Roger B., and Jessup, Paul F. "Returns from Bank Holding Companies." *The Bankers Magazine* (Spring 1972), pp. 59–62.

Varvel, Walter A. "A Valuation Approach to Bank Holding Company Acquisitions." Federal Reserve Bank of Richmond, *Economic Review* (July–August 1975), pp. 9–15.

Whitehead, David D., and King, B. Frank. "Multibank Holding Companies and Local Market Concentration." Federal Reserve Bank of Atlanta, *Monthly Review* (April 1976), pp. 34–39.

PART

VII

Banking Horizons

CHAPTER

20

Financial Intermediation in 1980 and 1985

Chapter 1 contained a description of the general and specific functions performed by commercial banks and the other major financial intermediaries. By creating loanable funds for creditworthy borrowers, and by providing a means by which savers can accumulate liquid and relatively riskless financial assets, financial intermediaries have facilitated and stimulated rapid economic development in the United States, especially since World War II. Financial intermediaries also will have an important role during the coming years if the nation is to maintain a satisfactory rate of economic growth and to solve its social problems, such as adequate housing for all citizens.

In this chapter we shall (1) explore the relationship between economic growth and the availability of funds to financial intermediaries, (2) examine some projections for the economy in 1980, (3) consider projections of the relative size of each of the major financial intermediaries in 1980 and 1985, (4) analyze the estimated sources and uses of funds at commercial banks in 1980 and 1985 and, (5) discuss some of the major groups of proposals in the *Report of the President's Commission on Financial Structure and Regulations*, commonly known as the Hunt Commission Report, and in Congress's study of *Financial Institutions in the Nation's Economy (FINE)*.

Economic Growth and the Availability of Funds to Financial Intermediaries

Growth in the availability of funds at commercial banks and other financial intermediaries is tied closely to growth in employment, production, and income in the economy. One reason for this is that financial savings, which are a primary source of funds to these intermediaries, tend to grow as income grows. Income is created by the production of goods and services. The level of production, in turn, depends largely on population growth, the educational and skill level of the population, the degree of labor-force participation, the amount of capital, and technological advances. In addition, the availability of funds to financial intermediaries is related to growth in the economy because the Federal Reserve provides reserve funds to commercial banks at a pace designed to facilitate and to stimulate orderly economic growth. As commercial bank deposits grow in the process of credit expansion, some of these funds are transferred to nonbank intermediaries, thereby augmenting the flow of financial savings to these institutions. Therefore, since increases in the two basic sources of funds to financial intermediaries depend closely on real growth in the economy, it is important that bank management and other financial officers take into account the projected expansion in employment, production, and income as they formulate their objectives and plans.

Projections for 1980 and 1985

Let us note some projections for 1980 and 1985 for GNP, total labor force, employment, and other important economic variables.

GNP

GNP represents the money value of all goods and services produced in the economy during a year. GNP projections usually are stated two ways: (1) in *constant* dollars, that is, as measured in terms of prices prevailing during a base year, and (2) in *current* dollars, that is, as measured in terms of prices prevailing in each year. Projections of GNP in terms of constant dollars tend to be reliable because *real* output is the result of population growth, labor-force participation, and other factors that tend to grow at a fairly stable and predictable rate over a relatively short period such as a decade. Projections of current-dollar GNP are more difficult because they involve a prediction of the rate of inflation or deflation.

Current-dollar GNP projections for 1980 and 1985 are shown in Table 20-1. The "basic" GNP projections for these years are $2.6 and $3.8 trillion, respectively. The key determinant of these projections is the estimated rate of inflation. The Bureau of Labor Statistics (BLS) assumes that inflation, as measured by the private GNP deflator, will average 4.8 percent between 1975 and 1980 and 4.1 percent between 1980 and 1985. These rates compare with 2.0 percent inflation between 1955 and 1968 and 4.1 percent between 1968 and 1972. The projected inflation rates are well below those experienced between 1972 and 1976, which averaged close to 8 percent. Given the political pressure to reduce unemployment, the assumed inflation rates and hence the current-dollar GNP estimates may be too conservative.

Population

According to a mid-range estimate prepared by the Bureau of Census, the total population is expected to rise from 213.4 million in 1975 to 222.8 million in 1980 and 234.1 million in 1985.[1] The annual growth rate is expected to be 1.0 percent during the early 1980s and then would decline to 0.6 percent by the end of this century as it converges toward zero in the long run.

The change in the age distribution of the population in the 1970s may have more important implications for financial intermediaries than the absolute growth in population. In 1970, there were approximately 25 million people in the 18–24 age group and 48 million people in the 25–44 age group. By 1980 about 29 million people will be in the 18–24 age group, but about 62 million people will be in the 25–44 age group. Because a higher percentage of the population will be in these younger age groups, financial intermediaries can expect to experience large increases in the demand for consumer loans and residential mortgage loans relative to business loans. Moreover, because younger families tend to be net borrowers rather than net suppliers of funds, financial intemediaries may have to step up their efforts to obtain funds from the older segments of the population and from businesses.

Employment

Civilian employment is expected to increase from 92.1 million in 1973 to 104.4 million in 1980 and to 112.1 million in 1985 (Table 20-2). This

[1]Bureau of Census, Population Estimates and Projections, Series p-25, No. 601, "Projection of the Population of the United States: 1975 to 2050," (Washington, D.C.: U.S. Government Printing Office, 1975), p. 3.

Table 20-1
The Derivation of Personal Income, Selected Years, 1955–1973, and Projected to 1980 and 1985

Component	Actual			Projected					
	1955	1968	1973	1980			1985		
				Basic	Alternate policy	Slower recovery	Basic	Alternate policy	Slower recovery
Gross national product	398.0	864.2	1,294.9	2,553.4	2,551.5	2,468.7	3,769.7	3,766.2	3,641.0
Less									
Corporate profits plus inventory valuation adjustment	46.9	84.3	105.5	233.4	232.2	221.1	311.0	308.0	303.5
Capital consumption allowances	31.5	74.5	110.8	207.3	207.5	203.7	320.6	322.0	308.1
Indirect buiness taxes	32.1	78.6	119.2	223.3	222.8	216.4	320.5	319.7	310.3
Social insurance contributions	11.1	47.1	91.2	176.3	176.1	174.1	243.1	242.3	263.2
Statistical discrepancy	2.1	-2.7	-5.0	0	0	0	0	0	0
Plus:									
Subsidies less current surplus of government enterprises	-.1	7	6	2.5	2.5	2.5	3.1	3.1	3.1
Government transfers to persons	16.1	56.1	113.0	247.1	251.6	232.9	352.3	368.5	328.0
Net interest paid by government and consumers	10.1	26.1	38.3	70.6	72.6	67.5	99.1	101.3	94.8
Dividends	10.5	23.6	29.6	68.6	68.6	64.7	98.2	98.2	99.6
Equals:									
Personal income	310.0	689.9	1,055.0	2,101.9	2,108.2	2,021.0	3,127.1	3,145.4	3,008.3
Less:									
Personal taxes, Federal	31.4	79.7	114.1	237.1	262.8	218.1	393.1	450.0	352.0
Personal taxes, State and local	4.1	18.3	37.2	86.2	84.2	83.8	159.1	157.5	150.3
Equals:									
Disposable personal income	275.3	591.0	903.7	1,778.6	1,761.3	1,719.2	2,574.9	2,538.0	2,506.0
Displays: (percents)									
Personal savings rate	5.7	6.7	8.2	7.1	7.0	7.1	6.4	6.3	6.4
Effective rate for Federal personal taxes	10.1	11.6	10.8	11.3	12.5	10.8	12.6	14.3	11.7
Effective rate for Federal corporate taxes	43.9	43.5	41.6	34.1	31.7	39.3	33.5	31.1	38.7

	Average annual rate of change								
	1955–68	1968–73	1955–73		1973–80			1980–85	
Gross national product	6.2	8.4	6.8	10.2	10.2	9.7	8.1	8.1	8.1
Less:									
Corporate profits plus inventory valuation adjustment	4.6	4.5	4.6	12.1	12.0	11.2	5.9	5.8	6.5
Capital consumption allowances	6.9	8.3	7.2	9.4	9.4	9.1	9.1	9.2	8.6
Indirect business taxes	7.1	8.7	7.6	9.4	9.4	8.9	7.5	7.5	7.5
Social insurance contributions	11.8	14.1	12.4	9.9	9.9	9.7	6.6	6.6	6.3
Plus:									
Government transfers to persons	10.1	15.0	11.4	11.8	12.1	10.9	7.4	7.9	7.1
Net interest paid by government and consumers	7.6	8.0	7.7	9.1	9.6	7.9	7.0	6.9	7.7
Dividends	6.4	4.6	5.9	12.8	12.8	11.8	7.4	7.4	9.0
Equals:									
Personal income	6.3	8.9	7.0	10.4	10.4	9.7	8.3	8.3	8.3
Less:									
Personal taxes, Federal	7.4	7.4	7.4	11.0	12.7	9.7	10.6	11.4	10.1
Personal taxes, State and local	12.2	15.2	13.0	12.8	12.4	12.3	13.0	13.3	12.4
Equals:									
Disposable personal income	6.1	8.9	6.8	10.2	10.0	9.6	7.7	7.6	7.8

Source: U.S. Department of Labor, Bureau of Labor Statistics, *Monthly Labor Review* (March 1976), p. 15.

NOTE: These figures do not reflect the January 1976 benchmark revision of the National Income Accounts.

Table 20-2 Labor Force, Employment, Productivity, and Gross National Product, Selected Years, 1955–1973, and Projected to 1980 and 1985

Item	Actual			Projected (basic version)		Average annual rate of change						
						Basic version					Slower recovery version	
	1955	1968	1973	1980	1985	1955–68	1968–73	1973–85	1973–80	1980–85	1973–80	1980–85
Total labor force (including military)	68,072	82,272	91,040	103,310	109,749	1.47	2.05	1.57	1.82	1.22	1.82	1.22
Unemployed	2,852	2,817	4,304	4,757	4,306	-.09	8.85		1.44	-1.97	3.75	-2.74
Employed (persons concept)	65,220	79,455	86,736	98,553	105,443	1.53	1.77	1.64	1.84	1.36	1.73	1.42
Adjustment factor (person to jobs)	4,033	5,447	5,318	5,888	6,654	2.34	-.48	1.89	1.47	2.48	.78	2.91
Employment (jobs concept)	69,253	84,902	92,054	104,441	112,097	1.58	1.63	1.66	1.82	1.42	1.67	1.51
General government	9,475	14,453	14,690	17,685	20,087	3.30	.33	2.64	2.69	2.58	2.50	2.62
Federal	4,741	5,609	4,305	4,246	4,339	1.30	-5.15	.07	-.20	.43	-.20	.43
Military	3,025	3,517	2,295	2,088	2,088	1.17	-8.18	-.78	-1.34		-1.34	
Civilian	1,716	2,092	2,010	2,158	2,251	1.54	-.80	.95	1.02	85	1.02	.85
State and local	4,734	8,844	10,385	13,439	15,748	4.92	3.26	3.53	3.75	3.22	3.51	3.28
Education	2,180	4,798	5,497	6,916	7,946	6.26	2.76	3,12	3,34	2.81	3.00	2.92
Noneducation	2,554	4,046	4,888	6,523	7,802	3.60	3.85	3.97	4.21	3.65	4.06	3.65
Private	59,778	70,449	77,364	86,756	92,010	1.27	1.89	1.46	1.65	1.18	1.51	1.28
Agriculture	6,434	3,805	3,423	2,750	2,300	-3.96	-2.09	-3.26	-3.08	-3.51	-3.08	-3.51
Nonagriculture	53,344	66,644	73,941	84,006	89,710	1.73	2.10	1.62	1.84	1.32	1.69	1.42
Private average annual hours per job	2,130	2,002	1.960	1,920	1,895	-.48	-.43	-.28	-.30	-.26	-.33	-.25
Agriculture	2,480	2,314	2,255	2,179	2,125	-.53	-.51	-.50	-.49	-.50	-.49	-.50
Nonagriculture	2,088	1,985	1,946	1,911	1,889	-.39	-.39	-.25	-.26	-.24	-.29	-.22
Private GNP per hour (1963 dollars)	3.30	4.86	5.41	6.39	7.30	3.02	2.18	2.53	2.40	2.71	2.26	2.71
Agriculture	1.24	2.51	3.16	4.77	6.30	5.57	4.72	5.92	6.07	5.71	6.07	5.71
Nonagriculture	3.59	5.01	5.53	6.45	7.33	2.60	1.98	2.38	2.22	2.60	2.08	2.60
Total GNP (billions of 1963 dollars)	468.7	759.2	898.5	1,154.7	1,375.8	3.78	3.43	3.61	3.65	3.57	3.34	3.67
General government	48.8	74.0	78.1	90.7	102.7	3.25	1.08	2.31	2.16	2.52	2.00	2.52
Private	419.9	685.2	820.4	1,064.0	1,273.1	3.84	3.67	3.73	3.78	3.65	3.46	3.76
Agriculture	19.8	22.1	24.4	28.6	30.8	.85	2.00	1.96	2.29	1.49	2.29	1.49
Nonagriculture	400.1	663.1	796.0	1,035.4	1,242.3	3.96	3.72	3.78	3.83	3.71	3.50	3.83

Source: U.S. Department of Labor, Bureau of Labor Statistics, *Monthly Labor Review* (March 1976), p. 11.

NOTE: These figures do not reflect the January 1976 benchmark revision of the National Income Accounts.

assumes that the rate of civilian unemployment drops steadily to 4.7 percent in 1980 and further downward to 4.0 percent in 1985. These rates may be overly optimistic given the fact that the rate of unemployment averaged 4.7 percent or less in only eleven of the twenty-six years between 1950 and 1976.

Per Capita Disposable Income

Per capita disposable income in current dollars is expected to rise from $5,494 in 1976 to $7,983 in 1980 and to $10,999 in 1985. On the other hand, per capita disposable income in 1972 dollars is expected to rise from $4,141 in 1976 to $4,661 in 1980 and to $5,403 in 1985. In other words, real income should increase by slightly more than one-third during the 1975-1985 period.

Assets of Financial Intermediaries in 1980 and 1985

If GNP, population, employment, and per capita income expand to the levels projected in 1980 and 1985, all financial intermediaries can expect a significant increase in assets. Table 20-3 contains a projection of assets for each of the major financial intermediaries for 1980 and 1985. It goes without saying that any projections of the growth of financial intermediaries is fraught with difficulties. Changing regulatory environment is just one of many factors that stands to upset any projections. Nevertheless, it seems beneficial to consider what the relative size of the major financial intermediaries will be under a relatively simple assumption, that is, that the rate of growth over the immediate past—1968–1976—will continue in the short run.

As shown in Table 20-3, the assets of all the major financial intermediaries are expected to increase from $2.1 trillion at the close of 1976 to $3.0 trillion in 1980 and to $4.7 trillion in 1985. Commercial bank assets are anticipated to increase to $1.4 trillion by 1980 and to $2.3 trillion by 1985. The annual growth rate in bank assets has been slightly below that for all intermediaries; therefore, their relative share of all assets of intermediaries is expected to slip slightly in the years ahead.

Inflation eroding the cash values of life insurance policies has made it difficult for life insurance companies to compete for funds. Since inflation is expected to continue, the growth rate of these companies should continue to lag behind that of other intermediaries. Savings and loan associations and credit unions should continue to enjoy above-average growth as they acquire and expand their range of consumer financial services offered.

Table 20-3

Actual and Projected Growth in Assets of Major Financial Intermediaries, Selected Years, 1968–1985 (billions of dollars)

	Actual Amounts		Projected Amounts		Annual Growth Rate	Percentage of Total	
	1968	1976	1980	1985	1968–1976	1975	1980, 1985
Commercial Banks	$ 501	$1016	$1447	$2251	9.24%	49.1%	47.4%
Life Insurance Companies	188	321	420	586	6.92	15.5	12.3
Savings and Loan Associations	153	392	627	1130	12.48	18.9	23.8
Mutual Savings Banks	71	135	186	278	8.36	6.5	5.9
Noninsured Pension Funds	83	160	222	335	8.55	7.7	7.1
Credit Unions	14	45	81	167	15.71	2.2	3.5
TOTAL	$1010	$2069	$2983	$4747	9.38%	100.0%	100.0%

Source: Actual amounts from *Federal Reserve Bulletin* and Securities and Exchange Commission, *Statistical Bulletin*. Projections by author.

NOTE: Details may not add due to rounding.

Sources and Uses of Funds at Commercial Banks: 1980 and 1985

Table 20-4 contains the actual and projected sources and uses of funds for all commercial banks in 1968 and 1976. On the sources side the most significant development during this period has been the shift in the composition of deposits from demand to time. It is uncertain to what extent this trend will continue. At the end of 1976, time deposits exceeded demand deposits as sources of funds by better than a 3-to-2 margin. An important question facing bankers today is just how much more economizing of demand deposits can be effected by their holders. Another trend on the sources side has been the increase in "other liabilities" as a source of funds. It is doubtful that this increasing trend has run its course, given the ingenuity of bankers to raise funds from nondeposit sources.

On the uses side, banks between 1968 and 1976 decreased the relative percentage of cash assets held and U.S. Treasury securities held and increased loans as a percentage of the total. The pressure for earnings is the chief explanation for this performance shift. It is unlikely that bank liquidity can be squeezed further in the foreseeable future. Thus, the relative future relationships on the asset side of the balance sheet appear to be more certain than those on the liability side.

Given the projection of bank assets from Table 20-3, and the percentage composition of sources and uses of funds at the end of 1976, the aggregate balance sheet for commercial banks in 1980 and 1985 were projected and are shown in Table 20-4. There are many reasons to expect some shifts in the composition of the sources and uses of funds from what they were at the end of 1976.

The purpose of the projection in Table 20-4 is to encourage consideration of the possible magnitudes and complexities involved in managing the sources of uses of bank funds in the early 1980s.

Uses of Funds

Cash Assets. As may be seen in Table 20-4, commercial bank cash assets in 1980 are projected to be $284 billion in 1985. These cash assets represent primarily required reserves, correspondent balances, and cash items in the process of collection. There would appear to be little room to economize on these assets.

U.S. Treasury Securities. In the past, banks have held U.S. Treasury securities primarily for liquidity purposes. Today, banks hold Treasury securities primarily because of the requirement to pledge high-quality securities as collateral for federal, state, and local deposits. Since it is anticipated that deposits of public funds will continue to grow as

Table 20-4
Actual and Projected Balance Sheet for All Commercial Banks, Selected Years, 1968–1980 (billions of dollars)

	Actual Amounts		Projected Amounts		Percentage of Total	
	1968	1976	1980	1985	1968	1976, 1980, 1985
Assets						
Cash assets	$ 84	$ 128	$ 182	$ 284	16.8%	12.6%
U.S. Treasury securities	64	102	145	225	12.8	10.0
Other securities	72	150	214	333	14.4	14.8
Loans	265	583	831	1292	52.9	57.4
Other assets	16	53	75	117	3.5	5.2
TOTAL	$ 501	$1016	$1447	$2251	100.0%	100.0%
Liabilities and Capital						
Demand deposits	230	319	454	707	45.9	31.4
Time deposits	204	497	708	1101	40.7	48.9
TOTAL DEPOSITS	$ 434	$ 816	$1162	$1808	86.6%	80.3%
Other liabilities	30	125	126	196	6.0	12.3
Capital	37	75	107	167	7.4	7.4
TOTAL	$ 501	$1016	$1447	$2251	100.0%	100.0%

Source: *Federal Reserve Bulletin* and Board of Governors of the Federal Reserve System, *Banking and Monetary Statistics: 1941–1970*. Projections by author.

NOTE: Details may not add due to rounding.

rapidly as they have in the recent past, the amount of high-quality securities needed to collateralize public deposits should grow commensurately. However, it is likely that a large percentage of this pledged securities requirement will be met with municipal securities because the yield on these issues should be much higher than the after-tax yield on Treasuries. Moreover, banks are expected to meet a large part of their liquidity needs with short-term agencies and through the various liability management techniques. In view of these considerations, relative bank holdings of U.S. Treasury securities should not change dramatically.

Other Securities. At the end of 1976, municipals comprised about two-thirds of the "other securities" held by commercial banks. Agencies accounted for most of the remaining portion of this asset category. Municipals are anticipated to account for most of the absolute increase in this category. The incentives for banks to acquire municipals should be the relatively high yield on these issues, the need to have additional securities to pledge against government deposits, and the social obligation to assist in the financing of public projects. Banks also should purchase a large amount of agencies for the same three primary reasons that they will acquire municipals, although the after-tax yields on these obligations should not be quite as high as that on municipals.

Loans. Loans are expected to rise to $831 billion in 1980 and to $1.3 trillion by 1985. In the period of 1985, several major trends are expected in the structure of bank loans. First, consumer loans should continue to increase as a percentage of total bank loans. This trend should be the result of the growth in population and consumer income and from the greater effort made by most banks to develop their retail banking business. Credit-card loans should account for a significant part of the increase in consumer lending.

A second major change expected in the structure of bank loans is the increase in residential real estate loans. The 1968 Housing Act set as its goal in the next decade the construction or rehabilitation of 26 million housing units. The Commission established to study housing finance estimated that it would require $465 billion (in 1969 dollars) to finance these housing needs. If the nation is to attain the housing goals established by the 1968 Housing Act, commercial banks will have to increase their share of the residential mortgage loans made and they probably will be under great political and social pressure to do so. Because of the 1969–1970 and 1973–1975 recessions, which severely affected residential construction, the nation has fallen far short of this stated goal.

Finally, it is expected that businesses will continue to finance more of their short-term credit needs through the sale of commercial paper.

Moreover, businesses may issue more intermediate-term securities in lieu of obtaining term loans from banks. In the period to 1985, banks may witness a slight decline in short-term business loans and business term loans as a percentage of total loans. The drop may be offset by increased bank purchases of business commercial paper and short-term notes in the open market.

Sources of Funds

As we have seen, time deposits now comprise more than three-fifths of total deposits. It is difficult to assess at what point the trend in time deposits will level out and stablilize as a percentage of total deposits. This continuing trend will place further pressure on bank costs.

The Hunt Commission Report Recommendations for Financial Intermediaries

Background

In the 1970 *Economic Report of the President*, President Richard Nixon disclosed his plans to appoint a commission to study the nation's financial structure. The President's mandate to the commission was to "review and study the structure, operation, and regulation of the private financial institutions in the United States, for the purpose of formulating recommendations that would improve the functioning of the private financial system."[2] The commission's immediate objective in carrying out this mandate was "to move as far as possible toward freedom of financial markets and equip all institutions with the powers necessary to compete in such markets."[3] The commission recognized that most of the regulations applicable to our financial institutions were enacted in the Depression environment of the 1930s. As a result, the commission contended that the nation's financial institutions were overly protected and were not sufficiently flexible or competitive to meet the financial needs of a growing and industrially advanced nation. In the light of this contention, the commission made a number of recommendations designed to improve the competitiveness and flexibility of the nation's financial intermediaries.

Some Major Recommendations

Interest-Rate Restrictions. One of the Hunt Commission's most important recommendations was to remove the interest-rate ceiling on

[2]The Hunt Commission Report is the commonly used title of *The Report of the President's Commission on Financial Structure and Regulation* (Washington, D.C.: U.S. Government Printing Office, December 1971).

[3]*Ibid.*, p. 9.

time and savings deposit and dividend restrictions on savings and loan association deposits.[4] The restrictions on commercial banks were enacted in the early 1930s to reduce "cut-throat" competition for deposits. It was believed that many banks failed in the early 1930s because they took on risky, high yielding loans in order to pay the higher interest needed to be competitive for deposits. Since the 1930s, as we have seen in previous chapters, bank failures have been reduced to a negligible level primarily through strict bank examination standards, more knowledgeable bank officers, and the institution of federal deposit insurance, which reduced the threat of bank runs. The Hunt Commission proposed the removal of interest-rate ceilings on deposits as an important step toward improving competition among all financial intermediaries.

The commission also recommended the removal of interest-rate restrictions on FHA and VA mortgages and the removal by states of statutory ceilings on mortgage loan rates. By permitting mortgage rates to be market-determined the flow of funds to finance the housing needs of the nation might be enhanced. Market-determined rates would assist borrowers especially during tight-money periods when some potential borrowers are prevented from obtaining funds by statutory restrictions on rates.

Operational Restrictions on Financial Intermediaries. In order to provide more operational flexibility for financial intermediaries, the Hunt Commission recommended the removal of the restrictions on branch banking, that savings and loan associations and mutual savings banks be permitted to accept checking accounts, and that all depository institutions be permitted to sell and manage mutual funds. The removal of restrictions on branch banking would increase competition in many areas of the country. However, the implications of the other two recommendations are so far reaching that they will require much additional study and evaluation.

Reserve Requirements. The commission recommended that all institutions holding demand deposits be required to become members of the Federal Reserve System and operate under similar competitive rules. In addition, the commission recommended the elimination of reserve requirements on time and savings deposits, equal reserve requirements for all banks, and the gradual reduction of reserve requirements. These recommendations are designed to achieve greater equity among all financial institutions.

[4]The grouping of the Hunt Commission's recommendations in this section follows closely that in Clifton B. Luttrell, "The Hunt Commission Report—An Economic View," Federal Reserve Bank of St. Louis, *Monthly Review*, 54 (June 1972), pp. 8–12.

Chartering. The commission recommended that the federal level of government have the authority to charter stock savings and loan companies, mutual savings banks, and mutual commercial banks. This proposal also is designed to increase competition among financial intermediaries.

Single Tax Formula. The commission recommended that Congress establish a uniform system of taxation for all depository institutions. Presently, depository institutions organized on a mutual basis receive more favorable tax treatment than those organized on a stock basis. Many observers argue that there is little justification for this tax differentiation.

Financial Institutions and the Nation's Economy (FINE)

In 1975, the Ford administration proposed the Financial Institutions Act, which contains many of the recommendations of the Hunt Commission. However, as of mid-1977, this proposal was still lodged in committee.

In 1976, the U.S. House of Representatives Committee on Banking, Currency, and Housing began to hold hearings on proposals to restructure the nation's financial institutions to promote greater efficiency and competition. This committee generated much discussion in the financial community through its *Financial Institutions and the Nation's Economy (FINE)* study. Many of the "discussion principles" of the FINE study made proposals very similar to those of the Hunt Committee.[5]

Major titles or sections in the FINE discussion principles include:

I. Depository Institutions
II. Housing
III. Depository Institutions Holding Companies
IV. Regulatory Agencies
V. The Federal Reserve System
VI. Foreign Banks in the United States
VII. United States Banks Abroad

Concluding Observations

It is highly unlikely that many of the Hunt Commission's proposals or the FINE study's "discussion principles" will be implemented in the

[5]U.S. Congress, House Committee on Banking, Currency, and Housing, *Financial Institutions and the Nation's Economy (FINE): Discussion Principles*, 94th Congress, First Session, November 1975, pp. 1–21.

near future. However, both efforts have led to a very beneficial evaluation and discussion of our financial system by academicians and members of the financial community.

Suggestions for Additional Reading

The American Bankers Association. *Summary and Interpretive Analysis of the Report of the President's Commission on Financial Structure and Regulation.* Washington, D.C.: The American Bankers Association, 1972.

Booz, Allen & Hamilton, Inc. "The Challenge Ahead for Banking." Chicago: Booz, Allen & Hamilton, Inc., 1970.

Bowman, C. T., and Morlan, T. H. "Revised Projections of the U.S. Economy to 1980 and 1985." *Monthly Labor Review* (March 1976), pp. 9–21.

Carter H. Golembe Associates, Inc. *Commercial Banks and National Housing Policy.* Chicago: Association of Reserve City Bankers, 1971.

Darnell, Jerome C. "Banking Structure: What Does the Future Hold?" Federal Reserve Bank of Philadelphia, *Business Review* (August 1973), pp. 3–9.

Editors of *Fortune. Markets of the Seventies: The Unwinding U.S. Economy.* New York: Viking Press, 1968.

Fischer, Gerald C. "Commercial Banking 1975 and 1980: A First Step in Long-Range Planning." Philadelphia: The Robert Morris Associates, 1970.

Haywood, Charles F., and McGee, L. Randolph. *The Expansion of Bank Funds in the 1970s.* Chicago: Association of Reserve City Bankers, 1969.

Kutscher, Ronald E. "Revised BLS Projections to 1980 and 1985: An Overview." *Monthly Labor Review* (March 1976), pp. 3–8.

Lovati, Jean M. "The Changing Competition Between Commercial Banks and Thrift Institutions for Deposits." Federal Reserve Bank of St. Louis, *Review* (July 1975), pp. 2–8.

Luttrell, Clifton B. "The Hunt Commission Report—An Economic View." Federal Reserve Bank of St. Louis, *Review* (June 1972), pp. 8–12.

Murphy, Neil B., and Gilbert, Gary G. "Competition Between Thrift Institutions and Commercial Banks: An Examination of the Evidence." *Journal of Bank Research* (Summer 1971), pp. 8–18.

Murphy, Neil B., and Weiss, Steven J. "Restructuring Federal Regulation of Financial Institutions." *The Bankers Magazine* (Winter 1972), pp. 71–77.

O'Brien, James M. "Capital Needs Projections: A Need for Perspective." Federal Reserve Board of Philadelphia (May–June 1976), pp. 3–11.

The Report of the President's Commission on Financial Structure and Regulation. Washington, D.C.: U.S. Government Printing Office, December 1971.

U.S. Congress, House Committee on Banking, Currency, and Housing. *Financial Institutions and the Nation's Economy (FINE): Discussion Principles.* 94th Congress, 1st session, November 1975, pp. 1–21.

CHAPTER

21

Areas of Opportunity for Commercial Banks in the Future

By 1985, assets of all commercial banks are expected to be approximately $2.3 trillion or more than 2.3 times the 1976 total of $1.1 trillion. Moreover, during this period growth of bank holding company assets is expected to be even more impressive. Each bank and holding company's participation in this growth essentially will depend on how well it takes advantage of the many opportunities for service to consumers, businesses, and governments.

The primary purpose of this concluding chapter is to consider the major areas of opportunity for banks and bank holding companies in the coming years. These principal areas include (1) consumer financial services, (2) business financial services, (3) real estate services, (4) leasing services, (5) money and capital markets, (6) investment management services, (7) financial and management advisory services, (8) computer services, and (9) international banking.

Consumer Financial Services

For most banks, the field of consumer financial services offers perhaps the greatest opportunity for growth and profits in the years ahead. There are several fundamental reasons for the anticipated gains in this area. First, population is expected to continue to grow in absolute terms even though this growth will be at a lower rate than in the past. Second, people 24–35 years of age are projected to increase as a percentage of the population. Third, families' incomes as measured in constant and current dollars should increase by a sizable amount. Because of these factors alone, banks will experience a sharp absolute increase in the demand for deposit services, consumer loans, credit-card services, safe deposit boxes, traveler's checks, and the myriad other possible services that banks can offer consumers. Finally, an important stimulus to the demand for consumer financial services will be the growing sophistication of consumers. At present, there are untold numbers of people who (1) do not have a checking or savings account, (2) have not borrowed from a bank, (3) do not hold a bank credit card, (4) do not have a bank safe deposit box, or (5) have not used any of the other more sophisticated consumer services offered by banks. As more and more people break away from the poverty level, banks have both an opportunity and a responsibility to seek these customers out and to introduce them to the many financial services that can assist them in their everyday affairs.

Business Financial Services

In the future, banks also have great opportunities to provide financial services to businesses. Moving from the $1.8 trillion economy of 1977 to the $3.8 trillion economy of 1985 will require that most firms in operation today undertake considerable capital investment in order to have the facilities to produce the goods and services that will be demanded. To finance this growth in plant and equipment, firms will have to raise considerable sums with bank term loans and through the sales of intermediate- and long-term debt instruments in the open market. The large sales volume expected in the future will mean a greater demand for working capital loans, inventory loans, accounts receivable loans, factoring services, lockbox services, and virtually all the other business financial services that banks or bank holding company subsidiaries can provide.

Real Estate Services

Adequate housing for all citizens ranks as one of this nation's most pressing needs. As we saw in Chapter 20, 26 million housing units are required to meet the nation's housing goal during the period between 1968 and 1978. Two recessions and severe inflations have delayed the accomplishment of this goal. Commercial banks and bank holding company subsidiaries can contribute in a number of ways toward increasing the quantity and quality of housing. First, banks, mortgage companies, and REITs have the opportunity to provide construction financing for individual houses and large apartment and condominium projects. Second, these institutions can provide permanent funds for such projects through a variety of financing arrangements. Third, these institutions can originate and service mortgages for other real estate lenders. Finally, banks can provide short-term loans to REITs, mortgage companies, and other real estate-oriented firms.

Leasing Services

Background

Although leasing is a relatively new field for banks in this country, as a financing arrangement it goes back at least to the days of ancient Rome when ship chandlers leased their ships for trade on the Mediterranean Sea. The impetus to bank leasing in the United States was provided by Comptroller of the Currency James J. Saxon, who ruled on March 18, 1963, that personal-property leasing is necessary to and included in the business of banking. Since that time, it is believed that every state banking authority has given its state-chartered banks the authority to enter lease financing arrangements.

There are two primary restrictions on the leasing activity of national banks. First, banks can engage only in full pay-out leases; that is, the lease payments at least must equal the cost of the equipment. This requirement is not a meaningful restriction because in order for the bank to earn income on the lease, the sum of the lease payments must exceed the cost of the equipment. The second restriction is that banks may buy equipment only at a customer's request. That is, banks are not allowed to stockpile for future leasing.

Why Banks Enter Leasing

There are three primary reasons why banks enter the field of leasing.

Profit. Leasing offers an opportunity for banks to earn a good rate of return. A lease arrangement is in the nature of an installment loan, which usually is the most profitable type of loan that banks make. Ordinarily, there are five direct sources of income associated with a lease: (1) the basic lease rate, (2) cash flow benefits from accelerated depreciation, (3) the investment tax credit—if applicable and in effect, (4) renewal option rentals, and (5) the residual value of the equipment.

A Complement to the Loan Function. Leasing complements the bank lending function by offering an alternative to customers who need intermediate-term loans to finance equipment.

New Accounts and Customers. A leasing department or holding company subsidiary can provide leads to new business deposit accounts and to customers for other bank services.

Opportunities for Banks

It is estimated that leasing and equipment finance account for about 25 percent of the annual expenditures on equipment. Moreover, the U.S. leasing market is growing at a rate of 10–12 percent a year. Bank leasing departments and leasing subsidiaries are making significant inroads into the equipment market. Many large banks lease such big-ticket items as aircrafts, ships, rolling stock, construction equipment, computers, pollution-control equipment, generators, medical and dental equipment, and nuclear cores for utilities. Other items leased by large and small banks alike include office equipment, furniture, automobiles, trucks, and machine tools. Because the growth of the equipment market should at least keep pace with the rest of the economy, equipment leasing offers most banks a great opportunity to enter this profitable field.

Money and Capital Markets

In the future, there are four avenues of profit and service for commercial banks in the money and capital markets. First, banks are expected to increase their holdings of municipals as a percentage of total bank assets. As we have seen, this is because of the attractive yield on these issues, because banks need high-quality securities as collateral for public deposits, and because of the social obligation of banks to finance worthwhile projects. Second, money market and regional banks have an opportunity to reap sizable rewards by underwriting and distributing the large amount of municipals and agencies that must be marketed in the future. Third, money market and regional banks stand to profit from commissions earned as money market makers for seasoned municipal, agency, and Treasury issues. Finally, astute investment managers will continue to have the opportunity to make significant profits as a result of the cyclical movements in interest rates.

Investment Management Services

Banks with trust departments have exceptional opportunities in the future. First, as a result of anticipated increases in employment and income, bank-managed pension and profit-sharing funds are expected to continue to grow at a rapid rate. Second, for most bank trust departments, the management of personal trusts, estates, and investment advisory accounts is perhaps the trust area with the greatest volume and profit potential in the coming years. Most of the population is unaware of the personal trust services offered by a trust department. However, as incomes and wealth continue to grow and as more people learn of the advantages of professional money management, the opportunity for service and profit in this area is almost unlimited. Finally, bank recordkeeping and safekeeping services for corporations, correspondents, and individuals should contine to grow significantly in the years ahead.

Financial and Management Advisory Services

Customers look to their bank for financial advice on all types of matters. In the past most banks had provided this counsel free. However, as financial organizations have grown in number, size, and complexity, banks have had to reassess the costs of continuing to provide free financial counseling to their customers. As a result of this reevaluation, many money market and regional banks have hired economic and financial experts to provide financial advice to the bank and its customers. Fees are established for this advice, which may include economic forecasts, sales and earnings projections, financial budgeting and planning, evaluation of alternative means of financing the firm, and credit analysis of a firm's customers. Several bank holding companies have acquired general management consulting firms with experts in virtually every area of business skills. However, the income potential in the field of financial and management advisory services for banks is virtually untapped.

Computer Services

In the 1960s, most banks found themselves with excess computer capacity and had to look for ways to offset some of the costs associated with owning or leasing the equipment. As a result, many banks began to offer payroll accounting services, maintenance of accounts receivable services, inventory analysis, billing services, maintenance of accounts for correspondent banks, and many other computer-oriented services. Today, a number of bank holding companies have gone a step further and have subsidiaries or working agreements with independent companies to provide the full range of computer services. Since many small- and medium-sized firms are not utilizing computer services, the opportunities for banks for profit and service in this area are great.

International Banking

Regulatory Background

For centuries, international banking was dominated by European banks. Prior to 1914, foreign activities by American banks were hampered because national banks were prohibited from establishing foreign branches and accepting bills of exchange. Only state-chartered banks and private, unincorporated banks engaged in any type of international banking.

The passage of the Federal Reserve Act opened the way for American banks to engage in international banking. This act permitted national banks to accept bills of exchange arising from international transactions, and any bank with capital and surplus of at least $1 million was authorized to establish foreign branches. In spite of this newly acquired authorization, only one national bank opened a foreign branch during the next three years. In 1916, Congress amended the Federal Reserve Act to permit national banks to invest in corporations engaged primarily in international or foreign banking. These corporations came to be called "agreement corporations" because banks were required to enter into an "agreement" with the Federal Reserve Board regarding the type and nature of their activities. In 1919 Congress gave banks further incentive to engage in international banking by authorizing the Federal Reserve Board to charter corporations for the purpose of engaging in international or foreign financial activities. These corporations are commonly called "Edge Act Corporations" because the sponsor of the act was Senator Edge of New Jersey. Edge Act Corporations were permitted to engage in a wide range of international banking activities, including buying and selling of foreign exchange; buying and selling of securities for foreign customers; receiving checks, bills, drafts, acceptances, and other securities for collection abroad; and even the acquisition of equity ownership in foreign corporations engaged in banking. In 1966, Congress passed legislation authorizing national banks with $1 million or more in capital and surplus, upon approval of the Federal Reserve Board, to invest an amount not exceeding 10 percent of capital and surplus in the stock of a foreign banking corporation.

Organizational Alternatives for Providing International Banking Services

Today, as a result of legislative authorization and banking ingenuity, American banks have a number of organizational alternatives for providing international banking services to their customers. These alternatives include (1) the establishment of an international banking department in the home office, (2) correspondent bank affiliations, (3) the establishment of foreign branches and representative offices,[1] (4) the acquisition of foreign banking subsidiaries or affiliates, (5) participation in financial consortia overseas with other domestic banks or with foreign banks, or (6) the establishment of Edge Act Corporations in major United States cities where international trade and finance is important.

For medium-sized banks, a home office international department and a number of correspondent affiliations in major European markets represent the minimum facilities needed. However, money market and regional banks at least should have a home office international department and an overseas branch that allow them access to the Eurodollar market in order to serve their customers adequately and to compete on a reasonable scale with banks that provide international banking services.[2] In the 1960s, a number of large money market banks became truly worldwide banking organizations by establishing branches and representative offices and subsidiaries in virtually every country where American corporations operate. For example, in 1976 Bank of America had 108 foreign branches, representative offices, subsidiaries, and affiliates in more than 100 countries. Citibank in May 1977 operated 209 foreign branches and 14 representative offices in 107 countries as well as five Edge Act Corporations in the United States.

Between 1960 and 1975 the number of banks with foreign branches rose from 8 to 125; the number of foreign branches increased from 131 to 732; and the assets of overseas branches climbed from $3.5 billion to $176.5 billion. The number of Edge Act and agreement corporations rose from 15 to 112.

Opportunities in International Banking

Money market regional banks are enjoying significant benefits from their international operations. BankAmerica Corporation reported for 1976 that 40.2 percent of its after-tax operating earnings was attributable to its international operations. At Citibank in 1976, 57.4 percent of "net interest revenue" (gross interest revenue minus interest expenses) was developed from international operations.

In the future, international banking operations for domestic banks should continue to grow for several reasons. First, money market and regional banks need access to the Eurodollar market in order to acquire funds during any future liquidity crises and to serve the overseas credit

[1]A branch office is authorized to provide a full range of banking services. On the other hand, representative offices provide only advisory services to commercial customers and expedite services performed by correspondent banks; representative offices are not branches because they are not authorized to receive and pay deposits. Douglas A. Hayes, *Bank Lending Policies: Domestic and International* (Ann Arbor, Mich.: University of Michigan, Graduate School of Business Administration, 1971), pp. 231–232.

[2]*Ibid.*, p. 229.

needs of their customers. Second, major banks will have to provide adequate international banking services to retain, especially, their multinational corporate customers and, to a lesser extent, individual customers.

A Perspective

From this brief discussion of the various areas of opportunity for banks, it should be apparent that large banks and large bank holding companies will have a greater range of opportunity for profit than will smaller banks. To compete effectively on a national or regional scale, banks will have to offer most of the financial services permitted by current Federal Reserve regulations. However, because of the growing importance of the consumer as both a source and a user of bank funds, small banks, by providing high-quality, personalized service, should also enjoy great success in the years ahead.

Suggestions for Additional Reading

The American Assembly. *Capital for Productivity and Jobs.* Eli Shapiro and William L. White, eds. Englewood Cliffs, N.J.: Prentice-Hall, 1977.

The American Bankers Association. *International Banking.* 2nd. ed. Washington, D.C.: The American Bankers Association, 1969.

Arthur D. Little. Inc. *The Outlook for the Nation's Check Payments System: 1970–1980.* Washington, D.C.: The American Bankers Association, December 1970.

Bee, Robert N. "Looking Ahead at International Banking." *The Journal of Commercial Bank Lending* (March 1976), pp. 31–35.

Debs, Richard A. "International Banking." Federal Reserve Bank of New York, *Monthly Review* (June 1975), pp. 122–129.

Eyre, Stephen C. "The New Future of International Banking." *The Journal of Commercial Bank Lending* (April 1974), pp. 44–48.

Frankel, Allen B. "International Banking: Part I." Federal Reserve Bank of Chicago, *Business Conditions* (September 1975), pp. 3–9.

———. "International Banking—Structural Aspects of Regulation." Federal Reserve Bank of Chicago, *Business Conditions* (October 1974), pp. 3–11.

Grun, Donald S., and Schuelke, Mary. *The Trust Activities of the Banking Industry.* Chicago: Association of Reserve City Bankers, 1975.

Haskew, Jerri R. "How Regional Banks Can Become International Lenders." *The Bankers Magazine* (Autumn 1976), pp. 40–43.

Hayes, Douglas A. *Bank Lending Policies: Domestic and International.* Ann Arbor, Mich. University of Michigan, Bureau of Business Research, 1971, chaps. 11–13.

Institute of Bankers. *Banking in the 1970s.* London: Blades, East and Blades, July 1970.

Jessup, Paul F., ed. *Innovations in Bank Management: Selected Readings.* New York: Holt, Rinehart and Winston, parts 7–8.

Kay, Douglas C. "Leasing for Your Bank." *The Journal of Commercial Bank Lending* (November 1969), pp. 20–32.

Leimone, John E. "Edge Act Corporations: An Added Dimension to Southeastern International Banking." Federal Reserve Bank of Atlanta, *Monthly Review* (September 1974), pp. 130–138.

Mastrapasqua, Frank, "U.S. Bank Expansion via Foreign Branching: Monetary Policy Implications." New York University Graduate School of Business Administration, Institute of Finance, *The Bulletin* (January 1973), pp. 87–88.

Mathis, F. John, ed. *Offshore Lending by U.S. Commercial Banks.* Philadelphia: The Robert Morris Associates, 1975.

McInnis, Edwin. *Trust Functions and Service.* Washington, D.C.: American Institute of Banking, The American Bankers' Association, 1971.

Nadler, Paul S. "A Look at the Future of American Banking." In *The Changing World of Banking.* Herbert V. Prochnow and Herbert V. Prochnow, jr., eds. New York: Harper & Row, 1966, chap.19.

National Banks and the Future: Report of the Advisory Committee on Banking to the Comptroller of the Currency. Washington, D.C.: U.S. Government Printing Office, 1962.

"New Edge Offices Participate in Expanding International Banking Market." Federal Reserve Bank of Dallas, *Business Review* (March 1976), pp. 1–5.

Timmerman, Ray J. "Direct Equipment Leasing by Banks." *Robert Morris Associates Bulletin* (January 1967), pp. 25-32.

U.S. House of Representatives, Subcommittee on Domestic Finance. *Commercial Banks and Their Trust Activities: Emerging Influences on the American Economy.* Vol 1. Washington, D.C.: U.S. Government Printing Office, July 8, 1968.

Wilmouth, Robert K. "International Banking: New Directions, New Dimensions." *The Journal of Commercial Bank Lending* (August 1976), pp. 9–15.

Index